Passages

COMPARATIVE LITERATURE AND CULTURE

Series Editors
TIMOTHY MATHEWS AND FLORIAN MUSSGNUG

Comparative Literature and Culture explores new creative and critical perspectives on literature, art and culture. Contributions offer a comparative, cross-cultural and interdisciplinary focus, showcasing exploratory research in literary and cultural theory and history, material and visual cultures, and reception studies. The series is also interested in language-based research, particularly the changing role of national and minority languages and cultures, and includes within its publications the annual proceedings of the 'Hermes Consortium for Literary and Cultural Studies'.

Timothy Mathews is Emeritus Professor of French and Comparative Criticism, UCL.

Florian Mussgnug is Reader in Italian and Comparative Literature, UCL.

Passages
Moving beyond liminality in the study of literature and culture

Edited by Elizabeth Kovach, Jens Kugele and
Ansgar Nünning

First published in 2022 by
UCL Press
University College London
Gower Street
London WC1E 6BT

Available to download free: www.uclpress.co.uk

Text © Authors, 2022
Collection © Editors, 2022
Images © Copyright holders named in captions, 2022

The authors have asserted their rights under the Copyright, Designs and Patents Act 1988 to be identified as the authors of this work.

A CIP catalogue record for this book is available from The British Library.

Any third-party material in this book is not covered by the book's Creative Commons licence. Details of the copyright ownership and permitted use of third-party material is given in the image (or extract) credit lines. If you would like to reuse any third-party material not covered by the book's Creative Commons licence, you will need to obtain permission directly from the copyright owner.

This book is published under a Creative Commons Attribution-Non-Commercial 4.0 International licence (CC BY-NC 4.0), https://creativecommons.org/licenses/by-nc/4.0/. This licence allows you to share and adapt the work for non-commercial use providing attribution is made to the author and publisher (but not in any way that suggests that they endorse you or your use of the work) and any changes are indicated. Attribution should include the following information:

Kovach, E., Kugele, J. and Nünning, A. (eds.) 2022. *Passages: Moving beyond liminality in the study of literature and culture*. London: UCL Press. https://doi.org/10.14324/111.978 1800083189

Further details about Creative Commons licences are available at https://creativecommons.org/licenses/

ISBN: 978-1-80008-320-2 (Hbk)
ISBN: 978-1-80008-319-6 (Pbk)
ISBN: 978-1-80008-318-9 (ePDF)
ISBN: 978-1-80008-321-9 (ePub)
DOI: https://doi.org/10.14324/111.9781800083189

Contents

List of figures vii

Notes on contributors viii

Acknowledgements xv

Introduction: approaching 'passages' from the perspective of travelling concepts, metaphors and narratives in the study of literature and culture 1
Elizabeth Kovach, Jens Kugele and Ansgar Nünning

Part I: Symbolic passages between media, genres, languages and cultures

1. The sound of Benjamin's arcades 19
Rolf J. Goebel

2. Spectral passages: Christian Petzold's *Transit* (2018) as a misadaptation of Anna Seghers's novel (1944) and allusion to Europe's 'Summer of Migration' 35
Max Bergmann

3. The passage from tragedy to novel in Álvaro Cunqueiro's *Un hombre que se parecía a Orestes* (1969) 56
Marta Mariño Mexuto

4. Translating behind bars: cultural passages from Shakespeare to the Italian dialects 72
Beatrice Montorfano

5. Cultural translation as a poetics of movement 89
Marie-Christine Boucher

Part II: Theoretical passages as transitions in art and (non)human life

6. The utterance as transgression: contextual liminality and the rhetoric of the verisimilar 105
Tomi Moisio

7. Kafka's actors: Josef K.'s journey to theatricality 119
   Tanja Marcotte

8. From passage to maturity to liminal critique: Foucault's care of the self as liminal practice 134
   Ruben Pfizenmaier

9. Traversing Hell: Carl Gustav Jung and the practice of visionary travelling 155
   Tommaso Alessandro Priviero

10. Multiple selves: understanding the nature of dissociation in *Black Swan* (2010) 173
    Büke Sağlam

11. Passage and flow: oceanic dystopia in the self-conscious Anthropocene 186
    Florian Mussgnug

Part III: Political passages related to identity, othering, supremacy and power

12. The gaze and the city: woman walking down the street 202
    Martina Hrbková

13. Passages: reading before/for responsibility in Elizabeth Bowen's *The Death of the Heart* (1938) 218
    Laura Lainväe

14. Thirdspace and hospitality: migratory passage and the labyrinth of national (in)difference in Rachid Boudjedra's *Topographie idéale pour une agression caractérisée* (1975) 237
    Eric Wistrom

15. Passage into new realities: Albania(ns) at the turn of the nineteenth and twentieth centuries through the eyes of European travel writers 257
    Oriol Guni

16. Unmaking silence and futureS in the midst of 'The passing dreams of choice' (Audre Lorde) 277
    Susan Arndt and Xin Li

Index 293

List of figures

2.1 Georg, turning around. Still from *Transit* (Christian Petzold; DE/F 2018; timecode: 1:33:38) © Hans Fromm/Schramm Film.   43

2.2 Letters. Still from *Transit* (Christian Petzold; DE/F 2018; timecode: 0:01:35) © Hans Fromm/Schramm Film.   47

2.3 Flatscreen in bar. Still from *Transit* (Christian Petzold; DE/F 2018; timecode: 0:02:49) © Hans Fromm/Schramm Film.   47

2.4 Surveillance camera image. Still from *Transit* (Christian Petzold; DE/F 2018; timecode: 0:18:06) © Hans Fromm/Schramm Film.   49

2.5 Police raid in hotel. Still from *Transit* (Christian Petzold; DE/F 2018; timecode: 0:41:40) © Hans Fromm/Schramm Film.   51 den Kulturen (Iudicium, 2001), *A Companion to the Works of Walter Benjamin* (ed.; Camden House, 2009) and *Klang im Zeitalter technischer Medien: Eine Einführung* (Passagen Verlag, 2017). His current research focuses on intersections of music and other sounds with literature, philosophy and media technologies. He was a member of the 2011 and 2012 German Studies Association (GSA) Conference Program Committees, and a member of the GSA task force on programme and structural changes.

Oriol Guni is a PhD candidate at the International Graduate Centre for the Study of Culture at the Justus Liebig University Giessen, Germany. His research focuses on the intersections of literature and culture between West and East. He is specifically concerned with modern encounters of orientalism, balkanism, Eurocentrism, semiospheres, discourse analysis, and vertical and horizontal perceptions created through the means of travel literature and cultural and religious encounters. His previous career was as a journalist and translator. He is currently working on travel writing about Albania, with the hope of producing a framework that is specific to Albanians in particular, and to some of the cultures of the Balkans.

Martina Hrbková is a PhD student in the Department of Anglophone Literatures and Cultures, Faculty of Arts, Charles University, Prague, Czech Republic. Her research interests include areas in British modernist and contemporary literature, spatial theory and literary space, corporeality, and topics related to feminism and gender studies. She is currently working on her dissertation entitled 'Corporeal Geographies: Women walking and inhabiting the city in the writing of Virginia Woolf and Jean Rhys'.

Laura Lainväe is interested in relations between literature, theory and climate change, and also in animal studies, deconstruction and contemporary art. She holds a PhD in English studies from Paul-Valéry University, Montpellier, France. She is a member of EMMA (Etudes Montpelliéraines du Monde Anglophone). Her thesis, 'A New Eco-logic: Rethinking modern identities through the notions of humility and mastery in the works of Elizabeth Bowen and Samuel Beckett', links a deconstructive reading of identities in the twentieth century to the current ecological crises (namely, climate change and accelerating species extinction), proposing, as its hypothesis, that they stem from an ethics based on patriarchal, capitalist and anthropocentric mastery. Based on a close reading of Elizabeth Bowen's and Samuel Beckett's post-war novels, the project proposes an eco-logic (or an ethics of humility) that would be better adapted to the needs of the vulnerable in the context of the anthropogenic global ecological crises in the twenty-first century.

Xin Li is conducting her postdoctoral research at the University of Bayreuth, Germany. Her research interests include post-humanism, postcolonialism, poststructuralism and the challenges presented to the totality at the foundation of Western epistemology. She holds a PhD in transcultural Anglophone studies. Her thesis is entitled 'Saying the Unsayable – Poethics of silence in contemporary North American narratives'.

Tanja Marcotte is a PhD candidate at the Graduate Centre for the Study of Culture at the Justus Liebig University Giessen, Germany. Her project is to explore the margins of theatricality in Kafka's work by analysing the text, *inter alia*, with the theatre techniques of Bertolt Brecht (*Theatralität bei Kafka – Techniken des Theaters als erzählerische Mittel*). She is a trained musical performer, and she has performed on stage across Europe since 2004, including two world premieres. In 2016, she received the Kulturpreis from the city of Butzbach for directing and writing the scenic city tour following the traces of F.L. Weidig. She graduated at the Justus Liebig University Giessen in 2016 with a degree in German and ethics. She is currently working as a teacher in a comprehensive school in Giessen, and as a coordinator for academic consultation for a theatre (BüchnerBühne).

Marta Mariño Mexuto recently obtained her PhD at the University of Santiago de Compostela, and she is now a researcher at the University of A Coruña, Spain. She graduated in classics at the University of Valladolid in 2015, where she achieved the Highest Grades Award that year. Afterwards, she obtained a master's degree in literary theory and comparative literature at the University of Salamanca, and a master's degree in teacher training at the University of A Coruña. Her research field is mainly the rewriting of ancient myths in modern literature, whether it can be classified as inspiration, or rather as a subversion of the classic conventions.

Tomi Moisio defended his doctoral dissertation in the Department of Art History, University of Helsinki, Finland, in September 2020. His thesis is entitled 'Composed Reality: The artistic discourse of Erik Enroth'. Moisio's theoretical interests include narrative, context and the complex relationship between word and image. Central to his thesis is the notion of conflict as context. Narratology and hermeneutics are both methods in his study. Moisio is currently working as a curator for the Serlachius Museums in Mänttä, Finland. His published articles include texts on contemporary artists, such as Erwin Wurm and Wilhelm Sasnal, as well as accounts of Finnish modernism, including an article on Erik Enroth's poetry and its relation to his paintings.

Beatrice Montorfano is a PhD candidate at the University of Siena, Italy (PhD degree in philology and literary criticism, modern literature), and at the Université Sorbonne Nouvelle – Paris 3 (ED 267 – Arts et Médias), France. As a collaborator with the digital platform Dislocazioni Transnazionali, she has authored a database mapping Shakespeare's presence on the contemporary Italian stage, and she has collaborated with Sara Soncini on a catalogue of the Italian productions of Sarah Kane's plays. She has published an article about the interaction between pop culture and Shakespeare in the context of prison theatre (in *Textus* 3, 2018). Her dissertation will focus on the role played by Shakespeare, as a global and transnational phenomenon, in marginalized experiences of contemporary Italian theatre.

Florian Mussgnug is Professor of Comparative Literature and Italian Studies, and Vice Dean International for Arts and Humanities, at UCL (University College London), UK. He has published widely on twentieth and twenty-first century literature in Italian, English and German, with a particular focus on the environmental humanities, creative critical practice and narratives of risk, crisis and care. Recent publications include *Dwelling on Grief: Narratives of mourning across time and forms* (Transcript, 2022, with Simona Corso and Jennifer Rushworth); *Thinking through Relation: Encounters in creative critical writing* (Peter Lang, 2021, with Mathelinda Nabugodi and Thea Petrou); *Mediating Vulnerability: Comparative approaches and questions of genre* (UCL Press, 2021, with Anneleen Masschelein and Jennifer Rushworth); *Human Reproduction and Parental Responsibility: Theories, narratives, ethics* (a special issue of *Phenomenology and Mind*, 2020, with Simona Corso and Virginia Sanchini); and *Rethinking the Animal–Human Relation: New perspectives in literature and theory* (Edinburgh University Press, 2019, with Stefano Bellin and Kevin Inston). He has held visiting and honorary positions at Sapienza University Rome, Roma Tre University, the Universities of Oxford, Siena and Cagliari, and at the British School at Rome.

Ruben Pfizenmaier is a PhD candidate at the International Graduate Centre for the Study of Culture at the Justus Liebig University Giessen, Germany. His PhD project is entitled 'Formations of Practice: The exercise of ancient rhetoric as mode of subjectification'. In this project, using manuals of antique rhetoric as primary material, he strives to sketch a theory of exercise as subjectification, using concepts and methodology from phenomenology, as well as practice theory. He studied philosophy, creative writing and cultural journalism at the University of Hildesheim, and philosophy and literature at University College Cork, and he holds a master of arts in philosophy from the Free University of Berlin. His research interests include theories of embodiment, subjectivity, intercultural/cross-cultural philosophy, ethics and aesthetics.

Tommaso Alessandro Priviero holds a PhD in history of psychology from UCL (University College London), UK, and is a trainee Jungian analyst based in London. His first monograph was dedicated to a study of the psychology of anarchism in the poetry of Lucretius. His second book, based on his doctoral research, is a study of Jung and Dante, appearing soon from Routledge in the book series Research in Analytical Psychology and Jungian Studies. He regularly publishes papers, and teaches modules at UCL on the history of madness and the intersections between depth psychology and hermeneutics.

Büke Sağlam is pursuing her PhD at the University of Santiago de Compostela, Spain, as a member of the programme Estudios de la Literatura y de la Cultura (Literary and Cultural Studies). She is writing her thesis, 'Inside the Original Fear: The representation of "cosmicism" in literature and popular culture', under the supervision of Professor César Pablo Domínguez Prieto. She studied English language and literature at Yeditepe University, Istanbul. During her BA, her article on Dostoevsky's *Crime and Punishment* was published in a Russian journal, *SputnikPlus*. Being enrolled in Master Mundus Crossways in Cultural Narratives, she did her MA in three countries: Adam Mickiewicz University (Poland), Universitá degli studi di Bergamo (Italy) and Universidade de Santiago de Compostela (Spain). She wrote her MA dissertation on unmotivated violence. She co-organized the seminar Small/Minor Literatures & Cultures: A Preliminary Debate, along with César Pablo Domínguez Prieto, held in Santiago de Compostela in 2017. She is also a member of the Small/Minor Literatures network.

Eric Wistrom is a doctoral candidate in the Department of French and Italian at the University of Wisconsin-Madison, USA. His thesis focuses on hybridity in postcolonial and postmigration studies, specifically the evolution of interlinguistic influences of French, Arabic and Berber dialects, and new practices of textual hybridity in Arabo-Francophone expression. He has a subspeciality in trauma studies, focusing on the literary representations of acute and post-traumatic stress disorder. In addition to his work at Madison, he is concurrently pursuing a second PhD in molecular and cell biology at the University of Texas at Dallas, where he studies post-transcriptional control in neuroplasticity and pain.

Acknowledgements

We would like to thank all who contributed to the event that initiated this volume: the annual conference of the Hermes Consortium for Literary and Cultural Studies, which took place at Rauischholzhausen Castle, Justus Liebig University Giessen (JLU) from 19 to 24 May 2019, and which was hosted by the JLU's International Graduate Centre for the Study of Culture (GCSC). Special thanks go to Doris Bachmann-Medick for her workshop on liminality, Florian Mussgnug for his keynote lecture and Max Bergmann for hosting a screening of the film *Transit*. We are very grateful to the faculty members of the Hermes Consortium and the two anonymous reviewers for UCL Press for their detailed and constructive feedback on the concept of the volume and its individual chapters. Thanks also to the team of the International PhD Programme 'Literary and Cultural Studies' of the JLU, particularly Silvia Casazza, who supported us in preparing the final manuscript. We also thank our UCL Press editor, Chris Penfold, for his guidance and support throughout the publication process, as well as UCL Press's Comparative Literature and Culture Series editors, especially Timothy Mathews for feedback on early drafts of our book proposal. Last but certainly not least, thank you to all the contributors for their ideas, enthusiasm and collaborative spirit.

Giessen, March 2022
Elizabeth Kovach, Jens Kugele and Ansgar Nünning

Introduction: approaching 'passages' from the perspective of travelling concepts, metaphors and narratives in the study of literature and culture

Elizabeth Kovach, Jens Kugele and Ansgar Nünning

Liminality's limits? Why passages deserve a closer look

In the study of literature and culture, use of the term 'liminality' to describe situations of uncertainty and states of the in-between is ubiquitous. The term's concrete meaning is consequently often taken for granted and undertheorized. This is a point that Bjørn Thomassen stresses in *Liminality and the Modern: Living through the in-between*, in which he advocates situating the term 'in its intellectual and anthropological history, and with due stress on the concepts of experience and transition' (Thomassen 2016, 7). This history began with anthropologist Arnold van Gennep's 1909 book *Les Rites de Passage*, in which liminality refers to 'the middle stage in concretely acted out ritual passages', the in-between of ritualized moments of status change – boy to man, single to married and so forth (Thomassen 2016, 2; van Gennep 1960). Victor Turner reinvigorated the term in the 1960s, linking it to modern experience in general (Turner 1977). While Thomassen acknowledges the productive avenues of research that the term has garnered across myriad disciplines, he also suggests that 'liminality must, at a minimum, stay close to one aspect of its original meaning … : namely, that it has to do with the passing of a threshold and therefore with transition' (Thomassen 2016, 15). The term is sharpened by the context of passage.

This volume is an exploration of the broader contexts and processes – passages – within which liminal experiences and encounters are situated. The study of literature and culture is, in fact, marked by various distinct understandings of passages beyond rites of passage in ritual praxis – for instance, the shopping arcades (*Passagen*) theorized by Walter Benjamin, the Middle Passage of the Atlantic slave trade, present-day forms of migration and resettlement, transitions depicted in the *Bildungsroman*, and passing racial and gendered identities. Whether structural, semiotic, spatial/geographic, temporal, existential, societal or institutional, passages refer to processes of (status) change. They connect and thereby engender difference. They enable entrances and exits, arrivals and departures, while they foster moments of liminality in the process. Unlike thresholds that are simply crossed, passages imply journeys of duration, prompting anticipation of the new and foreign, as well as a sense of existential finitude. Rarely smooth, passages come with challenges and risks, and bear the potential for breaks and ruptures. Unlike travel, which carries largely positive connotations of the bourgeois subject voluntarily moving, passage can be involuntary, forced and traumatic.

The aim of this volume is to establish an interdisciplinary dialogue on how this largely overlooked term can be theorized, how its various connotations can be productively synthesized, and how it can be fruitfully applied within specific research contexts and used to foster dialogue among various fields in the humanities and beyond. It is a term whose consideration begs for interdisciplinary thought and exchange, and it can act as a vehicle for bringing disparate research projects and perspectives together. Such an endeavour does risk some potential pitfalls. The danger is that virtually anything and everything can be conceived of as a kind of passage. Ubiquitous opportunity for application can quickly lead to a lack of theoretical specificity, as our opening discussion of liminality implies. A question we are most interested in, therefore, is how can concepts, metaphors or narratives of or related to 'passages' function in particular, heuristically valuable senses? Why could 'passages' be more productive in describing specific social, cultural, political or historical phenomena than other closely related or synonymous terms? How do attempts to theorize 'passages' demand interdisciplinary thought and exchange? How do understandings of passages sharpen the notion of liminality? These are the questions that we posed in conceptualizing this volume, which also quickly led us to discuss the broader potentials and pitfalls of interdisciplinary research within the humanities, and the formative role that metaphors, concepts and narratives play within it.

Concepts, as well as metaphors and narratives, are among the most central tools of academic discourse. Concepts such as 'genre', 'history', 'cultural memory', 'narration', 'performativity', 'space', 'identity' and 'intertextuality' constitute a common language for the study of literature and culture. They enable discussion and exchange between different disciplines, as well as between scholars from different national cultures of knowledge. Like metaphors and narratives, concepts shape and structure the way in which we discuss literature and culture, order our experiences and knowledge of the world, and greatly contribute to our ways of academic world-making. Rather than being univocal or firmly established, the meaning and operational value of concepts, methods, theories, metaphors and narratives tends to differ between cultures of research and education, as well as between historical periods. They are dynamic and changeable as they travel back and forth between different academic and national contexts. Answering the demands of the time and adhering to paradigms dominant in a specific field of research, their scope of meaning usually changes significantly as the cultural baggage attached to them differs.

Especially in the context of interdisciplinary research, concepts, metaphors and narratives are perpetually 'on the move', travelling across different cultural contexts, and gaining access to new fields of research while promoting continuous renegotiation and re-adaptation. This introduction will begin with a discussion of the three key (meta-)terms used in the subtitle of this introduction – concepts, metaphors and narratives – and the ways in which these three terms constantly gravitate into each other's fields. We then tease out some of the implications of the topic of this volume by exploring the uses of the metaphoric concept, or conceptual metaphor, of passages. Lastly, we outline examples of the application of the term 'passages' to literary and cultural studies research of today, exemplified by the contributions to this volume.

Considering travelling concepts, metaphors and narratives in the interdisciplinary and international study of literature and culture

Various specific notions of passages can be traced within the interdisciplinary and international study of literature and culture, to which we will return in more detail in the next section. 'Passage' can certainly be called a travelling concept in the sense of Mieke Bal (see Bal 2002). For Bal, travelling concepts are those that are taken up within various disciplinary contexts, and thereby perpetually shift in meaning according to the ways in which they are newly interpreted and employed. They are what enable interdisciplinary and international academic exchange in the humanities and beyond, because they act as vital points of orientation – the building blocks of a 'common language' (Bal 2002, 22) – through which researchers can communicate with one another. Throughout the past few decades, the studies of literature and culture have become increasingly interdisciplinary and international fields of research. Their objects of study often require interdisciplinary approaches and international perspectives, because '[t]he idea of locating the study of culture exclusively in the context of national and disciplinary constellations is surely losing plausibility in a world which is itself increasingly characterised by cultural exchange, globalisation, transnationalisation and interdependence' (Neumann and Nünning 2012, 1). Key concerns of today – ranging from systemic racism to global warming – can only be adequately addressed when disciplines and national research cultures and institutions come together and work collaboratively. A productive way to approach such pressing issues is to pursue a concept-based, interdisciplinary approach to the fields of literary and cultural studies.

The cross-pollination of thought caused by travelling concepts can stimulate new areas of interdisciplinary research, and occurs along four main 'axes of travelling': across disciplines, national cultures and cultures of research, historical periods, and between academia and society (Neumann and Nünning 2012, 11; Baumbach et al. 2012, 6). As mentioned at the beginning of this introduction, the concept of 'liminality' to which 'passage' is linked has travelled from the field of anthropology to dozens of other international research contexts, ranging from literary and cultural studies to 'marketing and consulting' (Thomassen 2016, 7). Its historical path of travel began with van Gennep's 1909 book, continued with Turner's interpretation of the term in the 1960s, and persists in humanities discourses today (van Gennep 1960; Turner 1977). The term is adapted to describe shifting social realities. For instance, sociologist Arpad Szakolczai suggests that 'the modern condition can be best characterised as a paradoxical state of "permanent liminality"', in which a sense of suspension from normalcy or stability finds no foreseeable end (Szakolczai 2017, viii). Cultural studies scholar Doris Bachmann-Medick has suggested the same paradoxical notion, which she calls 'persistent liminality', to describe the Covid-19 pandemic:

> We have to reckon with the possibility that the crisis experience of Covid-19 could endure as a permanent state. What seems to emerge

is a persistent border and transition experience with increased uncertainties of prognosis and continuing existential uncertainties of survival. In such a fundamental crisis there can hardly be any talk of transition anymore, since the stabilizing tripartite structure of the conventional (ritual) process has been massively disturbed. (Bachmann-Medick 2021, n.p.)

For Bachmann-Medick, the pandemic has created a liminal experience that, rather than being part of a larger process of passage, could potentially persist indefinitely.

These examples illustrate the way concepts can be quite radically redefined according to the phenomena they describe. The idea of 'permanent' or 'persistent' liminality divorces the idea of the liminal from its original anthropological meaning, as a state of in-between defined precisely by its position within an overall process of passage. Attempts to conceive of ways out of persistent liminality could thus revisit or newly conceptualize the notion of passage to find opportunities for thinking about and instigating change. An example of such an attempt is Franziska Hoppen's *Liminality and the Philosophy of Presence: A new direction in political theory* (2021), which theorizes presence as a way of moving beyond what she finds is the permanently liminal state of modern Western politics in crisis. Her work is part of a Routledge series, Contemporary Liminality, edited by Arpad Szakolczai, who positions liminality as 'a new master concept' that provides 'the basis of a new, anthropologically-focused paradigm in social theory' (Szakolczai n.d., n.p.). If liminality is indeed a 'master concept', and given the fact that it is used increasingly to describe political, social and cultural norms, rather than states of exception, we suggest that more rigorous engagement with notions of passage could enrich the discourse by initiating further thought about how liminal states can be disrupted and overcome.

This would require novel approaches to theorizing and identifying processes of passage. A staged ritual comprised of clear, repeatable steps is easier to delineate than processes of passage that occur on larger global and societal scales. This does not mean that passage is not productive for such contexts, but simply that, as a travelling concept, its meaning and interpretation must shift according to the academic disciplines and cultures, historical moments and phenomena it is used to describe. As Neumann and Nünning state, 'Working with travelling concepts involves multiple and different forms of analysis that allow us to focus on the production of difference and differentiation' (Neumann and Nünning 2012, 12). This volume, in providing a variety of literary and cultural studies approaches to the concept of passages, aims to demonstrate the production of varied approaches to, and interpretations of, a common term.

As is the case for most travelling concepts, many notions of passage are 'profoundly metaphorical' (Neumann and Nünning 2012, 15). Far from meaning the literal movement of passing from one point to another through space and time, 'passages' have come to function as metaphors for appearing as another race or gender, shopping arcades, coming-of-age rituals and much more. Metaphorical concepts of passage allow the term to proliferate, but this can also 'foster oversimplification: Concepts lose much of their analytical potential once they function as metaphors' (Neumann and Nünning 2012, 15–16). In addition, metaphorical concepts can 'also project "mininarrations" (Eubanks 1999, 437) onto [the phenomena they describe], thereby providing ideologically charged plots and explanations of historical changes rather than neutral descriptions thereof' (Baumbach et al. 2012, 11). On the one hand, metaphorical concepts run the risk of losing theoretical specificity and, on the other hand, of carrying narrative 'baggage' with them – invoking associations and implications to which scholars must remain sensitive.

Thus, while travelling concepts, metaphors and narratives such as 'liminality' and 'passage' can, and have proven to, stimulate and invigorate avenues of research within the humanities and beyond, such travel must be observed with sensitivity to the ways in which the proliferation of conceptual metaphors/metaphorical concepts and mini-narratives can lead to a loss of 'analytical potential' and invoke various preconceptions. One must also consider why some concepts travel better than others – why certain paths are open while others remain closed (see Baumbach et al. 2012, 2). The translatability of a given term, incompatible research traditions and language barriers all potentially impede conceptual travel. Issues of access to resources, privilege and power certainly play a role, and 'we also have to take into account the agents that prepare for and enable their journeys as well as the motives and methods of these facilitators' (Baumbach et al. 2012, 13). Yet, when successful transfers and re-appropriations do occur, they can lead to 'new theoretical frameworks, disciplinary research domains or new fields of interdisciplinary research' (Neumann and Nünning 2012, 16). New concepts, metaphors and narratives can introduce productive ruptures into the symbolic, conceptual systems and frames of reference with which researchers operate. And, as Neumann and Nünning emphasize, one of the most valuable aspects of travelling concepts is their ability to 'add a self-reflexive dimension to the study of culture' (4), through which we remain aware of, and transparent about, how concepts are conditioned by disciplinary, cultural, national, historical and societal contexts (16). Travelling concepts, metaphors and narratives contribute not only to the production of novel research perspectives and approaches, but also to heightened degrees of self-reflection among the researchers who encounter and work with them.

Implications, potentials and risks of the conceptual metaphors, metaphoric concepts or narratives of 'passages'

Having addressed travelling concepts, metaphors and narratives in general senses, we now turn specifically to the theme of 'passages'. It is a term whose consideration demands interdisciplinary exchange, and it can act as a vehicle for bringing disparate research projects and perspectives together. There are various well-established notions of 'passages' within the study of literature and culture. In each kind of 'passage' – be it a textual passage, a shopping arcade, the Middle Passage, passing in terms of identity, or rite of passage – the literal sense of physical 'passing' is entangled with further conceptual, metaphorical and narrative connotations.

Let us begin with the etymological origins of 'passage', which appeared in the thirteenth century to denote both 'a road' and the 'action of passing' (*Online Etymology Dictionary* 2001–22). The latter is a mini-narrative, in that it denotes an action through which a change of state (most basically temporal and spatial) occurs. Passage in eleventh-century Old French referred specifically to a 'mountain pass' (*Online Etymology Dictionary* 2001–22). Passage in the sense of 'a portion of writing' was first recorded in the early seventeenth century (*Online Etymology Dictionary* 2001–22). It continues to be used in common parlance, particularly by literary and cultural-studies scholars, who read, highlight and analyse passages of text daily, but its metaphorical nature is rarely reflected upon. The term positions grammatically ordered signs as metaphors for movement through time and space. Textual 'passages' are experiences, perhaps even mini-narratives, in themselves. They also act as spatial, temporal and mental corridors between further textual units that precede and follow.

Passage in the sense of 'building corridor' also first appeared in the seventeenth century (*Online Etymology Dictionary* 2001–22). Walter Benjamin famously describes the *Passagen*, or shopping arcades of Paris, in the *Passagenwerk* (written between 1927 and 1940). He describes the steel and glass structures as relics from the past (nineteenth-century France), commodity museums full of curious shops and objects. Their subject is not the close reader, but the *flâneur*, who wanders through them haphazardly. Benjamin presents the arcades, or *Passagen*, of Paris as both literal and metaphoric passages. They literally house and lend structure to the action of passing through. They are, in Benjamin's words, 'hybrid forms of house and street' in which 'every gate is simultaneously entrance and exit' (Benjamin 1999, 874). While they in this sense epitomize constant movement, they are simultaneously figured as static records of nineteenth-century city life. They represent what Benjamin calls 'Paris of the Empire', as well as a foregone heyday of industrialization, 'the last refuge of those infant prodigies that saw the light of day at the time of the world exhibitions'; Benjamin repeatedly lists the strange commodities he encounters, such as: 'the briefcase with interior lighting, the meter-long pocket knife, or patterned umbrella handle with built-in watch and revolver' (874). As Alexander Gelley notes, 'Benjamin's *Passagen* bear witness to a temporal lag, an arrestation of historical time' (Gelley 2015, 116). The act of physical passage of the *flâneur* contrasts with objects and businesses that are frozen in time. The *Passagenwerk* thus overlays many senses of passage and passing; the shopping structures – literal passages – function as vehicles for the consideration of further metaphorical senses of the term.

The Vulgar Latin *passare* means 'to step, walk, pass' and the Latin *passus* is 'step, pace'; it stems from the root 'pete-', meaning 'to spread' (*Online Etymology Dictionary* 2001–22). This last etymological detail makes 'passage' particularly interesting for African diaspora studies, as it reveals the term's history in denoting both movement and distribution – the Middle Passage and its resulting diaspora. In the last decades of the eighteenth century, the 'Middle Passage' was used mostly among Abolitionists to denote the Atlantic Ocean between the West Indies and west coast of Africa, the portion of the triangular trade in which Africans were forcibly captured, transported to the New World and sold into slavery. But, as the editors of the 2007 book *Many Middle Passages* state, today:

> the middle passage is not merely a maritime phrase to describe one part of an oceanic voyage; it can, rather, be utilized as a concept – the structuring link between expropriation in one geographical setting and exploitation in another ... the concept of the middle passage has relevance to a range of migrations involving the coerced

movement of people, sometimes simultaneously with the slave trade, as part of a worldwide process of capitalist development that spanned centuries and continues to this day. (Christopher et al. 2007, 2)

In the book, they address contemporary inequalities and injustices, such as the mass incarceration of African American men in the United States, as direct legacies and historical consequences of the Middle Passage. Here the Middle Passage has evolved from the name of a specific route to become a wide-ranging concept that denotes the everlasting legacy of the slave trade.

Another sense of passage is that of traversing identity categories – passage not as a thing, but as a performance. As Elaine K. Ginsberg writes in *Passing and the Fictions of Identity*, 'the genealogy of the term *passing* in American history associates it with the discourse of racial difference and especially the assumption of a fraudulent "white" identity by an individual culturally and legally defined as ... black by virtue of a percentage of African ancestry' (Ginsberg 1996, 3). The term metaphorically implies that an individual 'crossed or passed through a racial line or boundary – indeed *trespassed* – to assume a new identity, escaping the subordination and oppression accompanying one identity and accessing the privileges and status of another' (3). One form of passing usually involves others – that is, the traversing of categories of class, ethnicity, sexuality or gender. Such acts of passing expose the discursive and performative, rather than the biologically determinate, nature of these categories. And passing in identity also almost always involves spatial passage, as the passing individual leaves one environment and finds a place where he/she is yet unknown. Again, the literal is bound to the figurative sense of passage.

The traversing of identities and social positions is relatable to the ethnographic notion of 'rite of passage', coined in 1909 by Arnold van Gennep to describe rituals by which individuals pass from one group and identity to another through the tripartite phases of separation, transition and incorporation (Thomassen 2016, 3). Liminality, through the work of Turner, became an influential concept to denote the phase of indeterminacy between two states of being. As discussed at the beginning of this introduction, Bjørn Thomassen argues that liminality must be understood as a state that is always associated with 'transition' (15). By bringing the notion of liminality closer to its original ethnographic meaning, Thomassen heightens the importance of the term 'passage' in the process – that is, liminality must always be considered in conjunction with passage. Passage here is not an inconsequential passing by (like that of a *flâneur* casually strolling through an arcade), but rather a process of significant transition, one that engenders a change of state and status.

The contributions to this volume extend beyond the notions briefly described here to include further instances of migration and diaspora, processes of linguistic and cultural translation, historical change, transformations in literary expression, and other moments of transition, both literal and figurative. Can (and should) we try to draw these disparate notions into a common framework? There are certainly links to be made: some forms of racial passing and their politics could be thought about as legacies of the Middle Passage; Parisian shopping arcades, and the bourgeois culture they represented, were predicated on the passages involved in capitalistic accumulation via colonization.

Certain cultural objects also compel us to think about passages in myriad ways at once. Let us consider an example of contemporary cultural expression that exemplifies such a situation. Pajtim Statovci's powerful novel *Crossing*, originally published in Finnish in 2011, and in English in 2019, is narrated by a young man who flees his home country of Albania and wanders through different European cities (Berlin, Madrid, Helsinki), inventing new identities with each passage. He identifies as both male and female, and passes between genders and sexualities. The novel is comprised of alternating sections, told from the perspective of the narrator but about different times in his life – childhood and his later years as a migrant. This creates a continuous passing between times and places. The reader ultimately learns that not all the details of the protagonist's childhood are even his own, but rather those of his best childhood friend. Two lives are narrated as one, passing and bleeding into one another. Passage thus functions not only as a theme, but also as the novel's aesthetic, its organizing principle, its mode of expression.

In such an example, we encounter 'passages' compounded. The theme of passage (in terms of geography, culture, identity and history) is also expressed on a formal level. The novel cultivates passage as a way of seeing, as a mode of telling. Its visual and textual material is arranged to embody passage; it makes passage a perspective, a method of organization – not just a theme, but an approach, style, what we might even call a disposition for meaning making and understanding. It compels us to think about passages in many senses: in terms of coming-of-age rituals, in terms of border crossing, travel and migrations, both forced and voluntary, in terms of passing identity, and also in terms of the formal aspects of the text. This overlaying of many kinds of 'passage' on the levels of story and discourse turns the work into a form of expression that is determined by an overarching logic of 'passages'. By parsing the various senses of passages that contribute to this overarching logic, we can arrive at a nuanced understanding of its construction – how various kinds of passage function in distinct yet interlocking ways. This involves identifying and compiling layers of significance in the spirit of Clifford Geertz's anthropological notion of 'thick description' (Geertz 1973).

To conclude this section, we would like to return to the potential pitfall of framing 'passages' so broadly that virtually anything and everything could be identified as 'passage'. Even if 'passages' abound, as in the example just mentioned, they must be described in distinct terms and, ideally, linked to, or contrasted with, established definitions and theoretical frameworks. This can be challenging, because, as we see, the term 'passage' shifts in meaning according to the disciplines, frameworks and cultural objects in which it appears or functions. This exemplifies the difficulties that travelling concepts, metaphors and narratives can produce. At the same time, such difficulties are opportunities. Concepts live through travel and multiplicity. If they do not fluctuate in response to what Edward Said calls 'the essential untidiness, the essential unmasterable presence that constitutes a large part of historical and social situations', then they become 'ideological trap[s]' (Said 1983, 241). Their continued relevance depends upon acts of appropriation and redefinition. In thinking about 'passages' and other travelling concepts, metaphors and narratives, we have the opportunity to identify convergences and overlaps of various kinds, but we should also pay attention to the specific definitions of each instance to maintain precision and clarity in our interdisciplinary exchange.

Theorizations and applications of 'passages' in the contributions to this volume

Having addressed the potentials, conceptual horizons and challenges of 'passage' as an object of research and as an analytical tool, we now turn to the contributions to this volume and their respective approaches to notions of passage and liminality. In three main conceptual groupings, the contributions analyse a broad range of material as they explore the heuristic value of the term 'passage' and reflect on the role of metaphors, concepts and narratives. In addition to their direct engagement with the concept of passage and related theoretical frameworks, they have been selected with an eye for interdisciplinarity and the representation of current research, and novel arguments that are being pursued and formulated by a range of scholars, from early to advanced career researchers, within the studies of literature and culture.

The contributions to the first section explore symbolic passages between media, genres, languages and culture, as they engage with academic fields such as cultural theory, philosophy, literary criticism and film studies. Drawing on Hartmut Rosa's notion of resonance and Gernot Böhme's studies on atmosphere, Rolf J. Goebel offers new insights into Walter Benjamin's *Passagenwerk* (*Arcades Project*, 1927–40). Analysing the dreamworlds of the arcades as transitional spaces between the visual present and the mythological past, Goebel's contribution draws attention to Benjamin's sonic sensibility, highlighting the auditory experiences that significantly subvert the hegemony of seeing. In his discussion of Christian Petzold's film *Transit* (DE/FR 2018), Max Bergmann continues this interest in passages and their configurations of temporalities in urban space. Based on a novel by Anna Seghers of the same title from the 1940s, the film *Transit* transfers Seghers's World War Two story to contemporary Marseille. Bergmann shows that the film represents an uneasy medial transition from text to film, and his analysis demonstrates that the film engages with various forms and levels of passage, including the passage of time and the (attempted) passages of refugees to safer environments. Marta Mariño Mexuto focuses on Álvaro Cunqueiro's literary work as an example of genre passage. Her reading of Cunqueiro's *Un hombre que se parecía a Orestes* (1969) as the genre passage from Greek tragedy to modern novel pays particular attention to the role of parody in various moments of continuation and discontinuation that arise from this passage. Beatrice Montorfano focuses on the use of Italian dialects in Shakespearean productions as one of the most common features of Italian prison theatre. Challenging the notion of dialect as a popular, low-register means of expression, Montorfano analyses the temporal, spatial, linguistic and symbolic passages at work in the context of the transition from sixteenth-century English texts to the variety of dialects spoken in prison, as well as of the transition experienced by the actors involved in these projects. Marie-Christine Boucher highlights the potential of cultural translation for a poetics of movement, arguing that concepts developed in translation theory can provide helpful analytical lenses in our approaches to the complexity of movement and passage. Her reading of Nellja Veremej's *Berlin liegt im Osten* (2013) puts forth a conceptualization of literature without fixed abode as a transfictional phenomenon.

The second section of this volume directs our focus to theoretical passages as transitions and transgressions in art and (non)human life. Tomi Moisio's engagement with the work of Finnish artist Erik Enroth situates liminality and passage not only within the historical context of World War Two, with its destabilizations of social order, norms and values, but also within boundary negotiations of artistic discourse. He discusses artistic utterance as a rhetorical device, and promotes an understanding of artistic discourse as a defamiliarizing passage into new interpretations of everyday reality. Tanja Marcotte takes a closer look at aspects of theatricality in Franz Kafka's prose, examining how Kafka's novel fragment *Der Proceß* (*The Trial*, 1914–15) plays with transitions and transgressions between staged performance and 'real' life. Marcotte discusses various levels of theatricality, including the development of the protagonist as a theatrical character and theatrical dimensions in Kafka's narrative strategies, and her close reading sheds light on the in-between of passages at work in *The Trial*. Ruben Pfizenmaier shifts the focus to the transitional dimension of social passages, with reflections on education as an exemplary realm of social passage that are based on a deep engagement with the history of philosophy. Once a set of learning practices and rituals of initiation shaping the individual in a passage from childhood to maturity, education practices, as Pfizenmaier shows, have been transformed into ends in themselves. Tommaso Alessandro Priviero's chapter shifts the focus to a prominent trope in the history of religion and psychology, as he engages with the motif of travelling through Hell as a ritual and psychological passage of self-transformation. Priviero particularly discusses Carl Gustav Jung's esoteric interpretation of Hell as a place of transformation and purification vis-à-vis the Christian canonical vision of Hell as a place of eternal punishment. Büke Sağlam's study of Darren Aronofsky's contemporary Gothic movie *Black Swan* (US 2010) offers a psychological reading of the main characters, examining their roles in defining emotional passages and transformations. Sağlam's chapter pays particular attention to the concept of dissociation as a passage from one psychological state to another. The section ends with Florian Mussgnug's discussion of more radical forms of passage and transgression: imaginations of the world after the passing of human civilization in apocalypse fiction. Mussgnug's chapter discusses two recent examples of oceanic climate fiction – Clare Morrall's *When the Floods Come* (2016) and Helen Marshall's *The Migration* (2019) – through the dual conceptual lens of 'passage' and 'flow'. The 'productive ambivalence' of both concepts allows Mussgnug to challenge established boundaries of disciplinary enquiry, and to highlight the importance of relational thinking in the environmental arts, and the humanities more generally.

In the third section, political passages take centre stage, with chapters that address questions of identity, Othering, supremacy and power. In her analysis of texts by Virginia Woolf and Jean Rhys, Martina Hrbková turns our attention to the passage of female protagonists through urban space. Drawing on theoretical work on the internalization of the male gaze (John Berger), dynamics of power and self-regulation (Michel Foucault) and the production of space, Hrbková sheds light on aspects of visibility and the city–body relation in the context of passage. Laura Lainväe explores passages between the self and Other, with particular interest in dynamics of Othering. Taking Elizabeth Bowen's *The Death of the Heart* (1938) as a case study, Lainväe employs theoretical concepts by Jacques Derrida, Michel Foucault and others to analyse a number of social passages, including the protagonist's coming of age and attempted yet denied return home. In his analysis of Rachid Boujedra's *Topographie idéale pour une agression caractériseé* (1986), Eric Wistrom discusses the political implications of migratory integration that is often perceived as a challenge to the very foundation of the nation state's imagined communities. Informed by postcolonial approaches (Homi Bhabha) and cultural geography (Edward Soja), Wistrom also reflects on postcolonial contact zones as potential spaces for rebalancing cultural exchange. Oriol Guni shares this interest in the political dimensions of passage by offering insights into the representation of Albanians in the travelogues of the late nineteenth and early twentieth century. Through the heuristic lenses 'passage' and 'liminality', Guni's chapter explores the relation between these representations and the travel writers' cultures of origin, pointing to balkanist (Maria Teodorova) and orientalist (Edward Said) tropes in these cultural imaginations. In their co-authored chapter, Susan Arndt and Xin Li offer critical reflections on passage and liminality with regard to notions of future, futurity and the (un)making of silence. The authors discuss the role of White supremacy and, in particular, its silencing of autonomous passing into futures. Their readings of poetry by Marlene Nourbese Philip, Adrienne Rich, Samih Al-Quasim and Audre Lorde point to the potential of silence as a critical vehicle for passing into futures in an open, self-reflexive and non-totalized manner.

The chapters in all three sections challenge established disciplinary conventions, and encourage interdisciplinary dialogue on the potential of the term 'passage' and its fruitful application within specific research contexts, often in relation to the concept of 'liminality'. While the volume draws attention to various marginal, non-hegemonic perspectives, its contributions focus predominantly on European and Anglo-American cultural products and epistemologies. We thus hope that further conceptualizations of passages will take this volume as a productive starting point for research related to the Global South, non-Western and Indigenous cultures and forms of knowledge production, as well as further historical dimensions. In their explorations of an array of global literatures, sociopolitical concerns and cultural phenomena, the contributions demonstrate how a term such as 'passage' functions as a travelling concept and, as such, can be adapted and metaphorized to suit a variety of contexts. This is a source of potential pitfalls and promises. The term's flexibility poses the danger of a lack of theoretical specificity. When this danger is consciously addressed, however, 'passages' open new lines of thought and argumentation, while encouraging a high degree of self-reflexivity on the part of researchers. Such promises have been the driving motivations, and rewards, of creating this volume.

References

Bachmann-Medick, Doris. 2021. 'Persistent liminality: A driving force for the humanities in times of the pandemic'. Network of European Humanities.21. Accessed 25 February 2022. https://neh21.net/experts-report/doris-bachmann-medick/.

Bal, Mieke. 2002. *Travelling Concepts in the Humanities: A rough guide*. Toronto: University of Toronto Press.

Baumbach, Sibylle, Beatrice Michaelis and Ansgar Nünning, eds. 2012. *Travelling Concepts, Metaphors and Narratives: Literary and cultural studies in an age of interdisciplinary research*. Trier: WVT.

Benjamin, Walter. 1999. *The Arcades Project*, edited by Rolf Tiedemann, translated by Howard Eiland and Kevin McLaughlin. Cambridge, MA: The Belknap Press of Harvard University Press.

Christopher, Emma, Cassandra Pybus and Marcus Rediker. 2007. *Many Middle Passages: Forced migration and the making of the modern world*. Berkeley: University of California Press.

Geertz, Clifford. 1973. 'Thick description: Toward an interpretive theory of culture'. In *The Interpretation of Cultures: Selected essays*, 3–30. New York: Basic Books.

Gelley, Alexander. 2015. *Benjamin's Passages: Dreaming, awakening*. New York: Fordham University Press.

Ginsberg, Elaine K. 1996. *Passing and the Fictions of Identity*. Durham, NC: Duke University Press.

Hoppen, Franziska. 2021. *Liminality and the Philosophy of Presence: A new direction in political theory*. London: Routledge.

Neumann, Birgit and Ansgar Nünning, eds. 2012. *Travelling Concepts for the Study of Culture*. Berlin: de Gruyter.

Online Etymology Dictionary. 2001–22. 'Passage'. Accessed 25 February 2022. https://www.etymonline.com/word/passage#etymonline_v_7281.

Said, Edward. 1983. 'Traveling theory'. In *The World, the Text, and the Critic*, 226–47. Cambridge, MA: Harvard University Press.

Statovci, Pajtim. 2019. *Crossing: A novel*. New York: Pantheon.

Szakolczai, Arpad. n.d. 'Contemporary Liminality: About the series'. Accessed 25 February 2022. https://www.routledge.com/Contemporary-Liminality/book-series/ASHSER1435?pd=published,forthcoming&pg=2&pp=12&so=pub&view=list.

Szakolczai, Arpad. 2017. *Permanent Liminality and Modernity: Analysing the sacrificial carnival through novels*. London: Routledge.

Thomassen, Bjørn. 2016 [2014]. *Liminality and the Modern: Living through the in-between*. London: Routledge.

Turner, Victor. 1977 [1969]. *The Ritual Process: Structure and anti-structure*. Ithaca, NY: Cornell University Press.
Van Gennep, Arnold. 1960 [1909]. *The Rites of Passage: A classical study of cultural celebrations*. Chicago: Chicago University Press.

Recommended reading

Bachmann-Medick, Doris. 2016. *Cultural Turns: New orientations in the study of culture*. Berlin: de Gruyter.
Baumbach, Sibylle, Herbert Grabes and Ansgar Nünning, eds. 2009. *Literature and Values: Literature as a medium for representing, disseminating and constructing norms and values*. Trier: WVT.
Budick, Sanford and Wolfgang Iser, eds. 1996. *The Translatability of Cultures: Figurations of the space between*. Stanford, CA: Stanford University Press.
Clifford, James. 1997. 'Traveling cultures (remarks at a conference entitled "Cultural Studies, Now and in the Future", Champaign-Urbana, Illinois, April 6, 1990)'. In *Routes: Travel and translation in the late twentieth century*, 17–46. Cambridge, MA: Harvard University Press.
Cooke, Simon. 2009. 'English as a foreign literature', *European Journal of English Studies* 13 (1): 25–43.
Frank, Michael C. 2009. 'Imaginative geography as a travelling concept', *European Journal of English Studies* 13 (1): 61–78.
Galtung, Johan. 1981. 'Structure, culture, and intellectual style: An essay comparing saxonic, teutonic, gallic and nipponic approaches', *Social Science Information* 20 (6): 817–56.
Goodman, Nelson. 1991 [1978]. *Ways of Worldmaking*. Indianapolis, IN: Hackett.
Grabes, Herbert, Ansgar Nünning and Sibylle Baumbach, eds. 2009. *Metaphors Shaping Culture and Theory*. Tübingen: Narr.
Koepsell, Kilian and Carlos Spoerhase. 2008. 'Neuroscience and the study of literature: Some thoughts on the possibility of transferring knowledge', *Journal of Literary Theory* 2 (2): 363–74.
Lakoff, George and Mark Johnson. 1980. *Metaphors We Live By*. Chicago: University of Chicago Press.
Mayerhofer, Christine. 2014. *Living a Lie? Passing and concepts of identity in contemporary novels and life narratives*. Trier: WVT.
Neumann, Birgit, Vera Nünning and Ansgar Nünning, eds. 2010. *The Aesthetics and Politics of Cultural Worldmaking*. Trier: WVT.
Nünning, Vera and Ansgar Nünning, eds. 2010. *Methoden der literatur- und kulturwissenschaftlichen Textanalyse: Ansätze – Grundlagen – Modellanalysen*. Stuttgart: J.B. Metzler Verlag.
Nünning, Vera and Ansgar Nünning, eds. 2008. *Einführung in die Kulturwissenschaften: Theoretische Grundlagen – Ansätze – Perspektiven*. Stuttgart: J.B. Metzler Verlag.
Nünning, Vera, Ansgar Nünning and Birgit Neumann, eds. 2010. *Cultural Ways of Worldmaking: Media and narratives*. Berlin: de Gruyter.
Neumann, Birgit and Frederik Tygstrup. 2009. 'Travelling concepts in English studies', *European Journal of English Studies* 13 (1): 1–12.
Polster, Heike. 2009. *The Aesthetics of Passage: The imag(in)ed experience of time in Thomas Lehr, W.G. Sebald, and Peter Handke*. Würzburg: Königshausen & Neumann.
Sommer, Roy. 2007. 'From cultural studies to the study of culture: Key concepts and methods'. In *English Studies Today: Recent developments and new directions*, edited by Ansgar Nünning and Jürgen Schlaeger, 165–91. Trier: WVT.

Part I
Symbolic passages between media, genres, languages and cultures

1
The sound of Benjamin's arcades

Rolf J. Goebel

'The painted foliage on the ceilings of the Bibliothèque Nationale. As one leafs through the pages down below, it rustles up above' (S3,3; see also G°,15).[1] In characteristically self-reflexive fashion, this seemingly casual note, jotted down by Walter Benjamin while working on his *Arcades Project* (1927–40), points to the sonic undercurrent of his textual assemblage of excerpts and commentaries for his exploration of Paris as the capital of nineteenth-century high capitalism. Here, Benjamin is not focusing on the specific content of the piles of volumes on his desk, but on their auditory materiality. Reading in the sources for a vast network of surprising connections among disparate sources about shopping arcades, fashion, boredom, iron constructions, exhibitions, prostitution, panoramas, mirrors, railways and so forth, Benjamin listens to the acoustics of his own scholarly activity. The almost imperceptible sound produced by the turning of the pages of books (*Blätter*) seems to be answered by the painted leaves (*Blätter*) depicted in the wall paintings above him, creating surprising, almost mystical correspondences between textual and visual media, between printed culture and painted nature, between being bodily present in the here and now of the Bibliothèque Nationale and being mentally immersed, perhaps even lost, in the abysmal labyrinth of the cultural past. This relationship between book leaves and plant leaves is a special type of the resonance that Hartmut Rosa (2019) has described as the overarching 'metacriterion' of Western modernity. Following Rosa, resonances may be understood as spontaneous, intuitive and mutually transformative interactions, where human subjects respond to the objective world, or to one another, in an open, unpredictable manner. Resonant relationships, as Rosa summarizes, are not merely passive echoes but 'require that both subject and world be sufficiently "closed" or self-consistent so as to each speak in their own voice, while also remaining open enough to be affected or reached by each other' (Rosa 2019, 174). Similarly, Benjamin's book leaves resonate acoustically with the painted leaves, not in the manner of a mere echo, but as two independent, self-contained objects that nonetheless share a suddenly discovered affinity. This relationship could never reveal itself were it not for Benjamin's own auditory imagination, given to listening for wayward, secret, semi-forgotten or repressed voices secretly in tune with his own endangered position as an exiled intellectual. Thus, media – books and paintings – do not automatically resonate with one another but require the work of human subjectivity for their correspondences to materialize as textual representations of the sonic.

As Mirko M. Hall has shown (2010), this sonic resonance pervades Benjamin's notion of the dialectical image, whose visual metaphoricity is supplemented by the cognitive force of the auditory. The dialectical image rips forgotten, endangered or suppressed moments of the past out of their original contexts in order to juxtapose them with the crisis-ridden present. In these constellations, the past and the present come suddenly to an imagistic standstill, which opposes the complacent ideal of a preservation of archival treasures, as well as the overly optimistic ideology of historical progress. Instead, the dialectical image performs a last-minute rescue or redemption of a material that would otherwise be irretrievably lost: '[w]hat has been is to be held fast – as an image flashing up in the now of its recognizability' (N9,7). Because this cognitive illumination is as instantaneous, swift and short-lived as a flash of lightning in the sky, it needs a longer-lasting fixation in the text of the cultural historian, who assembles 'the rags, the refuse' of the past into a 'literary montage' (N1a,8) that is decidedly acoustic: 'In the fields with which we are concerned, knowledge comes only in lightning flashes. The text is the long roll of thunder that follows' (N1,1; see also Hall 2010, 89–94; Mettin 2019, 58–9). Like in a thunderstorm, marked by a temporal lag between the immediately visible flash of lightning and the eventual audibility of the thunder, there is an inevitable gap between the sudden recognizability of the past in the now and its eventual recording by the textual signifiers. Their sonic resonance echoes the signifieds rescued from oblivion while being necessarily belated, but this acoustic time lag is the cognitively productive mark of intellectual reflection, which, like the thunder, needs repetition and a certain duration to reveal its insights.

Sonic phantasmagoria in the arcades

The very fact that, in the montage-like textuality of the *Arcades Project*,[2] live sounds and media of sonic reproduction occur only as strangely dispersed events in increasingly obscure, marginalized or repressed places suggests that the mysterious aura of Paris is sustained by the uncanny effect of the temporal evanescence of the sonic.[3] In this sense, Martin Mettin's systematic study on dialectical instances of hearing traces quotidian sounds, street names and fragments of voices in the arcades as occasions for reflections on the philosophy of history in an urban echo chamber of dreamlike character, in which the historical past becomes audible (Mettin 2019, 115–23). Benjamin writes that high-industrial commodity capitalism's ideological deceptions were 'a natural phenomenon with which a new dream-filled sleep came over Europe, and through it, a reactivation of mythic forces' (K1a,8). These forces appear as visual surfaces in the architectural topography of Paris, which figures as a transitional space of musically inflected echoes and secret resonances between the past and the present. Nowhere can this sonic undercurrent of the metropolis be listened to more astutely than in the Parisian arcades, which mirror, in condensed, metonymic detail, the larger social and architectural transformation of urban modernity in their own transitional flux – between a rapidly vanishing past and the technological present, a mythic dreamworld and rational awakening, desire and repression and, last but not least, visual perception and auditory imagination.

According to Benjamin's 1935 Exposé for the *Arcades Project*, these spaces emerged after 1822 in the wake of the booming textile trade and the beginnings of iron construction, which was used in 'arcades, exhibition halls, train stations – buildings that serve transitory purposes' (Benjamin 1999a, 4). The shopping venues mentioned first in this series reflect such evanescent practices in their very name (*les passages, die Passagen*), which suggests an unstable combination of the solidity of architectural materiality with a dynamic, unpredictable process of social change, economic use value and ideological superstructure. This evocation of passages as unpredictable avenues leading the human subject towards open-ended experiences, the seemingly or actually new and the enticingly or frightfully foreign is somewhat effaced by the more static-sounding English term *arcades*. However, the title chosen for the English translation

(*The Arcades Project*) captures the infinite and provisional work-in-progress structure of the exposés, excerpts, citations and commentaries that Benjamin himself referred to as his process-driven *Passagenarbeit*, whereas the title of the original German edition (*Das Passagen-Werk*) has a double-meaning: *Werk* may be read as a synonym of *Arbeit*, but also evokes associations with the self-contained, seemingly complete autonomy of the classical-idealist or high-modernist work of art, a concept subverted by the avant-garde style of Benjamin's endeavours (see also Buck-Morss 1991, 1–7; Tiedemann 1999, 929–36). In fact, the translators of *The Arcades Project* stress that one should not lament the fact that Benjamin did not leave us a 'realized work'; rather, they argue that the fragmentary montage of the project transcends the 'conventional book form' together with Benjamin's philosophical intention of initiating the 'blasting apart of pragmatic historicism' premised on a 'continuous and homogeneous temporality' (Eiland and McLaughlin 1999, xi).[4]

Heinz Brüggemann has proposed that the arcades represent Benjamin's transfer of the ocularcentric bias of cultural modernity, which depends on the subject's fixating apperception of objects, into a state of intoxication and visionary experience. This hallucinatory ecstasy turns to the arcade as an image-space, where the visitor is gripped by tactile perception, kinesthetic sensibility, narrative imagination and remembrance (Brüggemann 2000, 576–9). What Brüggemann omits from this list, however, is the flux of the sonic imagination that unfolds in the arcades as a subversive, if unstable and elusive, alternative to the socially objectifying and epistemologically fixating hegemony of seeing. By contrast, Peter Rautmann and Nicolas Schalz (1992) have suggested that the multi-perspectival montage of textual material in the various convolutes of the *Arcades Project*, which allow spontaneous access by readers with diverse perspectives, anticipates the musical serialism and aleatory principles of composers such as Pierre Boulez and Karlheinz Stockhausen. The arcades themselves, as transitional spaces of indeterminate openness, are marked by a temporality akin to musical events; in the arcades, the *flâneur* enters a playful mode of walking, which evokes the tempi, rhythm, rests, accelerandi and retardandi of a musical performance, while the architecture of the arcades, with its sequence of gates, vestibules and intersections, corresponds to a musical composition's structure of introduction, main and secondary themes, variations and so forth (Rautmann and Schalz 1992, 11–13). Foregrounding the acoustic as a key principle of Benjamin's cultural analysis of urban modernity, this 'sonic turn' in Benjamin studies marks especially the important contributions in *Klang und Musik bei Walter*

Benjamin (Klein 2013), which explore issues such as Benjamin's metaphysical speculations about the messianic, redemptive promise of music; its ability to dissolve the visual regime of beautiful appearance (*Schein*); the connection between auditory sensation and remembrance; and the media-technological ramifications of music in urban modernity. Thus, Asmus Trautsch surveys the considerable range of Benjamin's music-theoretical vocabulary, his reflections on acoustic phenomena and the act of hearing, and the function of music as a sphere of semiotic indeterminacy between the super-sensuous and the corporeal (Trautsch 2013, 19–20). Specifically, Trautsch reconstructs the many ways in which sonic resonance functions as an echo of urban memory in text and image; as a resonance of the Word of God in human languages; or, in the form of music, as a medium of affects connecting other media of communication and knowledge (27, 39, 40). Tobias Robert Klein's more specialized essay on the arcades stresses the necessity of investigating the significance of musical and acoustic impressions for Benjamin's mediations of dream, myth, image and the world of commodities, which Klein puts into the historical context of musical orientalism (Klein 2013, 117).[5]

When Benjamin traced the history of the arcades, the venues, offering antiquated trades and shops, were already faced with historical decline, due to 'widened sidewalks, electric light, ban on prostitution, culture of the open air' and other such achievements of technological progress, changing morals and fashionable lifestyles (C2a,12). However, because of these threats of obsolescence, the arcades also figure as phantasmagoric sites of nostalgic desires for a dreamworld leading into the mythological past. 'Dream houses of the collective: arcades, winter gardens, panoramas, factories, wax museums, casinos, railroad stations' (L1,3), notes Benjamin, explaining that arcades 'are houses or passages having no outside – like the dream' (L1a,1). The 'dream house of the arcades is encountered again in the church', where the architectural style of the arcades encroaches on sacred architecture, lending the former a pseudo-mythical aura, while giving the latter an inappropriately fashionable splendour (L2,4). At other times, the arcade appears as a 'temple of Aesculapius, medicinal spring', which sometimes turns these venues into 'resort spas in ravines' (L3,1).

Galleries into the sonic past

For Benjamin, the arcades also exemplify the psychoanalytic structure of the modern city: like in ancient Greece, '[o]ur waking existence … is a land which, at certain hidden points, leads down into the underworld – a land full of inconspicuous places from which dreams arise' (C1a,2). By day, he notes, 'the labyrinth of urban dwellings resembles consciousness', whereas by night, the narrow, darkly menacing arcades appear as 'galleries leading into the city's past'; luring the 'nocturnal pedestrian' into their narrow lanes, they are part of a secret, mysteriously mythological underworld, presumably resembling the city's collective subconscious (C1a,2). Here, 'another system of galleries runs underground through Paris': the 'Métro', whose names – 'Combat', 'Elysée', 'Georges V', 'Etienne Marce' and so forth – when visually and acoustically encountered 'in the lightning-scored, whistle-resounding darkness' of the tunnels, 'are transformed into misshapen sewer gods, catacomb fairies' (C1a,2). Thus, 'Paris is built over a system of caverns', from which the noise of the Métro and the railway roars to the surface, 'and in which every passing omnibus or truck sets up a prolonged echo' (C2,1). In this noisy space of subterraneous resonances, the city's 'technological system of tunnels and thoroughfares interconnects with the ancient vaults, the limestone quarries, the grottoes and catacombs which, since the Middle Ages, have time and again been reentered and traversed' (C2,1).

If these noises signal the sonic unconscious of the city, the arcades are spaces where music resonates with uncanny force:

> Arcades – they radiated through the Paris of the Empire like fairy grottoes. For someone entering the Passage des Panoramas in 1817, the sirens of gaslight would be singing to him on one side, while oil-lamp odalisques offered enticements from the other. With the kindling of electric lights, the irreproachable glow was extinguished in these galleries, which suddenly became more difficult to find – which wrought a black magic at entranceways, and which looked within themselves out of blind windows. (T1a,8; see also Klein 2013, 120)

In this passage, the arcade figures as a luring, and lurid, space of nostalgic desire, conjuring up in the imagination of the (presumably male) visitor, the erotic dangers of the sirens of Greek antiquity, as well as the geographical exoticism of the female slaves or concubines of the Oriental harem. Thus, the arcade combines the classical topos of the affective irresistibility of music, which culminates in Nietzsche's notion of the irrationally intoxicating trance of the Dionysian principle, with the commodification of female sexuality for the voyeuristic enjoyment of the masculinist gaze. This motif links the arcade with the famous world exhibitions, which turn trade wares from foreign cultures, as well as the gazes of the distracted visitors, into mutually commodifying objects of the entertainment industry. If the world exhibitions 'are places of pilgrimage to the commodity fetish', as Benjamin notes in the Exposé of 1935 (Benjamin 1999a, 7), then this economic fetishization finds its equivalent in the arcades' spectacle of sexual perversion. The metaphoric association of buzzing gaslight fixtures and oil-lamps with sirens and odalisques populating a fairy grotto draws attention to the arcades' sonically illusionistic atmosphere, which is destroyed by the cold, glaring light of the more efficient electricity. Its technological reality principle is a threat to the dreamlike aura created by the mysterious, evocative glow of more old-fashioned modes of lighting, and while, physically speaking, the electric light is prohibitively brighter than its precursors, it produces its own regressive effects – black magic and the claustrophobic threat of blind windows.

Music's exile in the arcades

If the siren song of gaslight is a product of the auditory imagination, the arcades are also the hosts of real music exiled by historical progress: '[m]usic seems to have settled into these spaces only with their decline, only as the orchestras themselves began to seem old-fashioned in comparison to the new mechanical music. So that, in fact, these orchestras would just as soon have taken refuge there' (H1,5). As examples of this technically reproduced music, Benjamin mentions the 'theatrophone', a fashionable device introduced in 1881, which transmitted opera performances through telephone lines (H1,5; see also F°3 and Klein 2013, 124). Benjamin regards the theatrophone as a kind of 'forerunner of the gramophone' (H1,5) – rather anachronistically, considering the fact that the gramophone was invented more than half a century earlier. Although a newly opened arcade employed a 'monster orchestra in uniform' for its inaugural ceremony (Benjamin 1999a, 871), the commercial decline of most of these venues reflects the simultaneous obsolescence of live music in the emerging age of technological reproducibility. Music's traditional aura of authenticity – marking the unique and unrepeatable, if transitory, co-presence of musicians and audience in the here and now of the performance space – corresponds to the evanescence of enticing but mysterious trades and shops in the ageing arcades.

But it is important to note that the outdated live music seeks refuge from its impending displacement by new media of sound transmission and sound reproduction in the very venues – the arcades – that already host these same technologies as part of their consumerist appeal. As Klein points out, arcades, as sites of a spatialized past, figure as historical vantage points of an industrial objectification of music (Klein 2013, 123–4). In other words, the transitional character of the arcades is underscored by the clash between two historically conflictual modes of musical performance – old-fashioned, nostalgic live concerts and electrically produced sonic simulacra. 'Nevertheless', Benjamin continues, 'there was music that conformed to the spirit of the arcades – a panoramic music, such as can be heard today only in old-fashioned genteel concerts like those of the casino orchestra in Monte Carlo' (H1, 5; see also F°,3). Like the actual panoramas, round contraptions offering gigantic depictions of cities such as Paris, Rome, Amsterdam or Athens (Q1a,1), this music, exemplified by *Le Désert* and other compositions by Félicien César David (1810–76), offered a melange of exotic settings and plots appealing to the Parisian bourgeoisie's desire for far-away locales, while also satisfying the tastes of an Arab political delegation visiting Paris.[6] It is the phantasmagoric character of this music, its mixed aura of colonialist intrigue and historical obsolescence, that contributes to the similarity between the panoramas and the arcades, even though both venues are historically non-synchronous: while the arcades were decidedly outdated by the latest standards of commercial modernity, the panoramas anticipated fast-motion cinematography (Q1a,4 and Q1a,8).

Benjamin's musical references are crucial for registering the particular atmosphere of these transitional arcades. As Gernot Böhme argues, atmospheres are an 'intermediate phenomenon', unfolding as 'something between subject and object'; generated by 'eminently material, technical devices', they are felt through the bodily presence of human subjects 'in a state of affective resonance' (Böhme 2017, 168). As a special case of atmospheric space, musical space 'is experienced affectively' as the 'expanded space of the body' (Böhme 2017, 170), because music resounds 'whenever an acoustic event is about the acoustic atmosphere as such', in which hearing occurs as a self-reflexive act for its own sake, rather than as a merely pragmatic activity of hearing something (Böhme 2017, 173). Similarly, in Benjamin's note, the old-fashioned live performance of music, seeking refuge in the equally endangered arcades, allows their architectural surfaces to emanate an uncanny atmosphere of collective unconscious desires for a quickly vanishing past, whose traces nonetheless survive, in a fragmented and displaced manner, in the midst of urban progress.

Flânerie as auditory intoxication

Who, however, is the representative of the human subject position that resonates with these music-filled architectures? It is the *flâneur*, whose predominantly visual exploration of the city's 'vanished time' is stimulated by auditory sensations. Lutz Koepnick has argued that the acoustic is hostile to the visual preoccupations of flânerie: '[u]nable to shut down hearing entirely or to actively screen out unwanted acoustic stimulations, the urbanized ear seemed ill prepared to afford what, in Benjamin's eyes, rendered modern vision a catalyst of new aesthetic experiences: introspective reverie and aestheticizing flânerie' (Koepnick 2004, 119). But the *Arcades Project* contains several important passages that contradict this aversion to hearing. As Benjamin explains, the *flâneur* discovers a collective and mythic past that is not reducible to his own, private reminiscences; nonetheless, it always remains the past of the youthful life he has once lived: '[t]he ground over which he goes, the asphalt, is hollow. His steps awaken a surprising resonance; the gaslight that streams down on the paving stones throws an equivocal light on this double ground' (e°,1). As he walks over this stony ground, the *flâneur* feels 'as though driven by a clockwork mechanism', as if an old-fashioned children's toy music box is playing a tune: '[f]rom days of youth, / from days of youth, / a song is with me still' (e°,1). It is by the sudden remembrance of this nostalgic melody that the *flâneur* senses bodily the sonically affective atmosphere of his surroundings, recognizing the urban space around him as coming from a collective childhood 'that speaks to him, and it is all the same to him whether it is the childhood of an ancestor or his own' (e°,1).

This musical remembrance is an important, if usually overlooked, stimulus for the 'anamnestic intoxication' that drives the *flâneur*'s dreamlike discovery of 'sensory data' and 'abstract knowledge' about the Parisian cobblestones, shop signs, gateways and other such seemingly ordinary sites/sights, which are very different from the official monuments typical of a city such as Rome. The appreciation of these sights, Benjamin goes on to explain, is also significantly enhanced by the immense volume of literature written about the city (M1,4; M1,5). Thus, the *flâneur*'s experience of the dreamlike atmosphere is profoundly intermedial. Its predominantly visual perception is significantly shaped by a half-forgotten, wayward, but suddenly remembered song, which sounds as if playing from a mechanical sound reproduction device in the depth of his imagination, and this audiovisual sensation is, in turn, given discursive explanation by the remembrance of prior reading experiences.

Orpheus at the railway station

If the dreamworlds of the arcades are transitional spaces between the visual present and the mythological past, railway stations are similarly '[d]ream houses of the collective':

> The Gare Saint-Lazare: a hissing, wheezing princess with the stare of a clock. 'For our type of man,' says Jacques de Lacretelle, 'train stations are truly factories of dreams' ("Le Rêveur parisien," *Nouvelle Revue française*, 1927). To be sure: today, in the age of the automobile and airplane, it is only faint, atavistic terrors which still lurk within the blackened sheds; and that stale comedy of farewell and reunion, carried on before a background of Pullman cars, turns the railway platform into a provincial stage. Once again we see performed the timeworn Greek melodrama: Orpheus, Eurydice, and Hermes at the station. Through the mountains of luggage surrounding the figure of the nymph, looms the steep and rocky path, the crypt into which she sinks when the Hermaic conductor with the signal disk, watching for the moist eye of Orpheus, gives the sign for departure. Scar of departure, which zigzags, like the crack on a Greek vase, across the painted bodies of the gods. (L1,4; trans. modified)

In this scenario, it is the noisy acoustics of the railway station, produced by the hissing and wheezing of the steam locomotives, their whistles and the screeching of brakes, which releases the shadowy ghosts of the mythological past into the quotidian present. But like the arcades, this sonic space of travelling is in danger of fading into obsolescence, as it is rapidly being displaced by the faster, more fashionable and more convenient automobile and aeroplane. Because of its increasing marginalization in the marketplace of high-capitalist commerce and current technology, the railway station becomes the phantasmagoric stage of an eternal return of the same – the automatic, machine-like recurrence of stereotypical mythologies and stale, archaic images that, like recycled stage props and dusty costumes, surround the sentimental farewell scenes of everyday travellers with the superficial sheen of pseudo-historical importance. Under these circumstances, what happens to Orpheus' voice and lyre playing?

For an answer, we can turn to an earlier draft of this entry. It also mentions the railway station, with Orpheus, Eurydice and Hermes as the stationmaster, but links this mythological farewell scene to the neoclassicism of writers, painters and composers: Jean Cocteau, Igor Stravinsky, Pablo Picasso, Giorgio de Chirico and others (G°,26; see Klein 2013, 118). Rather cryptically, Benjamin suggests that the railway station as a space of travelling resembles neoclassicism, in that both are a 'transitional space of awakening in which we now are living' and which is, 'wherever possible, traversed by gods' (G°,26). Moreover, 'in neoclassicism, the muses who are so important for classical humanism mean nothing whatsoever' (G°,26). Outdated Greek gods and muses are part of a backward-looking aesthetics that lacks critical self-awareness of sociopolitical conditions: '[w]here neoclassicism is basically lacking is in the fact that it builds an architecture for the gods passing by which denies the fundamental relations of their coming-to-appearance. (A bad, reactionary architecture.)' (G°,26).

Benjamin's sketchy remarks become clearer when put into the context of Theodor W. Adorno's analysis of Stravinsky, Cocteau and Picasso.[7] In his essay from 1930, 'Reaction and progress', Adorno argues that musical material is not ahistorical and unchanging, but necessarily marked by history. Hence, progress in music means 'grasping the material at the most advanced stage of its historical dialectic' (Adorno 2017, 219). This dialectic involves the close interaction of the free ingenuity of the composer with the material; taking place within each composition, the success of this relationship can be measured only by the work's internal coherence (220). A particular challenge to the productive handling of musical material is the attempt to re-establish the 'primal meaning' of musical harmonies of the classical-romantic period represented by a composer such as Franz Schubert (223). For Adorno, one of the most fertile ways of addressing this issue is offered by the surrealist style, which he associates especially with the composer Kurt Weill. But he also discovers a tendency of musical surrealism in Stravinsky, whose works, like the traces of literary surrealism in Cocteau, show evidence of a 'subcutaneous connection' with the tendencies of painterly surrealism in Picasso (225). Their works, Adorno argues, are 'based on a recognition of the unrestorable nature of that "primal meaning"' (225). Surrealist compositions use 'obsolete means' by self-consciously foregrounding their own historically anachronistic character, and in so doing stage a kind of uncanny, ghostly return of the past, because such works derive their form 'from the "scandal" of the dead suddenly jumping to their feet among the living' (225). Thus, 'the surrealist technique can certainly provide constructive unity, coherent precisely in its illuminated, harshly exposed incoherence: a montage made of the ruins of things past' (226). Adorno differentiates this productive approach to past musical material from the mere pastiche of German Neoclassicism, which seeks to restore traditional musical means and materials in their presumably pure, original form, with the result that 'its means are so dead in themselves that not even the most accomplished copy could bring them back to life' (226–7). Adorno concludes his essay by stressing that the 'path to the "primal meaning" does not lead to the realm of archaic images but to the realm of images that appear to us as fresh' – a creative and critical reconfiguration of past material in the context of the present that he finds especially realized by the avant-garde (228).

Thus, Adorno discovers in Cocteau, Stravinsky and Picasso a productive technique of citing and reconfiguring selective motifs from musical tradition, whose ruinous, fragmentary and spectral strangeness inserts an invigorating sense of difference in the musical culture of the present, creating an effect similar to the visual montage technique of the avant-garde. This musical and painterly principle also resembles, of course, the technique of inscribing the redeemable past into the fleeting present, proposed by Benjamin's own dialectical image. Calling this procedure not neoclassical but surrealist, Adorno's terminology and analysis strikingly resembles Benjamin's own view that surrealism discovered the politically 'revolutionary energies that appear in the "outmoded" – in the first iron constructions, the first factory buildings, the earliest photos, objects that have begun to be extinct, grand salon pianos, the dresses of five years ago, trendy restaurants when the vogue has begun to ebb from them' (Benjamin 1999b, 210; trans. modified; see Brüggemann 2000, 588–93; Cohen 1993, 186–92). These outdated, unfashionable, enslaved and enslaving things, like social and architectural misery, can flip over into 'revolutionary nihilism' in the hands of the surrealist 'visionaries and augurs', who 'bring the immense forces of "atmosphere" concealed in these things to the point of explosion' (Benjamin 1999b, 210). For Benjamin, however, the noise level of this revolutionary energy and its ability to disrupt the homogeneity of the present – the reign of the bourgeoisie and industrial commodity capitalism – so as to instigate radical political change, is muffled by the racket of the railway station's technology. Here, Benjamin's aversion to the cacophony of the modern city resonates with the surrealists' distrust of the acoustic. As Koepnick argues, while the surrealists 'embraced the urban imaginary as a conduit to experiences of trance and intoxication, they disparaged the acoustical, including music, because external sounds restrained spontaneity and free imagination' (Koepnick 2004, 120). Hence, it makes perfect sense for Benjamin to have silenced the spectres of mythological prehistory: he briefly mentions the visual detail of Orpheus' teary eye, but the Greek singer's beautiful voice and his lyre, which in antiquity ecstatically moved beasts, trees and the denizens of the underworld, can no longer be heard. This, however, does not mean that Benjamin confirms the surrealist preference for visual sensations, as Koepnick suggests: '[w]hereas the eye, in the surrealists' perspective, was able to convert the discontinuous impressions into subversive visions, the ear could merely reaffirm the paucity of the real' (Koepnick 2004, 120). Rather, Benjamin seems to deplore the silencing of Orphic music – its quasi-surrealistic potential, as it were – by the phantasmagoric surface sights of modern technology, whose noisy evocations of sentimental mythologies displace the truth of music's disruptive and invigorating power, turning Orpheus' lyre-playing and singing into a precursor of neoclassical staleness.

Benjamin's reflections on the *Arcades Project* reveal themselves as the materialist equivalent to the metaphysical speculations of music in the essay on 'Goethe's *Elective Affinities*' (1919/22; Benjamin 1996).[8] Here, in a world marked by catastrophic fate, guilt, penitence and mythic sacrifice, music figures as the ultimately unattainable realm promising authentic redemption and reconciliation that is no longer subject to the deceptively reconciliatory semblance (*Schein*) of the visual in the world of the real. Of this musical ideal, only imperfect traces can be sensed in actual performance; hence, the 'deceptive harmony in the lovers' flute playing' in Goethe's novel is impermanent and marked by the mere appearance of reconciliation offered by sentimental emotion (*Rührung*) (Benjamin 1996, 348–9). A corresponding fragility is architecturally manifest in the old-fashioned arcades, railway stations, panoramas, wax museums and other dream houses of the collective, where music is simultaneously evoked and endangered by the metropolis's obsessions with the deceptively conciliatory semblance of historicizing architecture, mythological citations and the phantasmagoric transfiguration of social contradictions.

In this sense, the silence of Orpheus in the sentimental railway scene resembles the absence of authentic music from the life of Goethe's doomed lovers: '[t]heir world is wholly deserted by music' (Benjamin 1996, 349). This, however, does not mean that the silencing of music by the mythological phantasmagoria of urban modernity needs to be accepted as inevitable. Rather, in agreement with the surrealists' recognition of the revolutionary force of anachronistic material, Benjamin proposes that a critique of the nineteenth century should not focus on 'its mechanism and cult of machinery' – its fetishization of technological progress – but on 'its narcotic historicism, its passion for masks, in which nevertheless lurks a signal of true historical existence, one which the Surrealists were the first to pick up' (K1a,6). If the fields of Benjamin's investigation, as we saw earlier, are illuminated by the lightning flashes of a knowledge that give rise to thunderous texts, these same fields, 'where, until now, only madness has reigned', can be cultivated 'with the whetted axe of reason, looking neither right nor left so as not to succumb to the horror that beckons from deep in the primeval forest'; this critical reason clears the ground 'of the undergrowth of delusion and myth' (N1,4). While this statement appears simply to echo the classical Enlightenment critique of myth by analytical rationality, it can be associated with Benjamin's sonic sensibility, which ventures below the visual surfaces of industrial capitalism, technological advances and the fashionable commodity fetishism of modernity in order to rediscover noise, songs and orchestral music as parts of a shock-like illumination that promotes the collective subject's awakening from the mythic dreamworld into a utopian spacetime of revolutionary freedom and political emancipation.

Notes

1 This essay expands the analysis in Goebel (2017, 85–92) of Benjamin's comments on music and other sonic phenomena in the *Arcades Project*, mainly in the context of colonialist references. Entries in the *Arcades Project* (Benjamin 1999a) are cited by convolute numbers, except for passages not included in convolutes; these are cited by page numbers.
2 Susan Buck-Morss's magisterial *The Dialectics of Seeing* (Buck-Morss 1991) is still the most comprehensive study of the *Arcades Project*, focusing especially on the dialectical image, the dreamworld, myth, the phantasmagoria and surrealism. Brüggemann (2000) offers another succinct analysis of the *Arcades Project*, placing its portrayal of the arcades as outdated dreamscapes especially in the context of Sigfried Gidion's promotion of the new architecture of iron and glass.
3 In this sense, the arcades function as topographic media for the experience of the cultural past, as Skrandies (2005: 75) argues, not only in a visual, pictorial manner, but also acoustically.
4 Not accidentally, the translators discover acoustic reverberations in the formal structure of Benjamin's project, which displays 'significant repercussions for the direction and tempo of its reading', while its principle of citation and commentary sets up 'vibrations across the epochs of recent history' (Eiland and McLaughlin 1999, xi).
5 Alexander Honold stresses that, parallel to his obsession with the visual, graphic and graphological aspects of literature, Benjamin expresses a keen interest in voices, sonic cadences, timbres and rhythms. From such acoustic phenomena, Benjamin develops his particular understanding of literature as a sonic event [*Klanggeschehen*] (Honold 2005, 51).
6 For a detailed analysis of the musicological ramifications of David's compositions, see Klein (2013, 118–27).
7 See also the wide-ranging analysis of Benjamin's and Adorno's remarks on music and technological reproducibility, with a section on musical performance and recording in India, by Patke (2005).
8 My following remarks do not claim to recapitulate the enormous complexity of Benjamin's analysis of beauty, appearance and emotion in *Elective Affinities* but only to isolate the significance of music. See Trautsch (2013, 44–6) for an extensive discussion of Benjamin's

metaphysics of music, and Matassi (2013, 71–3) for a detailed analysis of the messianic primacy of music in the Goethe essay as the vehicle of redemption, hope and conscious dissolution of appearance opposing the deceptive regime of visual presence.

References

Adorno, Theodor W. 2017. 'Reaction and progress'. In *Night Music: Essays on music 1928–1962*, edited by Rolf Tiedemann, translated and introduced by Wieland Hoban, 218–29. London: Seagull Books.

Benjamin, Walter. 1996. 'Goethe's *Elective Affinities*'. In *Selected Writings, Volume 1, 1913–1926*, edited by Marcus Bullock and Michael W. Jennings, 297–60. Cambridge, MA: The Belknap Press of Harvard University Press.

Benjamin, Walter. 1999a. *The Arcades Project*, edited by Rolf Tiedemann, translated by Howard Eiland and Kevin McLaughlin. Cambridge, MA: The Belknap Press of Harvard University Press.

Benjamin, Walter. 1999b. 'Surrealism: The last snapshot of the European intelligentsia'. In *Selected Writings, Volume 2, 1927–1934*, edited by Michael W. Jennings, Howard Eiland and Gary Smith, translated by Rodney Livingstone and others, 207–21. Cambridge, MA: The Belknap Press of Harvard University Press.

Böhme, Gernot. 2017. *The Aesthetics of Atmospheres*, edited by Jean-Paul Thibaud. London: Routledge.

Brüggemann, Heinz. 2000. 'Passagen'. In *Benjamins Begriffe*, vol. 2, edited by Michael Opitz and Erdmut Wizisla, 573–618. Frankfurt: Suhrkamp.

Buck-Morss, Susan. 1991. *The Dialectics of Seeing: Walter Benjamin and the Arcades Project*. Cambridge, MA: MIT Press.

Cohen, Margaret. 1993. *Profane Illumination: Walter Benjamin and the Paris of surrealist revolution*. Berkeley: University of California Press.

Eiland, Howard and Kevin McLaughlin. 1999. 'Translator's foreword'. In *The Arcades Project*, by Walter Benjamin, edited by Rolf Tiedemann, translated by Howard Eiland and Kevin McLaughlin, ix–xiv. Cambridge, MA: The Belknap Press of Harvard University Press.

Goebel, Rolf J. 2017. *Klang im Zeitalter technischer Medien: Eine Einführung*. Vienna: Passagen Verlag.

Hall, Mirko M. 2010. 'Dialectical sonority: Walter Benjamin's acoustics of profane illumination', *Telos* 152: 83–102.

Honold, Alexander. 2005. 'Text auf der Tonspur: Benjamins Überlegungen zu einer akustischen Physiognomie der Literatur'. In *Walter Benjamins Medientheorie*, edited by Christian Schulte, 49–69. Konstanz: UVK Verlagsgesellschaft.

Klein, Tobias Robert. 2013. '"Musik in Passagen": Walter Benjamin und die Musik in der Hauptstadt des 19. Jahrhunderts'. In *Klang und Musik bei Walter Benjamin*, edited by Tobias Robert Klein and Asmus Trautsch, 117–27. Munich: Fink.

Klein, Tobias Robert and Asmus Trautsch, eds. 2013. *Klang und Musik bei Walter Benjamin*. Munich: Fink.

Koepnick, Lutz. 2004. 'Benjamin's silence'. In *Sound Matters: Essays on the acoustics of modern German culture*, edited by Nora M. Alter and Lutz Koepnick, 117–29. New York: Berghahn Books.

Matassi, Elio. 2013. 'Trauerspiel und Oper bei Walter Benjamin'. In *Klang und Musik bei Walter Benjamin*, edited by Tobias Robert Klein and Asmus Trautsch, 69–74. Munich: Fink.

Mettin, Martin. 2019. *Echo im Sprachwald: Figuren dialektischen Hörens bei Walter Benjamin*. Berlin: Neofelis.

Patke, Rajeev S. 2005. 'Benjamin on art and reproducibility: The case of music'. In *Walter Benjamin and Art*, edited by Andrew Benjamin, 185–208. London: Continuum.

Rautmann, Peter and Nicolas Schalz. 1992. 'Zu einer Theorie der Passage / Pour une théorie du passage'. In *Passagen: Nach Walter Benjamin / [D']après Walter Benjamin*, edited by Victor Malsy, Uwe Rasch, Peter Rautmann and Nicolas Schalz, 10–16. Mainz: Hermann Schmidt.

Rosa, Hartmut. 2019. *Resonance: A sociology of our relationship to the world*, translated by James C. Wagner. Cambridge: Polity.

Skrandies, Timo. 2005. 'Topographische Materialität: Die Passagen als Medien historischer Erfahrung'. In *Walter Benjamins Medientheorie*, edited by Christian Schulte, 71–85. Konstanz: UVK Verlagsgesellschaft.

Tiedemann, Rolf. 1999. 'Dialectic at a standstill: Approaches to the Passagen-Werk', translated by Gary Smith and André Lefevere. In *The Arcades Project*, by Walter Benjamin, edited by Rolf Tiedemann, translated by Howard Eiland and Kevin McLaughlin, 929–45. Cambridge, MA: The Belknap Press of Harvard University Press.

Trautsch, Asmus. 2013. 'Die abgelauschte Stadt und der Rhythmus des Glücks: Über das Musikalische in Benjamins Denken'. In *Klang und Musik bei Walter Benjamin*, edited by Tobias Robert Klein and Asmus Tratsch, 17–46. Munich: Fink.

2
Spectral passages: Christian Petzold's *Transit* (2018) as a mis-adaptation of Anna Seghers's novel (1944) and allusion to Europe's 'Summer of Migration'

Max Bergmann

At the beginning of 2020, the film *Transit* (DE/FR 2018), directed by Christian Petzold, became a surprise hit in the international press, and was included in many 'Best of 2019' lists – due to a later release outside Germany – and even featured prominently in a *New York Times* list of who *should* be nominated for the Academy Awards.[1] The reason for its global appeal is hard to pin down, but it might be its ambiguity, not letting itself be fixed in any genre or interpretation. Its blurring of time levels, and of fact and fiction, seems to fit perfectly with the end of the decade, which, just like the film, has felt open ended, transitory and in constant movement.

This chapter explores *Transit* as a film that works in multiple ways as a passage or transition between two states, and reads it as a film that is related in myriad ways to the 'Summer of Migration' of 2015 (Hess and Kasparek 2017), a high point in the steadily increasing number of migrants seeking asylum in Europe. *Transit*'s different levels of passage are complex and interwoven, not only within its narrative, but also in its mediality and visual strategies. The title itself already points towards movement, alluding to the characters' desire to flee, the bureaucratic details (*Transitvisum*) required to leave and Marseille as a space of transit. The fact that it is an adaptation or, as I will argue, a 'mis-adaptation' (Casetti 2004) of Anna Seghers's novel of the same name from 1944 muddles its medial status. It represents an uneasy passage from text to film, a transition of media that is not without complications in voice and perspective. By shooting the events of the book, set during World War Two, not in a staged past, but in contemporary Marseille, the film is able to reflect the passage of time, similarities between situations of flight and the persistence of memory. This context comes to haunt the film in many ways, and the spectral represents the final lens of analysis that this chapter will take up.

From Berlin to Marseille

Beginning his career in 1995, director Christian Petzold has always been occupied by passages or journeys of some kind. Early on, in his *Gespenster* (*Ghosts*) trilogy, the passage between life and death was foregrounded, as the characters either moved between the two realms or could not be clearly identified as belonging to either. Petzold is rooted in the Berlin School, a German film movement of the late 1990s and 2000s that seemed to be as much a creation of the media as it was tied to certain aesthetic choices (Schick 2018, 291–306). The long takes, the minimal dialogue, sober framing and monochrome colour palette suit the spectral topics and aimless, perpetually searching characters that Petzold depicts in his earlier films. Soon, Petzold's focus slowly shifted towards outright political, historical and economic passages. While such themes were present in his earlier work, at times unexpectedly, the story of a German soldier returning from Afghanistan in *Jerichow* (DE 2008) signifies a distinct shift (Fisher 2013, 119). This does not mean that these passages are not closely intertwined with the personal, but, as in *Barbara* (DE 2012) and *Phoenix* (DE 2014), situated in the German Democratic Republic of the 1980s and post-World War Two Berlin respectively, contexts larger than those related to the self come to the fore more definitively. In time, the director's visual style also evolved, not leaving the Berlin School behind entirely, but evolving towards a more dynamic image in almost every aspect.

Both developments are visible in *Transit* as well, for which Petzold developed the first ideas with his mentor and friend Harun Farocki. Seghers's novel had been an important book in their relationship for years (Brombach and Petzold 2018, 19–20). In the film, traces of the Berlin aesthetic can be easily spotted, but they are not dominant, and they are paired with less formally strict images. A moving and moveable camera effortlessly expands the image-space beyond the frame. The story, too, seems much less constrained, albeit just as laden with passages as previous Petzold films. Georg, the main character, tries to flee the German occupation of France during World War Two, and almost accidentally assumes the identity of the dead author, Weidel. In the process, he falls in love with Weidel's wife, Marie, who roams Marseille in search of her husband. She moves mysteriously in and out of view, until her and Georg's paths intersect. They are stranded in Marseille, looking for a way to leave Europe, like everyone else in the German refugee community, spending their time in cafes, embassies and consulates, waiting for visas and the confirmation of their safe passage abroad. Petzold arranges these locations as non-places – he mentions Marc Augé as inspiration (Petzold and Voelcker 2019) – where people spend time doing nothing and remain nearly anonymous, only caring about their own fates.

These places are clearly connected to the title of the novel and film. *Transit* seems to take it literally, by way of a definition of transit as a state of abeyance or limbo, a passage, as in, being *in transit*. This alludes to a transit visa, a certain kind of entry permit that allows one to pass through a country, in this case as part of a ship's journey. It is what most of the characters are seeking, whatever their final destination. Stuck for a time in Marseille, wandering around in search of said visa, they are in another kind of transit, making another kind of passage, as well: they are exiled from a Germany taken over by the Nazis. They have become truly homeless, in the sense that *Heimat*, for them, does not exist anymore – a topic Petzold has been concerned with throughout his career (Abel 2013, 69–110). The refugees are caught between this non-existent home and the destinations of their flight, safe fantasy spaces where jobs await and they can start anew, be it in Mexico City, Caracas or the United States. This liminal state of transit and permanent passage comes to define not only Georg, but also almost all of the film's ancillary figures.

In reaction, they incessantly tell their stories, holding on to their motivations and hopes by repetition. Georg, on the other hand, remains opaque, often shown in motion, on the way to somewhere or someone, in apparent contradiction to the deadlock of the complicated bureaucratic processes. But his physical movement remains empty, and mainly confined to Marseille, perhaps more closely related to the busy standstill of the applications and the never-ending requirements of consulates, as it may seem. Additionally, Georg embarks on yet another passage, taking on a dead man's identity that does not sit squarely with his own, even though one might argue that he would prefer to forget his prior existence. Finally, the multilingual nature of the refugee community's situation also places the characters once again in between, navigating the embassies, a foreign country and fellow refugees.

(Mis-)adapting Anna Seghers

The film is an adaptation of Anna Seghers's semi-autobiographical, identically titled novel, first published in French translation in 1944. It shares many of the same themes as the film: the delay of one's journey by heavy bureaucracy, lack of money or, at times, sheer coincidence. There is also the back-and-forth between waiting – in line at the embassy, at the grocery store, for a pizza in a restaurant – and endless movement – of refugees into the city, between consulates and ships, between hotels and the harbour (Schlenstedt 2001, 334–8). The film *Transit* transfers Seghers's story to contemporary Marseille, mixing time levels and objects while creating a mythic space that resonates with its fairy-tale-like character. As explicated by Silvia Schlenstedt in her commentary to the novel in Seghers's complete works, the text heavily mixes fact and fiction, intermingling real hotels, streets and locales that the author frequented during her time in Marseille with fictional events and characters: 'Such relations between real experiences and the world of the novel could be proven in many cases. They include details such as the locations in Marseille or events that are important for the whole story' (Schlenstedt 2001, 321).[2] In the film, this conflation of autobiography and fiction is transposed to a confusion of temporality, merging past and present.

When analysing *Transit* by Christian Petzold with a focus on the concept of passage, its status as adaptation would be the first passage. The film is a passage from written word to moving image. This includes a change of narrative voice, but it is the relocation of the story to present-day Marseille that makes the film neither a 'pure' or updated adaptation, nor a stand-alone film. The adaptation is caught in transit, highlighting the ruptures and tensions of intermedial passages. In this way, it consciously undermines the 'fidelity discourse' surrounding adaptations (Stam 2005, 14–16), making the usual categories of 'faithfulness' to the source text impractical.[3] It is also not a 'transcultural adaptation', a term that Linda Hutcheon uses to describe modernized adaptations that adjust the source text to contemporary values or regional contexts (Hutcheon 2013, 145–8). *Transit*'s adaptation is not cleanly executed and, as such, it could be best described as what Francesco Casetti calls a 'mis-adaptation' (2004). This term is not derogatory. It rather denotes an adaptation that is either too close or too far away from the source text – or, as in the case of *Transit*, somewhere in between, somehow slanted and not at a straight angle. Mis-adaptations are still valuable, as they are 'revealing in terms of the initial and final communicative situation' of both source and derivative text (Casetti 2004, 88). They stage an interplay of the different frames of production and discourse.

Casetti, influenced by Foucault's archaeological methods and discourse analysis, proposes that adaptations should be analysed by considering not only the source text and faithfulness to the source material, but also the contexts:

> I would like to suggest another perspective: both film and literature can also be considered as *sites of production and the circulation of discourses*; that is, as symbolic constructions that refer to a cluster of meanings that a society considers possible (thinkable) and feasible (legitimate). Consequently, film and literature are more revealing of the ways in which subjects interact with each other as either addressers or addressees, than of an author's ability to express him or herself. (Casetti 2004, 82, emphasis in the original)

Thus, literary and filmic works reveal more about interactions within society and the zeitgeist than any assumed authorial intentions. Hutcheon similarly refers to the notion of 'the vastness of context' that invariably influences adaptations (Hutcheon 2013, 142). To enable the kind of analysis that considers these aspects, Casetti uses the term 'communicative situation' to describe the various frames that influence and constitute texts (Casetti 1996; 2002; 2004). This is a complex process with many factors, essentially describing an adaptation as *'the reappearance, in another discursive field, of an element ... that has previously appeared elsewhere'* (Casetti 2004, 82, emphasis in the original), not as a repetition or juxtaposed expressive intention. In this way, the analysis goes beyond structural concerns or narrative comparisons and becomes a dialogue between text and context (83).

The frames that constitute the communicative situation are interactional, institutional, intertextual and existential. The interactional frame relates to the communicative interaction and the elements essential to it – how a text addresses its recipients. The institutional frame consists of 'institutionalized rules and manners' (Casetti 2004, 84), for example, the three-act structure of classical Hollywood films, perhaps at odds with a novel's structure. The intertextual frame refers to background discourses, the reception of the source text between publication and adaptation, and its relationships to other texts. Finally, the existential frame is 'a set of personal and collective experiences that operate as a reference' (84), including life experiences and connections to historical events. The text itself and the different frames work together and influence each other to result in a unique communicative situation, making a comparison of source and adaptation more fruitful.

Reading *Transit* as a mis-adaptation, and highlighting the passages that the text underwent on its way to becoming a film, the term becomes interesting as a description of an in-between state, of a film neither too close nor too far removed from the source, appearing in a peculiar relationship to Seghers's text. In the following, I will explore this relationship with particular reference to the communicative situation of the film, its different frames, and how they might have informed the film's aesthetic and narrative strategies. This will especially entail the existential frame, as the transposition of the story into modern Marseille alludes to many contexts related to the Summer of Migration. To account for the hauntings in the film, I will first turn to the notion of spectrality as a conceptual metaphor, and connect it to the concept of passage.

Spectrality, ghosts and haunting as conceptual metaphors

Always featuring remnants of the past, be it on a narrative or meta-referential level, Jaimey Fisher has called Petzold's cinema a 'ghostly archeology' (Fisher 2013, 1), even before *Transit* was made and released. Referencing his reconstruction of genre and generic elements in art-house cinema, as well as in many of his characters, Fisher links this concept to the work of Walter Benjamin, 'one of Petzold's stated influences' (Fisher, 2013, 16). Benjamin's *Arcades Project*, or *Das Passagen-Werk* (Benjamin 1999), is paramount here, a work 'in which he sought to create an archeological history of modernity by immersing himself in the past, tearing out quotes and images to "mortify" them, and then recontextualizing them in work that would illuminate the present' (Fisher 2013, 16).[4] This recontextualization, this illuminating of the present, is evident in *Transit* as well. Just like Benjamin's work, it tries to figure out: 'What is a remnant, a remain, and/or a ghost? Remnants, remains, and ghosts are things that, above all, recall the past – that underscore the so-called presence of the past' (Fisher 2013, 16). Fisher connects Benjamin and the concept of a 'ghostly archeology' to Petzold's oeuvre until 2013, but there could hardly be a more apt description of *Transit*, with its anachronistic temporality that is neither in the past nor fully in the present. Consequently, Alice Bardan connects the film to 'post-mortem cinema', a term referring to films that are 'able to convey a sense of haunting and to raise issues of memory, history and identity through a non-realistic configuration of temporality' (Bardan 2020, 120).

In *Transit*, 'the time is out of joint' indeed, to quote the famous *Hamlet* line that Jacques Derrida uses as a starting point in the founding text of the spectral turn in the humanities (Derrida 1994; del Pilar Blanco and Peeren 2013; Peeren 2014). Haunting, extensively theorized since the publication of *The Specters of Marx*, becomes a key term for the film as well. Closely related, spectrality and the ghost, understood as a 'conceptual metaphor' (del Pilar Blanco and Peeren 2013, 9), or 'traveling concept' (del Pilar Blanco and Peeren 2010, xi), redirect our attention to the spectres and hidden layers of the film. As Avery Gordon writes in her seminal book, *Ghostly Matters*: '[t]he ghost or the apparition is one form by which something lost, or barely visible, or seemingly not there to our supposedly well-trained eyes, makes itself known or apparent to us, in its own way, of course' (Gordon 2008, 8). In the film, the spectral moves beyond a sheerly temporal, Derridean haunting, as it turns out to be a central lens of many aspects, both intra- and extradiegetic.

In this regard, haunting can be productively coupled with passage, as the literary text haunts the film after its medial passage, appearing in the voice-over, possibly in the form of a physical manuscript passed around, and passively in the form of the dead author, Weidel, whose identity Georg assumes. Apart from this meta-level, the author comes to haunt the character as well, as he uncannily meets Weidel's wife Marie and falls in love with her, and is forced to philosophize about literature with the Mexican consul. As Malte Hagener has argued, permutation (*Vertauschung*), the ghostly exchange of identities, is a major theme in Petzold's oeuvre. (Hagener connects this recurring theme in Petzold's films to a text by Farocki: 'A permutation is also a spook – one existence takes possession of another' [1980, 274, quoted in Hagener 2018a, 167].)[5] Marie, on the other hand, is a spectre in her own right, coming into view suddenly and disappearing just as quickly, haunting the streets of the city. Marseille is an important marker of the spectral as well, as the contemporary city is haunted by its history as a hub for refugees during World War Two. But this spatial component of spectrality is not unilateral, as the events of the mid-2010s, the physical space of filming and its myriad connotations come to haunt the story. This point is especially pertinent for the existential frame, which will be discussed after examination of the other three frames.

The frames of *Transit*

In describing the communicative situation of the film *Transit*, the interactional frame will be the starting point for considering the ways in which the source text and adaptation address recipients and construct the story. The most important difference between the two texts in this regard is the change of perspective, and the frame narrative that the film adds. In the novel, the story is told by an unnamed first-person narrator, who experiences the same events as the film's Georg. The film, however, uses the bartender of the bar Mont Ventoux as its voice-over narrator, creating a frame narrative in which Georg has relayed the story to him. In one of the last scenes of the film, when the set-up is revealed in a mix of voice-over and dialogue, Georg hands over a manuscript to the bartender, asking if he can leave it with him. This manuscript could be the unfinished novel by the writer Weidel, which features earlier in the film, when Georg begins to read it and the voice-over appears for the first time. Conversely, it could also be *Transit*, the novel, making Georg the unnamed narrator writing the book, adding another layer to the film's relationship to the source text.

After this scene, the frame narrative is crucial for a Petzoldian twist, a ghostly haunting typical for his films: Marie, who should have left on a ship to Mexico earlier that day, suddenly enters the bar, looking for her husband as always. Georg turns around and sees her. A cut to his point of view reveals that she looks directly back at him. Georg rushes after her, but she has seemingly vanished again. He goes on to the port and learns, in a slight aberration from the book, in which the narrator only casually mentions it, that the ship Marie was supposedly on has sunk. The film ends ambiguously, Georg in the bar again, turning around to see if Marie comes in. The last shot is of him, suddenly looking hopeful at someone outside of frame, without disclosing whether it is Marie (Figure 2.1). In the novel, there is no doubt that the narrator has given up hope and, although it ends with an image of Marie forever roaming the streets like a ghost, it is clear that this is not reality.[6] Through the narratorial shift, the film is able to keep this in limbo, to make Marie one of those characters seemingly between the realms of life and death.

Apart from such concrete narrative effects, the change of narrator also contributes to the film's overall relationship to Seghers's novel. Even though the voice-over often recites her text verbatim, the altered perspective complicates matters. It simultaneously pulls together and distances the film from its source, adding to the uneasiness mentioned

Figure 2.1 Georg, turning around. Still from *Transit* (Christian Petzold; DE/F 2018; timecode: 1:33:38) © Hans Fromm/Schramm Film.

above. Again, the film develops and explores an in-betweenness. Petzold himself has spoken of this shift, and describes it as a cinematic decision. He believes a first-person narrator – contrary to the novel, where both narrator and addressee are equally alone – does not work in film because film addresses an audience, a shared space (Rogowski and Beer 2019, 9).[7] As Petzold notes in a different interview, it also speaks of the film's relation to *Heimat*, stating that the nameless narrator of the novel creates a home through the act of narrating (Brombach and Petzold 2018, 19). Instead of reproducing this situation, the film makes the act of making a home by narration visible (20). The interactional frame is important in this regard, as the conscious decision to give the protagonist a name while having someone else tell his story changes the dynamics of the story completely.

The institutional frame of *Transit*, meaning the way that institutionalized rules and conventions influence or shape an adaptation, is obvious in its rejection of standard adaptation practices. Neither a period drama with elaborate costumes and sets, nor a complete update for current times, it heightens the push-and-pull effect of the film as a passage, as being in transit itself. It is essentially two films in one, as Jonathan Romney summarizes succinctly:

> If you regard it as a story about World War Two manifestly filmed in the modern day, then you become increasingly conscious of the film *as* a film, as a fable recounted without historical set dressing. In this light, what we see is at once distanced and made more immediate. It's more immediate because it refuses the period illusionism which might have made the film a genre exercise and

therefore easy to disengage from. Conversely, *Transit* is distanced by being given the hard simplicity of a parable, of the demonstration of a theorem. (Romney 2019, n.p.)

Transit is not easy to categorize, unlike other 'genre exercises' and adaptations. On the other hand, and as part of the institutional frame as well, it fits neatly into the categories of art cinema, most prominently defined by David Bordwell (1985, 205–33). *Transit*'s general ambiguity, authorial presence, negation of cause and effect, and open-ended resolution are historical hallmarks of this type of narration. Of course, there have been many adaptations utilizing these stylistic and narrative devices, for example, Rainer Werner Fassbinder's *Fontane Effi Briest* (DE 1974), Stanley Kubrick's *Eyes Wide Shut* (UK/US 1999) and numerous others. Even the anachronism is not entirely new, and Petzold cites *The Long Goodbye* (Robert Altman; US 1973) and *Portrait d'une jeune fille de la fin des années 60 à Bruxelles* (Chantal Akerman; FR 1994) as influences (Petzold and Voelcker 2019, n.p.). This last point, while certainly part of the institutional frame, as these are historical precedents in cinema, already points toward the intertextual frame.

The intertextual frame is important in two respects: first, it again illuminates the film's relationship to the book, highlighting the consistencies, the aberrations and condensations of the story. Among others, the narrator's relationship to another woman named Nadine, which appears in the novel, is omitted to tighten the events. Second, it denotes the film's medial positioning, its conception as a film. One could argue that the intertexts above, which use a similar anachronistic setting, help to place *Transit* in a line of cinematic auteurs. In relation to the story, both the novel and the film make allusions to the film *Casablanca* (Michael Curtiz; US 1942). Writing about the parallels between Seghers's book and Curtiz's film, Heike Klapdor mentions two narrative levels related to the chase for a transit visa and the chase for a woman. She claims that the second dynamizes the first, creating love stories that follow the rules of melodrama (Klapdor 2008, n.p.). She also compares the stories' geographies, and their focus on port cities and public spaces: 'In *Transit* and *Casablanca*, the port and ship are of comparable symbolic power as the refuge in a public space that becomes private: the cafe, the bistro, the bar' (Klapdor 2008, n.p.).[8] Petzold's film leans into this; the city, its port and public/private spaces take centre stage. In another deviation from the novel, Petzold focuses on the works of architect Rudy Riciotti in modern Marseille. In a scene in which Georg is in conversation with a female fellow refugee, she remarks on the footbridge that connects the old fort with the new museum, Mucem, built in 2013 – another intertextual metaphor for the adaptation at hand.

There have been two other adaptations of *Transit*, both part of the intertextual network as well: *Fluchtweg nach Marseille* (Ingemo Engström and Gerhard Theuring; DE 1977) and *Transit* (René Allio; FR 1991). The film by Engström and Theuring, incidentally friends of Harun Farocki as well, is more pertinent to Petzold's version, since it is also not a straight adaptation.[9] It is rather a film essay, a mix of documentary, auto-ethnography and fiction film, using the novel more as a leitmotif than a template. In some scenes, we see the filmmakers in 1970s Marseille, sitting in the cafes of the novel and reading the text, in some ways strongly reminiscent of Petzold's clash of historical narrative and modern setting. In the German journal *Filmkritik* (later translated for *Framework*), the directors remark on the film, their research and the production:

> Finding a connection between a work situation (1977) and a material (1941) was both easy and difficult. The intersection point was quickly established as an idea ... In order to take the material seriously, the first requirement was to turn away from it, to initiate one's own choices ... Film adaptations were the bad habit of the TYCOONS who dominated the film industry, the genre of hollow filmic packaging, empty shells of speech and costume. Money to make money. So there was that too – an act of opposition ot [sic] the traditionally permitted routine. (Engström and Theuring 1982, 24)

This attitude, regardless of Petzold's actual stance, suits his film perfectly as well. Even though it is embedded in international production and distribution networks, if perhaps not part of the 'adaptation industry' (Murray 2011), and falls in line with recent production trends of German films on migration (Hagener 2018b),[10] it still seems to reject 'empty shells of speech and costume' with its anachronistic set-up. It opposes established conventions. The narrator in *Fluchtweg nach Marseille*, as in Petzold's *Transit*, tells his story to another person, not the bartender, but a fellow guest in a cafe. In this way, the narrative situation changes. The films' audiences witness a narrative enfolding, instead of being the addressees of a story told (Hagener 2018b, 26–7) – an effect that is apparent in both films. Asked about the film and text by Engström and Theuring, Petzold says that he was not aware of them before filming, but suggests that the film would make a good double feature with his own version (Arnold 2018).

The intertextual frame includes a wide range of further references, including to Kafka's *The Trial* and its adaptation by Orson Welles (see Helbig 2019; Bardan 2020), and marks a clear departure from Seghers's text, emphasizing the filmic medium. This interaction with film history is a major part of Petzold's filmmaking (Hagener 2018a, 171). Another reference is especially interesting in this regard: *Dawn of the Dead* (George A. Romero; US/IT 1978), which is alluded to when Georg visits the bar Mont Ventoux for the first time. Accompanying images of Georg eating pizza, the barkeeper/voice-over narrator says:

> It was on that afternoon that I first saw him. He had cashed the money order, was sitting at the window, eating hot slices and drinking chilled rosé. Outside, people were walking past carrying shopping bags. 'Fear and chaos will soon reign here, and all they can think of is going shopping', he said. I told him about a film in which zombies besiege a shopping mall. 'Yes', he said, 'even the dead are lost for ideas.' (Timecode: 31:07–31:38)[11]

This reference is no coincidence: it places *Transit* in a filmic network, and reinforces its interpretation as ghost story. Unlike in a horror film, in which ghosts and zombies are threatening presences, it is the principal characters and circumstances in *Transit* that are undead and come back to haunt the present. As another authorial intervention, this reference to *Dawn of the Dead* ties in with the anachronism, as well as with ideas of persisting memory and continuations of history that play a big role in the existential frame.

Existential frame and memory

For the existential frame, the concept of spectrality is especially useful, as '[f]or Derrida, hauntology reshapes history by disrupting its conventional structure of chronology' (del Pilar Blanco and Pereen 2013, 14). The film visualizes this and, quite literally, shows the ghosts of the past – history come back to haunt the present – and demonstrates the endurance of Holocaust memory. As Petzold has explained, this is intentionally kept ambiguous. The characters' clothes are timeless, and their interactions with the environment are calibrated so that they rarely interact with modern devices. But contemporary cars, ships and even technology are still prominent in the film and hard to miss, sometimes alongside historical ones. This stark contrast is immediately noticeable in the first

Figures 2.2–2.3 Letters; flatscreen in bar. Stills from *Transit* (Christian Petzold; DE/F 2018; timecode: 0:01:35; 0:02:49) © Hans Fromm/ Schramm Film.

scene of the film: Georg is in a bar in Paris, and modern French police cars drive by outside. An acquaintance comes in and tells him that Paris will be shut off and he will leave the city. He asks Georg for a favour. He then puts two letters on the counter, and they look jarringly dated, the address written in Sütterlin script, a historical form of German handwriting (Figure 2.2). Georg is to deliver the letters to the writer Weidel, and he agrees to do so in exchange for some money. Georg gets up and leaves the bar, revealing a modern flatscreen on the wall that was not visible before (Figure 2.3).

A cut, and more modern police cars in the street follow. In Weidel's hotel room, there is an old typewriter and manuscript, furthering the temporal confusion. These conflicting period markers in the first few minutes of the film leave viewers in a curious position, irritating and distracting them while they slowly realize the World War Two story unfolding in present-day France.

This becomes especially unsettling not long after, on the train ride to Marseille that Georg takes with his wounded friend Heinz. These scenes blur time levels, perhaps visualized by landscape shots, partly blurred by the speed of the moving train, which are interspersed throughout the journey. Temenuga Trifonova notes how the ensuing references zigzag across history:

> While the shots of the trains cannot fail to recall the trains transporting millions of Jews to the death camps, this reference to the past is deliberately conflated with the more recent visual memory of thousands of illegal migrants and refugees trying to enter Europe locked up in the back of TIR trucks, many of them suffocating to death – for example, before Georg and Heinz get on the train, another friend gives Georg instructions on how to get fresh air in the train compartment without attracting the Germans' attention. Here the political allegory flattens all temporal distinctions: the current refugee crisis is figured metaphorically through a reference to the Holocaust while, at the same time, the dystopian present/future day Holocaust, depicted by the film literally/realistically rather than metaphorically, is figured through a reference 'back' to the current refugee crisis. (Trifonova 2020, 220)

Once in Marseille, the film switches to an image from a surveillance camera (Figure 2.4), at once locating the events in the present and visualizing surveillance practices during the Nazi regime. The two layers of scenes that signify time periods are typical for the film, often referencing both past and present, letting the former come alive in a foreign environment. This directs our attention to the existential frame – the personal, collective and historical experiences that act as a reference point for Petzold's adaptation.

First and foremost, *Transit* brings to mind the refugee movements of the present and their reversal in the film, as Europe has become the place to leave.[12] As Bardan notes, it 'challenge[s] viewers to reflect on European history in light of the recent rise in anti-refugee sentiment' (Bardan 2020, 116). Consequently, just as World War Two haunts contemporary Marseille, the situation at the time of filming in 2017 comes to haunt the narrative, shortly after millions of refugees had fled to Europe and Germany. The 'Summer of Migration' of 2015, as Sabine Hess and Bernd Kasparek and others call it (Hess and Kasparek 2017; Hess et al. 2016; Yurdakul et al. 2018), saw unprecedented numbers of refugees fleeing to

Figure 2.4 Surveillance camera image. Still from *Transit* (Christian Petzold; DE/F 2018; timecode: 0:18:06) © Hans Fromm/Schramm Film.

the European Union. Displaced by the civil war in Syria and other conflicts, millions of civilians first fled to neighbouring countries such as Turkey or Lebanon, before beginning marches toward the European border, especially via the Balkan route (Kasparek 2016). Hess et al. (2016) argue that the situation is part of a long chain of events concerning the European border, including internal EU administrative acts, such as the treaties of Schengen (1985), Amsterdam (1999) and Lisbon (2009), as well as geopolitical, regional trends, especially the Arab Spring (Hess and Kasparek 2017, 6–9).

This led to a collapse of the European border regime, and made the politics that had been prevalent up to that point – externalization of the border to third countries and the Mediterranean; a smart, fortified border that capitalizes on digitalization and biometrization; an internal system of asylum practices (Dublin/Eurodac) (Hess and Kasparek 2017, 4) – impossible to maintain: 'This architecture of the European border regime broke down in summer 2015, they collapsed confronted by a new quality of migrant arrival. In the end, it challenged not only the European Union's border and migration regime, but the EU and the European project as a whole' (5). As is known, this culminated in the opening of the German border and Angela Merkel's instantly famous slogan '*Wir schaffen das!*' (We can do it!), and millions of refugees finding shelter in Germany and the EU. However, this development did not only have positive consequences. Merkel's (and the Christian Democratic/Socialist Union's) immigration politics quickly toughened afterwards (or returned to form, see Yurdakul and Koenitz 2019), and the EU moved to re-establish its border regime (Hess and Kasparek 2017; Buckel 2018). This deepened many trends that had been visible in the EU before. Perhaps due to a 'perfect storm' of circumstances (Lucassen 2018, 21), it led to the further strengthening of populist right-wing parties across Europe, nationalistic and anti-democratic tendencies in some member states, such as Hungary and Poland, and the militarization of the police in response to terror attacks that were quite often linked to migration movements. Hess et al., writing in 2016, summarize:

> Since last summer, every opportunity was taken to turn the Summer of Migration into a nationalistic *moral panic*: from conflicts in overflowing (mass) shelters, New Year's in Cologne and similar, less dramatic narratives of the 'conditions' in urban spaces, up to the often drawn connections between movements of migration and apparent or factual Islamistic terror attacks or plans.[13] (Hess et al. 2016, 15–16)

This was the situation at the time of *Transit*'s production: a multifaceted backlash against refugee movements and, in fact, refugees themselves, with reappearing moral panics concerning various aspects of the aftermath of the Summer of Migration, and a rising number of right-wing attacks (Staud 2018).[14]

In the film, the situation of flight is reversed, and countries of the Global South have become desirable destinations. With this, the film alludes to a wealth of topics: 'Fortress Europe' and the Mediterranean as a zone of defence and contact, EU deportation policies and the discourse around 'safe' countries of origin and third countries (or 'first countries of asylum'; see Hess et al. 2016, 14). Especially remarkable is a scene shortly after Georg's arrival in Marseille. In the hotel where he and many other refugees live, one woman is captured by military police and dragged outside (Figure 2.5). The other inhabitants stand in their doorways, silently watching, lowering their heads in shame. This scene, with its shocking details – the woman screaming, violently dragged across the floor, her clothes nearly torn off – evoke images of the evictions of refugee protest camps in Germany, or of the 'Calais Jungle' in 2016, directly referencing instances of the aforementioned backlash.

In *Transit*, rumours of sinking civilian ships on their way to the Americas make their rounds in the community and, given their surroundings in twenty-first-century Marseille, this may be seen as a reference to sinking refugee boats trying to reach European shores. This crisis at sea, existent but invisible for many years (see Last et al. 2017), and receiving varying degrees of humanitarian help from the EU (Heller and Pezzani 2016), has not abated since the closing of the Aegean/Balkan

Figure 2.5 Police raid in hotel. Still from *Transit* (Christian Petzold; DE/F 2018; timecode: 0:41:40) © Hans Fromm/Schramm Film.

route (Steinhilper and Gruijters 2018). Deprived of safer and, in effect, legal ways of migration, refugees were once again forced to try crossing the Mediterranean in precarious ways. Connected, but not as prominent in *Transit*, is a discourse about human trafficking and the facilitation of flight: at the end of the film, Georg has decided to stay in Marseille after all, and he thinks that people might view him as a trafficker. His role in acquiring the transit visas and passages for Marie and the doctor is indeed complicated.

The modern-day police officers on display in the streets of Marseille and Paris, on the other hand, could signal France's declaration of a state of emergency after the Paris terror attacks in 2015, which lasted until 2017. The subsequent militarization of the police and public space was a direct reaction to the attacks. Paranoia about sleeper cells coming to Europe disguised as refugees linked the declaration to refugee movements. In another storyline in the film, in one of the clear departures from the novel, the Maghreb is manifested in two characters. The region, deeply connected to France historically, and one of the larger geopolitical causes of the contemporary situation mentioned above, is inscribed into the film in the form of Melissa, the widow of Georg's friend Heinz, and Driss, their son. These characters allude to France's colonial past and the current situation of migrants in the country (Trifonova 2020, 220). Georg befriends the two, especially the boy, and reveals some of his past through this relationship (Helbig 2019, 36). In one of the key scenes, Georg helps Driss repair a broken radio, which instantly plays a song from his childhood, perhaps mending the broken link between past, present and future that the film portrays.

Conclusion

This analysis of the existential frame is not to suggest a simple comparison between the Holocaust, its memory and current circumstances. But all these associations, which are not openly mentioned but only alluded to in the visuals, and in the direct contradiction of a World War Two account in contemporary Marseille, are directly linked to the story that *Transit* tells. Through these links, *Transit* becomes a forceful enquiry into current matters, contextualizing historical events and bringing them into contact with the present. The frames of its communicative situation play a major role, as its intertextual references, change of narrator and rejection of institutionalized conventions contribute to the film's medial positioning and narrative strategies.

By highlighting the passage from text to image, from past to present, the film is able to provide commentary on contemporary issues by means of a mis-adaptation. This is emphasized in its in-betweenness, in its specific relationship to Seghers's text and in references and temporal markers that are often double-layered. It creates two kinds of passages in the film, within the narrative as well as on a meta-level, generating a complex web of references. This focus on flight, migration and a loss of *Heimat* connects it squarely with the Summer of Migration and its aftermath. *Transit*, with all its ambiguity, its uncertain ending and ghostly hauntings, makes clear that the present is neither clear-cut nor neatly closed off from history. Instead, the latter permeates contemporary surroundings, creating spectres that resonate with current realities.

Notes

1. See Dargis and Scott (2020), *Film Comment* (2019) and *Little White Lies* (2019). Even Barack Obama included it on his year-end list (Obama 2019).
2. 'Solche Bezüge zwischen Realerfahrung und Romanwelt ließen sich in vielen Fällen belegen. Sie betreffen Details etwa der Örtlichkeiten in Marseille, sie betreffen Begebenheiten, die gewichtig sind für die ganze Geschichte' (my translation).
3. For more on this discourse within adaptation studies, see Murray (2011, 7–9).
4. Benjamin also wrote about Marseille several times, and was a refugee himself in the city in 1940. For more, also regarding *Transit*'s relation to the *Arcades Project*, see Bardan (2020).
5. 'Auch eine Vertauschung ist ein Spuk – eine Existenz bemächtigt sich einer anderen' (my translation).
6. 'Sie läuft noch immer die Straßen der Stadt ab, die Plätze und Treppen, Hotels und Cafés und Konsulate auf der Suche nach ihrem Liebsten. Sie sucht rastlos nicht nur in dieser Stadt, sondern in allen Städten Europas, die ich kenne, selbst in den phantastischen Städten fremder Erdteile, die mir unbekannt geblieben sind' (Seghers 2018, 300). (My translation: 'She still walks the streets of the city, the squares and stairways, hotels and cafes and consulates in search of her beloved. She searches restlessly not only in this city, but in all the cities of Europe that I know, even in the fantastic cities of foreign continents that have remained unknown to me.')

7 'In einem Roman wendet sich ein Erzähler in seiner Einsamkeit an einen Leser, der genauso alleine ist. Ein Ich-Erzähler im Kino wendet sich aber nicht an ein einsames Subjekt, sondern an einen Raum, einen Zuschauerraum' (Rogowski and Beer 2019, 9). (My translation: 'In a novel, a narrator in his loneliness addresses a reader who is equally alone. A first-person narrator in cinema, however, does not address a lonely subject, but a space, an auditorium.')
8 'Von vergleichbarer Symbolkraft wie Hafen und Schiff ist in *Transit* und *Casablanca* die Zuflucht in einen öffentlichen Raum, der zu einem privaten Ort wird: das Café, Bistro, die Bar' (my translation).
9 For more on Allio's version, a rather conventional adaptation in a historical setting, see Winkler (2007, 192–5).
10 *Transit* was produced as a French–German co-production, with financing from several sources in both countries.
11 'An diesem Nachmittag sah ich ihn zum ersten Mal. Er hatte die Geldanweisung eingelöst, saß am Fenstertisch, aß die heißen Stücke und trank den kühlen Rosé. Draußen zogen die Menschen vorbei, mit ihren Einkaufstüten. "In wenigen Wochen wird hier die Angst und das Chaos sein, und ihnen fällt nichts Besseres ein als shoppen zu gehen," sagte er. Ich erzählte ihm von einem Film, in dem Zombies ein Einkaufszentrum belagern. "Ja," sagte er, "selbst den Toten fällt nichts Besseres ein"' (my translation).
12 *Transit*, the novel, was already associated with refugee movements in the past, for example, in the 1990s. See Schlensedt (2001, 353 and endnote 121); Thielking (1995).
13 'Seit dem letzten Sommer wurde jede Gelegenheit genutzt, um aus dem Sommer der Migration eine nationalistische moral panic zu kreieren: von Konflikten in überfüllten (Massen-) Unterkünften, über die Kölner Silvesternacht und ähnliche, weniger dramatische Erzählungen über die "Verhältnisse" in städtischen Räumen, bis hin zu den immer wieder gezogenen Verbindungslinien zwischen den Bewegungen der Migration und vermeintlichen oder tatsächlichen islamistischen Anschlägen oder entsprechenden Plänen' (my translation).
14 According to Staud (2018), who uses the official statistics of the German Department of the Interior, 2015–17, right-wing acts of violence increased drastically and were significantly higher than long-time averages.

Filmography

Barbara (Christian Petzold; DE 2012).
Casablanca (Michael Curtiz; US 1942).
Dawn of the Dead (George A. Romero; US/IT 1978).
Eyes Wide Shut (Stanley Kubrick; UK/US 1999).
Fluchtweg nach Marseille (*Escape Route to Marseille*; Ingemo Engström and Gerhard Theuring; DE 1977).
Fontane Effi Briest (Rainer Werner Fassbinder; DE 1974).
Jerichow (Christian Petzold; DE 2008).
The Long Goodbye (Robert Altman; US 1973).
Phoenix (Christian Petzold; DE 2014).
Portrait d'une jeune fille de la fin des années 60 à Bruxelles (*Portrait of a Young Girl at the End of the 1960s in Brussels*; Chantal Akerman; FR 1994).
Transit (René Allio; FR 1991).
Transit (Christian Petzold; DE/FR 2018).

References

Abel, Marco. 2013. *The Counter-Cinema of the Berlin School*. Martlesham: Boydell & Brewer.
Arnold, Frank. 2018. 'Interview mit Christian Petzold über seinen Film *Transit*', *epd Film*, 5 April. Accessed 24 March 2022. https://www.epd-film.de/meldungen/2018/interview-mit-christian-petzold-ueber-seinen-film-transit.

Bardan, Alice. 2020. 'Europe, spectrality and "post-mortem cinema": The haunting of history in Christian Petzold's *Transit* (2018) and Aki Kaurismäki's *Le Havre* (2011)', *Northern Lights: Film & Media Studies Yearbook* 18 (1): 115–29.
Benjamin, Walter. 1999. *The Arcades Project*, edited by Rolf Tiedemann, translated by Howard Eiland and Kevin McLaughlin. Cambridge, MA: The Belknap Press of Harvard University Press.
Bordwell, David. 1985. *Narration in the Fiction Film*. Madison: University of Wisconsin Press.
Brombach, Ilka and Christian Petzold. 2018. '"Ein Raum, in dem wir heimisch sind": Interview mit Christian Petzold'. In *Über Christian Petzold*, edited by Ilka Brombach and Tina Kaiser, 19–60. Berlin: Vorwerk 8.
Buckel, Sonja. 2018. 'Winter is coming: Der Wiederaufbau des europäischen Grenzregimes nach dem "Sommer der Migration"', *PROKLA: Zeitschrift für Kritische Sozialwissenschaft* 48 (192): 437–57. https://doi.org/10.32387/prokla.v48i192.907.
Casetti, Francesco. 1996. 'Communicative situations: The cinema and the television situation', *Semiotica* 112 (1/2): 35–48.
Casetti, Francesco. 2002. *Communicative Negotiation in Cinema and Television*. Milan: Vita e Pensiero.
Casetti, Francesco. 2004. 'Adaptation and mis-adaptations: Film, literature, and social discourses'. In *A Companion to Literature and Film*, edited by Robert Stam and Alessandra Raengo, 81–90. Oxford: Wiley-Blackwell.
Dargis, Manohla and A.O. Scott. 2020. 'And the 2020 Oscar nominees should be …', *New York Times*, 3 January. Accessed 24 March 2022. https://www.nytimes.com/interactive/2020/01/03/movies/critics-oscar-nominees.html.
Del Pilar Blanco, María and Esther Peeren, eds. 2010. *Popular Ghosts: The haunted spaces of everyday culture*. London: Bloomsbury.
Del Pilar Blanco, María and Esther Peeren, eds. 2013. *The Spectralities Reader: Ghosts and haunting in contemporary cultural theory*. London: Bloomsbury.
Derrida, Jacques. 1994. *Specters of Marx: The state of the debt, the work of mourning, and the New International*, translated by Peggy Kamuf. New York: Routledge.
Engström, Ingemo and Gerhard Theuring. 1982. 'Escape route to Marseille', translated by Barry Ellis-Jones, *Framework: The Journal of Cinema and Media* 18: 23–31. Originally published in 1978 as 'Fluchtweg nach Marseille', *Filmkritik* 22 (2): 66–97.
Farocki, Harun. 1980. 'Vertauschte Frauen', *Filmkritik* 282: 274–9.
Film Comment. 2019. 'Best films of 2019', 10 December. Accessed 24 March 2020. https://www.filmcomment.com/best-films-of-2019/.
Fisher, Jaimey. 2013. *Christian Petzold*. Urbana: University of Illinois Press.
Gordon, Avery F. 2008 [1997]. *Ghostly Matters: Haunting and the sociological imagination*. Minneapolis: University of Minnesota Press.
Hagener, Malte. 2018a. 'Konzentrische Kreise: Filmgeschichte als Matrix im Werk von Christian Petzold'. In *Über Christian Petzold*, edited by Ilka Brombach and Tina Kaiser, 159–71. Berlin: Vorwerk 8.
Hagener, Malte. 2018b. 'Migration and refugees in German cinema: Transnational entanglements', *Studies in European Cinema* 15 (2/3): 110–24. https://doi.org/10.1080/17411548.2018.1453772.
Helbig, Thomas. 2019. 'Die Gegenwart des Historischen in Christian Petzolds *Transit*', *all-over* 15: 33–44. Accessed 24 March 2022. http://allover-magazin.com/?p=3392.
Heller, Charles and Lorenzo Pezzani. 2016. 'Ebbing and flowing: The EU's shifting practices of (non-)assistance and bordering in a time of crisis', *Near Futures Online* 1. Accessed 24 March 2022. http://nearfuturesonline.org/ebbing-and-flowing-the-eus-shifting-practices-of-non-assistance-and-bordering-in-a-time-of-crisis.
Hess, Sabine and Bernd Kasparek. 2017. 'De- and restabilising Schengen: The European border regime after the Summer of Migration', *Cuadernos Europeos de Deusto* 56: 47–77. https://doi.org/10.18543/ced-56-2017pp47-77.
Hess, Sabine, Bernd Kasparek, Stefanie Kron, Mathias Rodatz, Maria Schwertl and Simon Sontowski. 2016. 'Der lange Sommer der Migration: Krise, Rekonstitution und ungewisse Zukunft des europäischen Grenzregimes'. In *Der lange Sommer der Migration: Grenzregime III*, edited by Sabine Hess, Mathias Rodatz, Bernd Kasparek, Stefanie Kron, Maria Schwertl and Simon Noori, 6–24. Berlin: Assoziation A.

Hutcheon, Linda (with Siobhan O'Flynn). 2013 [2006]. *A Theory of Adaptation*. London: Routledge.

Kasparek, Bernd. 2016. 'Routes, corridors, and spaces of exception: Governing migration and Europe', *Near Futures Online*, 2 February. Accessed 24 March 2022. http://nearfuturesonli ne.org/routes-corridors-and-spaces-of-exception-governing-migration-and-europe/.

Klapdor, Heike. 2008. '"Die Geschichte habe ich schon mal gehört.": Anna Seghers' Roman *Transit* und Michael Curtiz' Film *Casablanca*', *Argonautenschiff* 17: 174–88.

Last, Tamara, Giorgia Mirto, Orçun Ulusoy, Ignacio Urquijo, Joke Harte, Nefeli Bami, Marta Pérez Pérez, Flor Macias Delgado, Amélie Tapella, Alexandra Michalaki, Eirini Michalitsi, Efi Latsoudi, Naya Tselepi, Marios Chatziprokopiou and Thomas Spijkerboer. 2017. 'Deaths at the borders database: Evidence of deceased migrants' bodies found along the southern external borders of the European Union', *Journal of Ethnic and Migration Studies* 43 (5): 693–712. https://doi.org/10.1080/1369183X.2016.1276825.

Little White Lies. 2019. 'The 30 best films of 2019', 20 December. Accessed 24 March 2022. https://lwlies.com/articles/the-30-best-films-of-2019/.

Lucassen, Leo. 2018. 'Peeling an onion: The "refugee crisis" from a historical perspective', *Ethnic and Racial Studies* 41 (3): 383–410. https://doi.org/10.1080/01419870.2017.1355975.

Murray, Simone. 2011. *The Adaptation Industry: The cultural economy of contemporary literary adaptation*. New York: Taylor & Francis.

Obama, Barack. 2019. Twitter post, 29 December, 18:03. Accessed 24 March 2022. https://twitt er.com/BarackObama/status/1211331851358494720.

Peeren, Esther. 2014. *The Spectral Metaphor: Living ghosts and the agency of invisibility*. New York: Palgrave Macmillan.

Petzold, Christian and Becca Voelcker. 2019. 'Wartime out of joint', *Film Comment* 55 (1): 6.

Rogowski, Franz and Paula Beer. 2019. *Transit Presseheft*, 1 March. Accessed 24 March 2022. https://www.transit-der-film.de/downloads/artwork-texte/transit-presseheft.pdf.

Romney, Jonathan. 2019. 'Film of the week: Transit', *Film Comment*, 1 March. Accessed 24 March 2022. https://www.filmcomment.com/blog/film-of-the-week-transit/.

Schick, Thomas. 2018. *Filmstil, Differenzqualitäten, Emotionen: Zur affektiven Wirkung von Autorenfilmen am Beispiel der Berliner Schule*. Wiesbaden: Springer.

Schlenstedt, Silvia. 2001. 'Kommentar'. In *Transit*, by Anna Seghers, 311–64. Berlin: Aufbau Verlag.

Seghers, Anna. 2018 [1944]. *Transit*. Berlin: Aufbau Taschenbuch.

Stam, Robert. 2005. 'Introduction: The theory and practice of adaptation'. In *Literature and Film: A guide to the theory and practice of film adaptation*, edited by Robert Stam and Alessandra Raengo, 1–52. Malden, MA: Blackwell.

Staud, Toralf. 2018. 'Straf- und Gewalttaten von rechts: Was sagen die offiziellen Statistiken?', *Bundeszentrale für politische Bildung*, 13 November. Accessed 24 March 2022. https://www .bpb.de/politik/extremismus/rechtsextremismus/264178/pmk-statistiken.

Steinhilper, Elias and Rob J. Gruijters. 2018. 'A contested crisis: Policy narratives and empirical evidence on border deaths in the Mediterranean', *Sociology* 52 (3): 515–33. https://doi.org /10.1177/0038038518759248.

Thielking, Sigrid. 1995. 'Warten – Erzählen – Überleben: Vom Exil aller Zeiten in Anna Seghers' Roman *Transit*'. *Argonautenschiff* 4: 127–38.

Trifonova, Temenuga. 2020. *The Figure of the Migrant in Contemporary European Cinema*. London: Bloomsbury.

Winkler, Daniel. 2007. *Transit Marseille: Filmgeschichte einer Mittelmeermetropole*. Bielefeld: transcript.

Yurdakul, Gökce and Hartmut Koenitz. 2019. 'We can do it! (or can we?): Angela Merkel's immigration politics', Epicenter Blog at the Weatherhead Center for International Affairs, Harvard University, 24 May. Accessed 24 March 2022. https://epicenter.wcfia.harvard.edu /blog/we-can-do-it-angela-merkel-immigration-politics.

Yurdakul, Gökçe, Regina Römhild, Anja Schwanhäußer, Birgit zur Nieden, Folashade M. Ajayi, Charlotte Kneffel, Marnie Litfin, Hieu Hanh Hoang Tran and Aleksandra Lakić, eds. 2018. *Witnessing the Transition: Moments in the long summer of migration*. Berlin: Berlin Institute for Empirical Integration and Migration Research (BIM). https://doi.org/10.18452/18704.

3
The passage from tragedy to novel in Álvaro Cunqueiro's *Un hombre que se parecía a Orestes* (1969)

Marta Mariño Mexuto

Un hombre que se parecía a Orestes,[1] published in 1969, is a peculiar novel for many reasons. When it was first published, it surprised readers and critics alike with its mythical and fantastical elements, as the main literary movement in 1950s and 1960s Spain was social realism. At the time, Álvaro Cunqueiro (1911–81), aside from his poetry, had already published four novels, both in Spanish and Galician. All of them possessed some of the elements that distinguished *Un hombre que se parecía a Orestes* from other works of narrative fiction being released during those years. After the publication of Gabriel García Márquez's *Cien años de soledad* (1967), the time was right for Cunqueiro's fantastical narrative, which came very close to magical realism.

Álvaro Cunqueiro was born in the small town of Mondoñedo, in north-eastern Galicia. He wrote throughout his whole life, working as a journalist, and eventually managing one of Galicia's most popular newspapers, *El Faro de Vigo*. He first became known for his poetry, inspired by surrealism and medieval Galician poems that had been rediscovered and published a few decades earlier.[2] Along with Fermín Bouza Brey, Cunqueiro initiated the avant-garde lyric movement known as *neotrobadorismo*. His contributions to this literary trend were *Cantiga nova que se chama Riveira* (1933) and *Dona do corpo delgado* (1950).[3] It was well after the Spanish Civil War that Cunqueiro published his first novel, *Merlín e familia* (1955). The years following would be his most productive: he published six further novels until 1974, as well as short stories, essays, theatrical pieces and myriad articles.

Before starting an analysis of the novel, it is worth addressing the language issue in Cunqueiro's texts. Although it is by no means the focal point of this chapter, Cunqueiro's language could also be viewed in terms of passage. Cunqueiro's mother tongue was Galician, but he was used to hearing and speaking Spanish since childhood. At the time, Spanish was the only official language of the country, and no other language was allowed in government institutions or the school system. Galician, despite its tradition as the lyrical language used in the whole of Spain during the Middle Ages, was considered to be the language of peasants and uneducated workers. Cunqueiro recalls his first work of fiction, a western novel in which Native Americans speak Galician, as follows:

> I know that no one is bilingual; there is always a background language, but we spoke Galician constantly. And because I wanted the Amerindians to speak a language different than the whites', and since I couldn't speak any other language, I necessarily had to make them speak Galician. (Nicolás 1994, 121)[4]

His first poetic works were written in Galician, and they also match up with his political opinions at the time, as he was a fervent member of the nationalist Partido Galeguista.[5] He chose the same language for his first novel, *Merlín e familia*, but, from that moment on, he would alternate between Galician and Spanish in his narratives. However, he claimed that the novels he had first published in Spanish had already been translated by him, likely from his mother tongue. Galician was also the language of his short theatrical works, such as the remarkable *O incerto señor don Hamlet, príncipe de Dinamarca* (1958). Cunqueiro's explanation for this choice of language was economic: he considered himself a professional writer in Spanish, but: '[a]s a writer in Spanish, I am a professional. And as a writer in Galician I have no other option other than to be an amateur. It happens to all of us ... You lose money with works in Galician' (Nicolás 1994, 121–2).[6] He also admitted:

> Many of the great prosaists of our times may have started as poets, even the 'most prosaist' prosaists, such as André Gide and Jorge Luis Borges. In my case, the thing is, I couldn't naturally make a living

out of my writings in Galician. I had to write in Spanish. (Nicolás 1994, 122)[7]

An important part of Álvaro Cunqueiro's success and recognition comes from the fact that his works constitute a reworking of Galician narrative. Cunqueiro incorporated innovative literary resources without losing the spontaneity of Galician storytelling. Although heavily inspired by local landscapes and folklore, he inserted his texts in a wider tradition, through countless references to the classics, Arthurian literature and the *Arabian Nights*. Unfortunately, his place in the Spanish literary system was not prominent. As has been noted, Spanish literature at the time was dominated by social realism. There seemed to be no place for Cunqueiro's fantastical storytelling, which disregarded all rules and was considered 'escapist literature'. Appreciation for his novels grew in the 1970s and 1980s, as the literary landscape changed, thanks to American magical realism, but he still remains a little-known author for the general public.

This particular novel takes its inspiration from multiple literary systems, ranging from the Greek myth of Orestes and, in particular, the tragedies based on this story: Aeschylus' *Oresteia*, Sophocles' *Electra* and Euripides' *Orestes* and *Electra* (although many others also relate to the Trojan cycle and the characters in Cunqueiro's novel, such as Euripides' *Iphigenia in Aulis* and *Iphigenia in Tauris*). Cunqueiro's work is inspired by tragedy, but also by the Byzantine novel, chivalric romance and the codes of courtly love, and it includes several scenes from a theatrical play. Because its main inspiration is Greek tragedy, my aim is to describe and analyse the novel's passage between the genres of myth and the modern novel. I will also consider the role of parody in this process, which I describe as an important tool of passage.

Before getting started, a brief summary of the novel is in order: *Un hombre que se parecía a Orestes* focuses on the long wait for Orestes' return and enactment of revenge for his father Agamenón's[8] murder, allegedly perpetrated by his mother Clitemnestra's lover, Egisto.[9] All of these elements are taken from the original myth, but Cunqueiro's Orestes never seems ready to return to his hometown, and, when he finally does, fifty years have passed and the revenge has become meaningless. Readers familiar with ancient tragedies will find that many elements have been subverted: Clitemnestra, far from being a cold-blooded murderer, has become an air-headed housewife who cannot understand the situation she has been put into; Aegisthus is a mediocre king obsessed with Orestes' return; and Orestes is a disoriented young man who wishes he was not obliged to follow the rule of the tragedy. He has not become the criminal portrayed in Euripides' *Orestes*, but he has certainly ventured far from the heroic sphere.

Genre ambiguity

The concept of passage is useful to explain the transformation that the Orestes myth undergoes in Cunqueiro's novel, because this transformation is never complete. This is also why the idea of liminality, closely related to passage (from the Latin *limen*: doorstep or threshold), comes into play. Liminality, a term borrowed from anthropology, and used for the study of literature and culture in general,[10] 'involves a potentially unlimited freedom from any kind of structure. This sparks creativity and innovation, peaking in transfiguring moments of sublimity' (Thomassen 2016, 1). As we will see, this definition characterizes the effects of Cunqueiro's loose conception of genre, and why he did not want to be constricted by genre. The main characteristic of liminality is that it 'emerges in the in-between of a passage' (Thomassen 2016, 2). Cunqueiro's novel occupies a liminal space, because it cannot be considered a novel in a strict sense, although I employ the term for lack of a better one, and because it is certainly closer to a novel than a classic tragedy.

It is difficult to define any of Cunqueiro's works as novels, due to their fragmentary form, structured sometimes as a series of independent short stories.[11] In *Un hombre que se parecía a Orestes*, Cunqueiro includes sections that most resemble drama,[12] and two final chapters that are formally particular. The penultimate chapter, *'Seis retratos'* ('Six portraits'), consists of portraits of the six main characters, as well as the narration of the end of the story. The final chapter is an onomastic index (common to several of his novels), in which he explains a number of details about almost every character previously mentioned. His work clearly does not have a traditional form. Nonetheless, Cunqueiro was conscious of what he was doing: he considered genre to be a construction created mainly by the critics, and he did not see the point in making sharp distinctions between genres. The author:

> more than once questioned the existence of clear and strict borders between the genres in which he ventured; he was always spontaneous about the correlation between them, confessing that he found it difficult to differentiate them, and downplaying divisions

he found were typically made by critics and researchers. (Nicolás 1994, 76)[13]

Usually, when Cunqueiro was in the process of writing a novel, he also wrote poetry on the same theme as the novel. A good example of this is his novel *Las mocedades de Ulises* (1960), which inspired the unfinished cycle of poems *El retorno de Ulises*. Cunqueiro claimed that the same process happened during the writing of *Un hombre que se parecía a Orestes*, and that some of the poems written in parallel to the novel were later included in the novel itself. The reason was, as he stated, that the narrative genre was not enough for him: 'I hardly write a novel if I am not also writing poems that appear as facts or characters from the novel. I have always created a parallel poetry. This shows how the novel is not enough for me' (Nicolás 1994, 81).[14]

Given this generic mixing, *Un hombre que se parecía a Orestes* resembles a hyper-novel. As Franca Sinopoli defines it, the hyper-novel, or the postmodern novel in general, has the capacity to 'encapsulate other literary genres',[15] and introduces parody 'through intertextuality forcing the preceding texts (or hypotexts), hyper-textualizing them' (Sinopoli 2002, 191).[16] Aside from its extensive use of parody, Cunqueiro's narrative is an intricate web of hyper-texts. Sometimes, the preceding texts are mere literary references, but most of the time, the entire novel is based on a previous text: Orestes, Ulises, Sinbad and Merlin[17] are the protagonists of four of his seven novels. All of the postmodern narrative strategies included in the following list are displayed in the author's works: 'other traits of postmodern works are hybridity (of genre or otherwise), a very pronounced intertextuality, parody, temporal games, an accent on the abundance of short narratives and a deconstruction of rigid binary oppositions' (Aron 2002, 378).[18]

We cannot ignore the fact that Cunqueiro chose the novel form to recreate a story which had previously been treated mostly (but not exclusively) in tragedy. Myths can be formulated in any literary genre, the choice of which determines the final result:

> The very recreation of the myth, this is to say, of the mythical narration in a certain literary genre (a poem, a dramatic play, a novel) determines its sense and its forms. Lyrical poetry tends towards allusion, drama towards insistence on the characters' personalities, the novel towards description and longer narration. Myth, as a memorable scheme, is beyond all literary genres. We can

say that it transcends them, as it seems to transcend all its concrete literary executions. (García Gual 2008, 32)[19]

The novel is the genre that provides the author with possibilities for portraying characters' intimate lives and motivations, which are, in the case of the Orestes, a lot more important than action, given the fact that this is a story in which revenge, the event everyone is waiting for, never actually takes place. On the inevitable, but sometimes problematic, connection between the novel and other genres, Mikhail Bakhtin writes:

> We have already said that the novel gets on poorly with other genres. There can be no talk of a harmony deriving from mutual limitation and complementariness. The novel parodies other genres (precisely in their role as genres); it exposes the conventionality of their forms and their language; it squeezes out some genres and incorporates others into its own peculiar structure, reformulating and re-accentuating them. (Bakhtin 2002, 4)

The novel also allows Cunqueiro to offer several versions of the same fact, and to describe the general atmosphere, as well as the main characters, in detail, even though he also relies on the final '*Seis retratos*', which are basically descriptive. These changes of perspective are allowed by the novel genre, and they are essential in this work:

> It is probably in *Un hombre que se parecía a Orestes* where the changing perspective is used with more ability and complexity, not only in its ironic function, but also for the enrichment of the narrative. In this way, we successively share the kingdom chronicler's point of view and uncertainty, and Aegisthus' and Orestes' point of view in each of the three parts of the novel. (De la Torre 1988, 42)[20]

This generic flexibility, typical for postmodern narrative, enables the narrator, for example, to make King Egisto say '[i]t all seemed like the stuff of a psychological novel!' (Cunqueiro 1987, 116),[21] about the way he killed Agamenón, and to make Eumón confess to Egisto that he thought that 'you and Clitemnestra may be living in a comedy of errors' (96).[22] At one point, Egisto even pretends to be the protagonist of a chivalric romance, and there is also a moment at which the plot of a Byzantine romantic novel is read to Queen Clitemnestra:

the unhappy story of Persilida and Trimalchio, unfortunate lovers, whom she gave birth to on a beach, while he was in the tyrant of Syracuse's prison because he refused to dress up like a woman and please the sovereign. At the end of the novel, they meet in a flood, and Trimalchio recognizes the child as his in a lifeboat. (Cunqueiro 1987, 117)[23]

The fact that Cunqueiro, a folk-tale enthusiast, chose the novel instead of the folk tale as the most appropriate genre for combining many elements related to oral tradition is very meaningful. Maybe it has to do with what Mircea Eliade has stated about the novel's position in modern society: 'We need to highlight that narrative prose, especially the novel, has taken in modern societies the place of the recitation of myths and tales in traditional and popular societies' (Eliade 1999, 182).[24]

Even taking this into consideration, Cunqueiro did not forget about folk tales: some are inserted throughout the main plot of the novel, as well as in his other narrative works. Eleazar M. Meletinsky reminds us of the close link between myth and tale when he discusses the semantics of both: 'The semantics of the tale can be understood only by starting from mythological sources. Tales use the same semantic system as myth. Unlike myth, however, the social code dominates ... The fact that tales developed from myth is beyond all doubt' (Meletinsky 2000, 236). Cunqueiro gives fiction a peculiar treatment, calling attention to it, and making the characters conscious of their own fictional natures. This causes them to feel the conflict between their true personalities and the expectations placed on them as tragic characters. This is especially the case for Orestes, but it also applies to Egisto, Doña Inés and Ifigenia. For all of these reasons, Cunqueiro's novel is certainly fully self-conscious, defined by Robert Alter as follows:

> A self-conscious novel, briefly, is a novel that systematically flaunts its own condition of artifice and that by so doing probes into the problematic relationship between real-seeming artifice and reality. A fully self-conscious novel, however, is one in which from beginning to end, through the style, the handling of narrative viewpoint, the names and words imposed on the characters, the patterning of the narration, the nature of the characters and what befalls them, there is a consistent effort to convey to us a sense of fictional world as an authorial construct set up against a background of literary tradition and convention. (Alter 1978, XX–I)

The novel displays many of the elements mentioned above. The tragedy projected by one of the characters, Filón el Mozo, who is the city's playwright, is particularly meaningful – he is waiting for events to take place in order to finish his writing: 'he was secretly writing the well-known tragedy and had interrupted his work in the third scene of the second act, since it was there where he had planned to bring in Orestes' (Cunqueiro 1987, 53).[25] The characters that appear in the tragedy are conscious of their double existences in both narrative and dramatic fiction. Elements such as these are not exclusive to *Un hombre que se parecía a Orestes*. As Dolores Vilavedra summarizes, Cunqueiro's works are referential macrotexts:

> through the repeated presence of redundant themes and strategies, which generate the centrifugal character of his texts and make of them an independent and perfectly coherent universe ..., all this is, in good measure, the cause of the questioned and questionable definition of some of his novels as such. (Vilavedra 1999, 243–4)[26]

Nevertheless, we cannot forget that ancient myths have always been channelled through different literary genres: drama, epic poetry and even comedy.

Parody as a passage tool

In the process of passage from mythical tragedy to the novel that takes place in *Un hombre que se parecía a Orestes*, parody plays an important role. I am referring to the postmodernist form of parody, as it has been defined by Linda Hutcheon and Margaret Rose. Cunqueiro's novel can be considered as a parody of the *Oresteia*, according to Hutcheon's definition of parody:

> It will be clear by now that what I am calling parody here is not just that ridiculing imitation mentioned in the standard dictionary definitions ... While the *Odyssey* is clearly the formally backgrounded or parodied text here [in Joyce's *Ulysses*], it is not one to be mocked or ridiculed; if anything, it is to be seen, as in the mock epic, as an ideal or at least as a norm from which the modern departs. (Hutcheon 1986, 5)

Rose adds an interesting detail, which is particularly useful in this case:

> One other suggestion which can be made here is that the love of a parodist for the object of the parody need not exclude a desire to change and modernise it, and yet one more that the love of a work can help the parodist know and reproduce it better in the parody. Further to this, the desire of a parodist to change another text can lead to the production of something new from it, the love of which may lead the parodist to view the target text, and its contribution to the parody in question, with some sympathy. (Rose 1995, 46–7)

The original text is just a starting point, and it 'is often not at all under attack. It is often respected and used as a model – in other than artistic ways' (Hutcheon 1986, 103). That is, parody is a form of homage, rather than a way of ridiculing the original text, even if mockery is also possible. And mockery is certainly a part of *Un hombre que se parecía a Orestes*, but it does not justify the claim, supported by a number of critics, that what Cunqueiro accomplished here was a devaluation of the myth. The process of passage from one genre to another, even with the author's many parodic modifications, does not imply that the myth is by any means destroyed. All classical myths were continuously transferred from epic poetry to tragedy and comedy, and other minor genres, without losing any elements along the way. The Greek tragic trilogy was converted into satirical drama, which was usually developed around the same theme, and classical authors such as Plautus used heroes and gods as the protagonists of their comedies, as is the case in *Amphitruo*. For Bakhtin, this genre variation was crucial for placing myth under a new light:

> It was, therefore, a peculiar type of parodic-travestying *contre-partie* to the myth that had just received a tragic treatment on the stage, it showed the myth in a different aspect. These parodic-travestying counter-presentations of lofty national myths were just as sanctioned and canonical as their straightforward tragic manifestations. All the tragedians – Phrynicous, Sophocles, Euripides – were writers of satyr plays as well, and Aeschylus, the most serious and pious of them all, an initiate into the highest Eleusinian Mysteries, was considered by the Greeks to be the greatest master of the satyr play. (Bakhtin 2002, 53–4)

The audience would not feel that the hero they were watching in the performance of a tragedy was any less 'tragic' because he had previously been the protagonist of a comedy. If a myth such as that of Orestes, or those belonging to the Theban cycle, are often related to tragedy, this probably has a lot to do with the fact that some tragedies written by the most important Greek playwrights have been preserved to this day. We cannot forget that: '"[t]ragedy" is today a concept that we deduce from the contemplation of a heap of tragedies. For the Greeks and the men of the Renaissance, it was something different partly because their range of examples was different' (Leech 1989, 24).

The passage from tragic play to novel in Cunqueiro's novel is achieved by maintaining various tragic elements. Although this is not the right place for such an analysis, it is important to remember the number of tragic resources and allusions that Aristophanes included in his comedies.[27] In his parodic subversion of the main characters, Cunqueiro certainly uses humour, but the final result is by no means a work that could be qualified as humorous or light-hearted, even if some episodes are. During the last pages, Orestes realizes that the time that has passed has made revenge useless, but there is no forgiveness or reconciliation whatsoever; Orestes is condemned to exile:

> The wind had started to blow, the clouds covered the sky and it was starting to snow. Fine snowflakes were falling down like in the sifter's snowball. Big tears were rolling down the prince's face. He could never, ever live in his hometown. He would forever be a shadow lost on the roads. It was snowing. (Cunqueiro 1987, 227)[28]

And even if feelings of forgiveness were present, they would not erase the tragic background of the novel, because, as Lesky reminds us, the end does not necessarily define the play as a tragedy or a comedy:

> But the statement that a number of Attic tragedies end in happiness and harmony and are therefore not tragedies in the modern sense was not intended to imply that they did not contain a wealth of tragic motifs. Can one conceive anything more profoundly tragic than the fate of Orestes who had to strike down his mother and was then driven to madness by the Erinyes? (Lesky 1979, 13)

The modern, more simplistic, concept of tragedy that Lesky describes is based on Aristotle's own thoughts. Aristotle linked tragedy to a miserable ending, but, even in his time, this was not the only accepted definition of the genre. When he considers Euripides to be the 'most tragic' poet precisely because of his plays' endings, he admits that many people rejected the dramatist for the same reason: '[t]he critics, therefore, are wrong who blame Euripides for taking this line in his tragedies, and giving many of them an unhappy ending. It is, as we have said, the right line to take' (Aristotle 1984, 239). Aristotle does not agree with a 'happy' or harmonious ending, because he considers it to be typical of comedy, the kind of play 'where the bitterest enemies in the piece (e.g. Orestes and Aegisthus) walk off good friends at the end, with no slaying of any one by any one' (239).

It is problematic to define the preserved Greek tragedies in this way, since it is almost impossible to find a play that fulfils the criteria, aside from *Oedipus Rex*. That is why *Oedipus Rex* became a model for all tragedies, despite being unique in the combination of its elements. Some tragedies have happy endings, and, in some of them, the famous *anagnorisis* is absent. Maybe in *Un hombre que se parecía a Orestes*, the absence of *anagnorisis* could even add to the tragic effect, since, when the protagonist finally comes back, it is too late for anyone to recognize him, causing him to feel like a foreigner in his own city.

For all these reasons, it would be too much of a simplification to consider the tragic and the humorous as perfect opposites; rather, they are parts of a continuum:

> comedy is not and cannot be a proper opposite of 'tragedy'. There is a full and fully perceptible measure of continuity between all the comic phenomena just listed ... It follows that while we may distinguish between the various manifestations of comedy and the comic, we should distinguish them only as manifestations of this comic continuum. And that, on this basis, it is arbitrary to limit 'comedy' to the sphere of drama. The name might, with some plausibility, be applied to the whole continuum or to any part of it. (Silk 2000, 60–1)

Certainly, Euripides gave a peculiar treatment to mythical stories and characters. This treatment is criticized in Aristophanes' *The Frogs*, and many Athenians also found it inappropriate.[29] But that was not enough of a reason to stop considering their plays as tragedies, nor was Euripides accused of demythologizing Greek traditions, in the same way that the existence of a comedy based on Amphitruo did not exclude at that time a tragedy about the same character. Tragedy and comedy were complementary art forms. That is why the claim that Cunqueiro accomplished a 'disintegration of the myth', as González-Millán argues, sounds excessive:

> The reversion and dislocation of the intertextualized original myth and the tragic text – the first canonical literary formulation – are

such, that we should talk about a conscious will for demythologizing, so obvious in this text, although not less explicit in other novels or in other parts of *HPO* [*Un hombre que se parecía a Orestes*]. *HPO* constantly takes us back to the archetypical model of the *Oresteia* to disintegrate it through parody and, in this way, prevents the mythical image of Orestes from entering the novel. (González-Millán 1991, 144)[30]

Simplifications in this matter end up being far more problematic. A literary work can be perceived as a tragedy by readers even if it does not fulfil all the parameters of the tragic. What initially looked like the most undeniably tragic factor, the end of the play, turns out not to be the defining element of the genre, since several tragedies display what we would today call a 'happy ending'. This is when the concept of liminality comes into play again: not only does Cunqueiro's text occupy a liminal space in the passage from tragedy to novel, but it also represents a tragedy-to-comedy *continuum*.

Conclusion

Finally, it is important to take Cunqueiro's thoughts about myths into account. He did not consider mythical elements to comprise a mere background for his stories; instead, he acknowledged the value of myths for giving expression to the human condition:

> I simply believe that as important as daily reality is, myths, for example, are also important – they are not tales, although 'myth' means tale. They are answers instead. I do like to use them, reinvent them. I believe in the necessity of an imaginative literature and, in that sense, I do everything I can. (Nicolás 1994, 208–9)[31]

> All the Greek myths have a lot to say about any human situation ... They speak essentially about men, about the most elementary conditions, about the most complex things, about being ... When it was necessary to point out any limited situation of the human condition, its representation could be found in Greek tradition. You have the Oedipus complex, the Electra complex, etc. (Nicolás 1994, 207)[32]

In summary, *Un hombre que se parecía a Orestes* is a great example of genre passage and, since its inspiration comes from an ancient myth, we are able to see which elements survive, and which are modified or excluded. Cunqueiro foregrounded specific themes and elements of the story, such as the doubts that Orestes has about killing his mother, and the expectations created by Orestes, who has a great influence over the other characters, in spite of his rare appearances.

On the contrary, the desire for revenge that Clytemnestra wishes to take on her husband Agamemnon, who sacrificed their daughter Iphigenia to the gods, is completely absent from Cunqueiro's version of the story, because Iphigenia is still alive. Changes such as these affect the relationships between the characters, and reveal Cunqueiro's motivations and preferences regarding traditional myth and its value for storytelling during his own time. *Un hombre que se parecía a Orestes* also features a combination of postmodernist traits, such as the mixture of genres, the instrumental use of parody in the passage process from the original myth to a contemporary novel, and constant metafictional games. All of this makes of Cunqueiro's work a very interesting model of genre passage, as it continuously pushes the boundaries of the novel to assimilate elements of mythical tales, tragedy and even comedy, without losing its modernity.

Notes

1. The title could be translated as 'A Man Who Looked Like Orestes', although the novel has not been translated into English.
2. Between 1926 and 1932, the Portuguese professor José Joaquim Nunes published several volumes of *cantigas de amigo* and *cantigas de amor*, medieval songs written in Galician in the thirteenth and fourteenth centuries.
3. Although it was published in 1950, *Dona do corpo delgado* includes some poems related to *neotrobadorismo* and written before 1936.
4. 'Eu xa sei que non hai ninguén bilingüe, sempre hai unha lingua de fondo, pero falabamos galego constantemente. E como eu quería que os indios falasen unha fala diferente á dos brancos pois, naturalmente como tampouco sabía ningún outro idioma, tiven á forza que facelos falar en galego.' All translations from Galician and Spanish are mine.
5. Cunqueiro's ideology has been the subject of much speculation. Although he would always defend Galicia's idiosyncrasy and language, he became involved with Franco's regime immediately after the Civil War, collaborating with the Francoist newspaper *Era Azul*. However, for most of his life, he refused to speak clearly about his political ideas, stating that his only compromise was the one he had with the Galician language.
6. '... como escritor en gallego no tengo otra alternativa que ser un aficionado. Nos pasa a todos ... Con obras en gallego se pierde dinero.'
7. 'Quizá muchos de los grandes prosistas de nuestro tiempo empezaron por poetas, aun aquellos prosistas más prosistas como André Gide o Jorge Luis Borges. En mi caso el hecho es que yo no podía vivir naturalmente de mis escritos en gallego. Tenía forzosamente que escribir en castellano.'

8   I have transcribed the characters' names in their original Spanish form, which is also quite easy for the English-speaking reader to understand. I will keep the English form when talking about the original Greek characters who bear these names.
9   In different versions of the myth, there are variations in the details of the murder and the implication of the characters in it: Clytemnestra is sometimes just an accomplice, sometimes the instigator or even the murderer herself, without Aegisthus' participation.
10 For more on concepts travelling between different disciplines, see Bal (2002).
11 That is the case for *Merlín e familia* (1955) and *As crónicas do sochantre* (1956).
12 Originally written in Galician, and entitled *A noite vai coma un río*, this material had already been independently published in 1960.
13 '... máis dunha vez dubidou da existencia de fronteiras marcadas e estrictas entre os distintos xéneros nos que probou sorte; sempre foi espontáneo na interrelación daqueles confesando que lle custaba diferencialos entre si, restándolle importancia a esas divisións, segundo el, propias dos críticos e investigadores.'
14 'Yo difícilmente escribo una novela si al mismo tiempo no escribo unos poemas que aparecen como hechos, como personajes, de la novela. Siempre he creado una poesía paralela. Esto prueba que no me basta la novela.'
15 'sintetizar en sí a otros géneros literarios.'
16 'a través de la intertextualidad forzando los textos precedentes (o hipotextos) hipertextualizándolos.'
17 *Merlín e familia* (1955) and *Las mocedades de Ulises* (1960) have been previously mentioned in this study; the novel that revolves around Sinbad is *Si o vello Sinbad volvese ás illas...* (1961).
18 'D'autres traits des œuvres postmodernes comprennent l'hybridité (générique ou autre) une intertextualité très poussée, la parodie, les jeux temporels, un accent sur la multiplicité des petits récits et la déconstruction des oppositions binaires rigides.'
19 'La misma recreación del mito, es decir, del relato mítico en un determinado género literario (un poema, un drama, una novela) condiciona ya su sentido y sus formas. La lírica propende a la alusión, la dramatización a la insistencia en los caracteres de sus personajes, la novela a lo descriptivo y a la narración más larga. El mito, como entramado memorable, está más allá de los géneros literarios. Podemos decir que los trasciende, como parece trascender todas sus realizaciones literarias concretas ...'
20 'Probablemente es en *Un hombre que se parecía a Orestes* donde la perspectiva cambiante se utiliza con mayor destreza y complejidad, no sólo en función irónica sino para el enriquecimiento de la narración. Así, sucesivamente, compartimos el punto de vista y la distinta incertidumbre del cronista del reino, de Egisto, y del propio Orestes en cada una de las tres partes de la novela.'
21 '¡Parecía todo aquello asunto de novela psicológica!'
22 'tú y doña Clitemnestra quizás estéis viviendo una comedia de errores'. This expression is reminiscent of *A Comedy of Errors*, the play in which Shakespeare, creating confusion with the characters' identities, gave name to this kind of comedy. Shakespeare is referenced in almost all of Cunqueiro's works.
23 '... la infeliz historia de Persílida y Trimalción, amantes desventurados, que ella parió en una playa, de un pirata, mientras él estaba en prisiones del tirano de Siracusa por negarse a vestir de mujer y hacerle los gustos al soberano. Al final de la novela se encontraban en una inundación, y Trimalción reconocía al niño en una lancha de salvamento.'
24 'Lo que hay que subrayar es que la prosa narrativa, especialmente la novela, ha tomado en las sociedades modernas el lugar ocupado por la recitación de los mitos y de los cuentos en las sociedades tradicionales y populares.'
25 'Escribía en secreto la tragedia sabida, y tenía suspendida la labor en la escena tercera del acto segundo, que era allí donde tenía pensado dar la llegada de Orestes.'
26 '... por medio da reiterada presencia de temas e estratexias redundantes, que compensan o carácter centrífugo dos seus textos, e que fan deles un universo autónomo e plenamente coherente ..., en boa medida responsábel da discutida e discutible definición xenérica dalgunhas das súas novelas como tales.'
27 Silk (2000) goes deeply into the definitions of comedy and tragedy, and the relationships between both in Aristophanes' works.
28 'Se había levantado viento, las nubes cubrían el cielo y comenzaba a nevar. Caían copos finos como en la bola de nieve del cerero. Gruesas lágrimas rodaban por el rostro del príncipe.

Nunca, nunca podría vivir en su ciudad natal. Para siempre era una sombra perdida por los caminos. Nevaba.'
29 The fact that Euripides only won 4 dramatic contests, compared to Aesquilus' 13 victories and Sophocles' more than 20 triumphs, suggests that he aroused little enthusiasm in Athens.
30 'É tal a reconversión e dislocación do mito orixinal intertextualizado e do texto tráxico, primeira formulación literaria canonizada, que debe falarse dunha consciente vontade de desmitificación, tan obvia neste texto, aínda que non menos explícita noutras novelas e aínda noutros momentos de *HPO* [*Un hombre que se parecía a Orestes*]. *HPO* reverte incesantemente ao modelo arquetípico da *Orestíada* para desintegrala mediante a parodia e, así, facer imposible a entrada da imaxe mítica do Orestes clásico na novela … '.
31 'Simplemente creo que tanta importancia como tenga la realidad cotidiana, la tienen, por ejemplo, los mitos, que no son cuentos, aunque 'mito' signifique cuento, sino respuestas que están ahí. A mí me gusta tocarlos, reinventarlos. Creo que [sic] la necesidad de una literatura imaginativa, y en este sentido hago lo que puedo.'
32 'A cualquier situación humana actual … pues todos los mitos griegos tienen mucho que decir. Predican esencialmente del hombre, de las condiciones más elementales, de las más complejas, del ser … Cuando se ha querido señalar alguna situación límite de la condición humana se ha buscado en la tradición griega su representación. Tenéis los complejos de Edipo, de Electra, etc.'

References

Alter, Robert. 1978. *Partial Magic: The novel as a self-conscious genre*. Berkeley: University of California Press.
Aristotle. 1984. 'Poetics'. In *The Rhetoric and the Poetics of Aristotle,* translated by Ingram Bywater, 219–66. New York: Modern Library College Editions.
Aron, Paul, Denis Saint-Jacques and Alain Viala. 2002. *Le Dictionnaire du Littéraire*. Paris: Puf.
Bakhtin, Mikhail. 2002. *The Dialogic Imagination*, translated by Caryl Emerson and Michael Holquist. Austin: University of Texas Press.
Bal, Mieke. 2002. *Travelling Concepts in the Humanities: A rough guide*. Toronto: University of Toronto Press.
Cunqueiro, Álvaro. 1961. *Si o vello Sinbad volvese ás illas…* Vigo: Galaxia.
Cunqueiro, Álvaro. 1980. 'O incerto señor Don Hamlet, príncipe de Dinamarca.' In *Obra en galego completa* I, 187–253. Vigo: Galaxia.
Cunqueiro, Álvaro.1985. *Las mocedades de Ulises*. Madrid: Espasa-Calpe.
Cunqueiro, Álvaro. 1987. *Un hombre que se parecía a Orestes*. Barcelona: Destino.
Cunqueiro, Álvaro. 2004. *Poesía 1932–1933 (Mar ao norde/Cantiga nova que se chama Riveira/ Poemas do si e non)*. Vigo: Galaxia.
Cunqueiro, Álvaro. 2012. *Merlín e familia*. Vigo: Galaxia.
Cunqueiro, Álvaro. 2014. *Dona do corpo delgado*. Vigo: Galaxia.
De la Torre, Cristina. 1988. *La narrativa de Álvaro Cunqueiro*. Madrid: Pliegos.
Eliade, Mircea. 1999. *Mito y realidad*. Barcelona: Kairós.
García Gual, Carlos. 2008. 'Relecturas modernas y versiones subversivas de los mitos antiguos'. In *Reescrituras de los mitos en la literatura*, edited by J. Herrero Cecilia and M. Morales Peco, 31–44. Cuenca: Ediciones de la Universidad de Castilla-La Mancha.
González-Millán, Xoán. 1991. *Álvaro Cunqueiro: os artificios da fabulación*. Vigo: Galaxia.
Hutcheon, Linda. 1986. *A Theory of Parody*. Cambridge: University Printing House.
Leech, Clifford. 1989. *Tragedy*. New York: Routledge.
Lesky, Albin. 1979. *Greek Tragedy*, translated by H.A. Frankfort. London: Ernest Benn/Barnes & Noble.
Meletinsky, Eleazar M. 2000. *The Poetics of Myth*. New York: Routledge.
Nicolás, Ramón. 1994. *Entrevistas con Álvaro Cunqueiro*. Vigo: Nigra.
Rose, Margaret. 1995. *Parody: Ancient, modern, and post-modern*. Cambridge: Cambridge University Press.
Silk, Michael S. 2000. *Aristophanes and the Definition of Comedy*. New York: Oxford University Press.

Sinopoli, Franca. 2002. 'Los géneros literarios'. In *Introducción a la literatura comparada*, edited by A. Gnisci, 171–213. Barcelona: Editorial Crítica.
Thomassen, Bjørn. 2016. *Liminality and the Modern: Living through the in-between*. London: Routledge.
Vilavedra, Dolores. 1999. *Historia da literatura galega*. Vigo: Galaxia.

4
Translating behind bars: cultural passages from Shakespeare to the Italian dialects

Beatrice Montorfano

In Italy, the association between theatre and prison, and especially between Shakespeare and prison, cannot be said to be immediately understandable to everyone, but the presence of performing arts behind bars has spread in several countries, especially in the Anglosphere. In the UK, a research centre entirely dedicated to theatre in prison was established in 1991 by James Thompson and Paul Heritage (TiPP, Theatre in Prisons and Probation Research and Development Centre, in Manchester), while groups such as Clean Break Theatre Group and Geese Theatre Company have been active in prisons for decades. The phenomenon has also been thematized in a recent Shakespearean trilogy directed by Phyllida Lloyd for the Donmar Warehouse, with an all-female cast: *Julius Caesar*, *Henry IV* and *The Tempest* have been realistically set in a women's prison, thanks to the involvement of Clean Break and groups of women from several UK prisons. In the US, the San Quentin Drama Workshop was founded in 1957 and became a symbol of theatre in prison, because its actors were directed by Samuel Beckett himself in the 1984–5 trilogy known as 'Beckett Directs Beckett'. Nowadays, several drama and theatre projects involving prisoners are active in the country and, among them, a specific engagement with Shakespeare is widely diffused. The most famous is perhaps Shakespeare Behind Bars, founded in 1995 in

Luther Luckett Correction Complex (LaGrange, Kentucky) and led by Curt Tofteland, to which Hank Rogerson dedicated a homonymous documentary in 2005. I have knowledge of additional theatre projects inside prisons in Sweden, Austria, Germany, France, Greece, South Africa and Australia, but further interesting examples may likely be found elsewhere.

The popularity of the phenomenon has increased in recent decades in Italy, especially thanks to two projects. The experimental Compagnia della Fortezza, based in Volterra (Tuscany) and directed by Armando Punzo, has been awarded a significant number of important prizes in Italy and beyond, and has been active since 1988. The film *Cesare deve morire* (*Caesar Must Die*; IT 2012), filmed by Paolo and Vittorio Taviani while rehearsing and performing *Julius Caesar*, was the winner of the Berlinale Festival in 2012, and has largely contributed to the national and international fame of a theatre company active in Rebibbia prison (Rome). Another contributor to the established theatre prison movement in Italy is the Coordinamento Nazionale Teatro e Carcere (Ministero della Giustizia 2019), a national network of artists, companies and associations engaged in theatre projects within the penal system. Almost sixty groups and companies have joined the network, while the Minister of Justice website reports the presence of approximately eighty companies that are working (or have worked) in prisons (Ministero della Giustizia 2019).

Within this framework, this chapter focuses on one of the most common features of Italian prison theatre: the use of Italian dialects in Shakespearean productions. The transition from the sixteenth-century English texts to the variety of languages spoken in prison, and the transition experienced by the actors while performing Shakespeare's texts through their voices and words, represent two sides of a specific temporal, spatial, linguistic and symbolic passage. In order to maintain a focus on this theoretical frame, only one case study will be analysed here: *Julius Caesar*, translated into a mixture of standard Italian, locally coloured versions of it and southern Italian dialects, as performed in Rebibbia theatre between 2011 and 2013, and as filmed by the Tavianis in *Caesar Must Die*.[1] While the latter has become the subject of a number of interesting scholarly essays, the theatrical version has, as far as I know, never been taken into account. Therefore, the focus of this chapter is on language. The chapter will draw upon specific studies concerning the use of dialects in Italian theatre at large.

Translating Shakespeare in prison: a contact zone

In order to introduce the topic, it is important to underline that, in the prison context, theatre practice and the process of translation for the stage evolve in many ways. This depends upon the kind of prison and prison population involved. For example, a production of *The Tempest* was staged in 2015 by Artestudio, a company active in Regina Coeli (Rome), a prison[2] which is reserved for pre-trial detainees and for people who have received short sentences. There, the inmates' future is never predictable. Their release or relocation to another prison can be decided suddenly by the prison head, and theatre practice always has to adapt to these changes: it would be impossible, or unproductive, to work on a pre-existing script and to write a complete translation of the text in all the different dialects and languages spoken by the actors. Therefore, the performed lines that can be related to Shakespeare's play are based on a previous reading of the text in Agostino Lombardo's translation (Shakespeare 2014) – one of the most important and commonly used translations of Shakespeare into Italian – which is then retranslated in performance through improvisation practices guided by the director, Caterina Galloni.

The case of Rebibbia is considerably different. Prisoners have usually been given long sentences for being part of large criminal organizations, such as the Mafia or Camorra. As a result, they are in the position to commit to a long engagement with the text, and can translate it into Neapolitan and Sicilian, and dialects from Apulia, Calabria and other parts of Italy. In such cases, prisoners work as 'linguistic consultants', as Fabio Cavalli, the theatre director of the company, calls them.[3] The Tavianis go further in describing this process:

> One morning, however, in one of the larger cells, we discovered something that made us smile at the amazement and complicity that came about: a group of six or seven inmates were reading a text placed on the table around which they were sitting. Only later, we were told that that text was our screenplay, and that those inmates were our actors who were translating with the help of other inmates, not chosen for the film, our screenplay in their different dialects: Sicilian, Neapolitan, Apulian ... All the work was then supervised and integrated by Fabio Cavalli and Cosimo Rega, our Cassio. This anecdote helps to understand the reason for our choice. Even listening to the auditions, we were happily surprised to hear the squabbles of Prospero and Ariel in Neapolitan, or Romeo and

Polonio whispering and shouting in Sicilian or Apulian. We realized that the dialectal 'mispronunciations' did not diminish the tones of the tragedy, but on the contrary were able to express a new truth, by creating a deep connection between the actor and the character played through the use of a common language that allows the audience to follow the development of the drama, which after all in Shakespeare also has a strong popular aspect. Consequently, it was not we who chose the use of dialects, but our actors who took over the script and adapted it to their being, to their nature ... (*Cesare deve morire* 2012)[4]

The choice of the dialects as languages of translation is therefore based on the inmates' abilities and knowledge.

This was not the Rebibbia inmates' first encounter with Shakespeare. Their encounter dated back to 2005, when *The Tempest* was chosen by Cavalli as a way for them to experience something different from the classics of Neapolitan theatre (Eduardo De Filippo's plays, in particular) that had been performed by the company up to that time, without imposing a completely new theatrical tradition. As a basis, they used the version of *The Tempest* translated by De Filippo into a poetic Neapolitan dialect of the seventeenth century. By his own admission, De Filippo translated the play freely, using contemporary elements of language, as it would have been unnatural to look for 'complete adherence to a language not spoken for centuries' (De Filippo, in Shakespeare 1984, 187).[5] Then, the inmates reworked the text in order to make it shorter, and more accessible to themselves and to the audience, as well as more consistent with their linguistic and cultural backgrounds, both in the script and in the oral performance.[6] For example, the lines pronounced by Trinculo and Stephano, played by the Roman Renato Rotondi and Giovanni Arcuri, are translated into the vernacular spoken in Rome on stage, and not on the written page.

For *Caesar Must Die*, the actor-convicts used their translation to create a screenplay with the Taviani brothers. This has been the basis for a film that makes allusions to, but does not try to 'dig into the convicts' lives' (Tempera 2017, 273), and in which 'everything was scripted' (Gilbey 2013, n.p.), even the scenes where the camera records everyday prison life during the months of rehearsals. Indeed, the reworking of Shakespeare's text in the production has been accurately studied and produced, and its translation into dialect becomes an example of what Mary Louise Pratt defines as contact zones: 'social spaces where disparate cultures meet, clash, and grapple with each other, often in highly asymmetrical relations of domination and subordination' (Pratt 2003, 4). A perspective such as this 'emphasizes how subjects are constituted in and by their relations to each other', and considers these relations 'not in terms of separateness or apartheid, but in terms of co-presence, interaction, interlocking understandings and practices, often within radically asymmetrical relations of power' (7). In our case, translation into dialects enhances contact among worlds that could seem extremely distant: dominant and subordinated languages and cultures, pivotal authors and marginal places, performative arts and fixed characters (the prisoner, the convict, the criminal). Moreover, this framework sheds light on the reciprocal constitution of two subjects, which cross the *limen* of the passage. On the one hand, there is Shakespeare, the mobile, nomadic upmost symbol of a 'polyphonic world literature' (Soncini 2008, 73) and, on the other hand, there are the prisoners, who have generally been under-represented in education systems, and who spend long periods in spaces governed by regimentation, closure and immobility. It is primarily in the 'translation zone' (Apter 2006) that both the prisoners and Shakespeare undertake a process of transition from a previous state of being, a journey which 'does not describe a linear path between two unrelated poles. Instead, it involves complex, uneven and contradictory relations of mutual transformation' (Neumann and Nünning 2012, 6).

An interlinguistic and intersemiotic translation: some examples

I will now consider how Shakespeare has been changed in this experimental artistic production in prison. I will draw on a brilliant essay by Maurizio Calbi, who is one of the few Italian scholars concerned with Shakespeare's presence in prison. Calbi's '"In states unborn and accents yet unknown": Spectral Shakespeare in Paolo and Vittorio Taviani's *Caesar Must Die*' (2014) considers what we can call the performativity of Shakespeare and his works, namely, his ability to embody and reproduce a non-essentialist identity. Hans Rudolf Venten, in his clear description of the manifold changes that occurred to the twin concepts of performance and performativity in their travelling through time and space, illustrates how the latter transformed through its passage from Austin's research on the performativity of speech to Derrida's theory of iterability: '[w]ith his reception and criticism of Austin, Derrida tried to foster his theory of linguistic signs based on iterability and quotability. In his terms, "performativity" is the effect of altered meaning through the repetition of signs in shifted contexts in time and space' (Venten 2012, 253). Venten approaches what is regarded as a turning point in the definition of performativity: its application to gender and identity in the studies of Judith Butler. William B. Worthen, whose words are of great significance here on account of his interest in theatre, drama and, particularly, Shakespeare, also draws on Butler to define when a performance is performative: when it works 'as a "ritualized practice" that "draws on and covers over the constitutive conventions by which it is mobilized"' (Worthen 1998, 1101).

From this perspective, Worthen states that every new appearance of a Shakespearean work in a theatre worldwide, or in a cinema or elsewhere, becomes performative when it is considered not as a 'performance of' a text, but rather as what Roach (1996) defines as a surrogation, an iteration, 'an ambivalent replaying of previous performers and performances by a current behavior' (Worthen 1998, 1101). In dramatic performance, Worthen holds, the text is not at the centre of the iterative process. Consequently, it cannot prescribe a meaning for the performance. Instead, it is the other way round: '[t]he citational practices of the stage – acting styles, directorial conventions, scenography – operate on and transform texts into something performative: performances, behavior' (1098). On this basis, it becomes difficult to regard texts as firm repositories of authority, on which dramatic practices are inextricably dependent, even when stage performances enact the plays of authors as symbolic and monolithic as Shakespeare. In these cases, what occurs is a specific form of interaction, given that a challenge to 'the apparent authority of the text' (1102) is brought into conjunction with an engagement with classic drama.

Within the same theoretical framework, which looks at Shakespeare as a cultural phenomenon, rather than as the authoritative writer of fixed texts, Douglas Lanier advances the idea of a rhizomatic Shakespeare, shaped by his multiple afterlives (Lanier 2014). In our case study, the translation of one of his texts into a plurality of languages 'bears witness to the fact that "Shakespeare" does not *properly* belong, that it is an "entity" – what Jacques Derrida may call a "Thing" (*Specters* 22) – that lends itself to an almost infinite variety of "migrations"' (Calbi 2014, 240). This Shakespeare in Rebibbia is therefore something more than a canonical 'foreign Shakespeare', because 'it cannot be made to coincide with the discrete boundaries of an individual non-Anglophone national tradition' (241), since there is more than one target language, and these languages are also 'foreign' to most of the Italian audience – so much so that some lines in dialect, which are considered difficult to understand, are translated into standard Italian through subtitles in the DVD version of the film. For this Shakespeare, who remains 'in-translation', Calbi suggests a movement 'across and in-between, a rhyzomatic movement that frustrates – and irremediably defers – points of arrival or destination' (241), a movement that also retroactively affects the English text. Calbi quotes various examples of this displacement of meaning with respect to the English (as well as the standard Italian) version of *Julius Caesar*, which testify also to the interweaving of translational choices that are directly connected to a specific criminal vocabulary and language.

For example, as noted by both Calbi and Mariangela Tempera (another authoritative Shakespearean scholar in Italy), the phrase 'It must be by his death' (2.1.10) (Shakespeare 1998, 197), in the scene where the actor playing Brutus (Salvatore Striano) struggles to master the lines of his monologue, becomes the 'more personal, direct, abbreviated' (Calbi 2014, 241) Neapolitan version, 'He must die', that is to say, 'Adda murì', which is very different from the typical standard Italian 'Deve morire', or, more literally, 'Deve essere con la sua morte'. The line is repeated with an increasing violence and a sense of claustrophobia as 'Adda murì, mò, mò' ('He must die right now') at the end of the speech. Tempera holds that 'the syntactical construction may recall Eduardo De Filippo's most famous line: "Adda passà 'a nuttata" [The night will pass, eventually]' (Tempera 2017, 275), pronounced at the end of De Filippo's 1945 comedy *Napoli milionaria*, a phrase which has been turned into a proverb in current Italian language. Another example of many that can be drawn from the script of the theatrical version of the play is when Brutus invites the conspirators not to fear Antony, but to save him. While Brutus responds to Cassius' doubts about him with the sober phrase 'Alas, good Cassius, do not think of him' (2.1.184), the translation into dialect results in a more passionate, even violent, utterance, and it puts emphasis on the leading role that Brutus plays at this moment in the play: 'Aggio ritt' ca no! Nun dative penziero pe' isso' (literally, 'I have said no! Do not worry about him').[7]

Similarly, there are some instances of overlapping between the Roman backdrop depicted by Shakespeare and other places related to the actors' backgrounds. First, the film shows how, during the rehearsals of the second scene of the first act, the actor playing the Soothsayer (*Indovino*, in Italian) asks the theatre director, Fabio Cavalli, whether he could perform the part as if he was 'nu poco pazzeriello' ('a bit crazy'), as the soothsayers usually are in his town. Also, in a scene introduced by the Tavianis,[8] Cosimo Rega, playing Cassius, comments on the description of Rome as 'shameless' by comparing it to Naples, his hometown. These two examples highlight a wider form of translation, one which does not simply imply the transposition of words from one language to another, but which also enriches and expands the significance of the play thanks to the intersemiotic passage from text to stage (and to film). The enhancement is expressed by words pronounced in the native dialects of the interpreters, or in locally coloured and colloquial Italian, a choice which strengthens the affective connection between the actors and their lines.

Furthermore, 'the language of mafia culture informs the whole film, from the conspirators' greeting of Brutus with "Baciamo le mani" (a typical mafia-coded form of greeting) to the identification of the would-be dictator with a *capo*' (Calbi 2014, 242). In Antony's speech, the translation of 'honourable man/men' as 'uomo/uomini d'onore', an expression used to refer to members of the Mafia, is 'amongst the most emblematic examples of the extent to which notions of Roman honour resonate with the codes of honour of organized crime associations' (Calbi 2014, 242). The expression 'uomo/uomini d'onore' is also used in the canonical Italian translation by Agostino Lombardo (Shakespeare 2000, 129–39), but, in the film, it is particularly emphasized by the repetitions in both Italian and dialect, and by the ironic tone of the interpreter. In the script of the theatrical version of *Julius Caesar*, the modified and cut version of Antony's speech is translated into standard Italian up to the last two appearances of the expression, which are written in Neapolitan and highlighted by the structure of the phrase, typical of the dialect: 'Piuttosto che fare torto a loro, preferisco far torto a un morto, far torto a me, a voi, ma guai fare nu torto a n'ommo d'onore! A ommeni d'onore comm'a cchelli!' ('Rather than wrong them, I would wrong the dead, myself, you, but woe to me if I wrong a man of honour. Men of honour such as them!'). With such a translation, the Shakespearean sentence ('I will not do them wrong. I rather choose / To wrong the dead, to wrong myself and you, / Than I will wrong such honourable men' [3.2.126–8; Shakespeare 1998, 259]) acquires a new meaning, strictly related to a criminal code of behaviour: not only must one avoid wronging specifically the 'honourable men' who killed Caesar, but also, generally speaking, any honourable man ('n'ommo d'onore'). But Antony is clearly ironic, and these words propel his audience to a backlash against the conspirators, which follows his speech.

Another interesting translational feature relates to two words, which are also marked by a strong connection to the language and values of criminal organizations, *rispetto* and *infame*. Tempera observes that Eduardo De Filippo, in his above-mentioned translation of *The Tempest*:

is familiar with the sinister connotations that a word like 'respect' can acquire: Stephano's 'The poor monster's my subject, and he shall not suffer indignity' (3.2.34–35) becomes 'Stu povero mostro è suddito mio e se rispetta lu cane pe' lu patrone!' (De Filippo 1984, 117) [This poor monster is my subject and you should respect the dog because of the master]. (Tempera 2017, 267)

I have observed that the same happens with regard to the theatrical version of *Julius Caesar*. The substantive *rispetto* (respect) and the adjective *rispettoso* (respectful) are used nine times in the script, but there is only one direct correspondence with the English text. Otherwise, the words seem to have been chosen in order to cast light on a high-valued principle among those associated with Italian criminal organizations. For example, Cassius opens his famous dialogue with Brutus in the fourth act with the following words: '[t]hat you have wronged me doth appear in this' (4.3.1) (Shakespeare 1998, 277). In the script, the line becomes 'Senza ca ci giramm' attuorno: tu m'hai mancato di rispetto e o fatto è chesto' ('Without going around it: you disrespected me and here's the thing'). The same happens with *infame* (infamous), a highly significant word in the criminal culture of the convicts, used to accuse someone of the worst possible act: betrayal. The term appears seven times in the script (once with the colloquial apheresis of the first vowel), none of which is a translation of 'infamous' in English (but of 'vile', 'foul', 'unkind'). To offer just one instance of its appearance: when Shakespeare makes Antony say: '[j]udge, O you gods, how dearly Caesar loves him. / This was the most unkindest cut of all' (3.2.180–1) (Shakespeare 1998, 262), referring to Brutus, the adjective 'unkindest' becomes 'infame', and it defines the man, not his act.

Finally, the interplay between two realms of meaning – the Roman *Julius Caesar* as written and interpreted in early modern England, and the social and cultural background of the inmates – also resonates in the theatrical version through dramatic and performative choices. The text has been translated and tailored to the interpreter's needs, and many changes to the Shakespearean play have been made in order to make space for all the actors. Among them is the apocryphal scene featuring Caesar and Cicero, following the scene set at Brutus' house that opens the second act. The two characters are respectively interpreted by the Roman Giovanni Arcuri and the Calabrian Francesco De Masi, who are older than the majority of the other actors. Their dialogue deals with the themes of old age, lack of gratitude and power. Caesar feels the weight of unexpected facts that he cannot dominate – such as his public fainting – and complains that he is no longer appreciated by those for whom he won battles and conquered lands. Before they quarrel at the end of the scene, Cicero reminds him that politics is like a war, 'ma nu pocu cchiù 'nturcigghiata' ('but a bit more complicated'), with a Calabrian accent that marks the distance between the two characters.

These are only a few examples of how both the interlinguistic and intersemiotic translation embodies the actors' backgrounds, from their criminal vocabulary and their values, to their spatial and cultural reference points. This is the strategy whereby the Taviani brothers try to deconstruct and rewrite Shakespeare's *Julius Caesar*. Calbi goes even further in describing the phenomenon as the 'transformation of the "original" into an "intertext" that is made to cohabit' with other languages (Calbi 2014, 240). The distance between a monumental and despotic view of the author and his works, on the one hand, and a performative view based on the idea that the reiteration would be able to make the 'Thing', on the other hand, is broadly highlighted by Calbi elsewhere:

> Thus, the (Shakespearean) work – what Derrida calls in *Specters of Marx* the 'signature of the "Thing 'Shakespeare"'' (22) – cannot be clearly or absolutely separated from its afterlife. It takes place as a necessarily contaminated 'entity', in that it is structured from within – and 'de-structured' – by reproducibility and iterability. Its first time is inextricably intertwined with the second time of repetition; its time is the anachronistic time of spectrality. (Calbi 2013, 18)

Dialects as languages of culture and of contradictions

Concerning the process of deconstruction and rewriting into multiple dialects, Shaul Bassi (2016) raises a question about the translation choices, which leads us to consider the role of the actor–prisoners, and the means through which they undertake their own passage: who owns the language, and, more specifically, who owns the dialect in *Caesar Must Die*? Bassi argues that the filmmakers and the theatre director share a confidence 'in realigning the inner selves of the inmates with the high existential and philosophical truths of Western civilization' (Bassi 2016, 195). In order to reach this outcome, the inmates should 'be authentic, but only just so' (195). Cavalli, in his artificial, academic Italian, warns Giovanni Arcuri, who plays Caesar with an excessively Roman inflection, with the line: 'Non è un dialetto volgare. È un dialetto, però in bocca a personaggi nobili' ('Not too vulgar. It is dialect, but spoken by noblemen' [Tempera 2017, 275]).[9] By containing the actor's speech, he refers to the noble roots of the characters interpreted by the convicts, who, instead, belong to the lowest social classes. Bassi depicts both Cavalli and the Taviani brothers as 'old-fashioned, progressive, twentieth-century intellectuals' (Bassi 2016, 196), sharing a great faith in the redeeming power of highbrow culture and in the educational role of the canon: Shakespeare is what they think it is their duty to teach to the illiterate, in order to widen their horizons and to mix the 'high word of poetry' with the 'visceral word of life' (Canessa 2012, n.p.). While this insight rings true, one should not neglect the significant role of the actor–prisoners themselves in this controversy about their presumed salvation through so-called high culture. Somehow, Calbi helps us by highlighting the non-homogeneous use of a noble dialect in the film, and the massive presence of shifts 'from more formal to less formal registers; they refract and "rewrite" each other in a kind of Bakhtinian heteroglossia' (Calbi 2014, 241). This plurilingualism is not new in the Italian theatre, given that, as Marvin Carlson has observed, it has made appearances 'in a wide variety of forms, from the coexistence of different languages or dialects in the same text (sometimes called horizontal plurilingualism) to that of different stylistic registers of the same dialect (sometimes called vertical plurilingualism)' (Carlson 2006, 68). The feature has also been taken into account by Tullio De Mauro, one of the most important Italian linguists of the twentieth century, and among the few interested in contemporary theatrical language: far from being a 'fact of rustic lack of culture', the plurilingualism of Italian theatre represents one of the possible artistic manifestations of plurilingualism as 'a great fact of national culture, capable of guaranteeing Italy its international profile' (De Mauro 1987, 136).

This testifies to the inner adaptability of dialects, which can be variously employed by the speakers – in this case, the inmates – who master them. The inmates play an active role in the artistic development of the film that cannot be utterly denied or ignored, even though, as Thomassen has written, 'the relationship between structure and agency is not easily resolved' in liminal phases of passage (Thomassen 2014, 1).

In prison theatre, the choice not to use standard Italian becomes a way of fostering the communicative skills of the inmates, and it is motivated by the search for spontaneity and authenticity. In Italy, actors, directors, writers and poets representative of experimental forms of theatre have regarded dialects as languages of contradictions, reactions and resistance against the neo-colonial impact of standard Italian, which was imposed over the great linguistic fragmentation of the country by the new-born Kingdom of Italy in the second half of the nineteenth century and, later, by the Fascists. The opposition to standard Italian, which is felt to be televised, flat and stale – a 'defective organism' in need of 'prosthetics' (Ferrone 2006, 7) – is also the reason why Cavalli and the Taviani brothers consider dialects to be the language of authenticity and natural expression, perhaps from a slightly naive perspective that downplays their subversive potential. Nonetheless, Cavalli maintains that dialect can also be a language of culture, expanded to such an extent as to become able to express everything. The theatre director himself points out the high poetic potential of translation into dialects, which are anything but poor languages, unfit to reach literary status or transcend a local reality.[10]

This affirmation of non-standard language as the language of culture has parallels with the field of postcolonial Shakespeare, as Roshni Mooneeram argues in a study about the translation of *The Tempest* into Mauritian creole by Dev Virahsawmy, who, in his own words, used Shakespeare to 'enhance' his language (Mooneeram 2009, 140). Likewise, in prison theatre and, specifically, in Rebibbia, the recognition of dialect as a literary language is meant to counter an exclusion that has always been an issue for Italian theatre. Siro Ferrone calls into question a process of 'whitewashing' performed by the 'mystifying mask' of the national language since the sixteenth century and the invention of the printing press, in order to remove the prestigious mark of literature from the peripheral languages typical of the oral theatrical tradition:

> The search, by theatre-makers – often coming from 'minor' social categories or arts, when not illiterate (such as many actors of the society of the *ancien régime*) – for a certification of literary dignity, pushed the artists of the scene to dress themselves in costumes, forms, masks, languages that did not belong to them but that could still produce, on them, an ennobling effect. (Ferrone 2006, 1)

Moreover, here the dialect issue overlaps with the need for literary models that are part of the Western canon, such as Shakespeare, and implies not only the acceptance of the role of highbrow culture, but also the need to interact with it in order to open up spaces of critique. This seemingly contradictory approach is peculiar to the dynamic relationship between Shakespeare and popular culture, to which Italian dialects belong, as outlined by Douglas Lanier: '[i]ndeed, I will argue that the double-edged nature of this "and" – a sense of simultaneous attraction and tension between Shakespeare and popular culture, and the cultural constituencies they represent – is the distinguishing characteristic of their relationship' (Lanier 2002, 4). Lanier also tackles the problem of the role of the Bard as a Foucauldian author-function outside the realm of high literature, by casting light on its simultaneous presence in two reciprocally challenging cultural systems:

> Shakespeare's appearances in pop culture typically involve interplay between two cultural systems – high and pop culture – that operate in parallel realms, two bodies of reference, sets of cultural institutions, canons of aesthetic standards, modes of constructing cultural authority. That interplay takes many forms, some harmonious, some reciprocal, some recuperative, some competitive, some antagonistic, and even some unstable combinations of these. But at its heart is a contest for authority between the two cultural systems and the institutional interests they represent. (Lanier 2002, 16)

Rob Pensalfini stresses the interconnection between an elitist notion of Shakespeare as the foremost exponent of Western (and world) literature and his presence inside prisons: '[t]here may be one way, though, in which Shakespeare's contribution to the prison culture is unique, connected to his cultural prestige and notoriety. For many in the prison, particularly prisoners and custodial staff with limited education, Prison Shakespeare challenges long-held notions of Shakespeare's exclusiveness and inaccessibility' (Pensalfini 2016, 222). This tendency explains why it is correct to use the controversial term *appropriation* as conceptualized and defined by Lanier. In this case, indeed, it 'retains the connotation that this struggle to claim Shakespeare is contentious, a matter of a weaker party wresting something of value from unwilling or hostile hands' (Lanier 2002, 5), while the opposite meaning of the term, used when a dominant group adopts elements of a disadvantaged culture, is certainly less common in the field of Shakespearean studies, given the symbolic capital of the author involved. Within this framework, dialects stand as prisoners' commodities strongly tied to their life outside (and also inside) prison, through which they approach Shakespeare and gain back an active, performing role.

In fact, by controlling their words and their communication, the actor–prisoners contribute to overthrowing the Foucauldian prison panopticon: '[a]nd they tell me that, doing theatre, they can tell the viewer what they want. They say "I can also make mistakes, make fun of them, they don't notice, I pretend, and they stand there watching, they can't move, they have to cope with it"' (Marino 2019, 47). This is how Lello Tedeschi, speaking about the Teatro Kismet at the Trani prison,[11] describes the experience through the eyes of the prisoners, who are capable of grasping the contemporary reversal of the panoptic principle. In fact, the actors, while they are acting within the prison space, find themselves doubly under the gaze of the spectators – as inmates and as characters. However, the observer is also real, concrete, visible, and not de-materialized as the eye of disciplinary power described by Foucault, under whose gaze prisoners cannot control the limiting representation of themselves as criminals (Foucault 1975). The participants in the theatrical production, instead, are extremely aware of their position. They actively choose if and how to present and represent themselves, they hold the attention of the audience and, regarding the issue at stake here, they decide how much of their linguistic and cultural background they want to embody and express through their voices and words.

Obviously, if this is true in theatre, where the audience is physically present, cinema involves a totally different control over the attention and the gaze of the viewer. Nonetheless, in *Caesar Must Die*, the central and leading role of the actors is emphasized by the disorientation experienced by Italian spectators, who are not able to fully understand the film because of unclear and unintelligible dialogue in southern dialects. This feeling of uneasiness is much more likely to characterize the experience of the audience from the north of the country, while a more complete comprehension, even without the subtitles, is guaranteed only for those who are able to master these supposedly archaic and barbaric vernaculars. This sounds like a sort of double revenge: one is taken by the southern speakers against the traditionally richer, more developed and racist northern regions, and the other by those who speak dialects in contrast to the plain, sometimes even pretentious, Italian used by averagely educated cinema-goers. In both cases, prisoners, as actors, experience new hierarchies in the control of communicative power.

To conclude, I would like to consider the physical implications of prison as a form of limited passage. Being a sort of limbo, prison does not represent a threshold but a purgatorial phase of life, during which everything from outside is lost, and views of the future and new possibilities seem denied. With theatre behind bars, however, the restrictive fixity of this condition, a passage that leads nowhere, evolves into a different kind of Foucauldian heterotopia: 'the prison (an exemplary heterotopia of deviation) and the theatre (a heterotopia capable of bringing "onto the rectangle of the stage, one after the other, a whole series of places that are foreign to one another", Foucault 1984, 6) come to coincide' (Cavecchi 2017, 13). And it is exactly the appearance of these 'foreign places' that opens up spaces in which truly dynamic passages can happen.

Drawing on Victor Turner and Richard Schechner's considerations about the process of performing an already existing script during rehearsals, I wish to suggest that, through theatre, the actor-prisoners are involved in the process of passing through the land of the 'not-not-me' (Turner 1982, 121; Schechner 1986). The starting point is their personal and collective history and state, the 'biological-historical individual' (the 'me'). During the rehearsals, they are made to meet the 'not-me', that is to say, in our case, *Julius Caesar* by William Shakespeare, and his characters. This way, prisoners cross the threshold of the fixed and overdetermined character they are used to playing – that of the condemned criminal – and move towards something new and unknown. Despite this, they do not forget their backgrounds, their pasts and their memories. The director assists the 'alchemic or mystical marriage going on as the actor crosses the limen from not-me to not-not-me'; finally, 'the me at this third stage is a richer me than the me at the beginning' (Turner 1982, 121).

Within this frame of reference, I truly believe that the languages used in both of the Rebibbia versions of *Julius Caesar* play a key role in fostering the reaching and crossing of the not-not-me area, as they work exactly as 'aspects of the actor's experience surface which tincture the script-role he or she has undertaken' (Turner 1982, 121). In doing so, the languages of translation go a long way towards activating a truly transformative experience, a crucial passage for both the Shakespearean text and the actor-prisoners involved.

Notes

1. The script of the theatrical version has kindly been provided by Fabio Cavalli. I was part of the audience on the occasion of the open rehearsal *Giulio Cesare a Rebibbia* (15 May 2013), and a video recording of that show has also been provided by Cavalli. The DVD of *Caesar Must Die* was released in 2012.
2. *Casa circondariale*, in the Italian penal system.
3. This definition (of *esperti*) was used by Cavalli during an unpublished interview I conducted in Rome in 2012 for the research for my BA thesis.
4. Unless otherwise indicated, all translations are mine.
5. See also Mariangela Tempera (2017, 270).
6. Both the video recording of the show and the script have kindly been provided by Fabio Cavalli.
7. It is interesting to note that the sentence is pronounced in plain, standard Italian in the Tavianis' film, as another sign of the continuous process of translation and re-translation: 'Ti ho detto di no, Cassio' (timecode: 30:39).

8   'Città senza vergogna', pronounced while looking with Brutus at Antony offering Caesar the crown. There is no correspondence in Shakespeare's play, in which it is Casca who describes how Caesar has been offered the crown three times (1.2.214–91), and in which Cassius comments on Rome, talking with Brutus: 'Age, thou art shamed! / Rome, thou hast lost the breed of noble bloods!' (1.2.151–2).
9   Translated by Bassi.
10 From the unpublished interview I conducted in Rome in 2012 for the research for my BA thesis.
11 The interview was published as the output of European-based research on theatre in prison. The report has also been published in Mancini (2008).

Filmography

Cesare deve morire (Caesar Must Die; Paolo Taviani and Vittorio Taviani; IT 2012).

References

Apter, Emily. 2006. *The Translation Zone: A new comparative literature*. Princeton, NJ: Princeton University Press.
Bassi, Shaul. 2016. *Shakespeare's Italy, Italy's Shakespeare*. New York: Palgrave Macmillan.
Calbi, Maurizio. 2013. *Spectral Shakespeares: Media adaptation in the twenty-first century*. New York: Palgrave.
Calbi, Maurizio. 2014. '"In states unborn and accents yet unknown": Spectral Shakespeare in Paolo and Vittorio Taviani's *Cesare deve morire (Caesar Must Die)*', *Shakespeare Bulletin* 32: 235–53.
Canessa, Fabio. 2012. 'Fabio Cavalli, regista di *Cesare deve morire* "Il carcere è un teatro"', *La Nuova Sardegna*, 19 June. Accessed 13 February 2022. http://www.lanuovasardegna.it/regione/2012/06/18/news/fabio-cavalli-regista-di-cesare-deve-morire-il-carcere-e-un-teatro-1.5284336.
Carlson, Marvin. 2006. *Speaking in Tongues: Language at play in the theatre*. Ann Arbor: University of Michigan Press.
Cavecchi, Maria Cristina. 2017. 'Brave New Worlds: Shakespearean Tempests in Italian prisons', *Altre Modernità/Otras Modernidades/Autre Modernités/Other Modernities* 11: 1–22.
De Mauro, Tullio. 1987. *L'Italia delle Italie*. Rome: Editori Riuniti.
Ferrone, Siro. 2006. 'Una lingua in maschera: Vita artificiosa del parlato sulla scena teatrale italiana'. In *Lingua e dialetto nel teatro contemporaneo: Atti della giornata di studio (Prato, Ridotto del Teatro Metastasio, 12 marzo 2004)*, edited by Neri Binazzi and Silvia Calamai, 1–7. Padua: Unipress.
Foucault, Michel. 1975. *Surveillir et punir: Naissance de la prison*. Paris: Gallimard.
Foucault, Michel. 1984. 'Of other spaces: Utopias and heterotopias', translated by Jay Miskowiec, *Architecture/Mouvement/Continuité* 5: 46–9. Accessed 30 September 2019. http://web.mit.edu/allanmc/www/foucault1.pdf.
Gilbey, Ryan. 2013. 'Paolo and Vittorio Taviani: "For us, it was cinema or death"', *The Guardian*, 1 March. Accessed 13 February 2022. https://www.theguardian.com/film/2013/mar/01/taviani-cinema-or-death.
Lanier, Douglas. 2002. *Shakespeare and Modern Popular Culture*. Oxford: Oxford University Press.
Lanier, Douglas. 2014. 'Shakesperean rhizomatics: Adaptation, ethics, value'. In *Shakespeare and the Ethics of Appropriation*, edited by Alexa Huang and Elizabeth Rivlin, 21–40. New York: Palgrave Macmillan.
Mancini, Andrea. 2008. *A scene chiuse: Esperienze e immagini del teatro in carcere*. Corazzano: Titivillus.
Marino, Massimo. 2019. *Teatro e carcere in Italia*. Accessed 13 February 2022. http://www.ristretti.it/areestudio/cultura/teatro/index.htm.

Ministero della Giustizia. 2019. 'Teatro in carcere'. Accessed 13 February 2022. https://www.giustizia.it/giustizia/it/mg_2_3_0_6.wp.
Mooneeram, Roshni. 2009. *From Creole to Standard: Shakespeare, language and literature in a postcolonial context*. Amsterdam: Rodopi.
Neumann, Birgit and Ansgar Nünning. 2012. 'Travelling concepts as a model for the study of culture'. In *Travelling Concepts as a Model for the Study of Culture*, edited by Birgit Neumann and Ansgar Nünning, 1–22. Berlin: Walter de Gruyter.
Pensalfini, Rob. 2016. *Prison Shakespeare: For these deep shames and great indignities*. London: Palgrave Macmillan.
Pratt, Mary Louise. 2003. *Imperial Eyes: Travel writing and transculturation*. London: Routledge.
Roach, Joseph. 1996. *Cities of the Dead: Circum-atlantic performance*. New York: Columbia University Press.
Schechner, Richard. 1986. *Between Theater and Anthropology*. Philadelphia: University of Pennsylvania Press.
Shakespeare, William. 1984. *La tempesta*, translated by Eduardo De Filippo. Turin: Einaudi.
Shakespeare, William. 1998. *Julius Caesar*, edited by David Daniell. London: Methuen Drama.
Shakespeare, William. 1999. *The Tempest*, edited by Virginia Mason Vaughan and Alden T. Vaughan. London: Methuen Drama.
Shakespeare, William. 2000. *Giulio Cesare*, translated by Agostino Lombardo. Milan: Feltrinelli.
Shakespeare, William. 2014. *La tempesta*, translated by Agostino Lombardo. Milan: Feltrinelli.
Soncini, Sara. 2008. 'Diachronic translation in Tiezzi's *Hamlet*'. In *Crossing Time and Space: Shakespeare translations in present-day Europe*, edited by Carla Dente and Sara Soncini, 63–76. Pisa: Plus.
Tempera, Mariangela. 2017. 'Shakespeare behind Italian bars: The Rebibbia Project, *The Tempest*, and *Caesar Must Die*'. In *Shakespeare, Italy, and Transnational Exchange*, edited by Enza De Francisci and Christ Stamatakis, 265–76. New York: Routledge.
Thomassen, Bjørn. 2014. *Liminality and the Modern: Living through the in-between*. London: Routledge.
Turner, Victor. 1982. *From Ritual to Theatre: The human seriousness of play*. New York: Paj Publications.
Venten, Hans Rudolf. 2012. 'Performativity and performance'. In *Travelling Concepts as a Model for the Study of Culture*, edited by Birgit Neumann and Ansgar Nünning, 249–66. Berlin: Walter de Gruyter.
Worthen, William B. 1998. 'Drama, performativity, and performance', *Publications of the Modern Language Association* 113 (5): 1093–107.

5
Cultural translation as a poetics of movement

Marie-Christine Boucher

To migrate to a country, one has to physically pass a border – no matter if said border has been rendered virtually non-existent with the help of international treaties or if it is still highly controlled, and no matter if it coincides with a topographical obstacle or not.[1] This might seem so obvious that it hardly needs to be mentioned at all. It involves a movement in both space and time, one in which the *here* and the *there* usually correlate respectively either with *then* or with *now*. Yet any migration relies constantly on passages, much beyond the first crossing of that border. It entails many other passages: much smaller, less significant ones in everyday life, and, as a result, the culture of origin of a person cannot be located in a single place any more. Traditions are carried, communities develop their own spaces, particularly in large cities, and these spaces can be the location of everyday border crossings. In literature, the initial crossing of the border can be – and often is – a part of autobiographical narratives, but so can be the numerous back-and-forths that follow throughout the years. When Lena, the protagonist of Nellja Veremej's novel *Berlin liegt im Osten* (2013) enters her East German patients' apartments, or the Russian cafe where she meets compatriots, she crosses symbolic borders that have an impact on how she translates herself in relation to the people around her.

Today's migrant literature is not merely located in a third space. It is not hybrid, nor does it solely tell stories of liminality. It rather tells of a 'never-ending bouncing back and forth between places and times, societies and cultures' (Ette 2016, 7), and, in doing so, it becomes a source of 'knowledge-for-living' and 'knowledge-for-living-together'.[2] Taking into consideration the importance of migration phenomena in contemporary society, there needs to be – as Ottmar Ette claims – a theory that can take into account the movements, or passages, that take place through migration. In *Writing-between-Worlds* (*ZwischenWeltenSchreiben*), Ette speaks of 'Literatures without a fixed Abode' (*Literatur ohne festen Wohnsitz*), a category that 'queers the familiar distinction between national literature (the province of the still-dominant national philologies) and world literature (the domain of comparative literary studies)' (Ette 2016, 8). Literatures without a fixed Abode[3] are therefore plural by definition, and while they do not belong strictly to national literatures in the way they are still defined today, they are also not purely products of World Literature, which follows a very different logic.[4] Therefore, refusing to locate these literatures solely 'inside the nation'[5] does not mean to locate them in a no man's land or as part of a homogenized world literary canon. Literature without a fixed Abode is 'not literature without borders' (7); rather, it addresses the reality that borders 'are constantly being drawn and re-drawn' (9).

I argue that translation theory has already developed a set of concepts that can take into account the complexity of movements – and, therefore, of passages – that characterize contemporary society. In order to develop a poetics of movement, which Ottmar Ette calls for, one should acknowledge the insights that translation theory can provide. In order to do this, I will demonstrate how 'cultural grids' – a concept stemming from translation theory – can be integrated into the poetics of movement, using Nellja Veremej's *Berlin liegt im Osten* as a literary case study.

A brief detour through the translational turn

Before bringing translations theory into relation with a poetics of movement, it seems necessary to briefly define what is understood as (cultural) translation, and how this concept has been used as a methodological tool beyond translation proper. In the wake of the translational turn (see Bachmann-Medick 2014; Snell-Hornby 2006; Bassnett 1998), the concept of translation has been described by many as a necessary category to deal with the complexity of today's culture.

Translation is 'a basic social practice' (Fuchs 2009, 21), a kind of 'master metaphor epitomizing our present *condition humaine* ... in a perplexing context of change and difference' (Delabastita and Grutman 2005, 23):

> Thus, 'translation' [is] a methodological tool for breaking scenarios of intercultural encounter into smaller units, thereby taking notice of actors, mediators, and translators, and of their practices, steps, and emotional involvements ... From this stance translation can not only be seen as a research category that is 'good to think with' (Edmund Leach) but also as a social condition and mode of existence of migration itself. (Bachmann-Medick 2018, 274)

As Benjamin was perhaps the first to spell out in his seminal essay, 'The task of the translator', published in 1923, translation is a mediated process, and, most importantly, it *is* a process, period (Benjamin 1971). This led to an understanding of the concept that removes the illusion of immediacy (Ette 2016, 176), and that stresses the importance of embeddedness in a cultural context. Translation was therefore not to be understood as a purely linguistic process, as had been the case before. In translation studies, this idea became particularly prominent after the cultural turn, and its objects of study have since become much broader. Today, translation studies are 'concerned, not with languages, objects or cultures as such, but with communication across cultures' (Snell-Hornby 2006, 166). Following this logic, cultural translation 'can be understood as a process in which there is no start text and usually no fixed target text. The focus is on cultural *processes* rather than products. The prime cause of cultural translation is the movement of people (subjects) rather than the movement of texts (objects)' (Pym 2009, 138). This deconstructivist notion of translation as a process renders obsolete the necessary existence of an original. Therefore, it becomes possible to speak of translation without implying a linguistic transfer between two (equivalent) texts.

The call for a poetics of movement

In *Writing-between-Worlds*, Ottmar Ette calls for theories and terminologies to change with social change. Literatures without a fixed Abode, as literatures that are not located solely in national literatures, yet are also not part of universalistic world literature, require new conceptualizations, which should be articulated in a new *poetics of movement*:

> To analyze the Literatures without a fixed Abode, we need concepts that can articulate difficult vectoral processes. We still do not have any testable concepts of movement that correlate space and time in sufficiently complex ways to allow us to describe this vectorization with precision. This is why we have as yet no fully articulated *poetics of movement* to help decode the vectoral imagination of today's literatures in all its intricacy and multiplicity, so that we can retrieve from them the knowledge-for-living sedimented there in layers of overlapping movements. This is not to say that a 'vectoral turn' should now replace the spatial turn. Rather, we have to attune our critical analyses of cultural and literary phenomena more to the forms and functions of movement. (Ette 2016, 32)

With this in mind, Ette proposes that these movements, which are an essential feature of Literatures without a fixed Abode should be thought of as vectors, as these emphasize a type of movement in which time and space cannot be conceived of separately:

> These dynamics transform fixed structures anew and turn them into the kind of open, arrow-like structures that I call vectorized or vectoral. A mobile system of coordinates is sketched out …, one in which past experience creates places, where spaces grow out of movement, where the past grows out of having been lived and the present out of the process of becoming future. They form a mobile network in which … the movements in and of the past cannot be separated from the movements in and of the future. (Ette 2016, 3)

Ette criticizes the reduction of movement to its cartographic representation, and likens the loss of information that takes place to the transfer from a three-dimensional globe to a two-dimensional map:

> We have, it seems to me, more than enough spatial concepts. What we are urgently lacking is a sufficiently precise terminology for movement, dynamics, and mobility. One could go so far as to speak of a colonization of the concepts of movement by a flood of spatial models that arrest dynamic processes through obsessive spatialization and reduce them by painstakingly ignoring the

dimension of time ... Spatialization has its price, especially when it ignores movement. (Ette 2016, 31–2)

In Ette's view, Benjamin's arcades, for example, contrast with this idea, in that they are not mere spaces, but rather 'mobile spaces' (Ette 2016, 32). In a way, these are not fixed, and, just as the landscape of the city will change at each end of the arcade, the two points on the cultural grids that authors–translators are translating are not immutable. Yet, at the moment where this translation-act is taking place, they are two definite points in space and time, and it is the combination of the location in space and time of the source and of the target that determines the nature of the vectoral movement.

Of course, there are limits to the metaphor of the vector in the case of literature and culture. In mathematics, vectors can be placed anywhere on a grid; that is, a vector represents the distance between two points, but this distance can be located anywhere on a grid without changing the value of the vector. This is not the case with culture(s): movement from different points – places, locations – in the world will yield different results. Yet Ette's metaphor offers the definite advantage of emphasizing the importance of the sum of all movements that literature contains. This is where translation can complement the metaphor of the vector: as a theory of movement, translation requires that space and time be constantly taken into account.[6]

Culture(s) as grids

In 'Composing the other', an essay on postcolonial translation, André Lefevere challenges 'the supposedly primary or fundamental role played by linguistic codes in the operation known as "translating"' (Lefevere 1999, 75). As mentioned previously, translation theory has expanded its scope in the last decades, and, at least since the cultural turn in translation studies, purely linguistic definitions of translation have been challenged repeatedly. For that reason, a definition of translation that does not place language at its core might not seem particularly groundbreaking. Yet Lefevere's theory offers a productive solution to the definition of culture in (cultural) translation. He postulates the existence of two cultural grids: a 'conceptual grid' and a 'textual grid', which are 'both ... the result of the socialization process' (Lefevere 1999, 75).

The 'textual grid' is made up of the elements that texts usually contain in a given cultural context: 'certain texts are supposed to contain certain markers designed to elicit certain reactions on the reader's part, and ... the success of communication depends on both the writer and the reader of the text agreeing to play their assigned parts in connection with those markers' (Lefevere 1999, 76). Even texts that do not make use of those markers in the expected way depend on the reader's knowledge of the grid, as in the case, for example, of postmodernist texts that play with the reader's expectations. In order for the effect to be created, the reader has to be aware of which set of 'rules' are being broken (76).

The conceptual grid works in a similar manner, but it includes a wider range of cultural elements that are not limited to text. Any concept that is present in a certain cultural context has the potential to be (mis)interpreted. Lefevere illustrates this point with the marketing of Corn Flakes in India, which only became successful once they were rebranded as Basmati Flakes (Lefevere 1999, 77). Problems of translation, therefore, 'are caused at least as much by discrepancies in conceptual and textual grids as by discrepancies in languages' (76). There are clear advantages to conceiving of cultures as the interweaving of grids. Instead of thinking of a writer or a text as belonging to a single culture, with the fixed meaning this entails, thinking of culture as an overlapping or interweaving of grids forces us to locate the text in a much more precise and flexible manner.

Lefevere emphasizes the fact that, in a translation process, 'both the writer of the original and the translator are faced with the two grids ..., and that both have to come to terms with those grids' (Lefevere 1999, 77). The writer interacts with the combination of textual and conceptual grids of the time and place where they are writing. The place and time at which the narratives are being produced determine the location of the source text on the conceptual and textual grid. A translator must then also interact with the combination of textual and conceptual grids at the time and place where they are translating. A story about another time and place requires first determining the textual and conceptual grids from which the source text originates. In order for the translation to be successful, its retelling in the here and now will be influenced by local textual and conceptual grids. In a similar fashion, when writing transnational narratives, a writer must refer to the two grids in more than one location at a time. The place and time of the writing/publishing determines where that text is located on the conceptual and textual grids. In transnational storytelling, the result – in this case, a novel – is the sum of all vectors that it contains, that is, the sum of all movements on these two grids. If the translation proper of a source text into a target text can be seen as more or less unilateral – the translation is of a text written at one point in space and time, and one point on the interweaving of the conceptual and textual grids, into a second point in space and time on the conceptual and textual grids – transnational storytelling involves, as Ette points out, many vectors that point in many directions. The following section offers a reading of Nellja Veremej's transnational novel *Berlin liegt im Osten* in light of these two overlapping theories, as a collection of vectoral movements that can be located on interwoven cultural grids.

Locating vectors on cultural grids

Berlin liegt im Osten takes place over the course of one year, from Christmas to Christmas, approximately, and it is set in Berlin's Alexanderplatz and its surroundings. The main protagonist, Lena, is a woman in her early forties, who grew up in Soviet Russia and moved to Germany in the early 1990s, as Berlin was undergoing rapid changes. The novel contains some strong autobiographical elements, and, just as the author herself did at some point in her life, Lena works as a caretaker in a retirement home in the centre of Berlin, in what used to be East Berlin. As a first-person narrator, Lena recounts her own life story and, in parallel, the life of her patient, friend – and at some point even lover – Ulf Seitz. Seitz was a child during World War Two, and he became an adult in the German Democratic Republic (GDR). Seitz is portrayed as a very ordinary man, who has both suffered and profited from history and the political evolution of the country: he grew up without his father, whom he lost during the war, but he later profited from his position as a respected journalist and writer in the GDR. As a result, he could not quite understand the enthusiasm of a lot of people – including his then wife – about the West, and the time of the German Reunification. Lena tells his story in the way she has heard it from him personally, and she does mention that she is not a completely reliable narrator, and sometimes fills the gaps using her own imagination. Altogether, Lena goes into much greater detail about Ulf Seitz's memories than her own, which she recounts in a more brief and superficial manner. Early in the novel, before she dives into Ulf Seitz's past, she also recounts another patient's memories of the end of the war, shortly after this patient has died in the retirement home. This does not serve the general arc of the story, but it is, as Stuart Taberner notes, 'significant for its framing of Lena as a teller of German stories' (Taberner 2018, 415). She, the migrant worker, will be 'the sole custodian of his memories' ('die einzige Hüterin seiner Erinnerungen'; Veremej 2013, 39).[7]

The author of the novel, Nellja Veremej, was born in 1963 in the Soviet Union, and she lived in various cities there, including Maikop, a small city in the Russian Caucasus, approximately halfway between Krasnodar and Sochi. She first studied Russian philology in Leningrad, and, later, journalism in Novi Sad, Yugoslavia, and she has been living in the centre of Berlin since 1994. Mitte, the centre of Berlin, plays a prominent role in her novel *Berlin liegt im Osten*, which is set mostly in the district of Berlin-Mitte, around Alexanderplatz and its famous television tower. *Berlin liegt im Osten* was Veremej's first novel. It was originally published by Jung und Jung, a relatively small publisher in Salzburg, Austria, which mostly publishes books on topics related to Austria. The paperback edition of the novel was published two years later by Aufbau, a German publisher in Berlin. In contrast to some contemporary writers who also originate from the former Soviet Union, such as Olga Grjasnowa and Nino Haratischwili – who have been critiqued, discussed and translated a lot in the last five to ten years – this novel has not been as widely received, even though its media reception was mostly positive.[8] Sabine Berking, in the *Frankfurter Allgemeine Zeitung*, described it as a 'Berlin novel that had been missing' ('Ein Berlin-Roman, wie man ihn bisher vermisste'; Berking 2013, n.p., my translation). The translocal and transnational nature of the novel is underscored by the fact that this comment came from a journalist based in Frankfurt about a novel that was written by an author who is originally from Russia, and that was initially distributed by an Austrian publisher.

In its academic reception, the novel has been mostly analysed in the context of cultural memory studies, as an example of cosmopolitan or transcultural memory. Stuart Taberner locates the novel in the context of the recent enlargement of German memory culture. He reminds us that minorities and migrants have often been excluded from a German cultural memory that was necessarily ethnic. He quotes Yasemin Yildiz and Michael Rothberg: '[i]n the aftermath of the Nazi genocide, it has seemed necessary to preserve an ethnically homogeneous notion of German identity in order to ensure Germans' responsibility for the crimes of the past, even though that very notion of ethnicity was one of the sources of those crimes' (Taberner 2018, 408). The integration of migrants into German memory – as 'custodians of German memory', as Lena sees herself – therefore remains a topic of discussion, along with the integration of German memory into a universal history of conflict and cruelty. Shifting away from the question of memory culture, I would like to argue that an analysis of this novel can be complemented by a reading that emphasizes the creation of knowledge-for-living and knowledge-for-living-together through processes of cultural translation. Doing so can shed light on the dynamic origins of seemingly static presents.

About herself and her patient/friend Ulf Seitz, Lena says: 'We are Easterners, after all' ('Wir sind halt Ossis'; Veremej 2013, 44), *Ossis* being a derogatory term that was used in West Germany to describe East Germans, but which has since also been reclaimed by East Germans. With this expression of familiarity, Lena signals that she does not perceive herself to be a foreigner to Seitz in the same way that she might be perceived by other Germans – such as West Germans, or even younger (East) Germans who did not witness communism. Through this experience, they share a common vocabulary. In her account of her first visit to his apartment, she points out that the first thing she did when she entered the apartment was to put her hand down on the belly of his cream-coloured refrigerator, an almost fifty-year-old Zil Moskva model from the 'golden era of socialist civilization' ('goldenen Ära der sozialistischen Zivilisation'; Veremej 2013, 43). Seitz tells her, full of pride, that, except for the rubber seal, the machine is still working, and that Moscow was good competition to General Electric in the 1960s. Lena is puzzled by the fact that she feels pride at that moment, as if the compliment was addressed to her personally. From that moment on, she knows that they share a language:

> Why was I flattered on behalf of that grumbling monster? Mr Seitz did not say anything else, and it was not necessary – at that moment I knew that he, like me, was a fan of the cosmonauts and not of the astronauts, and that he did not believe in the moon landing of the Americans either. That we both belong to those people who find it outrageous when someone has not read Maxim Gorky, or could not pronounce the word *Khachaturian*. We still do not understand why the Soviet invasion of Afghanistan was a war and why NATO's is considered a peace mission. Complacent America is suspect to us in many ways, but at the same time we are secretly ashamed of our poor English skills. Both of us have spent much of our lives under red flags, our sensors and antennas are likely to remain tilted to the left forever, even if we make a sincere effort to keep them upright and in the middle. (Veremej 2013, 44)[9]

If we observe this scene from a translational perspective, we can see the sum of all vectors, of all movements that characterizes this very exchange. On the one hand, this scene tells of the reality of many migrants, particularly women, who do care work in nursing homes. Lena, a Russian woman, takes care of Seitz, an elderly German man. On the other hand, because borders 'are constantly being drawn and re-drawn' (Ette 2016, 9), it also tells of a much more complex situation, as the two characters lived a good part of their lives in two countries that do not exist any more. While Lena is talking about Seitz in the third person in this excerpt, she is also addressing her own past in doing so, and thereby tells the reader as much about herself as about him.

The title of the novel, *Berlin liegt im Osten*, suggests a relocation of Berlin towards the East, but it also suggests that today's Germany is still, at least partly, located on this 'Eastern' conceptual grid (Zil Moskva, cosmonauts, Maxim Gorky, Khachaturian), which is what allows Lena to successfully translate her experience of communism without much difficulty. What Lena shares with Seitz is the consequence of a redrawing of borders that took place in the middle of the twentieth century, and of another one that took place towards the end of that century; they share a reality through the existence (and disappearance) of these borders. The short exchange about the refrigerator not only refers to a foregone era; it also points to a time where power relations were different:

> Almost half a century old, still tough! – I like this thing too, said Mr Seitz proudly. The rubber sealing gives way, otherwise everything still works. Good work, I must say that Moscow seriously challenged General Electric with its machines back in the sixties. (Veremej 2013, 43–4)[10]

Lena is 'flattered on behalf of that grumbling monster', possibly because she feels Seitz is addressing her as a former Soviet citizen. At that moment, the narration shifts from 'ich' ('I') and 'er' ('he') to 'wir' ('we') and 'uns' ('us'), in opposition to 'Sie' ('they', 'them'), the 'West'. This interplay of time and space is what allows Lena, the migrant care worker, to feel suddenly less foreign. As cultural grids do not follow linguistic or territorial borders, in the presence of the old man, she may still have to speak German, yet she does not need to translate herself completely.

In addition to conceptual grids, texts also exist on specific textual grids. *Berlin liegt im Osten*, as is the case for many works that centre on Berlin, refers extensively to Alfred Döblin's 1929 classic *Berlin Alexanderplatz*. The protagonist tells an anecdote about Seitz's father appearing in the novel: 'Mr Seitz's father, Konrad Seitz, has actually made his way into a work of art, into the book *Berlin Alexanderplatz* – as the man who jumps off the 41 tram line with two yellow parcels in the middle of

Rosenthaler Platz' (Veremej 2013, 46–7).[11] Later, on a date with Roman, a German doctor, Lena tells Roman about the novel, as they take a walk through the centre of the city: 'then we walk through Berlin Mitte again with its narrow streets, and this time I show Roman all my knowledge about the universe of Franz Biberkopf ...' (Veremej 2013, 221).[12] Towards the end of the novel, she mentions that her Russian ex-husband, Schura, with whom she migrated to Germany in the early 1990s, resembles Franz Biberkopf: 'how could I have overlooked how much my ex-husband resembles poor Franz Biberkopf in his demeanour, who in the novel stood on exactly the same corner with his vendor's tray full of shoelaces?' (Veremej 2013, 314).[13] Lena uses these textual references to locate herself in the specific social and cultural context in which she now lives. While her destiny as a migrant has a lot in common with what others experience all over the world, the references she uses to convey it refer to a very specific textual grid. She does not live in New York or Paris; she lives in the centre of Berlin, so it is with Franz Biberkopf that she compares her ex-husband, and she references *Berlin Alexanderplatz* to impress her German suitor.

In sum, the refrigerator scene allows us to reflect on the relevance of conceptual grids when it comes to complex realities that do not follow any current linguistic or territorial borders, while, on the textual grid, references to *Berlin Alexanderplatz* inform us about how the novel locates itself through the use of certain markers that are typical of the type of text it represents in its specific context – in this case, the Berlin novel. The presence of these references anchors the protagonist in its specific reality: (East) Germany – more specifically, (East) Berlin.

In this chapter, I have argued that translation should serve as a source of methodological tools to describe literary phenomena that are the result of the movement of people across space and time. As has been asserted by many proponents of the translational turn, translation allows for an emphasis on movement, which must always take into account that cultures are entities that are neither stable over time, nor clearly geographically delineated. Using Nellja Veremej's *Berlin liegt im Osten* as a case study, I have demonstrated how cultural grids can complement the concept of vectoral imagination, thereby contributing to the development of a fully fledged poetics of movement. Ette's vectoral imagination, combined with Lefevere's (1999) concept of cultural grids, keeps the emphasis on movement in space and time, and takes the very specific directionality of passages into account, without needing to postulate a unidirectional linearity in those movements.

If a poetics of movement allows us to fully account for the movements that literatures are made of, and the complex interweaving of textual and conceptual knowledge-for-living that they contain, then vectors and vectoral imagination can become a useful part of a translational perspective's 'toolkit'. In addition to this, moving away from concepts such as hybridity, in-betweenness or liminality recognizes the agency of the actors involved in and around the text, be it the migrant authors or the protagonists that live in their work. Translation is not an accidental act. It requires intention, and a great deal of knowledge about the languages and cultures one is translating from and into. Transnational literature, much like translated texts, engages with cultural grids in an act of cultural translation. In telling stories of repeated passages – the big and the small – these literary texts convey a great deal of knowledge-for-living about multiple locations on these cultural grids. Looking at transnational literature through the lens of translation theory might therefore offer a way to position texts in the various specific cultural contexts from which they emerged, without the need to postulate that cultures exist as immutable entities.

Notes

1. This chapter is partly based on research conducted in the context of my dissertation project funded by the FRQSC (Fonds de recherche du Québec – Société et Culture).
2. 'ÜberLebensWissen' and 'ZusammenLebensWissen' in the German original. See Ette (2005). All English terms and quotations are borrowed from the 2016 translation by Vera M. Kutzinski.
3. 'Abode' is written with a capital 'A' in the translation by Vera M. Kutzinski, possibly in relation to 'World Literature', which is also generally capitalized.
4. Lower case 'world literature' refers to the 'sum of all forms of literary expression in all of the world's languages', while upper case 'World Literature' refers to the (re)emerging discipline, upon which Emily Apter critically reflects in *Against World Literature*: 'I do harbor serious reservations about tendencies in World Literature toward reflexive endorsement of cultural equivalence and substitutability, or toward the celebration of nationally and ethnically branded "differences" that have been niche-marketed as commercialized "identities." ... I have been left uneasy in the face of the entrepreneurial, bulimic drive to anthologize and curricularize the world's cultural resources, as evinced in projects sponsored by some proponents of World Literature' (Apter 2013, 2–3).
5. To play on the title of Azade Seyhan's 2001 monograph.
6. Ette himself does point to the direction of translation in certain cases, but mostly in a literal sense, and in some cases where he does describe movements as translation processes: '[t]he very figures of movement inscribed in the figure of roving Odysseus facilitate the process of translation and acquisition because they contain a spatio-temporal weave of movements structured as an itinerary' (Ette 2016, 60).
7. All translations from *Berlin liegt im Osten* are mine.
8. Although, as Stuart Taberner notes, a lot of the reviews contain the 'usual potentially patronising mention of the migrant writer's German-language competence' (Taberner 2018, 413).
9. 'Warum fühlte ich mich stellvertretend für dieses brummende Monster geschmeichelt? Herr Seitz sagte nichts weiter, und es war auch nicht nötig – in diesem Moment wusste ich, dass er,

wie ich, ein Fan der Kosmonauten war, und nicht der Astronauten, und dass er auch nicht an die Mondlandung der Amerikaner glaubte. Dass wir beide zu den Menschen gehören, die es empörend finden, wenn jemand Maxim Gorki nicht gelesen hat, oder das Wort Chatschaturjan nicht aussprechen konnte. Wir haben immer noch nicht kapiert, warum die sowjetische Invasion in Afghanistan Krieg war und die von der NATO als Friedensmission gilt. Das selbstgefällige Amerika ist uns in vieler Hinsicht suspekt, gleichzeitig aber schämen wir uns insgeheim über unsere miserablen Englischkenntnisse. Wir beide haben einen Großteil unseres Lebens unter roten Fahnen verbracht, unsere Sensoren und Antennen bleiben wohl für immer nach links gekippt, selbst wenn wir uns ehrlich bemühen, sie aufrecht und in der Mitte zu halten.'

10 'Fast ein halbes Jahrhundert alt, immer noch taff! Ich mag das Ding auch, hustete Herr Seitz stolz. Der Dichtungsgummi gibt nach, ansonsten alles noch in Gang. Gute Arbeit, notabene hat Moskau mit seinen Maschinen damals, in den Sechzigern, General Electric ernst herausgefordert.'

11 '… der Vater von Herrn Seitz aber, Konrad Seitz, ist tatsächlich in ein Kunstwerk geraten, eben in das Buch "Berlin Alexanderplatz" – als jener Mann, der mitten auf dem Rosenthaler Platz mit zwei gelben Paketen von der Linie 41 abspringt.'

12 'Dann laufen wir wieder durch Berlin Mitte mit seinen engen Gassen, und diesmal schenke ich Roman all mein Wissen über das Universum von Franz Biberkopf …'

13 'Wie habe ich nur übersehen können, wie sehr mein Ex-Ehemann in seinem Habitus dem armen Franz Biberkopf ähnelt, der im Roman an exakt der gleichen Ecke mit seinem Bauchladen voller Schnürsenkel stand?'

References

Apter, Emily. 2013. *Against World Literature: On the politics of untranslatability*. London: Verso.
Bachmann-Medick, Doris. 2014. 'From hybridity to translation: Reflections on travelling concepts'. In *The Trans/National Study of Culture: A translational perspective*, edited by Doris Bachmann-Medick, 119–36. Boston: De Gruyter.
Bachmann-Medick, Doris. 2018. 'Migration as translation'. In *Migration: Changing concepts, critical approaches*, edited by Doris Bachmann-Medick and Jens Kugele, 273–93. Boston: De Gruyter.
Bassnett, Susan. 1998. 'The translation turn in cultural studies'. In *Constructing Cultures: Essays on literary translation*, edited by Susan Bassnett and André Lefevere, 123–40. Clevedon: Multilingual Matters.
Benjamin, Walter. 1971. 'Die Aufgabe des Übersetzers'. In *Gesammelte Schriften* IV/I, 9–21. Frankfurt am Main: Suhrkamp.
Berking, Sabine. 2013. 'Nellja Veremej: Berlin liegt im Osten: Wem der Osten noch am Gaumen klebt', *FAZ.NET*, 7 June. Accessed 10 February 2022. https://www.faz.net/aktuell/feuilleton/buecher/rezensionen/belletristik/nellja-veremej-berlin-liegt-im-osten-wem-der-osten-noch-am-gaumen-klebt-12207057.html.
Delabastita, Dirk and Rainier Grutman. 2005. 'Fictional representations of multilingualism and translation', *Linguistica Antverpiensia: New series themes in translation studies* 4. Accessed 10 February 2022. https://lans.uantwerpen.be/index.php/LANS-TTS/article/view/124/66.
Döblin, Alfred. 1929. *Berlin Alexanderplatz: Die Geschichte vom Franz Biberkopf*. Berlin: S. Fischer.
Ette, Ottmar. 2005. *ZwischenWeltenSchreiben: Literaturen ohne festen Wohnsitz*. Berlin: Kulturverlag Kadmos.
Ette, Ottmar. 2016. *Writing-between-Worlds: TransArea studies and the literatures-without-a-fixed-abode*, translated by Vera M. Kutzinski. Berlin: De Gruyter.
Fuchs, Martin. 2009. 'Reaching out; or, nobody exists in one context only: Society as translation', *Translation Studies* 2 (1): 21–40.
Lefevere, André. 1999. 'Composing the Other'. In *Postcolonial Translation: Theory and practice*, edited by Susan Bassnett, 75–94. London: Routledge.
Pym, Anthony. 2009. *Exploring Translation Theories*. London: Routledge.

Seyhan, Azade. 2001. *Writing Outside the Nation*. Princeton, NJ: Princeton University Press.
Snell-Hornby, Mary. 2006. *The Turns of Translation Studies: New paradigms or shifting viewpoints?* Amsterdam: John Benjamins.
Taberner, Stuart. 2018. 'Memories of German wartime suffering: Russian migrant Nellja Veremej's *Berlin liegt im Osten* in context', *Monatshefte* 110 (3): 406–27.
Veremej, Nellja. 2013. *Berlin liegt im Osten*. Salzburg: Jung und Jung.

Part II
Theoretical passages as transitions in art and (non)human life

6
The utterance as transgression: contextual liminality and the rhetoric of the verisimilar

Tomi Moisio

Contextualizing the oeuvre of an artist means taking into account not only the discourse of the art institution, but also the society in which the artist is working. Liminality as a consequence of a conflict, such as war, often produces a destabilization of the social order, which means that the norms and values of a society are in a state of flux. Liminality as a concept is described by Bjørn Thomassen as referring 'to moments or periods of transition during which the normal limits to thought, self-understanding and behaviour are relaxed, opening the way to novelty and imagination, construction and destruction' (Thomassen 2016, 1). In a liminal social context, the concepts of reality and verisimilitude – if not truth itself – are at stake. Artistic utterances have the power to shape the social, as well as the artistic, context.

In this chapter, I shall address the question of artistic utterance as a rhetorical device in representing reality in post-war conditions. As theoretical tools, I apply Quentin Skinner's insights on the concept of context (1988, 2010), as well as Monika Fludernik's concept of *the rhetoric of the verisimilar* (1996). Skinner's views are partly inspired by John L. Austin's *speech act theory* (1962). This is important to bear in mind, especially when artistic expression is understood as *acts* and *utterances*. Finally, I shall clarify my view of artistic utterances as *interpretations of experience* with the help of Hanna Meretoja's narrative hermeneutics (2017).

The concept of *passage* is used here to refer to the instability contained in liminality, as well as the transgressing power of an utterance, and also as a metaphor for the hermeneutic back-and-forth movement entailed in contemplating artistic utterances and producing new interpretations of everyday experiences of reality. It is worth noting that the concept of *defamiliarization*, or estrangement, developed by the Russian literary theorist Viktor Shklovsky in his famous essay 'Art as technique' (1917), in fact comes close to how the concept of passage is understood in this chapter. 'The technique of art', Shklovsky writes, 'is to make objects "unfamiliar", to make forms difficult, to increase the difficulty and length of perception because the process of perception is an aesthetic end in itself and must be prolonged' (Shklovsky 2012, n.p.). Artistic discourse *is* a passage, resulting in 'seeing things out of their normal context' (Shklovsky 2012, n.p.).

Also of interest is the notion of 'travelling concepts', proposed by Mieke Bal (2002, 22), and referred to by Birgit Neumann and Ansgar Nünning (2012, 3), among others. Concepts are seen as 'miniature theories', or even as 'intellectual tools'. Consequently, it is necessary to delve into the essence of these concepts and probe their boundaries in different contexts. Central to my purpose are concepts that have travelled from literary theory (narratology) and political history to an art-historical context.

As a case in point, I shall use the artistic oeuvre of the Finnish-Swedish artist Erik Enroth (1917–75).[1] I consider Enroth's artistic expression to be a fine example of a discourse moulded in the liminal post-war conditions of Finland in the 1940s and 1950s. Enroth tried to find new ways to express his experience of a society undergoing change and transition. As a comparative context, I use the post-war society of the Weimar Republic, and the impact it had on the artistic expression of the time.

Art from the gutter

Erik Enroth held his first solo exhibition in Galerie Hörhammer in Helsinki, Finland, in December 1948. On display were works such as *Politicians* (1947–8), *At the Funfair* (1948) and *Stoking the Fire* (1948). The art critic Sigrid Schauman, who was a painter herself, described Enroth's artistic expression as 'slang' (Schauman 1948), referring probably both to his bold, unconventional style (at least unconventional in Finland in the 1940s) and to his subject matter, which bore a resemblance to the *Rinnsteinkunst* (art from the gutter) of the Berlin Realists at the turn of the century.[2] Although Enroth lacked the social agenda often attached to artists such as Heinrich Zille (1858–1929), Käthe Kollwitz (1867–1945) and Hans Baluschek (1870–1935), he nevertheless shared with them a sense of – or, better yet, an obligation to present – a certain verisimilitude in his artistic portrayal. This had, however, little to do with *mimesis* per se. Honesty and integrity were central ingredients in the painterly ethos of these artists, although this was at times challenged by rhetorical persuasion and exaggeration, the 'side effects' of painterly rhetoric.

Similar ethical tendencies to those that characterized the turn of the century continued in the Weimar Republic period (1919–33) in the works of younger artists who had been involved in World War One, such as Max Beckmann (1884–1950) and Otto Dix (1891–1969). Anna Grosskopf writes: '[t]he themes and motifs of the Berlin Realism of the Empire continued in the art of the Weimar Republic' (Grosskopf 2018, 21).[3] Representing reality in the chaotic conditions of post-war society posed a problem for artists. With millions dead and even more wounded, and with the economy ruined, it was time to reconsider artistic expression and the means to achieve verisimilitude in art. Franz W. Kaiser has suggested that in Germany in the 1920s, artists wanted to convey a visual truth that did not allow for romanticizing or idealization. The plain truth had to be presented and, furthermore, 'to an audience who did not wish to see it' (Kaiser 1995, 26). The artists 'poked their fingers in the wound of society', as Tobias Hoffman and Hannelore Fischer have stated (2018, 10).

In 1953, on the verge of his national breakthrough as an artist, Erik Enroth gave an interview in which he elaborated on his philosophy and artistic method: 'I wander around in factories, slaughterhouses, scrap warehouses – everywhere where you can meet life's sparkling display of colours – and then re-create the experience from memory. My art is difficult, a mockery of so-called "good taste", but it's honest' (*Hufvudstadsbladet* 1953). With this declaration, the artist takes an ethical stand against art seen as decoration or ornament. He also hints at the possibility that the process of perception is prolonged ('My art is difficult'), and that things are seen out of their normal context ('a mockery of so-called "good taste"'). Examples of these factories and slaughterhouses can be seen in works such as *Tampella Factory Worker I* and *II* (1948), *Workshop* (1950–3), *Meat* (1950–3) and *Oxen Skulls* (1953). In the painting *Workshop*, for example, the faceless foundry workers are depicted raw, with their veins exposed. It is not an image of the heroic working man rebuilding the nation, the likes of which you could see in abundance, especially in public paintings in post-war Finland, but a disillusioned display of continuous toil, set to provoke.

The utterance transgressing generally accepted boundaries

The *Oxford Modern English Dictionary* defines 'transgress' as 'go beyond the bounds or limits set by (a commandment, law etc.)', or 'violate', or 'infringe' (Swannell 1995, 1163).[4] In discourse, as well as in society in general, it is possible to 'go beyond' accepted boundaries, so to speak. However, this movement – a passage of a sort – is not merely the crossing of a threshold, since it also requires in-depth knowledge and analysis of the context in which it takes place.[5] This movement may also shift the boundaries themselves. The political historian Quentin Skinner has suggested that the context of a given text can be equally as important as the text itself: 'neither approach seems a sufficient or even appropriate means of achieving a proper understanding of any given literary or philosophical work' (Skinner 1988, 29). He has also emphasized how thoughts and ideas of the past can be seen as arguments, or deeds: '[t]he aim is to see such texts as contributions to particular discourses, and thereby to recognise the ways in which they followed or challenged or subverted the conventional terms of those discourses themselves' (Skinner 2010, 125). This does not just apply to texts in general, but to concepts as well, so to be able to:

> understand what a writer may have been doing in using some particular concept or argument, we need first of all to grasp the nature and range of things that could recognisably have been done by using that particular concept, in the treatment of that particular theme, in that particular time. (Skinner 2010, 102)

Skinner's theories are concerned with political history and the history of ideas, but I am going to apply his conceptual framework to the analysis of artistic expression.[6] Artistic ideas can therefore be seen as artistic arguments, uttered in a particular historical context with reference to other such ideas or arguments (Lukkarinen 1989, 19; Keane 1988, 205). In artistic discourse, it is not only the art institution (however vaguely defined) that sets the 'accepted boundaries' for the artist's expression, not to mention the whole history of art with its 'anxiety of influence' (to quote Harold Bloom's famous title), but also society in general, with its arbitrary assumptions of good taste, what is appropriate and so on. For example, seen from today's perspective, it did not take an awful lot to exceed the boundaries of what was generally seen as acceptable in Finland in the 1940s. Indeed, the art critic Olavi Veistäjä felt he needed to warn the audience of the unsettling effect of Enroth's art when his first solo exhibition travelled to Tampere in 1948. Admittedly, Enroth's expression had evolved from docile landscapes such as *Fields in Hämeenkyrö* (1946) to the more direct expression of *Woman and Flower* (1948), for example. Whether people should be warned about such images is another matter entirely.

Finland in the late 1940s was still a rural country, with two thirds of the population living in the countryside. Due to its peripheral location in the north-east corner of Europe, the avant-garde of the European art world did not reach Finland until years, in some cases decades, later. The rise of nationalistic tendencies in the 1930s did not exactly improve the dire situation, and World War Two finally disconnected Finland from the rest of Europe pretty much completely, at least artistically. Many art critics, for example, demanded that Finnish artists promote and maintain national values and depict motifs that suited these ends. The influential art historian Ludvig Wennervirta, who not only opposed modernism but also held National Socialist sympathies, wrote in 1942 that Finnish art was 'gradually recovering, foreign influences are absent' (Wennervirta 1942). Wennervirta was probably still inspired by the exhibition 100 Years of German Art, held at Helsinki Kunsthalle in 1936. In the exhibition, there were no works by the artists (Max Beckmann, for example) whose paintings adorned the walls of the Haus der Kunst in Munich a year later in the infamous exhibition Entartete Kunst (Degenerate Art). Artistic discourse, not willing to conform to the nationalistic agenda, could be seen as a form of transgression. It was at least undesirable, if not illegitimate.

So it was an introverted and reactionary art scene which Erik Enroth entered after being discharged from military service in 1944. In the war, Enroth had initially been in the front line operating a light machine gun, and then, after 1942, worked in the information service as a war artist. The reactionary art scene was, however, the least of the war veteran's worries. Men returning from the front struggled to readjust themselves to civilian life. Many suffered from shock or trauma. Poverty was widespread, and crime rates were at their highest immediately after the war (Ylikangas 2009, 177).[7] Finland also had to deal with tens of thousands of domestic immigrants, who had to leave their homes in the Karelia region, which was lost to the Soviet Union in the war. Erik Enroth continued his art studies after the war, and his artistic ambitions directed him towards international contexts. Contextual migration, understood both figuratively and literally, extends the notion of 'passage' from a spatial metaphor into something much more concrete. Enroth travelled extensively, and he was able to widen his artistic perspective in situ in different geographical locations as well.

Enroth first studied in Stockholm and then in Paris, in L'Académie André Lhote. However crucial these international modernist influences were for his artistic expression, they are of little avail in trying to explain his artistic character. Many Finnish art historians have labelled Enroth's art as either expressionist or cubist (or, usually, both). Picasso is the artist most often mentioned in connection with Enroth's artistic influences (see, for example, *Circus*, 1950–1). However true this may be formalistically speaking, it is something else that occupies the viewer when examining Enroth's oeuvre. It is more a question of an artistic method by means of which the artist perceives his experience of reality than of style as a formal construction. Style periods are not, I argue, a fruitful way to describe the characteristics of Enroth's artistic discourse.

The rhetoric of the verisimilar

In order to better define this 'something else', valuable help is offered by Monika Fludernik's concept of *the rhetoric of the verisimilar* in her magnum opus *Towards a 'Natural' Narratology*: '[t]he textual real, although supposedly accessible through a naturalistic reading of the discourse, in fact requires a sophisticated deployment of rhetoric (the rhetoric of the verisimilar) to mark its realism, and in historical discourse its historicity' (Fludernik 1996, 4).[8] With regard to pictorial art, Michael Fried has suggested that this 'reality effect' has been neglected by traditional art historical writing as nothing more than 'simply a function of the painter's skill in representing more or less exactly what lay or loomed before his eyes' (Fried 1992, 3). At this point, it needs to be emphasized, however self-evident it may seem, that pictorial art is in many ways different from literature. Nevertheless, I consider works of art to be, if not texts in a literal sense, at least utterances of a kind, discourse, and therefore suitable for (con)textual study. From a semiotic perspective, even context is a text, as Mieke Bal and Norman Bryson remind us in their influential article 'Semiotics and art history' (Bal and Bryson 1998, 243). So, in this chapter, paintings are often referred to as artistic utterances.

Fludernik equates the verisimilar with fiction, and its function with that of 'the textual "real" in the realist novel', as well as 'the function of the anecdote in historical writing'. It creates an 'illusion of veracity' (Fludernik 1996, 3–4). Without being certain of the plausibility of the project, I would like to venture into an experiment of recontextualization to test this concept in an art historical context. 'Re-creating an experience from memory' and at the same time claiming to be 'honest' – even if it is not meant in a realistic or historical sense – is too enticing a point of departure to ignore. (Quotations from Erik Enroth are from *Hufvudstadsbladet* 1953.)

If we stop for a moment to consider the word *rhetoric* and its semantics, we find two formulations: 'a) the art of effective or persuasive speaking or writing, b) language designed to persuade or impress (often with an implication of insincerity or exaggeration, etc.)' (Swannell 1995, 928). There is an interesting connection between verisimilitude on the one hand, and insincerity or exaggeration on the other, especially if we consider verisimilitude as 'a) the appearance or semblance of being true or real and/or b) a statement, etc. that *seems* true' (Swannell 1995, 1221, my emphasis). This might suggest that insincerity and exaggeration, as tools to persuade and impress, are acceptable, ethical even, as long as the result *seems* true, or has the appearance of truth. In conjuring up a picture, the artist seems to suggest that, instead of *being* true, this *could be* true, this *might have* happened. Erik Enroth was in pursuit of honesty and truth, but, paradoxically, he used persuasion and exaggeration to achieve these goals. There is a verisimilitude in his paintings that addresses the viewer, that confronts him or her with an utterance that needs an interpretation in the social and artistic context of the time. This, in turn, calls for an ethics of interpretation.

Fabian Reifferscheidt has described Germany's post-war condition as 'a world torn off its hinges', a world, it seems, where 'humour, allegory and merely allusive settings would be altogether inappropriate' (Reifferscheidt 2018, 109). Reifferscheidt also claims that 'the immediate brutality of realist postwar art … lacked predecessors in the realm of pictorial art' (109). There was, indeed, a direct brutality in the pictorial rhetoric of the era, but I cannot agree with Reifferscheidt that it was of a quality not depicted in art before. Especially Reifferscheidt's example, the series of lithographs *Memento 1914/15* (1914–15) by Willy Jaeckel, seems directly indebted to Francisco de Goya's famous and gruesome series of prints, *Los desastres de la guerra* (*The Miseries of War*, executed in the 1810s and published in 1863, 35 years after the artist's death).[9] The atrocities depicted in Goya's prints are indeed difficult to exceed. Not even the most appalling of, say, Otto Dix's *Lustmord* scenes compares with the spine-chilling atmosphere of some of Goya's prints. Neither the prints of Jaeckel nor those of Goya are the testimonies of an eyewitness, but they *could* be. The direct portrayal of the brutality is, supposedly, a hint in that direction, although it could also be seen as a rhetorical device. Goya went even further by naming one of his prints *Yo lo vi* (I saw this).[10]

Fabian Reifferscheidt makes an interesting point with reference to George Grosz's (1893–1959) series of offset prints, *Ecce Homo* (1916–22). He finds the fact that Grosz may well have included a self-portrait in the licentious society he depicts illuminating, since the artist has now transformed himself (or *transgressed*) from an objective observer into a participant in the fictional world of the picture, and thus has become a reference point for the spectator, increasing the authenticity of the work (Reifferscheidt 2018, 109–10). This, in turn, is a rhetorical device that creates a verisimilar effect.

In her book *Ethos and Narrative Interpretation: The negotiation of values in fiction*, Liesbeth Korthals Altes reminds us that 'the ethos an audience attributes to a speaker on the basis of his discourse is likely to determine deep down what message is conveyed, superseding actual semantic content' (Korthals Altes 2014, 5). This, in turn, suggests that 'to strategically fashion one's discursive ethos is crucial; and that ethos effects rely on psychological and moral codes, whether truly shared or strategically or deceptively deployed' (5). Although concerned with literary narratives, the notions advanced by Korthals Altes are interesting from the perspective of this study as well. Should artistic discourse 'be understood as expressing its enunciator's character' (5)? And, if so, '[a]re there particular conditions under which it is more appropriate for interpreters to attribute an ethos to authors, rather than to narrators or characters?' (6). It would be tempting to apply some of the concepts of classical narratology, namely *the unreliable narrator* or *implied author*, in the study of pictorial art. This would, however, be a tour de force beyond my powers in the present research.

The subjects depicted by Erik Enroth are not as gruesome as those of Goya or some of the Weimar artists. The 'immediate brutality' of his art was of a different kind, 'a mockery of good taste' perhaps. It is the verisimilar quality that is of essence here, the quest for truth. An interesting reference point is Max Beckmann, who stated in 1938: '[w]hat I want to show in my work is the idea that hides itself behind so-called reality' (Beckmann 1989, 117). Beckmann emphasized that 'it is, in fact, reality which forms the mystery of our existence' (117). By suggesting a possibility, a new perspective on something that is too obvious or mundane, the artist helps the spectator to observe different aspects of a reality that he or she has taken for granted. It is the artist's responsibility to portray those aspects as 'real' rather than 'naturalistic'. This is, I argue, quite close to Shklovsky's (2012) prolonging of the process of perception.

According to Monika Fludernik, realism 'closely corresponds to a mimetic representation of individual experience that cognitively and epistemically relies on real-world knowledge' (Fludernik 1996, 37–8). In other words, realism means the 'mimetic evocation of reality from both a sociological and a psychological perspective. Verisimilitude and realism, in fact, correlate very closely with one another' (37–8). So the quest for truth does not concern the mimetic re-presentation of nature per se, but is a rendition of a person's experience of the surrounding context, be it artistic or social. It does not have to be illusionistic in a photorealist sense, as long as it 'relies on real-world knowledge' and is – at least supposedly – honest. This, in turn, would suggest that it is indeed more a question of an artistic method than of style, at least in a formalistic sense referring to a certain style period.

However, Fludernik reminds us that 'our understanding of what is real derives precisely from well-worn clichés of what should happen, has been known to happen, conventionally does happen, reflecting an array of frames and scripts, conventionalised expectations, moral attitudes and common-sense notions of the agentially and psychologically verisimilar' (Fludernik 1996, 162–3). This results in the fact that, according to Fludernik, '[v]erisimilitude, and the lack thereof, lies in the eyes of the beholder' (162–3). So, once more, verisimilitude is a matter of reading the context. However, one of the points being made in this chapter is that the context can also be challenged, perhaps even subverted.

Conflict as context: the ethics of artistic utterances

A friend and colleague of Erik Enroth has described how he 'continued his struggle in artistic expression'.[11] He 'lived all senses alert and mediated his truth of post-war times unscrupulously' (Kunnas 1961, 140). Hence, the social context became entwined with the artistic context. Painting a representation of an individual experience functioned as a means of coming to terms with the chaotic conditions of a conflict-ridden society. Liesbeth Korthals Altes, among others, notices the connection between the social context and the artistic context: '[t]hroughout history, the social functions of literature and of the author have been invested with changing, but always strong, norms and values, extending in particular to the author's or artist's ethos' (Korthals Altes 2014, 8). I must emphasize once more that even though literature and painting are not commensurate, in this sense it is not irrelevant to think about the social functions of pictorial art from an ethical perspective.

Artistic expression, including fiction, can be seen as a means to process the experience of the 'real world'. It can also function as an aid in coming to terms with chaotic social conditions. In her article 'On the use and abuse of narrative for life: Toward an ethics of storytelling', Hanna Meretoja (2017) quotes Hans-Georg Gadamer (particularly with reference to the concept *Etwas-als-etwas-Verstehen*) by emphasizing how 'even the most elementary perception interprets reality by structuring it and giving it shape' (Meretoja 2017, 82). In narrative hermeneutics, stories can be seen as '*interpretations* of experience, instead of equating them with experience per se' (82).[12] Avoiding a discussion of narrativity in pictorial art in the limited context of this chapter, I would suggest that too much emphasis should not be put on narrative form. If we think of utterances as interpretations of experience, as 'structuring and giving it shape', there is no need to distinguish 'storytelling' from the objective 'reporting of facts'. An artistic utterance, such as a painting, can be seen as structuring reality instead of merely reproducing it. It is a strategy of history to construct coherent narratives from objective facts.[13] But fiction and imagination are also valid means for processing our experience of the real world.

We must take into account artists' intentions in performing their 'speech acts'. Quentin Skinner's methodology is inspired by John L. Austin's speech act theory, with its emphasis on the potential of illocutionary meaning, which means that of interest is not only what is said, but what is *intended* by what is said. Skinner emphasizes the fact that '[t]o know about motives is to know what prompted those particular speech acts, quite apart from their character and truth-status as utterances' (Skinner 2010, 96).[14] So, to be clear, we should ask whether it was the social (and, of course, to some extent, the artistic) context of the post-war era that prompted Erik Enroth to paint a picture such as *Faces on the Street* (1950–3), instead of enquiring whether he actually saw such a grotesque show. The nightmarish cast of characters is a result of painterly rhetoric exaggerating to an uncanny level the experience of everyday encounters in a liminal post-war society.

According to Meretoja, there is a *double hermeneutic* structure at work in cultural utterances (again, *stories* in the original), because they are interpretations of experiences that are already interpretations: '[t]hese second-order interpretations weave together experiences by showing how they are related and by creating meaningful connections between them' (Meretoja 2017, 82). Meretoja also proposes the possibility of a *triple hermeneutic*: '[w]hen we reinterpret our everyday experiences, identities and life plans in the light of these cultural narratives, this process can be seen to embody a "triple hermeneutic"' (82). To use the terminology of this chapter, Meretoja suggests that an artistic utterance and the context in which it is interpreted are intertwined: 'we are constituted in a dialogic relation to culturally mediated narrative models through which we constantly reinterpret our experiences' (82).[15] How does this notion correlate with the possible obligation for verisimilitude – if not truth – in art?

Contextualizing everyday experiences in a 'dialogic relation to culturally mediated models' helps to provide a *raison d'être* in a chaotic social context. For example, in 1947, Otto Dix said: '[p]ainting is an attempt to create order; order in oneself. There is a lot of chaos in me, there is a lot of chaos in our times' (Heller and Granof 1991, 169). According to Monika Fludernik: '[e]xperiences of liminality (insanity, schizophrenia, shock or trauma) are frequently adduced to explain such disruptions of ordinary human experience' (Fludernik 1996, 316). Even though Fludernik's insight is made with reference to 'radically experimental texts' (316), it is in my opinion also applicable to the context of visual art. The connotation of fracture (referring, among other things, to breaks and ruptures created by passages) can be as powerful in pictorial rhetoric as in literature, and in some instances even more so. What it boils down to is the dispute between man and the world, between the individual and society. However, at the bottom of this dispute, there always lies a dialogue. A hermeneutic movement is a passage as well, but instead of seeing it as a *circulus vitiosus*, it could best be described in a Heideggerian sense as moving back and forth, returning to something already left behind, gathering and enriching information along the way. An artistic utterance not only comments on or challenges the social and artistic context in which it is created. By engaging in a constant dialogue with it (moving back and forth), it also bears the potential to actually renew it. This dialogue continues in the context in which the utterance is interpreted.

It seems, at times, a futile project to try to come to terms with a reality that exceeds even the worst nightmare scenario pictured in art or fiction.[16] However, we do need means to help us comprehend the society that surrounds us. As Quentin Skinner reminds us: '[o]ur concepts are not forced upon us by the world, but represent what we bring to the world in order to understand it' (Skinner 2010, 46). Or, as Birgit Neumann and Ansgar Nünning propose, '[t]he cultural power of a concept resides in the scholarly activities it propels, i.e. in travelling processes, rather than in what it is "in itself"' (Neumann and Nünning 2012, 4). A concept has the ability to propel scholarly activities, and one aspect of a speech act is its *perlocutionary* possibilities, what can actually be achieved with, for instance, an artistic utterance (Austin 1962, 101–2). The potential of travelling concepts is not limited to a scholarly context but can be extended to society at large.

Disillusioned by the war and its aftermath, Erik Enroth (as, of course, the Weimar artists before him) struggled to make sense of the liminal conditions of a post-war society. Art is a rhetorical device which, by playing with and drawing parallels between possible interpretations of reality, provides us with a verisimilitude that can be used as a reference point in trying to grasp 'the idea that hides itself behind so-called reality' (Beckmann 1989, 117). Or, to quote Neumann and Nünning again, art (literature in the original) 'plays a crucial role in probing new epistemological constellations' (Neumann and Nünning 2012, 13). Passage is a central concept in this process, helping to 'see things out of their normal context', providing inspiration and enabling opportunities for contextual migration as well.

Notes

1. I defended my doctoral dissertation 'Composed Reality: The artistic discourse of Erik Enroth' in the Department of Art History at the University of Helsinki in September 2020. As a theoretical framework in my thesis, I apply both cognitive narratology and narrative hermeneutics, as well as Quentin Skinner's insights about the concept of context, so the problematics of this chapter are central to my study.
2. On *Rinnsteinkunst*, see, for example, Grosskopf (2018, 14–15).
3. All translations are my own, unless otherwise indicated.
4. Scientifically speaking, the term 'transgression' also means 'a relative rise in sea level' (Swannell 1995, 1163), but I must disappoint my readers by not pursuing this interpretation further.
5. 'Context' means 'the circumstances relevant for something under consideration' (Swannell 1995, 223).
6. In his doctoral thesis, later published as *Classicism and History: Anachronistic architectural thinking in Finland at the turn of the century: Jac. Ahrenberg and Gustaf Nyström* (1989), Ville Lukkarinen applies Skinner's theories to the art historical study of architecture.
7. This, I argue, is true of any post-war society.
8. Fludernik's notion bears a resemblance (a *vraisemblance*, perhaps) to Roland Barthes's concept *effet de réel*, but the rhetoric of the verisimilar lends itself to a wider range of applications. Instead of being merely a naturalistic detail, the rhetoric of the verisimilar alludes to representing *and* interpreting experientiality.
9. Goya's series of prints was, in turn, influenced by Jacques Callot's etchings *Les Grandes Misères de la guerre* (1633), depicting the miseries of the Thirty Years War.

10 It is unlikely that Goya would have seen all the miseries he depicted in his prints. Robert Hughes suggests that Goya's art was somehow similar to pictorial journalism (Hughes 2004, 272).
11 My interview with Kirsi Kunnas, 11 April 2012.
12 Experientiality is also essential to Monika Fludernik's views on narrativity.
13 Hayden White, among others, has written about this narrativization. See, for example, *The Content of the Form: Narrative discourse and historical representation* (1989). However, Monika Fludernik has suggested that White should actually use the term *storification* instead of *narrativization* (Fludernik 1996, 34).
14 Martin Heidegger was, of course, interested in the 'truth-status' of art. Unfortunately, it is beyond the limits of this chapter to delve more deeply into Heidegger's philosophy.
15 Meretoja is also referring to Mikhail Bakhtin's views on the 'dialogic fabric of human life' (Meretoja 2017, 82).
16 For example, during the exhibition *Wedding* in the district of the same name in Berlin, organized by the artist Otto Nagel in 1926, there was criticism that the dreadful works of art were futile when every visitor to the exhibition knew that reality was even more dreadful (Hoffmann 2018, 135).

References

Austin, John L. 1962. *How to Do Things with Words: The William James lectures delivered at Harvard University in 1955*. Oxford: Oxford University Press.
Bal, Mieke. 2002. *Travelling Concepts in the Humanities: A rough guide*. Toronto: University of Toronto Press.
Bal, Mieke and Norman Bryson. 1998 [1991]. 'Semiotics and art history'. In *The Art of Art History: A critical anthology*, edited by Donald Preziosi, 243–55. Oxford: Oxford University Press.
Beckmann, Max. 1989 [1938]. 'On my painting'. In *Max Beckmann: Tradition as a problem in modern art*, edited by Hans Belting, translated by Peter Wortsman. New York: Timken.
Fludernik, Monika. 1996. *Towards a 'Natural' Narratology*. London: Routledge.
Fried, Michael. 1992 [1990]. *Courbet's Realism*. Chicago: University of Chicago Press.
Grosskopf, Anna. 2018. 'Kunst aus dem Rinnstein – Berliner Realismus in Kaiserreich'. In *Berliner Realismus: Von Käthe Kollwitz bis Otto Dix: Sozialkritik – Satire – Revolution*, edited by Tobias Hoffmann, 13–21. Cologne: Wienand.
Heller, Reinhold and Corinne D. Granof. 1991. 'Otto Dix: Lustmord'. In *Vom Expressionismus zum Widerstand: Kunst in Deutschland 1909–1936: Die Sammlung Marvin und Janet Fishman*, edited by Reinhold Heller, 169. München: Prestel Verlag.
Hoffmann, Tobias. 2018. 'Was ist proletarische Kunst? Berliner Realismus zwischen Proletkult und heroischem Realismus'. In *Berliner Realismus: Von Käthe Kollwitz bis Otto Dix: Sozialkritik – Satire – Revolution*, edited by Tobias Hoffmann, 123–37. Cologne: Wienand.
Hoffmann, Tobias and Hannelore Fischer. 2018. 'Vorwort'. In *Berliner Realismus: Von Käthe Kollwitz bis Otto Dix: Sozialkritik – Satire – Revolution*, edited by Tobias Hoffmann, 10–12. Cologne: Wienand.
Hufvudstadsbladet 1953. 'Erik Enroth "exploderar fram sina dukar"', *Hufvudstadsbladet*, 19 September.
Hughes, Robert. 2004 [2003]. *Goya*. London: Vintage.
Kaiser, Franz W. 1995. 'Taiteen vastarinta – erään yksityiskokoelman teemoja'. In *Konst som motstånd. Vastavirta: Tysk konst från mellankrigstiden. Saksan taide sotien välissä. Samling Marvin och Janet Fishman. Marvin ja Janet Fishmanin kokoelma*, edited by Folke Lalander, Louise Fogelström, Timo Valjakka and Sointu Fritze, 22–32. Stockholm: Liljevalchs Konsthall.
Keane, John. 1988. 'More theses on the philosophy of history'. In *Meaning and Context: Quentin Skinner and his critics*, edited by James Tully, 204–17. Princeton, NJ: Princeton University Press.
Korthals Altes, Liesbeth. 2014. *Ethos and Narrative Interpretation: The negotiation of values in fiction*. Lincoln: University of Nebraska Press.

Kunnas, Kirsi. 1961. 'Erik Enroth – suomalainen ja eurooppalainen maalari'. In *Tampereen taidetta ja taiteilijoita*, edited by Matti Petäjä, 138–54. Tampere: Tampereen taiteilijaseura r.y.

Lukkarinen, Ville. 1989. *Classicism and History: Anachronistic architectural thinking in Finland at the turn of the century: Jac. Ahrenberg and Gustaf Nyström*. Helsinki: Suomen muinaismuistoyhdistyksen aikakauskirja.

Meretoja, Hanna. 2017. 'On the use and abuse of narrative for life: Toward an ethics of storytelling'. In *Life and Narrative: The risks and responsibilities of storying experience*, edited by Brian Schiff, A. Elizabeth McKim and Sylvie Patron, 75–93. Oxford: Oxford University Press.

Neumann, Birgit and Ansgar Nünning. 2012. 'Travelling concepts as a model for the study of culture'. In *Travelling Concepts for the Study of Culture*, edited by Birgit Neumann and Ansgar Nünning, 1–22. Berlin: De Gruyter.

Reifferscheidt, Fabian. 2018. 'Sexualität und Realismus – Wahrhaftig, grob unzüchtig und überprüfenswert'. In *Berliner Realismus: Von Käthe Kollwitz bis Otto Dix: Sozialkritik – Satire – Revolution*, edited by Tobias Hoffmann, 107–22. Cologne: Wienand.

Schauman, Sigrid. 1948. 'Erik Enroth's utställning', *Nya Pressen*, 7 December.

Shklovsky, Viktor. 2012 [1917]. 'Art as technique'. In *Russian Formalist Criticism: Four essays*, translated by Lee T. Lemon and Marion J. Reis. 2nd edn. Lincoln: University of Nebraska Press.

Skinner, Quentin. 1988. 'Meaning and understanding in the history of ideas'. In *Meaning and Context: Quentin Skinner and his critics*, edited by James Tully, 29–67. Princeton, NJ: Princeton University Press.

Skinner, Quentin. 2010 [2002]. *Visions of Politics, Volume 1: Regarding method*. Cambridge: Cambridge University Press.

Swannell, Julia, ed. 1995. *The Oxford Modern English Dictionary*. Oxford: Clarendon Press.

Thomassen, Bjørn. 2016. *Liminality and the Modern: Living through the in-between*. London: Routledge.

Wennervirta, Ludvig. 1942. 'Nykyhetken taidetta kotoisella pohjalla', *Ajan suunta*, 3 February.

White, Hayden. 1989 [1987]. *The Content of the Form: Narrative discourse and historical representation*. Baltimore: Johns Hopkins University Press.

Ylikangas, Mikko. 2009. *Unileipää, kuolonvettä, spiidiä: Huumeet Suomessa 1800–1950*. Jyväskylä: Atena.

7
Kafka's actors: Josef K.'s journey to theatricality

Tanja Marcotte

'one doesn't have to take everything as the truth, one just has to accept it as necessary'

Franz Kafka, *The Trial*[1]

Considerations of processes of movement from one point to another, and the in-between spaces that these entail, have recently become prominent in the humanities, as this volume shows. Moving away from binary thinking, the concepts of passages and liminality offer a new perspective on cultural entities. This chapter will examine the passage of Josef K. in *The Trial (Der Proceß)*, and how liminality is entangled with theatricality in Kafka's writing.

The arrest

In the first chapter of Kafka's *The Trial (Der Proceß)*, Josef K. is arrested without knowing why and without having to go to jail. Just before his arrest, he lies in bed before his usual breakfast, when he notices that he has an audience of sorts: '[f]or a while K. waited – from his pillow he saw the old woman who lived opposite watching with, for her, quite unusual curiosity – but then, both perplexed and hungry, he rang' (Kafka 2009,

5).[2] The scene is immediately set for K.'s signal – the ringing of the bell. Next to being an obvious theatrical motif, an interesting aspect of the scene is the simultaneity of two impulses: K. feels perturbed by the unusual situation of being observed, but he is hungry at the same time. And then: 'Immediately there was a knock at the door and a man he had never seen in the apartment came in' (5).[3] All of the characters, except the protagonist, behave according to the procedure of the arrest and treat K. as the arrested one.

This short passage already provides a first hint of what will become clearer when one continues reading Kafka's fragment: Kafka's characters are kept unsettled by theatrical elements within the narration. In the case of Josef K., this impression is fostered by the development of Josef K. as a theatrical character. He hovers indecisively between being a normal man and an actor in a role – that is, in a liminal position. Bjørn Thomassen proposes that '[l]ife and death, day and night, light and dark, girl and woman, novice and expert: liminality emerges in the in-between of a passage' (Thomassen 2018, 2). Josef K.'s journey towards becoming a performing character, as well as Kafka's unique narration with strong theatrical allusions that leave its characters in an in-between, contribute moments of liminality in *The Trial*. This element of in-betweenness, I argue, produces new insights into the role that theatricality plays in Kafka's work.

The liminal as well as theatrical aspects in Kafka's work have been frequently discussed.[4] Interestingly, both the theme of transition and transit *and* theatrical motifs can be found on the story levels of Kafka's oeuvre.[5] Works such as 'Josephine the singer, or the mouse folk', 'A report to an academy' and 'Before the law'[6] contain theatrical elements and hybrid species or spaces that resist definition. In *The Trial*, various explicit and implicit theatrical markers can be located. Just like the liminal state of the protagonist, theatricality needs to be defined by a careful examination of the relevant parameters. For this chapter, the theoretical aspects will be derived from various text samples, and the theatrical development of the protagonist Josef K. will be made visible by analysing segments of the first and last chapter, as well as two exemplary passages from the middle of the text.

'"Who are you?" K. asked, immediately half-sitting up in bed. But the man ignored the question, as if his presence there were simply to be accepted, and merely said, "You rang?"' (Kafka 2009, 5)[7] The man does not answer K.'s question. In the English version, the theatrical marker is an explicit 'as if'. In the German original, it is indicated by the grammatical form of the subjunctive. Either way, the narration takes on a phenomenological tone. With the appearance of the man 'as if', actual presence is entangled with a theatrical in-between. The narration's reference to something else is an aspect that Joseph Vogl localizes in an in-betweenness of perspective:

> The narration moves in a floating interference, which unsettles the relation between I and He, narrator and character, from sentence to sentence. But, at the same time, this smooth transition is a fact of the narrated character. The character acts as a self-referenced 'I', which repeats itself in the 'he' and therefore initiates an endless recursive reference: 'he' means an 'I', which again means a 'he' ... (Vogl 1994, 750, my translation)[8]

These aspects leave the narration in a timeless nowhere, according to Vogl. The oscillation between 'He' and 'I' is congruent with the oscillation between the subject/object relation on stage in a live performance.

Acting 'as if' is a basic element of theatre practice. For this chapter, it is crucial to understand that stage actors move between two entities. The actor on stage is a person, a subject, but he acts within a role that was created on paper by an author; the role on paper can be called an object. When both entities come together on stage, after being rehearsed, the aim is that the audience perceives a new subject, the actor *in* the part and *as* the part at the same time (Soeffner 2004, 237). The spectator sees both the actor and the character simultaneously – there is no either/or.[9] Yet it can also be said that the spectator's perception oscillates between these entities. The amplitude of such oscillation depends on the performance. For example: consider an actor performing Hamlet's famous monologue on stage, in which Hamlet struggles with his conscience. A man in the audience mistakes the performance for a comedy, and bursts into laughter. The actor turns his head to the man. While he does not change his lines, he addresses the man directly and accentuates some lines differently than usual. Everyone in the audience is aware of both the disturbance and the actor's reaction to it. They acknowledge the professional actor's decision to react to the disturbance, but they still regard him as Hamlet. The actor oscillates between the part of Hamlet that he created and himself, the actor. It is a constant in-between: '[h]e [the actor] is his own medium, he divides himself in himself, but he remains on this side of the gap behind the character he embodies, to stay in the picture' (Roselt 2005, 315, my translation).[10] This means that the actor never vanishes behind his part, and he has a certain amount of freedom in shaping his performance, even though he maintains the rehearsed script. Disturbances change the performance without changing the plot. Of course, this requires a certain amount of sovereignty. For a novice actor, it will be hard to react to a disturbance while staying in character. Nevertheless, this liminal state of the actor creates a space for creative and performative actions: 'Liminality refers to moments or periods of transition during which the normal limits to thought, self-understanding and behaviour are relaxed, opening the way to novelty and imagination, construction and destruction' (Thomassen 2018, 1). Between the rehearsed and the new arises the possibility for theatrical uniqueness. Theatrical performances (the ones that actors are truly engaged in) will surely be liminal ones, but not every liminal state of a person is theatrical.

Kafka's text continues with K. walking to the neighbouring room, where another man is sitting next to a window. The old woman from across the way has moved to a different window to continue watching. It is not clear whether the man sits in a position where he can be seen by the old woman, or how K. interprets the situation. Nonetheless, K. makes a strong theatrical gesture in this moment: '"But I just want to tell Frau Grubach –", K. said, making a movement as if to tear himself free from the two men, who, however, are a good distance away from him, and sets off towards the door' (Kafka 2009, 6).[11]

Now it is up to K. to act *as if*. He pretends to be captured by the two men, miming a situation. Yet, the gesture refers to the two men who are actually in the room but standing far away. The effect of this gesture is a circular one. It is neither mimetic nor realistic, since the object to which it is referring is in the room. It comes across as a failed theatrical gesture by an actor, since it is too exaggerated. This is typical for Kafka's writing: 'Just like the bell, too loud for a door bell, rings up to the sky, the gestures of Kafka's characters are too resounding for the environment and break through into a more spacious one' (Benjamin 1977, 418, my translation).[12] However, K. adapts to the moment by using the tools of an actor. He decides: 'If it was a hoax, he was going to play along with it' (Kafka 2009, 7).[13] The English version does not express the exact meaning of 'Komödie', which actually translates to 'comedy'. K. obviously recognizes the theatrical nature of his situation, and decides to play along.[14]

The decision to initiate a theatrical action is of major relevance for understanding the concept of theatricality.[15] In her definition of theatricality, Josette Féral offers three potential scenarios (Féral 2002, 95–8). In setting one, an audience waits in a theatre for the performance. The location is connected to the expectation of an event, which leads to theatricality (Fischer-Lichte 2012, 59–60). Anything that will happen on stage will be acknowledged as part of the performance, even if a fireman crosses the stage. In setting two, actors perform a rehearsed fight in a subway, and the passengers are not aware of the artificial set-up. The space in this case has no theatrical implications at all, but the actors are aware of the performance that is about to take place. In this context, the actors intend to perform and, therefore, behave *as if* they are having an argument. In the final setting, a person sits in a cafe and watches people passing by, deciding to regard them as theatre. In this case, the spectator creates theatricality. In each scenario, theatricality does not occur by accident. The intention behind the action is crucial: '[m]any activities are done intentionally, and they gather an audience. They may even be made available to spectators or be presented to an audience, but the way the activities are carried out is not related to their effect on the audience, and they are not theatre' (Kirby 1990, XI). If none of the participants has the intention of theatricality, theatricality will not exist. And this is why theatricality begins when a person consciously decides to initiate a theatrical action.

In Kafka's text, K. undergoes the typical learning process of an actor: he starts to overact. On the same evening of his arrest, K. sets up the scene one more time for Fräulein Bürstner, his neighbour, in whose room the interrogation with the supervisor had taken place. Again, explicit theatrical markers appear. K. wants to show Fräulein Bürstner what happened by recreating the arrest. It is a humorous twist, as Fräulein Bürstner is extremely tired and bored by K. She reluctantly acknowledges the theatrical setting that K. tries to create: '"Oh well, if you need it for demonstration, just move the table"' (Kafka 2009, 24).[16] She continues to perceive K. as a real-life person, while K. insists that she behave like his audience. The pact between audience and actor has failed in this constellation. The narration time and the narrated time are congruent in this text passage. Without any narrative distance, Fräulein Bürstner witnesses K.'s mise en scène[17] of the arrest. In the moment that K. engages himself with the performance and imitates the supervisor by shouting, a neighbour knocks, a classic disturbance. He does not stay in character, and he closes the scene by kissing Fräulein Bürstner excessively, which she simply tolerates (Kafka 2011, 39/2009, 26).

In the evening, K. lays down in his bed and evaluates his performance: '... but first he thought about the way he had behaved; he was satisfied with it, but was surprised that he wasn't even more satisfied ...' (Kafka 2009, 26).[18] Again, the text refers to itself, as Vogl postulates (Vogl 1994, 750). What is more, K.'s thoughts are split into two parts. One evaluates his behaviour, while the other evaluates his evaluation. He thinks on two levels, or, to be more precise, in a liminal area between two levels. As Jens Roselt (who refers to Plessner) formulates: '[i]f one pictures how he affects someone else, one in a way becomes the other, who is watching. This is why there is a distance *to* oneself and not *from* oneself, this means even in the detachment one stays related to oneself ...' (Roselt 2005, 310, emphasis in the original, my translation).[19] The liminal state of K. displays explicit parallels to the in-betweenness of an actor acting. The aforementioned scene is only K.'s first attempt at acting. Soon, he learns more about the rules of the 'Komödie' (Kafka 2011, 13) with which he has decided to play along.

The hearing

The story continues with several chapters that reveal no explicit information to the reader or K. regarding what the trial is about. One day, K. is informed by a phone call that he will have a hearing the next Sunday in a block of flats, but he is not informed about the time or exact floor. In order to remain inconspicuous, he asks the inhabitants of the flat where he can find a carpenter called Lanz, who could help him have a look at the flats. He eventually knocks on the door of a woman on the fifth floor, who lets him in straight away. '"Does a carpenter called Lanz live here?" he asked. "Through here," said a young woman with lustrous black eyes who was washing nappies in a tub, and gestured with her wet hand at the open door to the neighbouring room' (Kafka 2009, 31).[20]

Obviously, the woman and K. understand each other on a level beyond that of their verbal utterance. Their conversation is framed[21] in a particular manner. K.'s question about a carpenter does not irritate the woman. Theatrical frames have their own references and codes, and feature an internal axis of communication that is different from that featured in real life (Stricker 2007, 47). Framing determines, and is determined by, theatricality: the frame of unreality immediately causes us to interpret entities differently from how we would interpret them in real life. This is an aspect that can be found in the way in which Kafka's characters interact with each other (as well as in the narration). His characters are like actors and spectators engaged in a 'social game' – both actors and spectator are the game's participants (Herrmann 1981, 19).[22] The communication between actors, as well as between actors and spectators, follows the rules of the 'intratheatrical situation' (Lazarowicz 1997, 97).[23] They regard each other *as if* they were somebody else. And this *as if* is a crucial element of theatricality.

In this kind of game, the participants share the same knowledge about the situation: '[n]ot only do the various participants imagine many of the same things; each of them realizes that the others are imagining what he is, and each realizes that the others realize this' (Walton 1993, 18). If this presupposition is applied to the characters of *The Trial*, there is still room for surprises or unpredictable behaviour, even though everyone is aware of the theatrical game. Benjamin comments on K.'s dialogues with other characters: '[i]t seems like there is nothing new, as if the protagonist has been asked to remember what he has forgotten' (Benjamin 1977, 429, my translation).[24]

So this intratheatrical situation (or game) is validated by the woman's approval of K.'s question when he knocks on her apartment door. She obviously understands what K. wants to know: whether her apartment is the location of his hearing.[25] The next sequence is characterized by extremes: a small crowded room, noisy reactions from the audience, and strong verbal and physical interactions. Interestingly, K.'s only interest is in gaining the audience's approval: '"They're easily won over", K. thought; the only thing that bothered him was the silence from the left-hand side, which was immediately behind him and from which only isolated applause had come' (Kafka 2009, 32).[26]

K. constantly adapts his speech according to the audience's reactions: 'K. does not identify himself, above all with himself; he views himself through the eyes of the others, without accepting any of these mirror images and projections' (Simons 2007, 276, my translation).[27] This constant evaluation of his actions works like the 'autopoietic feedback-loop' (Fischer-Lichte 2012, 55, my translation)[28] of the theatre, in which the audience reacts to the actor's performance and the actor adjusts his performance accordingly. K.'s intention with his speech shifts from that of gaining the audience's sympathy to addressing it intellectually: '[h]e no longer thought it was necessary for all to applaud, it was sufficient if the assembly as a whole started to think about the matter ...' (Kafka 2009, 35).[29] This first hint of sovereignty (and this Brechtian approach to performance) collapses after he witnesses 'a secret sign' (36)[30] and a couple engaged in a sexually connotated fight (Kafka 2011, 57/2009, 38).

The hearing is the text's only scene in which a mass of characters gathers together. K. has his first real audience with which to interact, and he clearly lives through all the advantages and disadvantages of live performance. His mishandling of disturbances shows his inability to keep the interaction under his control.

A week later, K. travels, again unannounced, to the place of the hearing, only to find the apartment in its normal condition, inhabited by the woman who engaged in the sexual disruption of his hearing (Kafka 2011, 60/2009, 40). The place, the audience, the judge, the disruption – all of these factors are unstable and seem replaceable: 'Kafka does not negotiate a specific liminal border experience only on the level of the characters but also by destabilizing clarity and identity markers' (Geisenhanslüke 2012, 208).[31] So, due to Kafka's 'variety of voices' (Wagner 2011, 69), the narration as well as the story remain in an in-between.

The painter

Over several chapters, K. continues to seek help, until a recommendation leads him to a painter called Titorelli, who lives in a very small and airless room next to some court offices in an attic (Kafka 2011, 173/2009, 117). Here the framing seems to take on a different meaning than in the beginning. On his way up the staircase, he meets a few girls and asks them for Titorelli, telling them that he would like to be painted by him. One of them, who was 'quite depraved already' (Kafka 2009, 101),[32] '... opening her mouth as wide as she could and flapping her hand at K., as if he'd said something exceptionally surprising or inept, lifted up her skirt, which was very short anyway, with both hands, and ran as fast as she could after the other girls' (101).[33] The girls continue to giggle, as the painter opens the door wearing nothing but a nightshirt. K. enters a clearly sexually connotated scene, in which he wants to address the matter of his trial.

The girls interrupt the men's conversation every now and then with giggling or questions, asking whether Titorelli has started to paint him yet. Titorelli responds to them in a rather harsh way, and tells them that they are supposed to stay quiet. K. observes, but he does not react to the girls at all. 'He [Titorelli] paused, as if to give K. time to come to terms with this. Now the girls could be heard on the other side of the door again. They were probably crowding round the keyhole, perhaps it was possible to see through the gaps in the door' (Kafka 2009, 105).[34]

K. leaves the painter, the only artistic character in the story, responsible for the audience: 'K. had hardly turned towards the door at all, he had left it entirely up to the painter whether and in what way he would stand up for him' (Kafka 2009, 107).[35] In this moment, K. becomes part of the audience, and he watches the painter speak, with interruptions from another audience – the girls. This small sequence has so many variations of character constellations that the who-is-watching-who/what interaction becomes rather blurry. For this study, it is relevant that K. does not react to the relationship between the girls and the painter, but rather stays focused on talking about the trial. All the actions that make him uncomfortable, such as Titorelli positioning himself on his bed, or the heat in the room, are initiated by the painter. At one point, K. is unable to stand the temperature in the room any more: '[h]ardly had he taken his jacket off when one of the girls cried out, "He's got his jacket off already", and they could all be heard crowding round the gaps to see the spectacle for themselves' (111–12).[36] Here it becomes very clear that, first, the girls think that they are watching a sexual interaction between Titorelli and K. Second, Titorelli performs a speech for K., in which K. is allowed to take part every now and then. Third, Titorelli thinks that K. is watching him interact with the girls, even though K. is not very interested: '"You see, the girls think I'm going to paint you," the painter said, "and that you're getting undressed for it." "Do they now", K. said only mildly amused ...' (112).[37] K. sticks to his own script, and obviously does not become distracted by the frame that the girls create together with the painter. Still, he has some difficulties acting in the scene, as the heat and lack of fresh air make him uncomfortable. Interestingly, he exits Titorelli's room through a small door next to the bed (on which he has to step to get through the door) and walks through the court offices, finally able to breathe properly again (Kafka 2011, 173/2009, 117). The narrowness of the painter's room, and its proximity to the court offices, evoke the theatre,[38] since the arrangement of the space resembles a stage, where rooms are built without realistic distances from one another. But it is the multidimensional acting of the characters that shows the 'limitless in-between worlds in Kafka's stories' (Benjamin 1977, 430, my translation).[39]

The end

In the last chapter of *The Trial*, which is rich with explicit theatrical markers, K. waits in his apartment without knowing for whom. Two men arrive 'pale and fat, wearing frock coats and top hats that looked as if they were stuck on' (Kafka 2009, 161).[40] K. classifies them: '"They send old, second-rate actors for me", K. said to himself, looking round to confirm that' (161).[41] Besides the obvious theatrical marker, we learn that K. judges the two men in a professional theatrical manner. He tries to talk to them privately, as he did with two policemen in the first chapter, but the balance of competence has switched:

> 'At which theatre are you engaged?' 'Theatre?' one of the men, the corners of his mouth twitching, asked the other. The other grimaced, like a mute desperately trying to produce a sound from a recalcitrant vocal organ. 'They're not prepared for my questions', said K. to himself, and went to fetch his hat. (Kafka 2009, 161)[42]

The men try to stay in their parts. K., on the other hand, tests the two by directing questions at their real-life personas. Now it is K. who tries to interrupt the scene that the gentlemen are playing, and he perceives them immediately as colleagues: '[p]erhaps they're tenors, he thought, at the sight of their large double chins' (Kafka 2009, 162).[43] K. is presuming to know at this point what theatre people look like. This passage is not so much about whether tenors have double chins or not; it is more about what K. thinks he knows. He is convinced of being in a theatrical context. According to this, the narrative framing is very clear: '[w]hen the matrices are strong, persistent and reinforce each other, we see an actor, no matter how ordinary the behavior' (Kirby 1990, 5–6). Even though the scene started in K.'s own apartment, the theatre is a constant reference. In this chapter, K. acts more sovereign than in the first chapter or during the hearing – on a theatrical level.

K. and the two gentlemen walk as a 'single unit' (Kafka 2009, 161)[44] directly towards the site of K.'s planned execution. Yet, K.'s primary concern is how he is perceived by the others. Even shortly before his execution, the position of his naked upper body worries him: '[d]espite all the efforts they made, and despite all the cooperation K. showed, his posture remained very strained and unconvincing' (164).[45] Both of the German terms that describe K.'s posture ('gezwungen', 'unglaubwürdig') are frequently used in theatre jargon to criticize actors' bad performances (it is left open for whom his posture is hard to believe). K. evaluates his actions, but this time his vocabulary is more professional, and he differentiates between his physical presence and his effort. Concerned about projecting believable behaviour, K. seems to be performing for someone else. Close to his death, he feels that he understands:

> K. knew very well that it would have been his duty to grasp the knife himself as, going from hand to hand, it hung in the air above him, and plunge it into his own body. But he didn't do that, instead he

turned his neck, that was still free, and looked around. (Kafka 2009, 164)[46]

Now K. is not bewildered by his situation, but knows what needs to be done in advance. At the very end of the text, when he finally understands the story, he fails. He can see a person in a window, leaning and stretching his arms out (Kafka 2011, 241/2009, 164), which mirrors the opening scene with the old woman in the window. This time, however, K. is not disturbed by the audience. He hopes for help, as his life depends upon it. He does not receive any, as he watches two men watch him. The text ends at this point. It is uncertain whether K. really passes away, or if he is able to free himself:

> When a person ... for example dies on stage, he does not really die. If he were really dying, it would be a matter for the doctors and not for the audience. But the spectator would be just as unsatisfied, if he would not see how a person dies. So, he has to die for real without dying *for real*. (Hiss 1993, 17, emphasis in the original, my translation)[47]

The reality of the theatre is so strong that the oscillation between real-life subject and character produces a liminal state for the actor.

This takes the analysis back to the quotation at the very beginning of this chapter: '"one doesn't have to take everything as the truth, one just has to accept it as necessary"' (Kafka 2009, 159).[48] This statement functions as a guideline for theatre, as well as for Kafka's narration, and it is a strong reference to liminality. The narrator in Kafka's text is equally easy *and* impossible to define. That is why Vogl believes that Kafka writes in the 'fourth person' (Vogl 1994, 745),[49] instead of in the first or third person. Or, as Walton proposes in reference to the execution of K.: '[t]he narrator plays a game in which it is fictional that he [the narrator] wonders thus' (Walton 1993, 380).

Kafka's *The Trial* was never finished. Because Kafka named the last chapter 'end', it can at least be assumed that this was the intended ending – in contrast to the last pages of his other two larger fragments, *The Man Who Disappeared*[50] and *The Castle*,[51] which stop mid-sentence. Even though the protagonist seemingly dies at the end of the text, 'as if the shame would live on after him' (Kafka 2009, 165),[52] there is no closure. The process of adapting, adjusting and searching is unfinished.

The main points discussed in this chapter concern the framing and the starting point of theatricality – acting *as if* and the theatrical game, and the oscillation between the actor as real-life subject and character. Understanding theatricality as a situation of the in-between leads to the fact that an actor acting in a part exists in a liminal state for the time of the performance: '[t]he human is a body and at the same time he *has* a body that he can use in a certain manner' (Roselt 2005, 311, emphasis in the original, my translation).[53] Kafka's narration offers a double perspective on the story, since the protagonist sees himself through his own eyes and through the eyes of the other characters (Vogl 2006, 223–4).

Reading Kafka's texts through the lens of theatricality, as this chapter demonstrates, can help us understand what makes Kafka's narration so unique and what shapes his writing. Josef K. is caught in a constant in-between, and his passage merges with the oscillation between the subject and object, or real-life person and character. Even though he manages to adapt theatrical behaviour during the story, he does not achieve any kind of closure. Whether a final passage occurs at the fragment's close or not, it is liminality that is foregrounded and that persists.

Notes

1. Kafka (2009, 159); '..."man muß nicht alles für wahr halten, man muß es nur für notwendig halten"' (Kafka 2011, 233).
2. 'K. wartete noch ein Weilchen, sah von seinem Kopfkissen aus die alte Frau die ihm gegenüber wohnte und die ihn mit einer an ihr ganz ungewöhnlichen Neugier beobachtete, dann aber, gleichzeitig befremdet und hungrig, läutete er' (Kafka 2011, 9).
3. 'Sofort klopfte es und ein Mann, den er in dieser Wohnung noch niemals gesehen hatte trat ein' (Kafka 2011, 9).
4. For liminality, see, for example, Geisenhanslüke (2012), Vogl (2006; 1994). For theatricality, see, for example, Mihály (2015), Simons (2007), Liebrand (1998), Gronius (1983), Kurz (1980).
5. On the level of discourse, Kafka's unique narration challenges assumptions about perspective, time and mode. See, for example, Auerochs and Engel (2010, 441), Benjamin (1991), Wagner (2011, 58–80), Zimmermann (2004).
6. *Josephine, die Sängerin oder das Volk der Mäuse, Ein Bericht für eine Akademie, Vor dem Gesetz* (Kafka, 2019).
7. '"Wer sind sie?" fragt K. und saß gleich halb aufrecht im Bett. Der Mann aber ging über die Frage hinweg, als müsse man seine Entscheidung hinnehmen und sagte bloß seinerseits: "Sie haben geläutet?"' (Kafka 2011, 9).
8. 'Das Erzählen bewegt sich in einer schwebenden Interferenz, die das Verhältnis zwischen Ich und Er, Erzähler und Figur und Satz zu Satz erneut zu verunsichern scheint. Zugleich aber ist dieser gleitende Übergang ein Faktum der thematisierten Figur. Sie agiert als sich selbst nennendes Ich, das sich im "er" der Erzählung bloß wiederholt und damit einen endlos rekursiven Verweis initiiert: "er" meint ein "ich", das wiederum ein "er" meint ...'.
9. But at the same time, the actor as a private person will not overrule the part he is playing. 'We are not to attribute to Hamlet what we think we know about Laurence Olivier's private life' (Walton 1993, 172).

10 'Er selbst ist sein eigenes Mittel, d.h. er spaltet sich selbst in sich selbst, bleibt aber, um im Bilde zu bleiben, diesseits des Spaltes, hinter der Figur, die er verkörpert, stehen' (Plessner, as cited in Roselt 2005, 315).
11 '"Ich will doch Frau Grubach –", sagte K., machte eine Bewegung, als reiße er sich von zwei Männern los, die aber weit von ihm entfernt standen, und wollte weitergehen' (Kafka 2011, 10–11).
12 'Wie diese Glocke, für eine Türglocke zu laut, zum Himmel auf tönt, so sind die Gesten Kafkascher Figuren zu durchschlagend für die gewohnte Umwelt und brechen in eine geräumigere ein.'
13 '... war es eine Komödie, so wollte er mitspielen' (Kafka 2011, 13).
14 See also Burns: 'Behavior is not therefore theatrical because it is of a certain kind but because the observer recognizes certain patterns and sequences which are analogous to those with which he is familiar in the theatre' (Burns 1972, 12).
15 Recent research is based on Erika Fischer-Lichte's concept of theatricality. For her, the performance lies in the centre, which is connected to staging, corporeality and perception (Aufführung, Körperlichkeit, Wahrnehmung, my translation). The uniqueness of the event is indicative, and influences every aspect of theatricality (Fischer-Lichte 2004, 10–26). Due to the fact that there is no live performance in literature, elements besides the physical presence of both the actor and the spectator have to be specified. Or, to be more precise, aspects that are evoked by the actors' and spectators' physical presence need clarification.
16 '"Ja wenn Sie es zur Darstellung brauchen, dann rücken Sie das Tischchen ruhig fort"' (Kafka 2011, 36).
17 The term is used according to Mieke Bal (2002, 97–9).
18 '... vor dem Einschlafen dachte er noch ein Weilchen über sein Verhalten nach, er war damit zufrieden, wunderte sich aber, daß er nicht noch zufriedener war ...' (Kafka 2011, 40).
19 'Wenn man sich eine Vorstellung davon macht, wie man auf den anderen wirkt, wird man in gewisser Weise zu dem anderen, der einen betrachtet. Deshalb ist es eine Abständigkeit *zu* sich und nicht *von* sich, das heißt auch in der Distanz bleibt man auf sich selbst bezogen ...'
20 '"Wohnt ein Tischler Lanz hier?" fragte er. "Bitte", sagte eine junge Frau mit schwarzen leuchtenden Augen, die gerade in einem Kübel Kinderwäsche wusch, und zeigte mit der nassen Hand auf die offene Tür des Nebenzimmers' (Kafka 2011, 47).
21 The 'framing' of an event, which dominates the interpretation of the event, is a concept that was coined by Erving Goffman (1974).
22 '[Der] Ursinn des Theatres ... besteht darin, daß das Theatre ein soziales Spiel war, ein Spiel aller für alle. Ein Spiel in dem Alle Teilnehmer sind, – Teilnehmer und Zuschauer.'
23 'intratheatrale Situation'.
24 'Es ist als wäre da nichts Neues, als ergehe nur unauffällig an den Helden die Aufforderung, sich doch einfallen zu lassen, was er vergessen habe.'
25 Even K. is taken by surprise by the woman's reaction: '"I was asking about a carpenter, a man called Lanz?" "Yes", said the woman, "please go in"' (Kafka 2009, 31). '"Ich habe nach einem Tischler, einem gewissen Lanz gefragt?" "Ja", sagte die Frau, "gehn Sie bitte hinein"' (Kafka 2011, 47).
26 'Ein Beifallklatschen wieder aus der rechten Saalhälfte folgte. "Leicht zu gewinnende Leute", dachte K. und war nur gestört durch die Stille in der linken Saalhälfte, die gerade hinter ihm lag und aus der sich nur ganz vereinzeltes Händeklatschen erhoben hatte' (Kafka 2011, 49).
27 'K. identifiziert sich nicht, vor allem nicht mit sich selbst, er sieht sich mit den Augen Anderer, aber auch dies, ohne eines der Spiegelbilder und Projektionen anzunehmen.'
28 'autopoietische Feedbackschleife'.
29 '... er hielt es jetzt gar nicht mehr für nötig, daß alle Beifall klatschten, es genügte, wenn die Allgemeinheit über die Sache nachzudenken begann ...' (Kafka 2011, 53).
30 'ein geheimes Zeichen' (Kafka 2011, 54).
31 'Kafka [verhandelt] nicht nur auf der Ebene der Figuren eine spezifisch liminale Erfahrung von Grenzsituationen, indem er Eindeutigkeiten und Identitätszuweisungen beständig außer Kraft setzt.'
32 'schon ganz verdorben' (Kafka 2011, 148).
33 '... öffnete übermäßig den Mund, schlug mit der Hand leicht gegen K., als hätte er etwas außerordentlich überraschendes oder ungeschicktes gesagt, hob mit beiden Händen ihr ohnehin schon sehr kurzes Röckchen und lief so schnell sie konnte hinter den anderen Mädchen ...' (Kafka 2011, 148).

34 'Er [Titorelli] machte eine Pause, als wolle er K. Zeit lassen, sich mit dieser Tatsache abzufinden. Man hörte jetzt wieder hinter der Tür die Mädchen. Sie drängten sich wahrscheinlich um das Schlüsselloch, vielleicht konnte man auch durch die Ritzen ins Zimmer hineinsehn' (Kafka 2011, 155).
35 'K. hatte sich kaum zur Tür hingewendet, er hatte es vollständig dem Maler überlassen, ob und wie er ihn in Schutz nehmen wollte' (Kafka 2011, 158–9).
36 'Kaum hatte er den Rock ausgezogen, rief eines der Mädchen: "Er hat schon den Rock ausgezogen" und man hörte wie sich alle zu den Ritzen drängten, um das Schauspiel selbst zu sehen' (Kafka 2011, 164).
37 '"Die Mädchen glauben nämlich", sagt der Maler, "daß ich Sie malen werde und daß Sie sich deshalb ausziehn." "So", sagte K. nur wenig belustigt ...' (Kafka 2011, 164).
38 Jan Kott writes, 'All of these objects do not only exist. They mean something. But except for them, there is nothing' (Kott 1972, 68, my translation). 'All diese Gegenstände existieren nicht nur, sie bedeuten auch etwas. Aber außer ihnen gibt es nichts.'
39 'unerschöpfliche Zwischenwelt in Kafkas Geschichten'.
40 'Gehröcken, bleich und fett, mit scheinbar unverrückbaren Cylinderhüten' (Kafka 2011, 236).
41 '"Alte untergeordnete Schauspieler schickt man um mich", sagte sich K. und sah sich um, um sich nochmals davon zu überzeugen' (Kafka 2011, 236–7).
42 '"An welchem Theater spielen Sie". "Theater?" fragte der eine Herr mit zuckenden Mundwinkeln den andern um Rat. Der andere geberdete [sic] sich wie ein Stummer, der mit dem widerspenstigen Organismus kämpft. "Sie sind nicht darauf vorbereitet, gefragt zu werden", sagt sich K. und ging seinen Hut holen' (Kafka 2011, 236).
43 'Vielleicht sind es Tenöre dachte er im Anblick ihres schweren Doppelkinns' (Kafka 2011, 237).
44 'eine solche Einheit' (Kafka 2011, 237).
45 'Trotz aller Anstrengung, die sie sich gaben, und trotz allen Entgegenkommens, das ihnen K. bewies, blieb seine Haltung eine sehr gezwungene und unglaubwürdige' (Kafka 2011, 240).
46 'K. wußte jetzt genau, daß es seine Pflicht gewesen wäre, das Messer, als es von Hand zu Hand über ihm schwebte, selbst zu fassen und sich einzubohren. Aber er tat es nicht, sondern drehte den noch freien Hals und sah umher' (Kafka 2011, 241).
47 'Wird ... auf jener Fläche gezeigt, wie ein Mensch stirbt, stirbt er nicht wirklich. Würde er tatsächlich sterben, wäre es eine Sache der Ärzte, nicht die des Publikums. Aber die Zuschauer wären ebenso unzufrieden, wenn sie nicht sehen würden, wie ein Mensch stirbt. Er muss also wirklich sterben ohne in *Wirklichkeit* zu sterben.'
48 '"... man muss es nicht für wahr, man muss es nur für notwendig halten"' (Kafka 2011, 233).
49 'Vierte Person'.
50 *Der Verschollene*.
51 *Das Schloß*.
52 '... es war, als sollte die Scham ihn überleben' (Kafka 2011, 241).
53 'Der Mensch ist ein Körper und zugleich *hat* er seinen Körper, den er gezielt einsetzen kann.'

References

Auerochs, Bernd and Manfred Engel, eds. 2010. *Kafka Handbuch: Leben – Werk – Wirkung*. Stuttgart: J.B. Metzler.
Bal, Mieke. 2002. *Travelling Concepts in the Humanities: A rough guide*. Toronto: University of Toronto Press.
Benjamin, Walter. 1977. *Franz Kafka – Zur zehnten Wiederkehr seines Todestages: In der Fassung von: Walter Benjamin – Gesammelte Schriften II.2*. Frankfurt am Main: Suhrkamp.
Burns, Elizabeth. 1972. *Theatricality: A study of convention in the theatre and in social life*. New York: Harper Torchbooks.
Féral, Josette. 2002. 'Theatricality: The specificity of theatrical language', *SubStance: A review of theory and literary criticism* 31 (98/99): 94–110.
Fischer-Lichte, Erika. 2004. 'Theatralität als kulturelles Modell'. In *Theatralität als Modell in den Kulturwissenschaften*, edited by Erika Fischer-Lichte, 7–27. Tübingen: Francke.
Fischer-Lichte, Erika. 2012. *Performativität*. Bielefeld: transcript-Verlag.

Geisenhanslüke, Achim. 2012. 'Kafkas schmutzige Kinder: Schwellenerfahrung in Der Verschollene'. In *Liminale Anthropologien: Zwischenzeiten, Schwellenphänomene, Zwischenräume in Literatur und Philosophie*, edited by Jochen Achilles, Roland Borgards and Brigitte Burrichter, 199–208. Würzburg: Königshausen & Neumann.

Goffman, Erving. 1974. *Frame Analysis: An essay on the organization of experience*. Cambridge, MA: Harvard University Press.

Gronius, Jörg W. 1983. *Kafka im Theater: Über Adaptionen des 'Proceß' und Menschen im Hotel*. PhD dissertation, Berlin: Frei Universität Berlin.

Herrmann, Max. 1981. 'Über die Aufgaben eines Theaterwissenschaftlichen Instituts'. In *Theaterwissenschaft im deutschsprachigen Raum*, edited by Helmar Klier, 15–24. Darmstadt: Wissenschaftliche Buchgesellschaft.

Hiss, Guido. 1993. *Der theatralische Blick: Einführung in die Aufführungsanalyse*. Berlin: D. Reimer.

Kafka, Franz. 2009. *The Trial*, translated by Mike Mitchell. Oxford: Oxford University Press.

Kafka, Franz. 2011. *Der Proceß*. Frankfurt am Main: Fischer-Taschenbuch-Verlag.

Kafka, Franz. 2019. *Metamorphosis and Other Stories*, translated by Michael Hofmann. London: Penguin.

Kirby, Michael. 1990. *A Formalist Theatre*. Philadelphia: University of Pennsylvania Press.

Kott, Jan. 1972. *Spektakel, Spektakel: Tendenzen des modernen Welttheaters*. Munich: Piper Verlag.

Kurz, Gerhard. 1980. *Traum-Schrecken: Kafkas literarische Existenzanalyse*. Stuttgart: Metzler.

Lazarowicz, Klaus. 1997. *Gespielte Welt: Eine Einführung in die Theaterwissenschaft an ausgewählten Beispielen*. Frankfurt am Main: Peter Lang.

Liebrand, Claudia. 1998. 'Theater im Prozess: Dramaturgisches zu Kafkas Romanfragment', *Germanisch-romanische Monatszeitschrift* 48 (2): 201–17.

Mihály, Csilla. 2015. *Figuren und Figurenkonstellationen in Kafkas Erzähltheater: Zur Erklärungsfunktion der Wiederholungsstrukturen im mittleren Werk*. Vienna: Praesens Verlag.

Roselt, Jens. 2005. *Seelen mit Methode: Schauspieltheorien vom Barock bis zum postdramatischen Theater*. Berlin: Alexander.

Simons, Oliver. 2007. 'Schuld und Scham: Kafkas episches Theater'. In *Kafkas Institutionen*, edited by Arne Höcker and Oliver Simons, 269–94. Bielefeld: Transcript.

Soeffner, Hans-Georg. 2004. 'Die Wirklichkeit der Theatralität'. In *Theatralität als Modell in den Kulturwissenschaften*, edited by Erika Fischer-Lichte, 235–47. Tübingen: Francke.

Stricker, Achim. 2007. *Text-Raum: Strategien nicht dramatischer Theatertexte: Gertrude Stein, Heiner Müller, Werner Schwab, Rainald Goetz*. Heidelberg: Winter.

Thomassen, Bjørn. 2018. *Liminality and the Modern: Living through the in-between*. London: Routledge.

Vogl, Joseph. 1994. 'Vierte Person: Kafkas Erzählstimme', *Deutsche Vierteljahresschrift für Literaturwissenschaft und Geistesgeschichte* 68: 745–56.

Vogl, Joseph. 2006. 'Gespiegelte Szenen'. In *Franz Kafka: Neue Wege der Forschung*, edited by Claudia Liebrand, 222–32. Darmstadt: Wissenschaftliche Buchgesellschaft.

Wagner, Benno. 2011. 'Lightning no longer flashes: Kafka's Chinese voice and the thunder of the Great War'. In *Franz Kafka: Narration, rhetoric, and reading*, edited by Jakob Lothe, Beatrice Sandberg and Ronald Speirs, 58–80. Columbus: Ohio State University Press.

Walton, Kendall L. 1993. *Mimesis as Make-Believe: On the foundations of the representational arts*. Cambridge, MA: Harvard University Press.

Zimmermann, Hans Dieter. 2004. *Kafka für Fortgeschrittene*. Munich: C.H. Beck.

8
From passage to maturity to liminal critique: Foucault's care of the self as liminal practice

Ruben Pfizenmaier

An understanding of philosophy as a practice, form of life and set of exercises has been reinvestigated and propagated in recent decades. Pierre Hadot's *Philosophy as a Way of Life* (2010) provided a particular impetus, and Martha Nussbaum's (1994) work on ancient philosophy, Richard Shusterman's (2008; 2012) project of somaesthetics and Peter Sloterdijk's *You Must Change Your Life* (2013) have contributed significantly to this discourse. One of the trailblazers in approaching ancient philosophy as a set of practices is Michel Foucault. With the second and third volume of his *History of Sexuality*, Foucault turned to European antiquity, ascesis and modes of subjectivity (Foucault 1990; 1988a). Many contemporaries were surprised by this shift: Foucault, the philosopher in the archive who investigated topics such as madness, the institution of the prison and bio-power now read Plato; the thinker who had declared the 'death of the subject' now centred his work on subjectivity. Yet Foucault, on many occasions, explained this shift as a natural development of his thought, and presented subjectivity as his work's third axis, alongside knowledge and power.[1]

This chapter focuses on Foucault's last lectures at the Collège de France: *The Hermeneutics of the Subject* (1981–2), *The Government of Self and Others* (1982–3) and *The Courage of the Truth* (1983–4) (Foucault

2005; 2010; 2011). It analyses the practices of the care of the self, and their transformations in antiquity as liminal practices, premised on Arnold van Gennep's, Victor Turner's and Bjørn Thomassen's understandings of passage and liminality (van Gennep 1960; Turner 1967; Thomassen 2014).

After a brief introduction to the concepts of passage and liminality, the chapter addresses three forms of the care of the self, as discussed in Foucault's lectures:

(1) The Socratic, specifically Platonic, form of the care of the self. Foucault starts his analysis of the care of the self with Plato's dialogue *Alcibiades*. I want to describe this manifestation of a practised philosophy as liminal practice, preparing an individual at the edge of adolescence for his role as a mature citizen in the Athenian *polis*.[2]
(2) The Hellenistic, particularly Stoic, form of the care of the self. In a socially and politically transformed context, the Platonic care of the self lost its original field of application. In reaction, it sprawled and turned into an encompassing form of life, a *techne tou biou*. This section will focus on Foucault's reading of the Stoics, especially Seneca and Marcus Aurelius.
(3) The Cynic form of the care of the self. In Foucault's analysis of the Cynics and their way of life, the care of the self becomes an embodied, radical critique of society. My claim here is that the Cynic embodies liminality as a mode of critique.

The concepts of passage and liminality

In 1909, Arnold van Gennep published his *Rites of Passage*. In this anthropological study on rites of transition, van Gennep introduces liminality as the middle, or transitional, stage of the ritual passage. Every rite of passage, regardless of its specific context (whether it be the initiation to a social group or class, the path from childhood to adulthood or a spatial journey), follows a tripartite structure: separation, liminality and incorporation. Individuals are separated from their social group's members, but also from their own previous life or state of being. They then undergo a process of transformation and are, finally, reintegrated as matured, healed, initiated or otherwise transformed individuals (van Gennep 1960, 11).

About six decades later, Victor Turner rediscovered van Gennep's almost forgotten work. Via Turner and, especially, Turner's student Richard Schechner, the concept of liminality travelled to performance, theatre and literary studies. In his essay 'Betwixt and between: The liminal period in rites de passage', Turner explores the manifold aspects of liminality in ritualistic practices (Turner 1967). More recently, anthropologist and social scientist Bjørn Thomassen set out to transport the concept of liminality from ethnography and ritual theory to social theory in *Liminality and the Modern: Living through the in-between* (Thomassen 2014). He positions liminality as a universal concept on the same level as structure and practice, and conceptualizes 'moments where the relationship between structure and agency is not easily resolved' (Thomassen 2014, 1). Thus, liminality refers to complex situations in which the status quo dissolves and 'structuration and meaning formation take form' (1). Thomassen's main aim is to use the concept of liminality to analyse modernity and modern experience. Accordingly, in *Liminality and the Modern*, he discusses the theoretical formation of modernity in Descartes and Hobbes in light of liminality, but he also looks at gambling, discusses an anthropology of revolution and even presents a cross-cultural analysis of (bungee) jumping.

Building on Turner, whose early adoption of liminality was explicitly directed towards anthropologists, and in line with Thomassen's thoughts, I want to apply passage and liminality as analytical concepts to Foucault's reading of the care of the self. Although the care of the self in ancient philosophy is clearly not a ritual like van Gennep's object of study, it displays many aspects of liminality.[3]

An understanding of the care of the self can be established with passage and liminality – without referring to core concepts from the history of philosophy. As analytical concepts, liminality and passage enact a strong schematizing, structuring effect, which can be used to organize the various historical shifts of the care of the self. At the same time, this perspective stays focused on the performance of these practices, as well as their social and cultural embeddedness, without succumbing to a nonreflective anachronism by transforming Foucault's genealogical project into a universal theory. Liminality and passage as concepts are broad enough to constitute new starting points, without losing sight of cultural and historical specificities. Finally, and by describing the performance of ancient Cynics as liminal critique, the concept of liminality will prove useful to the understanding of Foucault's own concept of critique. Consequently, this chapter will contribute to an understanding of Foucault's thinking, and shed light on his interest in ancient philosophy.

In contrast to many publications on Foucault's technologies of the self, my chapter does not examine the soundness of Foucault's concepts (Schäfer 1995; Menke 2003; Butler 2004) or the historical foundation of his observations (as Wolfgang Detel brilliantly did, 2005), nor do I reflect on the critical value of the care of the self, as several authors have previously done.[4] Instead, I will focus on the mechanism of the care of the self in order to highlight Foucault's complex perspective and framing. His lectures on ancient philosophy are close readings of many, sometimes obscure, sources. Still, his interest is clearly informed by concepts such as power, subjectivity, knowledge and truth, and how they shape contemporary society (especially in his interviews and lectures, Foucault 1982; Foucault and Sennett 1981). However, instead of actualizing ancient practices, Foucault only highlights their potential as models or schemes for his own present in passing (Foucault 1982, 234, 236; 2005, 251–2). Most of the time, he stays in the 'resonance chamber' (Stiegler 2012, 51, my translation) of antiquity. Passage and liminality can generate a new and productive understanding of Foucault's lectures.

Foucault and the care of the self

In *Discipline and Punish*, Foucault describes how subjects are produced in discursive and non-discursive practices through techniques of surveillance, within structures of knowledge, by architecture and by modes of evaluation (Foucault 1995). To Foucault, power is a relation immanent to economic processes, sexual relations and relations of knowledge. Foucault claims that the individual is not passive within this constellation, but rather actively participates in his or her own subjugation by perpetuating normalization, repeating disciplines, giving accounts of themselves, and performing various examinations and assessments.[5] Foucault's interest in practices of ancient philosophy must be considered against this backdrop.

The care of the self appears as a set of concepts and practices related to subjectivity: they address the relations of the subject to others, as well as the way one relates to oneself. The care of the self is a process of focusing one's attention on oneself, by writing letters, reflecting on one's life in specific terms or engaging in a dialogue and being questioned about one's own convictions. The aim is to establish 'a certain kind of constant relationship to the self' (Foucault 2005, 86). This relationship can take on different shapes: a 'mastery of the self', 'having pleasure in oneself' or 'being content with oneself' (86). In all of these variations, the subject is not rooted in self-knowledge in the sense of the Cartesian *cogito*.

Quite contrary to institutions and practices, such as the Christian confession or the handling of suspects at the intersection of psychology and criminal prosecution, the subject of the care of the self does not submit him or herself to rules and laws. They do not discover or reveal truth about themselves and their deeds, but rather reflectively address themselves in practice.[6] Foucault discusses the care of the self as a 'technology of the self', distinct from 'technologies of production', 'technologies of sign systems' and 'technologies of power' (Foucault 1988b, 18). Technologies of the self allow:

> individuals to effect by their own means or with the help of others a certain number of operations on their own bodies and souls, thoughts, conduct, and way of being, so as to transform themselves in order to attain a certain state of happiness, purity, wisdom, perfection, or immortality. (Foucault 1988b, 18)

The care of the self is an etho-poetic endeavour: 'making ethos, producing ethos, changing, transforming ethos, the individual's way of being, his mode of existence. Ethopoios is something that possesses the quality of transforming an individual's mode of being' (Foucault 2005, 237).[7]

As mentioned in the introduction, this chapter will focus on three specific manifestations of the care of the self discussed by Foucault in his late works: the care of the self in Plato's dialogue *Alcibiades*, the care of the self in the Stoic art of living and, finally, the care of the self in Cynic philosophy. These manifestations are the focal points of a dynamic development, which began with archaic practices that persisted within Christianity, and the scope of which exceeds the limits of this chapter.[8]

Education and preparation for politics: Plato's *Alcibiades*

The *Alcibiades* begins with a discussion of politics. Alcibiades, offspring of a good family, wants to make a career in the *polis*. Socrates, in his famous fashion, confronts the young man with his ignorance, since he does not know what it means to govern others. He lacks the knowledge to succeed in politics. This can be rectified if he starts taking care of himself. And what is this self? It is his soul. Socrates demands that Alcibiades work on his soul as that which governs his deeds. This relation between soul and body must be reflected upon and moderated (Foucault 2005, 54). Only when Alcibiades is able to govern his desires and passions, and control his fears and anger, will he be able to govern others. Philosophy, in Plato's understanding, has to take on the form of a dialogue. Only when the self is directed towards another self as a 'reflecting surface' (69) can it know itself and access philosophical truth (which, in the case of Alcibiades, and according to Plato, is necessary for governing well). In this example, the appeals to 'know thyself' (*gnothi seauton*) and to 'take care of oneself' (*epimeleia heauto*) are reciprocally and dynamically entangled (69).

The master's position in Plato's model is essential: Socrates serves as *spiritus rector*, who monitors the practice of the care of the self, supervises the practitioner and guides his soul (*psychagogy*). It starts with a test, as Socrates first ensures that Alcibiades is ready and able to accept his flaws and tend to himself.[9] In this regard, philosophical exercises differ from many rites of passage, since they rely strongly on the willingness to actually change. The test not only makes Alcibiades aware of his shortcomings, but also separates him from his former convictions. By accepting that he knows nothing, he cuts himself loose from his former self-understanding and from anything he had taken for granted. The second phase is the process of acquiring philosophical knowledge. Unlike many rituals discussed by van Gennep and Turner, the adolescents engaging in the care of the self are not strictly separated from society and do not fall under special laws. They are also not stripped of their possessions, names or ranks, nor do specific commandments apply (van Gennep 1960, 65; Turner 1967, 98–9). They gather publicly but do not pursue accepted professions. Instead, they go for walks and talk. By discussing abstract, philosophical issues, they actively interrupt daily routines and distance themselves from what is commonly considered to be self-evident.

In this context, care means paying specific attention to one's thinking and ideas, but it is also a set of practices and exercises, meditations and tests (Foucault 2005, 10–11). Embedded in an ancient understanding of truth that differs from scientific truth in modernity, ancient philosophy, and especially the care of the self as a spiritual practice, 'postulates that for the subject to have right of access to the truth [it] must be changed, transformed, shifted, and become, to some extent and up to a certain point, other than himself' (15). Although it has over time been overshadowed by the Delphian notion of 'knowing thyself', the care of the self does not exhaust itself in an intellectual approach towards the self, but is a necessary condition for accessing truth.[10]

Socrates approaches Alcibiades at a crucial moment of his life. Described as a beautiful boy, Alcibiades has almost reached adulthood, and his former lovers are not interested in him any longer. Although Socrates seduces Alcibiades, he only wants his spiritual submission (Foucault 1988b, 23). Plato's *Alcibiades* is a critique of pedagogy (although part of the Athenian elite, Alcibiades has not received the education needed to rule as a free man among free men) and a problematization of the eroticization of boys. In *The Use of Pleasure*, the second volume of *The History of Sexuality*, Foucault investigates the isomorphism between sexual and social relations: activity and passivity, as well as penetration and being penetrated. The transition from the passivity of the boy to the activity of the adult man was essential in Greek antiquity.[11] It had to be ensured that the boy would not identify himself as an object of desire. This was achieved through a structuring, fashioning and mastery of the adult's desires (Foucault 1990, 224–5).

To be a free man allowed to govern others meant, among other things, to be free from one's desires. Freedom was not discussed as free will, or in opposition to natural determination, but as a relation to oneself, a mastery of those parts of the soul that are unable to regulate themselves.[12] For Foucault, the (primarily ethical) subject is constituted through an ongoing relationship to oneself as well as to others. It is guided by pragmatic advice, experiencing testing itself in light of shared values and ideals.

Building on self-awareness and reflective practices, Alcibiades must perform what I would like to call a liminal practice. In doing so, he not only educates himself and gains access to philosophical truth – in particular, regarding the question of 'what is justice?' – but he will also be enabled to take care of others and govern as a free man among free men. The care of the self appears as a passage to maturity, situated in the liminal period between youth and manhood. One might object that nothing is gained by describing a practice of education as a passage. But education related to the care of the self works differently: its aim is not to pass on shared values or a canon of general knowledge, but to support the development of an individual towards autonomy and maturity. To achieve this goal, it is directed towards a transformation of the very structure of subjectivity. It is not only interested in the embodiment of a moral code; it also aims to shape perception, habits and thinking. In the Socratic, or rather Platonic, sense, this is achieved by evoking and undergoing a specific Socratic 'non-knowing' and engaging in philosophical dialogue, before finally gaining access to philosophical truth.

The care of the self as the art of living: Marcus Aurelius and Seneca

With the end of Athenian democracy after the Macedonian conquest, philosophy and the care of the self as a preparation for political life lost their main purposes. Yet, the care of the self did not disappear. In the first and second centuries CE, it had become a general imperative, and had adopted the form of a comprehensive technology of the self, or an art of living (*techne peri tou biou*; *ars vivendi*) for potentially everyone's entire life. It was no longer directed towards or mediated by the city-state (Sellars 2003, 54).[13]

The various exercises of testing and paying attention to oneself, and, in doing so, freeing oneself, were no longer connected to a preparation for political practice. The erotic component disappeared, as did the limitation to a specific age. The care of the self was practised 'independently of any professional specification, to withstand in the right way all the possible accidents, misfortunes, disgrace, and setbacks that may befall' the individual (Foucault 2005, 94). Foucault states that a downright '"culture" of the self' emerged (178–9).

This care of the self was primarily aimed at freeing the individual from errors, bad habits, ingrained behaviours and dependencies. The unlearning of childhood imprints and the overcoming of the so-called 'family ideology' (Foucault 2005, 94–5) were at issue here. The focus was on the improvement of the self, rather than on education (94–5). While philosophy has always been entangled with medicine,[14] this relationship now becomes central: Stoics and Epicureans understood *pathos* as passion as well as illness; schools of philosophy became 'clinic[s] for the soul' (99).

Foucault stresses that this practice was not performed along the lines of the 'dos' and 'don'ts' of any law or codex, but that it was guided by philosophical concepts. The knowledge which has to be anchored in one's existence is supposed to transform one's life. It is not merely a propositional but rather a relational knowledge that constitutes the subject in relation to the world. This knowledge is not an answer to the question 'What is the subject?' (which would imply that the subject can be treated as an object), but rather: 'What should I make of myself?' (Foucault 2005, 318). This does not mean that a clear cut from formation through, for instance, social institutions, could be easily enacted. Nonetheless, Foucault sees the potential for a critical, highly attentive self-relation, which focuses on specific aspects of one's life and turns this aspect into the substance of a potentially critical practice.

Yet what did Stoic practices actually look like? Here, I will refer to two brief examples. Marcus Aurelius mentions a spiritual exercise, or meditation, which consisted of the detailed description of the ideas passing through the mind. The corresponding object is not only described in its essence, but also dissipated into all its parts. It has to be analysed and then evaluated in its value for the cosmos. Objects of such exercises were, for example, a charming dance (which, in the end, is only a series of banal motions) or one's own body (which is nothing but matter and will decay; only the *logos* will remain). The aim in both cases is to become free of temptations and misconceptions, such as singularity and individual independence, and to adopt an almost universal point of view, the point of view of the cosmos.[15]

Seneca tells us that he used to reflect on the events of the day before going to bed: What had happened? What had gone as planned? What had not worked? The schema he applied is not that of a judge or priest, but that of an accountant: the wrong doings are not moral failures, but strategic neglects. The rules and prescripts are not used to judge the past, but to guide the present (Foucault 1988b, 33). Other exercises, especially the writing of letters or journaling, similarly worked as a mode of self-examination. Foucault also mentions exercises against curiosity (Foucault 2005, 221), practices of hardship and deprivation, and listening exercises as preparations for philosophical education (333–8).[16]

One of the overarching aims of the Stoic art of living was the preparation for old age and death. In 65 CE, Seneca was sentenced to death by his former student, Nero. He re-enacted Socrates' death: he opened his veins, drank a cup of hemlock and suffocated in his bath (Tacitus 1937, 311–19). In one of his letters, he writes: 'Every man ought to make his life acceptable to others besides himself, but his death to himself alone' (Seneca 1920, 63).

Although its direction is inverted in a way, the care of the self as part of the technologies of the self can still be described as a liminal practice: instead of focusing on the integration of the young individual into society, the care of the self now aims entirely at a transformation of subjectivity. Van Gennep's tripartite structure is reduced to an ongoing liminality: taking care of oneself and exercising philosophy turns life into a journey that will not come to an end. Indeed, the metaphors of an ongoing journey and movement are widespread to describe the effort of the subject, as Foucault demonstrates (Foucault 2005, 248–52). Since the care of the self is not guided by strict, prescriptive laws or one clear model, the individual cannot anticipate the insights gained through this practice. Before wisdom and *apatheia* (the absence of desires) are found, the novice cannot know how they will feel, and thus never sees the actual objective prior to its conclusion.

Additionally, a social liminality is cultivated: a separation between those who practise the care of the self and those who do not. The technologies of the self introduce a vertically positioned spectrum. According to Peter Sloterdijk, this separation can be described as vertical tension. Sloterdijk constructs an entire theory of culture, centred around optimization, enhancement and self-conquest of the human through exercise and training. Culture, according to Sloterdijk's *You Must Change Your Life*, emerges as the secession of the truly cultivated from the rest, who only enact and are shaped by a mere agglomerate of habits (Sloterdijk 2013, 216). In this regard, the care of the self can be described as a passage not primarily directed towards a specific aim, but as a motion distinguishing one from those unable to cultivate themselves.

Foucault writes that the care of the self was understood as a decision for a specific way of life that could differ strongly in its execution. Foucault distinguishes two poles of the care of the self in Hellenism: 'a more popular, religious, cultic and theoretically unpolished pole', and 'more individual, personal, and cultivated' practices related to 'privileged classes and often depending on friendship networks' (Foucault 2005, 115). Since the general access to the technologies of the self was not restricted by status or birth, the gap between those who were able to conduct these exercises and those who were not necessarily reflects the social hierarchy. Apart from the fact that one needed the leisure to actually perform cultivation, the main obstacles were '[l]ack of courage, strength, or endurance, an inability to grasp the importance of the task or to see it through; such is the destiny of the majority in reality' (118). This relation between 'universal appeal and rarity of salvation' is eventually assimilated into Christianity (120). Regarding the anthropological function of technologies of the self and the art of living, Foucault remarks that, despite the importance of law and religion in times of Hellenism, these practices were 'inserted in the gaps left equally by the city-state, the law, and religion regarding this organization of life' (447), and thus provided a loophole for work on one's own societal status.

By looking at the care of the self in Hellenism, and in its Stoic manifestation, in terms of liminality, the strong link between modes of cultivation and social status becomes apparent – as does the potential for technologies of the self to work against the power of institutions and mainstream ideals. A strong connection to the liminal time of adolescence disappeared in this period. However, the care of the self still marked a space not entirely structured or governed by the status quo. Although practised by many, the care of the self and the philosophical life was often understood (and criticized) as an opposition to the status quo. In his 114th letter to Lucillius, Seneca opts for a comprehensive societal reform, which must begin with a philosophical cure (Seneca 1925, 314–16). Practising the care of the self potentially means to subject oneself to another truth. In this vein, the care of the self slowly turned into a passage into another life. This aspect of liminality became central to the Cynic's performance of the care of the self.

Dogs and scouts: the Cynic life as a scandalous manifestation of truth

Foucault analyses the Cynics and their way of life at the end of *Hermeneutics of the Subject* and then, more prominently, in his subsequent lecture series *The Government of Self and Others* and *The Courage of Truth* (Foucault 2005; 2010; 2011). In this third manifestation, the care of the self turns into a radical critique – one that I want to call a liminal critique. This is a form of critique that not only assesses with the intent of change, but that, also and mainly, has to be understood as a performance of a life not yet realized. It turns the Cynic's life into a passage into a different life.

Foucault mainly analyses the Cynics in the light of *parrhesia* and as part of what he calls a 'genealogy [of] political discourse', as well as a 'dramatics of true discourse' (Foucault 2010, 69).[17] The Greek word *parrhesia* originally meant to 'say everything', but it can also be translated as 'free-spokenness' or 'free speech' (43). In performing *parrhesia*, an individual is, in a nutshell, telling truth to power in a specific situation. Neither a rhetorical figure (as Foucault is eager to claim, and as especially contested by Melanie Möller, 2012) nor a kind of argumentation, *parrhesia* is rather the utterance of blunt and unadorned truth, thrown in the face of the other (Foucault 2010, 54). In speaking such truth, the *parrhesiast* ties himself to this truth and, since unpredictability is another of *parrhesia*'s core elements, takes a risk of potentially the utmost proportions. In Foucault's last two lectures, the Cynic life represents a third form of *parrhesia*, following discussions of political *parrhesia* of the Athenian *polis* and Socrates' irony. With the Cynics, a militant and revolutionary life, as Michael Hardt highlights (2010, 159), enters the stage. My discussion, however, will examine the Cynics in the light of the care of the self, which is understood as the condition and performance of *parrhesia* as an embodied, liminal critique.

The Cynics saw themselves as Socrates' true heirs. While Socrates described himself as a horse-fly constantly disturbing the besetting lethargy of Athens, the name Cynic literally refers to the Greek word *kynikos*, meaning dog-like (Foucault 2011, 242–3). Usually dressed in an overcoat and carrying a staff, the Cynic is a vagabond drifting through most parts of Greek and Roman antiquity (170). His feet are dirty, his beard ragged. Without spouse or family and a non-native to any fatherland, he is a free man under an open sky. The most famous Cynic is, of course, Diogenes of Sinope, who is usually depicted as living in a barrel. When the famous philosopher is approached by Alexander of Macedonia and granted a wish, he replies that Alexander should move out of his sun (Plutarch 1919, 259).

The Cynic lives the life of a dog. Living on the street, he is indifferent and beyond shame, reducing life to itself, beyond all conventions (Foucault 2011, 171). He is a citizen of only the cosmos, a true cosmopolite (Laertius 1925, 75). Almost every aspect of his life is public, be it eating or having sex. Like a dog's bark, his speech is sharp, direct and unflattering. This is no provocation for its own sake, but a dramatization of traditional philosophical principles of the true life. The principle of non-concealment was paramount. Already in Plato, a true life is a life that does not hold back: '[a]n unconcealed life would neither hide anything bad nor do anything bad, since it would not conceal anything' (Foucault 2011, 254). Natural desires cannot be evil and, hence, do not have to be concealed. Only acquired habits can be evil, because they are not given by nature.

The Cynics are a 'dramatization' of the scandal of truth (Foucault 2011, 253) and an 'extrapolation of the themes of the true life' (228). They live a transition. The Cynics are always and simultaneously inside and outside of society, as well as philosophy, inscribing themselves consciously to tradition and, at the same time, radicalizing philosophy to absurd proportions in order to challenge hypocrisy, abuse of power, moral decay and mendacity. The medium of this critique is not discourse but life itself: the Cynic life as the dramatic manifestation of truth. The critique itself consists of:

> getting people to condemn, reject, despise, and insult the very manifestation of what they accept, or claim to accept at the level of principles. It involves facing up to their anger when presenting them with the image of what they accept and value in thought, and at the same time reject and despise in their life. (Foucault 2011, 234)

Socrates has been described as *atopos*, as placeless: being part of society without actively taking part in the *polis*. Only this neglect of active participation gave him the independence to act as a public teacher of the care of the self (*Apology* 31 c–e; Plato 2017, 157–9; Foucault 2011, 78). In Cynicism, this relation to 'place' is further developed. Cynic life is a life of exile with a message – namely, that another life is possible, yet not effective. In reference to Epictetus' *Discourses*, Foucault writes that the Cynics exposed themselves to the most difficult tests and went beyond the margins of society. The Cynic was a 'night-watchman of his own thought' (Foucault 2011, 311) and a scout for society:

> It is these scouts of hardship, misfortune, and suffering who, on the one hand, will set especially tough and difficult tests for themselves but, as good scouts, will then return to their city in order to tell their fellow citizens that, after all, they should not worry themselves so much about those dangers they so greatly fear, since they themselves have experienced them. Sent as scouts, they faced up to these dangers and were able to vanquish them, and since they were able to vanquish them, so will the others be able to as well. (Foucault 2005, 441)

By constantly displaying that a true life is actually possible, the Cynic acts as a scandalous challenge to society, challenging others to take care of themselves by breaking with the current conventional limits.

The Cynic not only embodies a challenge and a rupture to society, but he also carries something other or exterior into the very heart of public life. The Cynic is not a fortune-teller who predicts Armageddon or revolution; he is neither preacher nor prophet. His subjectivity has incorporated the truth for which he speaks. He inscribes a difference and mode of transgression into society: the Cynic is the one who has left society, but still stays in its centre; he is proof of another life, which is yet to be collectively realized. He embodies a utopian mode of life: something that has no place. This makes the Cynic a figure of liminality, a life on the threshold between the status quo, and a mode of life considered impossible to be actually lived. Paradoxically, he lives the wrong life correctly, to borrow from Adorno (2006, 39). Kelly E. Happe connects this aspect of Cynic life with Occupy Wall Street: instead of discursively arguing for another life, activists turned Zuccotti Park 'into a public space of speech, care, and labor organizing' in 2011, 'a mini-city based on mutual aid' (Happe 2015, 214).

As a critic, the Cynic is speaking in the name of a truth, which is not recognized by the status quo – although he shaped his life according to commonly praised principles. The Cynic's critique is not uttered from a transcendental point of view, but it is rather situated in the here and now. Still, he occupies and utters his truth from a position that is not recognized. As an embodied critique, incorporated by and through an ongoing practice and cultivation of his relation to the world and his current historical situation, the Cynic is what he claims. He (almost satirically) already subjects his life to a truth, which is commonly considered to be aloof and utopian. In its radical liminality, his existence testifies to the fact that other formations of experience are possible, and that they can constitute other types of subjectivity.

For good reason, many tropes and aspects of Cynicism have been adopted in Christianity, especially by early martyrs. Yet Foucault goes further, as he proposes to consider Cynicism as a transhistorical category that plays the role of 'establishing a relationship between forms of existence and manifestation of the truth' (Foucault 2011, 180). Foucault brings the Cynic manifestation of the true life as a radically different life in relation with revolutionist practices – Russian nihilism, anarchism, as well as terrorism, and the life of the modern artist as a life that expresses the internal human forces underneath subjectivity and culture (184). Already in *The Hermeneutics of the Subject*, and in his discussion of *metanoia* (conversion) in the context of the idea of becoming free from imprints and bad habits via technologies of the self, Foucault leaps forward and looks at the role of conversion in nineteenth-century politics: '[o]ne day the history of what could be called revolutionary subjectivity should be written' (Foucault 2005, 208).[18] Unfortunately, the project of revolutionary subjectivity remains unfinished and the referenced lectures are merely rough drafts (Foucault himself called his consideration of Cynicism as a transcultural category 'no more than a stroll, an excursus, a wander', 2011, 177).

In 'What is critique?' (1978), Foucault defines critique as an expression of the intention to *not* be governed *like that*. He highlights that critique is not about not being governed at all, but about not being governed in the name of specific principles, objectives or procedures – or simply not by those who are governing (Foucault 2007, 44–5). Unable to be founded in an already existent right or convention, this form of radical critique speaks in the name of a future unable to enforce its claims (42). Foucault describes critique as a 'bundle of relationships', power, truth and subject 'tied to one another' (47). Critique, then, means to 'question truth on its effects of power and question power on its discourses of truth' (47).

It means to voluntarily insubordinate, it means the 'desubjugation of the subject' (47), to not accept the limits of the subject already given, to not accept the options of existence that are laid out. Judith Butler pointed out that, in the act of desubjugation, a new mode of existence is risked, unsupported by the current regime (Butler 2004, 306). With Foucault, critique is not only another way of judging, but it also brings 'into relief the very framework of evaluation itself' (Butler 2004, 307). This is precisely what the Cynic does. In his life, the Cynic cultivates an ethical experience that is not, or not yet, regulated or defined by the status quo, an experience that transcends the epistemological field (Vogelmann 2012, 228). In this indefiniteness, he dramatizes liminality.

Foucault's discussion of critique continues in his reading of Kant's 'Answering the question: What is Enlightenment?'. In 1984, Foucault argues that the 'critique of what we are' must not only involve the analysis of the 'limits imposed on us'; it also has to 'experiment with the possibility of going beyond them' (Foucault 1997b, 317). Critique 'consists of analyzing and reflecting upon limits' (Foucault 1984, 315). Especially in the late twentieth century, Foucault highlights, this analysis has to 'transform ... into a practical critique that takes the form of a possible crossing-over [*franchissement*]' (315). This is exactly what the Cynic's liminality does: instead of only engaging in discourse, challenging the normative grounds of the status quo, he transcends cultural and societal limits through his existence.

Conclusion

The practice of the care of the self can be fruitfully described with the concept of passage and the phases of liminality that passages engender. In its Platonic form, the care of the self constitutes and shapes the passage from youth to adulthood. In Stoic exercises, it shapes life itself as an ongoing inner journey, leading subjects away from unwanted imprints acquired in early life. Finally, embodied as the liminal critique of the Cynics, the care of the self cultivates a peculiar in-betweenness: rooted in the here and now, yet pointing to a different life that is already experimentally embodied.

The value in applying passage and liminality to Foucault's understanding of the care of the self can be summarized in three points. First, liminality highlights the specific mode of critique that the Cynic life displays. It not only provides the basis for an account of Foucault's interest in ancient philosophy, but it is also useful for understanding the concept of immanent critique. In several shorter pieces such as 'What is critique?' and 'What is Enlightenment?', Foucault sketches a form of critique that does not rely on transcendental truth, but stays entangled with what it deals with (Foucault 2007; 1984). Beyond the interpretation of Foucault's line of thinking, this interpretation of Cynic critique can be extended in various ways – for instance, in a dialogue with Donna Haraway's post-humanist concept of critique (1997), or with Seyla Benhabib's concept of 'social critique' (1992, 227), as Kristen Kennedy has suggested (1999, 27, 41–2).

Second, in his analysis of technologies of the self, Foucault mainly looks at how an *'ethical substance'* is formed through *'elaboration'* and *'ethical work'*, and which *'mode[s] of subjection'* are used to achieve a certain *'telos'* (Foucault 1990, 26–7, emphasis in the original). The concept of liminality adds to this scheme, as it sheds light on the social embeddedness of self-practices and the connection between self-practices and social hierarchy (both in Hellenism and Plato's *Alcibiades*). It also works as a schema to describe their concrete performance. Foucault was mainly interested in what an ethics that is not structured by codes and laws could look like – in this regard, the in-depth study of ancient philosophical practices often shifts to the sidelines, but it is crucial to think about self-practices beyond the frame of antiquity.

Third, passage and liminality can open the care of the self for broader research interests. In his investigations, Foucault mainly refers to the terminology of his sources – for instance, the Greek term *metanoia*, or the conversion to the true life, central to Stoic and Cynic philosophy, as well as to Christianity. In doing so, Foucault's analysis becomes rather detailed and specific. As a concept originally from anthropology, passage and liminality can open Foucault's discussion for interdisciplinary and intercultural comparisons on practices that aim to transform subjectivity. On many occasions, Foucault seems to be interested in the manifold practices and techniques developed by different cultures (for instance, he draws upon his visit to a Japanese Zen temple in 1978). Liminality and passage could help to recover this 'treasury of devices, techniques, ideas, procedures' among 'the cultural inventions of mankind' (Foucault 1982, 261). Foucault continues and clarifies that these practices 'cannot exactly be reactivated but at least constitute, or help to constitute, a certain point of view which can be very useful as a tool for analyzing what's going on now – and to change it' (261).

Rooted in anthropology, the concept of liminality has already been applied productively to many different cultures and practices. In *The Ritual Process: Structure and antistructure*, Victor Turner looked at examples as diverse as the community of St Francis, Ndembu rituals and hippies of the twentieth century.[19] In his studies, Turner paid close attention to ritualistically induced reflections, and examined how practices and techniques bring about manifold cognitive transformations (Turner 1967, 103). The concept of liminality could therefore contribute to an expansion of the history of philosophy in Foucault's fashion – as a 'history of forms, modes, and styles of life' (Foucault 2011, 210) that contributes to the comprehensive project of cross- or intercultural philosophy and the study of culture.

Notes

1. See especially the first lecture, 'The government of self and others', held on 5 January 1983, as well as the interview 'The ethics of the concern for self as a practice of freedom' from January 1984 (Foucault 1997a, 281). Many scholars have contributed to this debate, defending Foucault's self-assessment (McGushin 2007; Elden 2016; Deleuze 1988; Allen 2003), or arguing against the coherence of his oeuvre (Flynn 1985; Dreyfus and Rabinow 1982; Dews 1989).
2. Since the access to philosophy and politics in Greek and Roman antiquity was given to men, this chapter mostly refers to that gender.
3. A short note on ritual in Foucault's writings: although there are a few publications on the notion of ritual in Foucault (for instance, on rituals of juridical institutions such as punishment or examination, Shapiro 2005; McCall 2016), Foucault's thoughts generally kept a distance from the concept. This is likely due to the prominent use of ritual by Durkheim and his successors, as well as the *Annales* School – from which Foucault also kept his distance (McCall 2016, 57).
4. See especially the comprehensive collected volume by Axel Honneth and Martin Saar (2003), Heubel (2002), and Zamora and Behrent (2016).
5. Regarding Foucault's concept of power and the way subjectivity is produced, see especially his concept of the *dispositive* in the fourth chapter of *The History of Sexuality, Volume 1: The will to knowledge*: 'The deployment of sexuality' (Foucault 1998).
6. Foucault concisely discusses the development of the care of the self and various philosophical exercises from Socrates to Christianity in 'Technologies of the self' (Foucault 1988).
7. In this definition, Foucault mainly builds on Plutarch (Foucault 2005, 237).
8. Foucault discusses the origins of the care of the self briefly in *The Hermeneutics of the Subject* (Foucault 2005, 46–50). I will not be able to address the critique formulated against Foucault's reading of ancient philosophy. A thorough and critical reconstruction of the second and third volume of *The History of Sexuality* has been brought forward by Wolfgang Detel (2005). Pierre Hadot, who surely had an influence on Foucault, criticized Foucault's reading of the care of the self as being too strongly focused on ethics and, particularly, on the self; see Chapter 7: 'Reflections on the idea of the "cultivation of the self"' in *Philosophy as a Way of Life* (Hadot 2010).
9. Foucault discusses this especially in his lecture on 16 February 1983 in 'The government of self and others' (Foucault 2010, 223).
10. See the first hour of Foucault's lecture on 6 January 1982, 'The hermeneutics of the subject'. Looking back from our own present, Foucault proclaims the 'Cartesian moment' to be mainly essential for the disqualification of the care of the self: with Descartes, the self-evidence of the subject becomes the beginning of modern philosophy (Foucault 2005, 14). This was a crucial disruption in the long tradition of spirituality based on the assumption that the subject must first undergo a transformation to access truth (15). A few pages later, he writes: 'I think the modern age of the history of truth begins when knowledge itself and knowledge alone gives access to the truth. That is to say, it is when the philosopher (or the scientist, or simply someone

who seeks the truth) can recognize the truth and have access to it in himself and solely through his activity of knowing, without anything else being demanded of him and without him having to change or alter his being as subject' (17).

11   In *The History of Sexuality. Volume 2: The use of pleasures* Foucault writes: '[b]ut while the boy, because of his peculiar charm, could be a prey that men might pursue without causing a scandal or a problem, one had to keep in mind that the day would come when he would have to be a man, to exercise powers and responsibilities, so that obviously he could then no longer be an object of pleasure – but then, to what extent could he have been such an object?' (Foucault 1990, 220–1).

12   See especially Foucault, *The History of Sexuality. Volume 2: The use of pleasures*, Part One: 'The moral problematization of pleasures' (Foucault 1990).

13   Sellars shows in detail that the term τεχνη περι τον βιον and the concept of an art of living is mainly present in Stoic philosophy (Foucault 2005, 83; Sellars 2003, 54).

14   Democritus already wrote in fragment B31 that philosophy should free the soul from passions, just as medicine heals the defects of the body (Diels and Kranz 1966, 416; Horn 2014, 22).

15   Sellars describes Aurelius' aim as follows: 'a perspective that takes as its point of departure the large-scale process and movements of the cosmos itself, a perspective far removed from the first-person perspective of ordinary human affairs' (Sellars 2003, 151).

16   Foucault presents a classification of philosophy and spiritual exercises in his discussion of the etymology of the care of the self (Foucault 2005, 84–6) and in his analysis of philosophical ascesis in his lecture on 24 March 1982 (Foucault 2005, 453–89). Christoph Horn (2014) presents a detailed typology of ancient exercises, while Lars Leeten (2019) has recently analysed the interaction of various exercises in ancient self-cultivation.

17   The publications on Foucault's *parrhesia* are countless in philosophy, classics and political sciences, yet also literary studies, education and (art) history have adopted the concept. In philosophy and cultural studies, *parrhesia* is approached in different ways: analysing Occupy Wall Street (Happe 2015), thinking about the philosopher's relation to power (McCormick 2009) and contributing to the framework of Black philosophy (Havis 2013). The collected volume *Parrhesia: Foucault und der Mut zur Wahrheit* contains articles on Foucault's reading of *parrhesia* from various disciplines (Gehring and Gelhard 2012). Whereas authors such as Nancy Luxon suggest a comprehensive interpretation of Foucault's critical thinking, starting with the concept of *parrhesia* (Luxon 2004; 2008), others have pointed out the ambivalence of Foucault's reading (despite its value for a theory of subjectivity; Posselt 2013), and have published a disillusioning examination of the critical value of *parrhesia* for theories of democracy (Suntrup 2018). Seitz and Posselt (2018), like Suntrup, not only discuss *parrhesia* in Foucault and its relevance for critical theory, but also – in the context of *parrhesia* – look at strategies of 'word seizure' by right-wing activists.

18   Foucault also mentions festivals and carnival as 'manifestations of Cynic life' (Foucault 2011, 187) – both are among the standard examples of liminal events (Thomassen 2014, 8–10; Turner 1982, 42–4) and heterotopic spaces.

19   See Chapters 3 and 4 in Turner's *The Ritual Process: Structure and anti-structure* (1995).

References

Adorno, Theodor W. 2006. *Minima Moralia: Reflections from damaged life*, translated by Edmond F.N. Jephcott. London: Verso.

Allen, Amy. 2003. 'Foucault and Enlightenment: A critical reappraisal', *Constellations* 10 (2): 180–98.

Benhabib, Seyla. 1992. *Situating the Self: Gender, community, and postmodernism in contemporary ethics*. Cambridge: Polity.

Butler, Judith. 2004. 'What is critique? An essay on Foucault's virtue'. In *The Judith Butler Reader*, edited by Sara Salih, 302–22. Malden, MA: Blackwell.

Deleuze, Gilles. 1988. *Foucault*, translated by Seán Hand. Minneapolis: University of Minnesota Press.

Detel, Wolfgang. 2005. *Foucault and Classical Antiquity: Power, ethics, and knowledge*, translated by David Wigg-Wolf. Cambridge: Cambridge University Press.

Dews, Peter. 1989. 'The return of the subject in late Foucault', *Radical Philosophy* 51: 37–41.
Diels, Herrmann and Walther Kranz. 1966. *Die Fragmente der Vorsokratiker: Griechisch und Deutsch, Zweiter Band*. Dublin: Weidmann.
Dreyfus, Hubert L. and Paul Rabinow, eds. 1982. *Michel Foucault: Beyond structuralism and hermeneutics*. Chicago: University of Chicago Press.
Elden, Stuart. 2016. *Foucault's Last Decade*. Cambridge: Polity.
Flynn, Thomas. 1985. 'Truth and subjectivation in the later Foucault', *Journal of Philosophy* 82: 531–40.
Foucault, Michel. 1982. 'On the genealogy of ethics: An overview of work in progress'. In *Michel Foucault: Beyond structuralism and hermeneutics*, edited by Hubert L. Dreyfus and Paul Rabinow, 229–52. Chicago: University of Chicago Press.
Foucault, Michel. 1984. 'What is Enlightenment?'. In *The Foucault Reader*, edited by Paul Rabinow, translated by Catherine Porter, 32–50. New York: Pantheon.
Foucault, Michel. 1988a. *The History of Sexuality. Volume 3: The care of the self*, translated by Robert Hurley. New York: Vintage.
Foucault, Michel. 1988b. 'Technologies of the self'. In *Technologies of the Self: A seminar with Michel Foucault*, edited by Luther H. Martin, Huck Gutman and Patrick H. Hutton, 16–49. London: Tavistock.
Foucault, Michel. 1990. *The History of Sexuality. Volume 2: The use of pleasures*, translated by Robert Hurley. New York: Vintage.
Foucault, Michel. 1995. *Discipline and Punish: The birth of prison*, translated by Alan Sheridan. New York: Vintage.
Foucault, Michel. 1997a. 'The ethics of the concern for self as a practice of freedom'. In *Ethics: Subjectivity and truth*, edited by Paul Rabinow, translated by P. Aranov and D. McGrawth, 1: 281–301. New York: New York Press.
Foucault, Michel. 1997b. 'What is Enlightenment?'. In *Ethics: Subjectivity and truth*, edited by Paul Rabinow, translated by Catherine Porter, 1: 303–19. New York: New York Press.
Foucault, Michel. 1998. *The History of Sexuality. Volume 1: The will to knowledge*, translated by Robert Hurley. London: Penguin.
Foucault, Michel. 2005. *The Hermeneutics of the Subject: Lectures at the Collège de France 1981–1982*, edited by Frédéric Gros, translated by Graham Burchell. New York: Picador.
Foucault, Michel. 2007. 'What is critique?'. In *The Politics of Truth*, edited by Sylvère Lotringer, translated by Lysa Hochroth, 41–81. Los Angeles: Semiotext(e).
Foucault, Michel. 2010. *The Government of Self and Others: Lectures at the Collège de France 1982–1983*, edited by Frédéric Gros, translated by Graham Burchell. Basingstoke: Palgrave Macmillan.
Foucault, Michel. 2011. *The Courage of the Truth (Government of Self and Others II): Lectures at the Collège de France 1983–1984*, edited by Frédéric Gros, translated by Graham Burchell. Basingstoke: Palgrave Macmillan.
Foucault, Michel and Richard Sennett. 1981. 'Sexuality and solitude', *London Review of Books* 3 (9): 3–7.
Gehring, Petra and Andreas Gelhard, eds. 2012. *Parrhesia: Foucault und der Mut zur Wahrheit*. Zürich: Diaphanes.
Hadot, Pierre. 2010. *Philosophy as a Way of Life: Spiritual exercises from Socrates to Foucault*, edited by Arnold I. Davidson, translated by Michael Chase. Malden: Blackwell.
Happe, Kelly E. 2015. 'Parrhēsia, biopolitics, and Occupy', *Philosophy & Rhetoric* 48 (2): 211–23.
Haraway, Donna. 1997. *ModestWitness@Second_Millenium: FemaleMan_Meets_OncoMouse: Feminism and technoscience*. New York: Routledge.
Hardt, Michael. 2010. 'Militant life', *New Left Review* 64: 151–60.
Havis, Devonya N. 2013. 'The Parrhesiastic enterprise of Black philosophy', *The Black Scholar* 43 (4): 52–8.
Heubel, Fabian. 2002. *Das Dispositiv der Kreativität*. Darmstadt: Wissenschaftliche Buchgesellschaft.
Honneth, Axel and Martin Saar. 2003. *Michel Foucault: Zwischenbilanz einer Rezeption: Frankfurter Foucault-Konferenz 2001*. Frankfurt am Main: Suhrkamp.
Horn, Christoph. 2014. *Antike Lebenskunst: Glück und Moral von Sokrates bis zu den Neuplatonikern*. 3rd edn. Munich: C.H. Beck.
Kennedy, Kristen. 1999. 'Cynic rhetoric: The ethics and tactics of resistance', *Rhetoric Review* 18 (1): 26–45.

Laertius, Diogenes. 1925. *Lives of Eminent Philosophers:, Volume 2*, translated by Robert Drew Hicks. London: Heinemann.
Leeten, Lars. 2019. *Redepraxis als Lebenspraxis: Die diskursive Kultur der antiken Ethik*. Freiburg im Breisgau: Alber.
Luxon, Nancy. 2004. 'Truthfulness, risk, and trust in the late lectures of Michel Foucault', *Inquiry* 47 (5): 464–89.
Luxon, Nancy. 2008. 'Ethics and subjectivity: Practices of self-governance in the late lectures of Michel Foucault', *Political Theory* 36 (3): 377–402.
McCall, Corey. 2016. 'Rituals of conduct and counter-conduct', *Foucault Studies* 21: 52–79.
McCormick, Samuel. 2009. 'The political identity of the philosopher: Resistance, relative power, and the endurance of potential', *Philosophy & Rhetoric* 42 (1): 72–91.
McGushin, Edward F. 2007. *Foucault's Askēsis: An introduction to the philosophical life*. Evanston, IL: Northwestern University Press.
Menke, Christoph. 2003. 'Two kinds of practice: On the relation between social discipline and the aesthetics of existence', *Constellations* 10 (2): 199–210.
Möller, Melanie. 2012. 'Am Nullpunkt der Rhetorik? Michel Foucault und die parrhesiastische Rede'. In *Parrhesia: Foucault und der Mut zur Wahrheit*, edited by Petra Gehring and Andreas Gelhard, 103–20. Zürich: Diaphanes.
Nussbaum, Martha C. 1994. *The Therapy of Desire: Theory and practice in Hellenistic ethics*. Princeton, NJ: Princeton University Press.
Plato. 1925. *Lysis. Symposium. Gorgias*, translated by W.R.M. Lamb. Cambridge, MA: Harvard University Press.
Plato. 2017. *Euthyphro. Apology. Crito. Phaedo*, translated by Chris Emlyn-Jones and William Preddy. Cambridge, MA: Harvard University Press.
Plutarch. 1919. *Lives, Volume VII: Demosthenes and Cicero. Alexander and Caesar*, translated by Bernadotte Perrin. Cambridge, MA: Harvard University Press.
Posselt, Gerald. 2013. 'Wahrsprechen, Wortergreifung und "Collateral Murder": Zur Aktualität von Michel Foucaults Begriff der Parrhesia', *Rhetorik* 32 (1): 71–92.
Schäfer, Thomas. 1995. *Reflektierte Vernunft: Michel Foucaults philosophisches Projekt einer antitotalitären Macht- und Wahrheitskritik*. Frankfurt am Main: Suhrkamp.
Seitz, Sergej and Gerald Posselt. 2018. 'Sprachen des Widerstands: Zur Normativität politischer Artikulation bei Foucault und Rancière'. In *Foucault und das Politische: Transdisziplinäre Impulse für die Politische Theorie der Gegenwart*, edited by Oliver Marchart and Renate Martinsen, 185–209. Wiesbaden: Springer VS.
Sellars, John. 2003. *The Art of Living: The Stoics on the nature and function of philosophy*. Aldershot: Ashgate.
Seneca, Lucius Annaeus. 1920. *Epistles, Volume II: Epistles 66–92*, translated by Richard M. Gummere. Cambridge, MA: Harvard University Press.
Seneca, Lucius Annaeus. 1925. *Epistles, Volume III: Epistles 93–124*, translated by Richard M. Gummere. Cambridge, MA: Harvard University Press.
Shapiro, Gary. 2005. *Archaeologies of Vision: Foucault and Nietzsche on seeing and saying*. Chicago: University of Chicago Press.
Shusterman, Richard. 2008. *Body Consciousness: A philosophy of mindfulness and somaesthetics*. New York: Cambridge University Press.
Shusterman, Richard. 2012. *Thinking through the Body: Essays in somaesthetics*. Cambridge: Cambridge University Press.
Sloterdijk, Peter. 2013. *You Must Change Your Life*, translated by Wieland Hoban. Cambridge: Polity.
Stiegler, Bernd. 2012. 'Unzeitgemäße Betrachtungen und philosophische Episkopie: Philosophie und Geschichte in Michel Foucaults parrhesia-Vorlesungen'. In *Parrhesia: Foucault und der Mut zur Wahrheit*, edited by Petra Gehring and Andreas Gelhard, 49–62. Zürich: Diaphanes.
Suntrup, Jan Christoph. 2018. 'Die "Dramatik des wahren Diskurses"'. In *Foucault und das politische: Transdisziplinäre Impulse für die Politische Theorie der Gegenwart*, edited by Oliver Marchart and Renate Martinsen, 329–52. Wiesbaden: Springer VS.
Tacitus. 1937. *Annals: Books 13–15*, translated by John Jackson. Cambridge, MA: Harvard University Press.
Thomassen, Bjørn. 2014. *Liminality and the Modern: Living through the in-between*. London: Routledge.

Turner, Victor. 1967. 'Betwixt and between: The liminal period in rites de passage'. In *The Forest of Symbols: Aspects of Ndembu ritual*, 93–111. Ithaca, NY: Cornell University Press.

Turner, Victor. 1982. *From Ritual to Theatre: The human seriousness of play*. New York: Performing Arts Journal Publications.

Turner, Victor. 1995. *The Ritual Process: Structure and anti-structure*. New Brunswick, NJ: Aldine Transaction.

Van Gennep, Arnold. 1960. *The Rites of Passage*, translated by Monika B. Vizedom and Gabrielle L. Caffee. London: Routledge & Kegan Paul.

Vogelmann, Frieder. 2012. 'Foucaults Parrhesia – Philosophie als Politik der Wahrheit'. In *Parrhesia: Foucault und der Mut zur Wahrheit*, edited by Petra Gehring and Andreas Gelhard, 203–29. Zürich: Diaphanes.

Zamora, Daniel and Michael C. Behrent, eds. 2016. *Foucault and Neoliberalism*. Cambridge: Polity.

9
Traversing Hell: Carl Gustav Jung and the practice of visionary travelling

Tommaso Alessandro Priviero

In this chapter, the concept of 'passage' is examined by drawing mainly on the ideas of the Swiss psychiatrist and founder of analytical psychology, Carl Gustav Jung (1875–1961), while focusing on his most important work, the *Red Book* or *Liber Novus*. The object of interest is the motif of travelling through Hell, a liminal experience of self-transformation. Transformation as such, one may say, represents the cornerstone of Jung's dynamic vision of psychic energetics. Therefore, in this context, a notion such as liminal passage (the transitional 'experience of a threshold', from Latin, *'limen'*, 'threshold', but also 'harbour', 'refuge') denotes the subject's coming to terms with a special condition and practice in which self-transformation can take place. In other words, it is what Mircea Eliade calls 'a break in the homogeneity' of time and space that paves the way for the experience of the 'sacred' (Eliade 1987, 37). In the ancient mysteries or rituals of passage, the hero descends into a dark cave, crater or Hell, in order to give birth to a new consciousness and gain access to a new stage of life. The symbolism of passage plays a fundamental role in the context, indicating transition, movement, mobility, initiation, renewal, progress, change, diversity, transgression of norms and, most importantly, self-regeneration (passing from one's previous identity or mental state to a new and higher one). Eliade essentially defines the act of entering into a liminal sacred space as equivalent to 'a basic change in existential condition; the novice emerges from his ordeal endowed with a totally different being from that which he possessed before his initiation; he has become *another*' (Eliade 2012, 18). Analogously, Jung argues, man's life is regulated by archetypal stages of continuous transformation that far transcend the narrowness of the personal 'ego' or conscious will. In this sense, however little noticed thus far, the concept of liminal passage provides a valuable perspective for highlighting several aspects of Jung's hermeneutics. The 'limen', in the works of Jung, is mostly referred to in relation to the activities of the 'sub-liminal' mind, a constantly evolving order of perceptions beneath the threshold of the habitual or ordinary self. The idea of the subliminal mind, first conceived by Frederic W.H. Myers in 1886, and taken up later by William James in *The Varieties of Religious Experience* (1902), and by Théodore Flournoy, denotes a creative, transformative and healing potential residing in 'unconscious' content, revealing itself in dreams, meditation and visions. Man's capacity to release this material and integrate it in life leads to a proper journey of increasing self-awareness, technically referred to, in the Jungian world, as the 'individuation process'.

As examined by Craig E. Stephenson (2009), Jung's psychological approach to the liminal establishes a few compelling analogies with the seminal works of anthropologists and ethnographers such as Arnold van Gennep (who coined the term 'liminality' in 1909; van Gennep 1960), Victor Turner and Edward Schieffelin, not to mention figures such as James Frazer and Lucien Lévy-Bruhl, whom Jung extensively read and cited. The main difference is that, for anthropologists, liminality is primarily associated with a change in social status ('social liminality'); for Jung, it is associated with a shift in thinking. The liminal represents man's direct experience of different stages (horizontal axis) and degrees (vertical axis) of psychic reality. It is a symbol of plurality, complexity and, in one word, self-transformation. For Jung, the energy which is found in any system, including the human one, gradually becomes spent and must be somehow renewed. Man must find a practice of some sort to live and renew communion between himself and the laws of nature. In this regard, the experience of passage instantly evokes an intuitive understanding of the 'mobility' of reality, which Henri Bergson summarizes as follows: 'not *things* made, but things in the making, not self-maintaining *states*, but only changing states, exist. Rest is never more than apparent, or, rather, relative' (Bergson 1999, 49, emphasis in the original). For Bergson, one becomes aware of the mobility of reality (an idea very close to the Buddhist principle of the impermanence of all things) not through logic or conceptualization, but rather through a form of 'intellectual sympathy' for life, which he calls 'intuition' (51). Jung similarly interprets the function of sub-liminal imagination, which allows man to give up attachment to the ego and enter a liminal space of creative potential. Not by chance, one of the favourite and most cited Greek deities in the pantheon of Jung is Hermes, the god of boundaries and their transgression, as well as the protector of travellers to the underworld.

The liminal quality of the *Red Book*

In Jung's works, the archetypal pattern of visiting the underworld is not only a highly relevant matter for psychological discussion, but a first-hand experience. In a period stretching from 1913 to the late 1920s, Jung embarked on a visionary experiment – entitled *Liber Novus* (the *New Book*), yet popularly known as Jung's *Red Book* (2009) – which he repeatedly describes as a 'visit to Hell', or a *katabasis*, the cathartic journey to Hades undertaken by several heroes in ancient Greek and Latin mythologies. The appearance of previously unpublished records of this experiment in 2009 has revolutionized the field of Jung studies, almost half a century after their author's death.

Shortly before the commencement of this experiment, Jung was about forty, at the peak of honours and success. He was an acclaimed man of science, a professor at the University of Zurich, and president of the International Psychoanalytical Association, established in Nuremberg in 1910. He published *Transformations and Symbols of the Libido* (1911/1912),[1] a comparative study of an impressive amount of mythological and religious symbols, representing a crucial turning point away from Freud's theories, and presided over the foundation of analytical psychology, or 'complex psychology' ('komplexe Psychologie'), as he preferred to call his psychotherapeutic method. He recounts the experience of writing the whole book as a forceful eruption of psychic transformation, which, approximately one year later, was described in the *Red Book* (Jung 2012, 27–36). Shortly thereafter, Jung began to experience a growing state of inner turmoil that culminated in a series of waking visions, which were the beginning to what later became known as his 'confrontation with the unconscious' (Jung 1962, 174). In response to this situation, he developed a technique of creative visualization, adapted from the long-standing artistic and spiritual tradition of 'active imagination', which later served as one of the most recognizable psychotherapeutic tools in analytical psychology. In a liminal state between sleep and waking ('hypnagogia'), he plunged into deep meditational states in order to let psychic content appear as spontaneously as possible. At first, he noted his visions in private notebooks, the *Black Books*, for personal use, which were only first published in 2020. Then he began revising his material by interpreting the visions according to his then evolving psychological model. Later on, he added illustrations to the text, and began to faithfully transcribe the whole work into a quasi-medieval calligraphic manuscript. The final outcome (the *Red Book*) is a large folio volume of more than six hundred pages, with gothic characters, miniatures, historiated initials and paintings, which gives the work a notable resemblance to William Blake's illuminated books.

Against this backdrop, the *Red Book*, an incredibly rich, complex and multifaceted work, conveys a fundamental liminal quality. By recording a life-changing method of self-exploration, Jung's notebooks furnished him with a proper '*temenos*' (an ancient Greek term used to designate a piece of land cut off from common uses and dedicated to a shrine, which in this case indicates a 'mental space' marked off from ordinary thinking and allotted to exceptional meditative experiences). Later on, on the basis of what he first explored within himself, Jung often guided patients and pupils in explorations of the liminal quality of their own creative and transformative potentials, in the dedicated space of the psychotherapeutic setting. Among numerous themes which can be related to the liminal quality of the *Red Book*, the one which we will explore in the following pages is 'Hell'. In Jung's 'book of visions', Hell should not be understood as an afterlife abode of condemnation, but rather as a present living condition of utter bewilderment, encompassing a momentous existential change. As in the imagery of secret depths, cavities, holes and extreme isolation that accompany the adepts in the ancient mysteries, Jung's descent to Hell in the *Red Book* heralds the threatening emergence of a radical psychological reversal. And, just as in the mysteries, the time spent in the dark abyss was meant to enact a ritual death before the passage into a new life, such as narrated in Apuleius' *Metamorphoses*. What Jung initially perceived as a deeply critical time leading him to the brink of madness eventually came to represent the source of the most creative and significant period of his life:

> The years of which I have spoken to you, when I pursued the inner images, were the most important time of my life. Everything else is to be derived from this. It began at that time and the later details hardly matter anymore. My entire life consisted in elaborating what had burst forth from the unconscious and flooded me like an

enigmatic stream and threatened to break me. That was the stuff and material for more than one life. (Jung 1962, in Jung 2009, vii)

Grappling with his visions of Hell, Jung was in good company. He had in mind those who, since Odysseus and Aeneas, claimed to have visited similar places. Among them are two particularly striking examples. These are, first, Dante's journey to *Inferno* in the *Commedia* (Alighieri 1987), in which Hell, as gloriously portrayed by Botticelli, is shaped by nine circles progressively going from the widest to the smallest, where Lucifer abides, and, second, Christ's descent into the Land of the Dead, in the less popular apocryphal Apocalypse of Peter (Elliott 1993). In using these sources, Jung contrasts the Christian theological understanding of Hell as a place of eternal condemnation with a Blakean conception of Hell as a place of mental purification and transformation. The former view envisages a fixed, irreversible condition of immobility. The latter one evokes a dynamic, temporary situation leading to a process of change, as suitably described by images of circles, levels, thresholds, doors, transitions, initiations and narratives of passages – all of which characterize Jung's material.

Radical mental change

At the very beginning of the *Red Book*, Jung points out that, in the fortieth year of his life, desire for 'honour, power, and every human happiness' suddenly ceased and 'horror came over' him (Jung 2009, 231–2). This moment of radical conversion brings forth another crucial nuance to the current discussion of passage. It marks the pivotal crisis of a successful intellectual and man of science, which leads him towards a new phase of life. It is a radical transition from the 'habitual centre of personal energy' (one of William James's definitions of the 'ego', James 1902, 193) to the unfolding of something completely different, yet seemingly threatening. Jung's opening words echo a biblical passage from Isaiah: 'I said in the cutting off of my days, I shall go to the gates of the grave' (Isaiah 38:10; Carroll and Prickett 2008, 799). The 'cutting off' of days refers in this context to the traditional division of life in two halves, according to which the thirty-fifth year would represent the exact symbolical half of what man's lifespan is said to be in the Psalms, that is, seventy years: '[t]he days of our years are three-score years and ten' (Psalms 90:10; Carroll and Prickett 2008, 691). More famously, the same biblical motif of travelling to Hell at the midpoint of life inspires the illustrious beginning of Dante's

Commedia, in which the Florentine poet sets off in search of the beloved Beatrice on a visionary journey into Hell, Purgatory and Paradise, with the help of the Roman poet Virgil:

> Half way along the road we have to go,
> I found myself obscured in a great forest,
> Bewildered, and I knew I had lost my way. (*Inferno*, I, 1–3, Alighieri 1987, 43)[2]

Well aware of this reference, in a lecture at the Swiss Federal Institute of Technology in 1935, Jung claims that 'we can learn a great deal from Dante', by noting the following:

> He began to write his 'Divine Comedy' in his thirty-fifth year. The thirty-fifth year is a turning point in life – it is an interesting fact that Christ died in his thirty-fourth year ... A point in life exists at about the thirty-fifth year when things begin to change, it is the first moment of the shadow side of life, of the going down to death. It is clear that Dante found this point and those who have read *Zarathustra* will know that Nietzsche discovered it. When this turning point comes people meet it in several ways: some turn away from it; others plunge into it; and something important happens to yet others from the outside. If we do not see a thing, Fate does it to us. (Hannah 1959, 223)

Therefore, at the beginning of his self-explorations, Jung finds that he is involved in the same liminal experience of change that inspired Dante's journey. This is a critical phase of existential transformation (*Lebenswende*), which the ancient Greeks called *metanoia* ('radical mental changing'), and which William James relates to a fundamental principle of psychological and spiritual transformation (the phenomenon of 'conversion') (James 1902, 186–253). What is more, while heading to the gates of Hell, Dante appears to have another similar, controversial episode of transformation in mind, which is of great importance for Jung's experiences as well: the *metanoia* of Christ, whose crucifixion at the age of 33 occurs in the Gospels at the stroke of noon on Good Friday (Matthew 27:45–6; Mark 15:33; Luke 23:44), thus furnishing Dante with a primary model for his own descent to the Dead (Alighieri 2014, 744–6). In this episode, one can observe a remarkable analogy between the symbolical midpoint of life (the thirty-fifth year) and the midpoint of day (the stroke of noon). In *Wandlungen und Symbole der Libido*, Jung interprets the leitmotif of the hero's journey along similar lines, in an analogy with the development of solar myths:

> Just as the sun, guided by its own internal laws, ascends from morn till noon, and passing beyond the noon descends towards evening, leaving behind its splendor, and then sinks completely into the all-enveloping night, thus, too, does mankind follow his course according to immutable laws, and also sinks, after his course is completed, into night, in order to rise again in the morning, to a new cycle in his children. (Jung 1916, 191)

The first half of the hero's journey reflects the movement of the sun sailing over the sea, like a god being born anew every morning from the depths of the waters. This part of the myth depicts the awakening of the hero, or, in Jung's terms, the birth and rising of the ego over the realm of nature (Jung 2012, 30). The zenith of the heroic trajectory occurs at the stroke of noon, when the sun reaches the middle of the sky. Hence, this passage acquires the uncanny function of binding the brightest point of the day, the apotheosis of sensual life, to the appearance of death, the beginning of the sunset. Nietzsche calls noontide a 'death with waking eyes' and 'a very heavy kind of happiness', for 'he to whom an active and stormy morning of life is allotted, at the noontide of life feels his soul overcome by a strange longing for a rest that may last for months and years' (Nietzsche 1924, 350). Similarly, midday in Latin cultures is the 'sacred and dangerous' threshold par excellence, for the shadow of the sun is at its minimum length, and the worlds of darkness and light at maximum proximity (Caillois 1991, 91). Traditionally, midday provokes the incursion of a *demonio meridiano* (a 'noonday demon'), which Bernard of Clairvaux thought was nothing less than Lucifer himself (Scott-Macnab 2018). Thus, the midday of life is considered to be the favourite liminal context in which the living are granted access to the land of the Dead (Caillois 1991, 33). In light of this, the time Dante spends in Hell in the *Commedia*, before moving to the realms of *Purgatorio* and *Paradiso*, precisely mirrors the time and days of Christ's death, from Good Friday to Sunday (the time of the Passover, a capital rite of passage).[3] Analogously, if we return our focus to Jung's *Red Book*, Jung describes the puzzling burst of his visions as follows: '[t]his is really Good Friday, upon which the Lord died and descended into Hell and completed the mysteries' (Jung 2009, 304). With these words, he enigmatically refers, at least at first glance, to the Apostles' Creed, in which we get to know that, after his death, Christ visits Hell and, on the third day, arises from the Dead (Cross

1978, 75).[4] An astonishing representation of this event appears in a painting by an imitator of Hieronymus Bosch, which depicts Christ entering Hell in a citadel populated by naked humans, animals and demons of all sorts, disgorged from the mouth of a monster. As to the problematics presented by Christ's venture to a place of this sort, theologians since Thomas Aquinas (Goris 2018) have mainly answered by way of 'Christ's harrowing of Hell', that is, Christ descends to the land of the Dead and triumphantly conquers the power of evil. Be it as it may, no details are given about such a visit. Moreover, the theological understanding of the passage ingeniously opts for a distinction between *Inferno* (Hell), which supposedly indicates the eternal destiny of those condemned at the Final Judgement, and *inferos* (Hell, from *locus inferos*, the 'place beneath'), such as the Hell of the Old Testament, the Hebrew Sheol, the Greek Hades and the underworld of Odysseus, Aeneas and the heroes of European literature up to Dante. It follows that *inferos*, rather than *Inferno*, would be the place into which Christ descends for three days. At any rate, should one want to learn more about this event, one has to turn to apocryphal literature.

The function of the Antichrist

Christ's descent into Hell, which has never been recognized as part of the authoritative canon of Christian scriptures, is described in depth in several apocryphal accounts, such as the Gospel of Nicodemus (Hulme 1907), also known as Acts of Pilate after a section of its text, and the Apocalypse of Peter, a text Jung was very familiar with, especially thanks to Albrecht Dieterich's *Nekyia* (1913). The Apocalypse of Peter is an early apocalyptic Christian text (c.150 CE), not to be confused with the Gnostic Revelation of Peter, and the earliest extant paleo-Christian description of Hell (Elliott 1993, 595). It is framed as a series of visions of Heaven and Hell that Christ offers to the faithful Peter, including, among other things, blasphemers hanged by the tongue, apostates tormented by angels in a lake of mire, murderers cast in a gorge of 'creeping things', some people gnawing their tongues with fire in their mouths, some others in torment having heated iron in their eyes, and other similar delights (Elliott 1993, 603–11). The influence of Peter's account of Hell on subsequent Christian texts is considered to be great. As argued by Montague R. James, it inspired the *pandemonium* of demons and visions that appear in Dante's *Inferno*, in which a combination of Christian and traditional Greco-Roman representations of Hell attains its medieval apogee (Elliott 1993, 594–5).

The story began to widely circulate in the Middle Ages in many translations, spreading parallel to the rising status of the image of Satan in European medieval thought (Potestà and Rizzi 2019). At any rate, the extent to which Dante's text was informed by the apocryphal tradition at a literal level is for us a secondary aspect. Our primary concern is that Jung's long-standing confrontation with the apocryphal sources enables him to conceive of Christ's and Dante's journeys to the underworld as similar examples of the archetypal *nekyia*, and to bring such parallelism into his *own* experiences at the time of the *Red Book*, in which Jung's direct reading of Dante's *Commedia* plays a most significant role. That the apocryphal Christ's and Dante's travelling to Hell would essentially be comparable experiences cannot be overemphasized. It means, in short, to radically call into question the barrier between religious and poetic authority in spiritual matters. Or, in other words, to transfer such competence to the direct secular experience of poets and visionaries. For Jung, in fact, Dante's journey to Beatrice does not occur *ad imitationem Christi*, 'according to the model of Christ', as traditionally conceived from a theological perspective. It actually occurs *ad experientiam Christi*, 'according to the same experience of Christ', that is, by substantiating the subjective participation of the individual with the mystical realm, as declared by Dante himself, who ascribes his work to a type of sacred text (*Paradiso* XXV, 1; Alighieri 1987, 1020). This analogy, Jung argues, is fundamentally based on the fact that both narratives convey the motif of entering Hell as a living, liminal and transformative experience of passage, rebirth and regeneration. They convey the alchemical transition from 'darkness', or 'first death', to a different and higher state of consciousness, or 'second birth' (Jung 1944, CW12, §61, n2; 1955–6, CW14, §475). This view positions Dante's *Commedia* as a proper 'meditation book' ('Meditationsbuch'), or medieval 'book of visions'. A liminal space of visionary travelling and meditative interaction with the book serves as a landmark for Jung's evolving practice of meditation and inner visioning, later termed 'active imagination'. Along similar lines, the following appears later in the records of the *Red Book*:

> After his Death, Christ had to journey to Hell, otherwise the ascent to Heaven would have become impossible for him. Christ first had to become his Antichrist, his underworldly brother. No one knows what happened during the time Christ was in Hell. I have experienced it. (Jung 2009, 243)[5]

In a markedly apocalyptic vein, this short passage encapsulates a few compelling aspects of Jung's 'confrontation with the unconscious'. First of all, one reads that Hell is a bewildering 'experience' entailing a startling mental reversal, leading to an encounter with the opposite side of one's mind. And, most importantly, descending into Hell harbours a potential movement toward inner regeneration. In short, going to Hades in the *Red Book* is experienced as an in-between state ('*intra limen*'), revealing a challenging and self-transforming conversion to a hidden psychic world. It is an experience, yet it is no longer only a personal experience, for it is the subject's first glimpse beyond I-ness, into the mental space which Kant called the 'dark and stormy' waters of the irrational (Kant 1919, 270). This Hell is not a hypostatized principle of discrimination between good and evil with no fixed moral connotation, nor does it describe an irreversible condition. It is a place of suspension, which takes the mental traveller to the roots of his or her self-deceptions. Similarly, the initiation rites in the Eleusinian or Orphic mysteries involved Hell-scenarios that, through the experience of a ritual death (sometimes enacted through a proper burial in a cave), laid the foundations for a process of rebirth. 'Entering Hell' implies in this context the first stage in a journey of purification. In a similar manner, Jung interprets Dante's gradual advancement towards the bowels of the earth, representing, according to medieval views, the seat of the individual microcosm, as the radical egocentricity. Therefore, to plunge into Hell implies exploring the full extent of egocentric delusions, while progressively preparing oneself to enact their sacrifice. Analogously, the German mystic and contemporary of Dante, Meister Eckhart, the 'greatest thinker of that age', in Jung's view (Jung 1921, CW6, §410), empties Hell of images of sin, punishment and eternal regret, substituting them with the condition of those who cannot yet free themselves of the isolation of the cultivated ego (Potestà and Vian 2010, 265–6; Vannini 2018). Hence, as Irma Brandeis has poignantly captured, Dante's Hell is essentially a situation of mental obscuration, 'not *given* by the heavens, but made by eyes which are dull to light' (Brandeis 1962, 190). For Jung, purifying one's vision while travelling through Hell involves, first and foremost, the acknowledgment and integration of an evil counterpart. Dante's Satan (*Inferno*, XXXIV, 1–3), whose fall after his rebellion against God forms the funnel-like cavity of the *Inferno* in which the poet has to plunge to find the light, provides a most suitable model. Just as Dante's 'I' must come to terms with Lucifer, the 'emperor of the despondent kingdom' (*Inferno*, XXXIV, 28; Alighieri 1987, 334), to regain his freedom, so, too, does Jung's 'I' announce in the *Red Book* that Christ (or the hero) must first become the Antichrist (the anti-hero or dragon), in order to make the advancement of the journey possible. Later, Jung ascribes this process, in psychological terms, to the acknowledgement of the 'shadow' archetype (Jung 1953, CW7, §103n; 1951, CW9, 2, §§13–19) – that is, in brief, the unknown, rejected side of oneself, and the least desirable and most unfamiliar aspects of one's personality. The less recognized one's 'shadow' is, the blacker and more powerful its influence is over the conscious attitude, to the extent that it can possibly drag one to a visit to Hell or analogous undesirable places. By drawing on Dante's *Inferno* and the apocryphal literature, this motif appears in Jung's experiment under the guise of Lucifer or the Antichrist. This can be explained with the fact that much of what Jung recognizes as the cultural deficiency of the Western mindset has to do with all that Christian morality historically rejected as 'evil' or reproachable – that is, as he essentially argues in an unpublished seminar held in Polzeath, 'sexuality, animality, and creative imagination' (Jung forthcoming, 74–5), the primordial sources of psychic energy. Not too far from Nietzsche's view in the *Anti-Christ*, for which man would be the 'sickliest' animal 'most dangerously strayed from its instincts' (Nietzsche 1990, 136), Jung points out that real self-transformation shall never be complete without man's reconciliation with these great exclusions. Thus, the landscape of Hell, instead of depicting a condition of permanent exile, acquires the function of representing man's direct engagement with the opposite, excluded, neglected and unknown aspects of the mind – *'Die andere Seite'*, as Austrian illustrator and visionary writer Alfred Kubin (1909) phrases it. In this sense, Lucifer comes to play a primary role with regard to inner self-development, one which comes close to Blake's view of Satan as the light-bringer (*lux-fero*, Isaiah 14), the *stella mattutina* of personality, the catalyst of 'Energy' and the bearer of mental reversals. The whole debate is crucial to Jung, since it conveys one of the major issues regarding the relationship between modern psychology and religion: the suppression of the ambivalence of psychic functioning. This mainly occurred, according to his view, by hierarchically ascribing, following Augustine's theory of *privatio boni* ('absence of the good'), all the goodness to God (*summum bonum*) and all the evil to Satan (*infimum malum*), with the result of rejecting, in the name of a deceptive 'monotheism of consciousness' (Jung 1929, CW13, §51),[6] everything in the human mind that belongs to the natural play of opposites and regulates life (*enantiodromia*). Different was the view of the ancients, Jung argues, who felt, like Heraclitus, that '[t]he god is day and night, winter and summer, war and peace, surfeit and anger; but he takes various shapes, just as fire, when it is mingled with spices, is named according to the savor of each' (Heraclitus 1979, DK B67).

The 'Marriage of Heaven and Hell'

All things considered, Hell certainly remains a threatening and dreadful place in Jung's visionary experiences. It is a place, to borrow from Virgil, that is easy to get into but very difficult to exit (Virgil 1916, *Aeneid*, 6, 126–8). Hence, Jung warns the reader in the manner of Nietzsche:

> He who journeys to Hell also becomes Hell; therefore do not forget from whence you come. The depths are stronger than us; so do not be heroes, be clever and drop the heroics, since nothing is more dangerous than to play the hero. (Jung 2009, 244)

Despite the risks involved, the perils of Hell also epitomize a process of self-transformation similar to what the alchemists intended with the *nigredo* (blackening) or *putrefactio* (self-putrefaction): a dangerous, yet healing, descent into one's inner underworld. By interpreting the *katabasis* in this manner, Jung advocates a markedly non-dualistic perspective, as clearly evoked, among many similar occurrences, in this passage:

> What do you think of the essence of Hell? Hell is when the depths come to you with all that you no longer are or are not yet capable of. Hell is when you can no longer attain what you could attain. Hell is when you must think and feel and do everything that you know you do not want. Hell is when you know that your having to is also a wanting to, and that you yourself are responsible for it. Hell is when you know that everything serious that you have planned with yourself is also laughable, that everything fine is also brutal, that everything good is also bad, that everything high is also low, and that everything pleasant is also shameful. But the deepest Hell is when you realize that Hell is also no Hell, but a cheerful Heaven, not a Heaven in itself, but in this respect a Heaven, and in that respect a Hell. (Jung 2009, 244)

Leaving aside the somewhat religious tone, the proposed vision here positions Hell, or 'descent', as the necessary counterpart to Heaven, or 'ascent'. Only one-sidedness (that is, an excessive attachment or fear of what the ego wants and feels for itself) makes Hell look like an isolated, unchangeable external reality. When man is able to free himself from one-sidedness (that is, by realizing that 'everything serious that you have planned with yourself is also laughable'), Hell may begin to function in a compensatory way. Thus, the motif of travelling to Hell as the inception of a passage of rebirth aligns Jung's visions in the *Red Book* with the ancient tradition of Orphic myths, Eleusinian Mysteries and Homeric narratives, as well as symbolical readings of Dante's *Commedia*. Only 'in the region of danger (watery abyss, cavern, forest, island, castle, etc.)', Jung points out with the words of Hölderlin, 'can one find the "treasure hard to attain" (jewel, virgin, life-potion, victory over death)' (Jung 1944, CW12, 438). Accordingly, examples of *nekyia*, or journeys to Hades, lead courageous travellers to brighter places or states of being beyond their initial bewilderment. In the visions of Swedish scientist and mystic Emanuel Swedenborg (another man of science who experienced a radical mental switch around the midpoint of his life), this motif is developed through the doctrine of 'correspondences'. According to this view, with which Jung had been deeply familiar since his youth (Taylor 2007), a necessary equilibrium between 'Heaven' and 'Hell' must exist to respect the concordances between 'natural' and 'spiritual', 'outer' and 'inner', 'literal' and 'symbolic', 'external' and 'internal', and 'visible' and 'invisible' levels of perception (Swedenborg 2016, 57, 163). Swedenborg, too, explored methods of breathing concentration and visualization to have first-hand experiences of the law of 'correspondences', which he recorded in meditative notes. Once more, passage indicates in this context a transition to a special mental space, a *'temenos'*, in which one nourishes awareness of the balance of opposites that regulate life. In the *Red Book*, Jung comes to understand the time in Hell as the compelling counterpart to a continuous movement of renewal. He increasingly adopts a point of view that William Blake expresses at the beginning of *The Marriage of Heaven and Hell*:

> Without Contraries is no progression. Attraction and Repulsion, Reason and Energy, Love and Hate, are necessary to Human existence.
> From these contraries spring what the religious call Good and Evil. Good is the passive that obeys Reason. Evil is the active springing from Energy.
> Good is Heaven. Evil is Hell. (Blake 1974, 149)

Despite his admiration for the 'English mystic', as Jung used to refer to Blake (Jung 1921, CW6, §460; 1958, CW11, §905, n41), differences in their views about Hell remain. Nevertheless, in Jung's general understanding of Blake, Swedenborg, Dante, the apocryphal Christ and other examples, there is an underlying line of connection: the belief that, without balance of psychological opposites, such as the equilibrium of Heaven and Hell, no psychic functioning and self-transformation is possible. Therefore, Jung points out that Dante must first traverse Hell circle by circle until he reaches the bottom of Hell, in order to be able to invert the direction of his journey towards Heaven, where the beloved Beatrice abides. Maud Bodkin has expressed a similar dynamic view of Dante's journey:

> The horror of Dante's Hell is made bearable for the reader by the fact that interest is concentrated upon a forward moment. The torments of the damned are described as unending, but they have their effect as incidents in a journey – a transition from darkness to light, from the pangs of death to new life ... Opening the way of the pilgrim through the depth of Hell toward the light of Heaven, appears as the supreme motif of the story. (Bodkin 1951, 136)

Interestingly, in a capital work in the history of psychiatry, *The Discovery of the Unconscious*, Henri Ellenberger has summarized this crucial aspect of our discussion with a Dantesque analogy:

> One characteristic feature of any journey through the unconscious is the occurrence of what Jung called *enantiodromia*. This term, originating with Heraclitus, means the 'return to the opposite'. Certain mental processes are turned at a given point into their opposites as if through a kind of self-regulation. This notion has also been symbolically illustrated by poets. In the *Divine Comedy* we see Dante and Virgil reaching the deepest point of hell and then taking their first step upward in a reverse course toward purgatory and heaven. This mysterious phenomenon of the spontaneous reversal of regression was experienced by all those who passed successfully through a creative illness and has become a characteristic feature of Jungian synthetic-hermeneutic therapy. (Ellenberger 1994, 713)

This succinctly summarizes why Jung draws on Dante's hermeneutics of Hell as inspiration for the *Red Book*: it is a pathway to rebirth and psychological renewal. Jung's original understanding of the apocryphal

Christ follows a similar logic. Christ has to become his Antichrist, he argues, in order for the ascent to Heaven, that is, reaching a new state of consciousness, to be possible. If the dogmatic splitting of good and evil would inevitably lead to a one-sided vision of *staying in* Hell as a place of punishment and fear, Christ's temporary descent to Hell, like Dante's journey to *Inferno*, leads to a vision of *traversing* Hell as a deeply transformative human experience.

Conclusion

The image of Hell in the *Red Book* enlivens Jung's interpretation of the experience of liminal passage. By envisioning a journey through Hell as a transformative experience (a transitional stage along the process of self-transformation), three variations of this motif in the *Red Book* have been explored: the motif of 'radical mental change' (the beginning of the journey), the encounter with the 'other side' (the middle stage), and the incubation of a new vision (the potential future development of the journey). This chapter has probed Jung's original interpretation of the liminal quality of passage, which can be summarized by the following: the creation of a *'temenos'* and the enactment of a process of change. The first aspect describes a particularly dedicated space and time (a book, an artistic expression, a therapeutic setting, a meditational exercise, a 'special' activity) in which man ritually experiences and makes use of sub-liminal, or trans-liminal, sources of energy. In this sense, the liminal experience describes a passage to an in-between mental space beneath the threshold of ordinary perceptions, with substantial transformative effects. In Jung's scientific theorization, this practice is mainly referred to as the *'transcendent function'*, by which he intended 'nothing mysterious or metaphysical', but rather a specific technique arising 'from the union of conscious and unconscious contents' (Jung 1960, CW8, §131), aimed at widening consciousness and bringing to light elements of emotional disturbance. At the same time, the concept of passage aptly evokes the essentially dynamic nature of Jung's model of the mind. In this sense, the work of Jung highlights particularly well the metamorphic nature of liminal experiences of change. For Jung, in fact, psychic reality does not depend on isolated transitions from 'A' to 'B' (for example, from Hell to Heaven, or from 'madness' to 'sanity'), but on a constant experience of the in-between (the 'Marriage of Heaven and Hell'), the inherently transitional nature of the journey, the ever-changing process of transformation of things, from which man deludes himself to be separated. In this respect, man's experience of liminal passages indicates a capacity to embrace change. By giving up egocentric hopes and fears, individuals can access in themselves the passages that rule the rhythmic transformation of life.

Notes

1. In the English-speaking world, the work is more commonly known as the *Psychology of the Unconscious* (Jung 1916).
2. 'Nel mezzo del cammin di nostra vita / mi ritrovai per una selva oscura, / ché la diritta via era smarrita.' As Dante was born in 1265, the reference to 35 years dates the beginning of his journey as 1300, the first year of the new century, and the year of the first jubilee in Rome, organized by Pope Boniface VIII.
3. Dante's journey in the *Commedia* lasts a week, precisely the Holy Week between 8 and 14 April 1300, following the first Christian Jubilee established by Pope Boniface VIII, or from 25 to 31 March, following the anniversary of Christ's death.
4. 'Mortuus, et sepoltus, descendit ad inferos, tertia die resurrexit a mortuis.'
5. Later, in 1938, Jung notes: 'The three days descent into Hell during death describes the sinking of the vanished value into the unconscious, where, by conquering the power of darkness, it establishes a new order, and then rises up to heaven again, that is, attains supreme clarity of consciousness' (Jung 1958, CW11, §149).
6. 'We lack all knowledge of the unconscious psyche and pursue the cult of consciousness to the exclusion of all else. Our true religion is a monotheism of consciousness, a possession by it, coupled with a fanatical denial of the existence of fragmentary autonomous systems' (Jung 1938, CW11, §149).

References

Alighieri, Dante. 1987 [1306/1321]. *Commedia*. Milan: Garzanti.
Alighieri, Dante. 2014. *Opere: Convivio, monarchia, epistole, egloghe*. Milan: Mondadori.
Bergson, Henri. 1999 [1912]. *An Introduction to Metaphysics*, translated by T.E. Hulme. Indianapolis, IN: Hackett.
Blake, William. 1974. *Complete Writings*, edited by Geoffrey Keynes. Oxford: Oxford University Press.
Bodkin, Maud. 1951 [1934]. *Archetypal Patterns in Poetry*. Oxford: Oxford University Press.
Brandeis, Irma. 1962 [1960]. *The Ladder of Vision*. New York: Anchor.
Caillois, Roger. 1991. *Les démons de midi* [The demons of midday]. Montpellier: Fata Morgana.
Caroll, Robert and Stephen Prickett, eds. 2008. *The Bible: Authorized King James version*. Oxford: Oxford University Press.
Cross, Frank Leslie, ed. 1978. *The Oxford Dictionary of the Christian Church*. Oxford: Oxford University Press.
Dieterich, Albrecht. 1913. *Nekyia: Beiträge zur Erklärung der neuentdeckten Petrusapokalypse*. Leipzig: B.G. Teubner.
Eliade, Mircea. 1987 [1957]. *The Sacred and the Profane: The nature of religion*, translated by Willard Ropes Trask. San Diego, CA: Harcourt.
Eliade, Mircea. 2012 [1958]. *Rites and Symbols of Initiation: The mysteries of birth and rebirth*. New York: Harper & Row.
Ellenberger, Henri. 1994 [1970]. *The Discovery of the Unconscious*. 2 vols. London: Fontana.
Elliott, James Keith. 1993. *The Apocryphal New Testament: A collection of apocryphal Christian literature in English translation*. Oxford: Oxford University Press.
Goris, Harm J.M.J. 2018. 'Thomas Aquinas on Christ's descent into Hell'. In *The Apostles' Creed*, edited by Marcel Sarot and Archibald van Wieringen, 93–114. Leiden: Brill.

Hannah, Barbara. 1959. *Notes on Lectures given at the Eidgenossische Technische Hochschule, Zurich by Prof. Dr. C.G. Jung*. Zürich: private printing.
Heraclitus. 1979. *The Art and Thought of Heraclitus*, edited by C.H. Kahn. Cambridge: Cambridge University Press.
Hulme, William Henry, ed. 1907. *The Middle-English Harrowing of Hell and Gospel of Nicodemus*. London: Early English Text Society.
James, William. 1902. *The Varieties of Religious Experience*. London: Longmans, Green and Co.
Jung, Carl Gustav. 1916 [1911/1912]. *Psychology of the Unconscious: A study of the transformations and symbolisms of the libido*, translated by Beatrice M. Hinkle. New York: Moffat, Yard & Company.
Jung, Carl Gustav. 1921. *Psychologische Typen* [*Psychological Types*], CW, vol. 6. *The Collected Works of C.G. Jung*, edited by Sir Herbert Read, Michael Fordham and Gerhard Adler, translated by R.F.C. Hull. Princeton, NJ: Bollingen Series, Princeton University Press.
Jung, Carl Gustav. 1929. 'Das Geheimnis der goldenen Blüte: Ein chinesisches Lebensbuch' [Commentary on 'The Secret of the Golden Flower'], CW, vol. 13. *The Collected Works of C.G. Jung*, edited by Sir Herbert Read, Michael Fordham and Gerhard Adler, translated by R.F.C. Hull, §§1–84. Princeton, NJ: Bollingen Series, Princeton University Press.
Jung, Carl Gustav. 1944. *Psychologie und Alchimie* [*Psychology and Alchemy*]. CW, vol. 12. *The Collected Works of C.G. Jung*, edited by Sir Herbert Read, Michael Fordham and Gerhard Adler, translated by R.F.C. Hull. Princeton, NJ: Bollingen Series, Princeton University Press.
Jung, Carl Gustav. 1951. *Aion*. CW, vol. 9. *The Collected Works of C.G. Jung*, edited by Sir Herbert Read, Michael Fordham and Gerhard Adler, translated by R.F.C. Hull. Princeton, NJ: Bollingen Series, Princeton University Press.
Jung, Carl Gustav. 1953. *Zwei Schriften über Analytische Psychologie* [*Two Essays on Analytical Psychology*]. CW, vol. 7. *The Collected Works of C.G. Jung*, edited by Sir Herbert Read, Michael Fordham and Gerhard Adler, translated by R.F.C. Hull. Princeton, NJ: Bollingen Series, Princeton University Press.
Jung, Carl Gustav. 1955–6. *Mysterium Conjunctionis*. CW, vol. 14. *The Collected Works of C.G. Jung*, edited by Sir Herbert Read, Michael Fordham and Gerhard Adler, translated by R.F.C. Hull. Princeton, NJ: Bollingen Series, Princeton University Press.
Jung, Carl Gustav. 1958. *Zur Psychologie westlicher und östlicher Religion* [*Psychology and Religion: West and East*]. CW, vol. 11. *The Collected Works of C.G. Jung*, edited by Sir Herbert Read, Michael Fordham and Gerhard Adler, translated by R.F.C. Hull. Princeton, NJ: Bollingen Series, Princeton University Press.
Jung, Carl Gustav. 1962. *Erinnerungen, Träume, Gedanken von C.G. Jung: Aufgezeichnet und herausgegeben von Aniela Jaffé* [*Memories, Dreams, Reflections*]. Zürich: W. Verlag.
Jung, Carl Gustav. 2009. *The Red Book: Liber novus*, edited by Sonu Shamdasani. New York: W.W. Norton & Company.
Jung, Carl Gustav. 2012 [1925]. *Introduction to Jungian Psychology: Notes of the seminar given by Jung on analytical psychology in 1925*, edited by William McGuire, revised by Sonu Shamdasani. Princeton, NJ: Princeton University Press.
Jung, Carl Gustav. 2020 [1913–32]. *The Black Books 1913–1932: Notebooks of transformation*, 7 vols, edited by Sonu Shamdasani, translated by Martin Liebscher, John Peck and Sonu Shamdasani. New York: W.W. Norton & Company.
Jung, Carl Gustav. Forthcoming. *Notes on the Seminar in Analytical Psychology. Conducted by Dr. C.G. Jung. Polzeath, England, July 14–July 27, 1923*. Arranged by members of the class. Philemon Foundation.
Kant, Immanuel. 1919 [1781]. *Kritik der reinen Vernunft* [*Critique of Pure Reason*]. Leipzig: Verlag Von Felix Meiner.
Kubin, Alfred. 1909. *Die andere Seite: Ein phantastischer Roman*. Munich: Georg Müller.
Nietzsche, Friedrich. 1924 [1878–80]. *Menschliches, Allzumenschliches, II* [*Human, All Too Human II*], translated by Paul V. Cohn. London: Allen and Unwin.
Nietzsche, Friedrich. 1990 [1895]. *Der Antichrist* [*The Anti-Christ*], translated by R.J. Hollingdale. London: Penguin.
Potestà, Gian Luca and Marco Rizzi. 2019. *L'Anticristo: La scienza della fine* [*The Antichrist*]. 3 vols. Milan: Lorenzo Valla.
Potestà, Gian Luca and Giovanni Vian. 2010. *Storia del Cristianesimo* [*History of Christianity*]. Bologne: Il Mulino.

Scott-Macnab, David. 2018. 'The many faces of the noonday demon', *Journal of Early Christian History* 8 (1): 22–42.
Stephenson, Craig E. 2009. *Possessio: Jung's comparative anatomy of the psyche*. London: Routledge.
Swedenborg, Emmanuel. 2016 [1758]. *Heaven and Hell*. West Chester, PA: Swedenborg Foundation.
Taylor, Eugene. 2007. 'Jung, Swedenborg, redivivus', *Jung History* 2 (2): 27–31.
Van Gennep, Arnold. 1960 [1909]. *The Rites of Passage*. London: Routledge.
Vannini, Marco. 2018. *Introduzione a Eckhart* [Introduction to Eckhart]. Florence: Le Lettere.
Virgil. 1916. *Eclogues. Georgics. Aeneid I–VI*, translated by H.R. Fairclough. London: Heinemann.

10
Multiple selves: understanding the nature of dissociation in *Black Swan* (2010)

Büke Sağlam

The concept of dissociation, which plays a prominent role within the field of psychology, has time and again been addressed and explored within literary expression. Gothic fiction has in particular been a pioneer in representing not only phenomena and experiences of dissociation, but also many other kinds of mental illness that have a profound impact on the human psyche. As Margaret McAllister and Donna Lee Brien state in their article 'Haunted: Exploring representations of mental health through the lens of the Gothic': '[t]he linking of mental illness and the Gothic is prevalent and persistent historically, and has set up and reinforced vivid, often terrifying and horrifying images of mental illness and its treatment in the popular imagination' (McAllister and Lee Brien 2015, 73).

The aim of this chapter is to analyse the representation of dissociation in Darren Aronofsky's contemporary Gothic film *Black Swan* (US 2010) in order to better articulate the nature of this mental phenomenon. I believe that the Gothic genre is one of the most helpful resources for investigating this condition. As the genre's main objective is to discover and represent what is underneath the surface in order to deal with the deepest fears, emotions and desires of human beings, it becomes a suitable platform to study various kinds of mental disorders. Moreover, by profoundly analysing and narrating all these conditions, Gothic fiction makes what is 'fearful' and 'strange' visible, revealing how normal, humane and mundane they are. Dissociation, through narratives about the double, is one of the most recurrent themes, and it is treated allegorically in many classic Gothic works, such as *Dr Jekyll and Mr Hyde*, *Frankenstein*, *The Picture of Dorian Gray* and *The Double* (Stevenson 1991; Shelley 1994; Wilde 2005; Dostoyevsky 1972). Even today, it is possible to see various examples of the representation of dissociation, not only in literature, but also in films such as *Black Swan*, which is inspired by Dostoevsky's *The Double*. As Aronofsky commented during an interview about his film:

> I had the idea of the ballet world and I was thinking of doing something with 'The Double' with Dostoevsky. I saw Swan Lake, I had never been to the ballet, and suddenly I saw a black swan and a white swan played by one dancer and I was like 'oh'. It was a eureka moment, because it was The Double in the ballet world ... The ballet Swan Lake is gothic. The story is: during the day she is a swan, and at night she is like a half-swan-half-human creature. (Thompson 2010, n.p.)

The dissociation of the protagonist is represented perfectly in the film through a process of physical and mental transformation. To better understand the nature of dissociation, I will begin by clarifying the key terms and concepts that will constitute the backbone of this chapter, which include an understanding of 'passage' that I claim enriches our understanding of dissociation as both a psychic phenomenon and a subject of cultural representation.

Passage, dissociation and psychosis

In the Merriam-Webster dictionary, 'passage' is defined as 'a continuous movement or flow' (Merriam-Webster Online 2022). Because of its multifaceted connotations, the concept of passages embraces various ideas in the study of culture, and it is particularly suited to discussing dissociation. Dissociation itself is a kind of passage, as it makes the subject oscillate between mental states, adopting various perceptions and realities. This passage is rather amorphous and hard to define. Indeed, it is this indefinable and personal nature that makes the phenomenon unique and incomparable.

Dissociation is clearly present and particularly acute in the disorder schizophrenia. Andrew Moskowitz, from the Department of Psychology at Touro College Berlin, mentions Eugen Bleuler's definition of schizophrenia in his article, 'Schizophrenia, trauma, dissociation, and scientific revolutions':

> Bleuler's 1911 'definition' of *schizophrenia* reads almost as a calling card for dissociative disorders: 'If the disease is marked, the personality loses its unity; at different times different psychic complexes seem to represent the personality ... one set of complexes dominates the personality for a time, while other groups of ideas or drives are "split off" and seem either partly or completely impotent.' (Moskowitz 2011b, 349)

Moskowitz discusses different paradigms of schizophrenia and dissociation, beginning with the thoughts of Bleuler, who coined the term 'schizophrenia', and ending with the latest trauma/dissociation paradigm, indicating differences among them:

> Over the past several decades, the study of schizophrenia and the study of dissociative disorders have been dominated by opposing paradigms. For schizophrenia, the assumption of a genetic basis and biological causation has reigned supreme ... in contrast, the overriding paradigm for the study of dissociative disorders has focused almost exclusively on life events – traumatic or otherwise – that *are* assumed to be meaningfully related to the symptoms a person experiences ... at the same time, many trauma-oriented clinicians and researchers think of schizophrenia only as something dissociative disorders are *not* – but are often confused with; schizophrenia's validity as a biologically based entity is rarely questioned. (Moskowitz 2011b, 347–8, emphasis in the original)

Should the process of dissociation be defined as something pathological, that is to say, as a mere mental disease, or can it also be a natural outcome of an overly sensitive psyche? This seemingly simple question raises many more questions, such as: What is a sensitive psyche? What is the psychological profile of the specific person experiencing dissociation? What kind of dissociation is being referred to? And, last but not least, what is considered normal and natural, or abnormal and pathological?

Moskowitz begins this discussion by recalling an event that had a huge effect on him when he was at the beginning of his training as a clinical psychologist. One day he was leading a men's group as a substitute therapist when one of the patients said:

> 'You think you are better than us, don't you? You think this could never happen to you.' ... Perhaps I didn't think I was better than them, but I certainly thought I was *different* from them. Like most of us in Western societies, I had grown up believing that psychiatric disorders were illnesses – *diseases* like any other – and there had been nothing in my training until then to convince me otherwise. But learning about trauma, dissociation, and attachment in the ensuing decades has changed my mind. (Moskowitz 2011b, 347, emphasis in the original)

Point of view, belief and definitions of mental disorders shape the way the disorders are approached and understood. Therefore, before continuing with a psychological analysis of the protagonist of *Black Swan*, Nina Sayers, I would like to talk about one last term, psychosis. The concept of psychosis is another blurry term, and it is very hard to deal with. One major issue is how to categorize and name sets of symptoms or mental conditions with a term that is itself ambiguous. In another article, 'On the relation between trauma, dissociation, psychotic symptoms and schizophrenia', Moskowitz comments on the definition of psychosis:

> The term psychosis itself is not unproblematic. Earlier definitions of psychosis emphasizing 'impaired reality testing' are no longer popular as positivistic views of consensually-based reality existing 'out there' to be assessed by selves contained in bodies 'in here' are no longer tenable. But the current definitions are no better. For example, the DSM-IV diagnosis is entirely circular – 'psychosis' is defined as experiencing delusions or hallucinations or, most broadly, as all the positive symptoms of schizophrenia! Clearly such an approach is not helpful. (Moskowitz 2011a, n.p.)

The basic problem with defining these terms derives from the subjectivity of certain concepts, such as 'reality', as well as the ambiguity and fluidity of the human psyche. Our mental system is too complicated to be easily explained or categorized. As Moskowitz commented on the definition of psychosis in the DSM-IV (the fourth edition of the *Diagnostic and Statistical Manual of Mental Disorders* of the American Psychiatric Association (APA 1994)), the description of such a term is barely sufficient. When we look at the latest version, the DSM-V, we see that the problem with defining psychosis continues (APA 2013). David B. Arciniegas states:

> In their current conceptualization of psychosis, both the APA and the World Health Organization define psychosis narrowly by requiring the presence of hallucinations (without insight into their pathological nature), delusions, or both hallucinations without insight and delusions. In both of these current diagnostic classification systems, impaired reality testing remains central conceptually to psychosis. (Arciniegas 2015, 716)

These insufficient definitions once again demonstrate the impossibility of concretely defining such fluid conditions. Indeed, these mental states belong to a continuum that exceeds the artificial limits of diagnoses (or labels), which mainly serve to define the sane and insane and, thus, to separate one from another. Therefore, thinking of this necessary movement between states as a passage rather than as an anomaly helps us understand the true nature of the psyche, without stumbling on man-made categories, prejudices and judgements. Clearly, the need for categorizing mental disorders or conditions derives from the desire to treat them. A disease is something that needs to be cured. And, once such conditions are considered diseases, they will be investigated with cures in mind. However, one may ask if 'fixing' and understanding are the same thing, or if something needs to be cured in the first place.

Nina's dissociation

Gilles Deleuze and Felix Guattari's controversial *Anti-Oedipus*, published in 1972, introduced radical ideas about the nature of psychosis and schizophrenia (Deleuze and Guattari 1983). More importantly, the work protests the ideas of psychoanalysis, providing some theories of Freud as examples. The basic objective of psychoanalysis seems to be to give names to certain mental conditions, to categorize them, and to treat patients based on these so-called categories and complexes. While in some cases the treatment is necessary, and categories are required in order to define the condition and to be able to treat certain cases, the aim, according to Deleuze and Guattari, should not be about ambitiously 'fixing' them, nor reducing their conditions to diagnoses and complexes. The main aim in *Anti-Oedipus* is to introduce a different perspective regarding some mental disorders, such as schizophrenia and dissociation, from a philosophical point of view. As the title suggests, *Anti-Oedipus* refers to Freud's famous Oedipus complex and, throughout the book, Deleuze and Guattari try to explain how reductive and insufficient Freud's psychoanalysis is for explaining psychosis. As was stated by Gisela Brinker-Gabler:

> Based on a radical critique of Freud's psychoanalysis, Deleuze and Guattari develop an image of the 'body without organs' as a counter to the organic model of the (privatized) body and the centered self. They present this undifferentiated and 'organless' body as the flow of energies and drives that ontologically precedes the shaping of the individual into an 'organic' whole. (Brinker-Gabler 2012, 48)

The 'body without organs' is one of Deleuze's most important concepts. As can be clearly understood from the description of Brinker-Gabler, it refers to a decentred and fluid body full of multiplicities. As opposed to psychoanalysis, which defends the unity of the ego, schizoanalysis is inspired and fuelled by the dynamic and multiple nature of the psyche. As Deleuze and Guattari comment in *Anti-Oedipus*:

> In order to resist organ-machines, the body without organs presents its smooth, slippery, opaque, taut surface as a barrier. In order to resist linked, connected and interrupted flows, it sets up a counterflow of amorphous, undifferentiated fluid. In order to resist using words composed of articulated phonetic units, it utters only gasps and cries that are sheer unarticulated blocks of sound. We are of the opinion that what is ordinarily referred to as 'primary repression' means precisely that: it is not a 'countercathexis,' but rather this *repulsion* of desiring-machines by the body without organs. (Deleuze and Guattari 1983, 9, emphasis in the original)

According to Deleuze and Guattari, various symptoms of schizophrenia, such as dissociation and speech disorders, are far from being the evidences of a disease; rather, they are considered as a kind of reaction against the dominance of a centred self and the established 'truths' regarding the human psyche that psychoanalysis has attempted to maintain.[1] Another important point might be the difficulty to uphold unity when confronted with remarkable stress and pressure.

In *Black Swan*, the selection of the place and environment is perfectly suited for representing a situation in which daily stress creates the mentioned fracture in the protagonist of the movie. The story takes place in the New York City Ballet company and, because the world of ballet is known for its rigidity, obsession with perfection and ruthlessness, the audience does not have any difficulty understanding one of the main sources of stress for the protagonist. The psychological problems of Nina become more visible after she is selected for the role of the Swan Queen in Tchaikovsky's *Swan Lake*. She is asked to perform not only Odette (the White Swan), but also Odile (the Black Swan). At this point, it is important to emphasize the fact that the main cause of Nina's dissociation is not a sudden traumatic event; rather, it seems to be the consequence of constant daily emotional burden, stress and pressure. While she does not experience any problems in performing the part of the White Swan, the dissociation and so-called psychotic episodes start when she tries to embody the Black Swan. The Black Swan, the evil twin of the White Swan, represents the sensual self and the dark side of one's personality. According to the original story, Odile deceives the prince, who would save Odette, trapped in the body of a White Swan, by giving her his true love. Tricked, the prince falls in love with Odile, believing she is Odette. This event leads Odette to commit suicide.[2] Nina's dark side starts to show as she tries to fully perform Odile's part. During this process, Nina experiences visual hallucinations, while also struggling with eating disorders, anxiety and obsession. This inner fracture is provoked by the arrival of her double (shaped in flesh and bones as the character of Lily, another dancer in the same dance company).

Before continuing with an analysis of Lily, it will be useful to examine and understand Nina's psychological oscillation, or passage, through the hallucinations. Although auditory hallucinations are more common in real life,[3] in the case of Nina, visual hallucinations dominate, which enables the audience to fully engage with the mind of the protagonist more easily. As Moskowitz states:

> The current diagnostic criteria for schizophrenia, with a strong emphasis on psychotic symptoms, differs substantially from Bleuler's original conception, which saw delusions and hallucinations as only secondary features of schizophrenia. For the past 30 years, specific psychotic symptoms derived from the writings of Kurt Schneider (so-called 'first rank' symptoms), particularly certain forms of auditory hallucinations (voices conversing or commenting on one's behavior) and delusions (so-called 'passivity phenomena') have been central to the diagnosis of schizophrenia. These symptoms, common in DID [dissociative identity disorder] and easily understandable from a dissociation perspective, have led

to considerable diagnostic confusion and most likely frequent misdiagnosis of DID patients as schizophrenic. (Moskowitz 2011a, n.p.)

In the film, various visual hallucinations indicate the transformation of Nina into the Black Swan, such as seeing black swan feathers grow out of her body, her feet becoming webbed and changes in her legs and neck. During her last appearance as the Black Swan on stage, we see her total transformation into Odile: she grows wings while performing her famous 32 fouettés. Aronofsky perfectly emphasizes both her transformation and dissociation by showing Nina in her own body as she finishes the coda, with her shadow in the form of a swan. Again, while all these episodes can be considered to be evidence of psychosis and symptoms of schizophrenia, we need to keep in mind the ambiguity of the term psychosis and, as commented by Moskowitz above, the existence of the same symptoms in DID. As far as DID is concerned, there are two main approaches, as defined in the article 'Dissociative identity disorder and the sociocognitive model: Recalling the lessons of the past':

> Over the past decade, two competing views concerning the genesis and nature of DID have emerged. One perspective, referred to by Gleaves (1996) as the posttraumatic model (PTM), maintains that DID is an etiologically distinct condition that is best conceptualized as a defensive response to childhood trauma, particularly severe sexual and physical abuse ... An alternative perspective on DID is afforded by the sociocognitive model (SCM). The SCM conceptualizes DID as a syndrome that consists of rule-governed and goal-directed experiences and displays of multiple role enactments that have been created, legitimized, and maintained by social reinforcement. (Lilienfield et al. 1999, 507)

As far as these two models of DID are concerned, it is safe to suggest that Nina's condition seems to include elements of SCM. We also see various episodes related to sexual harassment and pressure enacted by her abusive director, Thomas,[4] and her pathological relationship with her dominant mother,[5] all of which can be considered traumatic events. Moreover, Thomas's abusive behaviours seem to be legitimized and ignored (in one scene, Nina's mother says that he has a 'reputation'), although his abuses are known by everyone. This turns the abuse into a part of everyday life at the ballet company, rather than a tragic and shocking traumatic event, although it may have the same traumatic effect on the subject. As Steve Lamberti from the University of Rochester Medical Center says about the character of Nina:

> Natalie Portman's character was involved in a highly stressful competition, she had conflicted relationships with her mother and with her understudy, and she was the object of sexual advances by her director. Any of these issues alone would be stressful, but experiencing all of them at once could be emotionally devastating, particularly for a young woman who is somewhat naïve and sheltered. (Donaldson James 2010, n.p.)

One question would be how traumatic events can become part of a daily routine, and if it is possible to consider anxiety and dissociation as natural outcomes of this situation. As commented by Lamberti, Nina is portrayed as a fragile young woman, and she may be more sensitive than others, although this does not change the fact that she is in a highly stressful environment. Her director is a symbol of power and is an almost fascist, authoritative figure who makes and exerts continuous demands and pressure. In his preface to *Anti-Oedipus*, Foucault comments on this kind of fascism as being one of the three adversaries confronted by the book:

> The major enemy, the strategic adversary is fascism ... And not only historical fascism ... but also the fascism in us all, in our heads and in our everyday behavior, the fascism that causes us to love power, to desire the very thing that dominates and exploits us. (Deleuze and Guattari 1983, xiii)

The film clearly tells us that Nina's main desire is to be perfect, although she is also dominated by this very concept of perfection and its promulgators, such as Thomas. The source of her self-harm and obsessive behaviours, as well as her anxiety and eventual dissociation, is this very desire that dominates her daily life. Moreover, the role enactment, one of the main elements of the SCM, is encouraged in her daily life both by her director (pushing Nina to lose control and release her 'dark side' to transform into the Black Swan) and by her mother, who insistently wants her to remain as her 'sweet girl'. In this sense, Nina is torn between two opposing demands. As discussed further by Lilienfield et al.

> By *role enactment*, proponents of the SCM mean that DID patients adopt and enact social roles geared to their aspirations and the demand characteristics of varied social contexts. According to this

view, the metaphor or concept of *role* does not imply that role-related behaviors are the products of conscious deception. Instead, role enactments tend to flow spontaneously and are carried out with little or no conscious awareness and with a high degree of 'organismic involvement' such that the role and 'self' (or 'multiple selves' as the case may be) coalesce so as to become essentially indistinguishable. (Lilienfield et al. 1999, 508, emphasis in the original)

It would be possible to explain certain aspects of Nina's dissociation with the SCM, emphasizing role enactment, rather than seeing it as a mere psychotic episode. It is also interesting to note that one refers to the literal meaning of the role when one discusses Nina's embodiment of Odile. In that sense, once again, we come to understand that this specific role enactment is indeed required in her daily life. Thus, Nina's dissociation is the consequence of a social role, rather than of psychosis or disease.

Another element that signals Nina's dissociation is the arrival of her double, Lily. As mentioned at the start of this chapter, the concept of the double is widely used in the Gothic genre to represent the subject's dissociation. Given that Aronofsky's film was inspired by Dostoevsky's *The Double*, we see a very similar situation with Nina. In *The Double*, while we are never sure whether the protagonist's double, Golyadkin Jr, exists (Dostoyevsky 1972), in *Black Swan*, the audience knows that Lily exists and represents everything that Nina would like to have, such as freedom and sensuality, in order to embody the main characteristics of the Black Swan. Nina's anxieties increase when Lily's dance is praised by Thomas, and when Lily is selected as Nina's alternate. In one scene, Nina begs her director not to select Lily as her substitute, saying: '[s]he is after me. She is trying to replace me!', just as Golyadkin Jr does to Golyadkin Sr in *The Double*. The source of anxiety is the same for both Nina and Golyadkin. Both fear being replaced by their doubles, who are somehow better than them in many ways. Their inner dissociation is complemented, or represented, by the external factor of the double, another person with the same or similar physical appearance. Gary Saul Morson comments on Golyadkin's condition: '[t]he real horror, which the hero constantly tries to ward off, is that while subjectivity is indeed unique and only one of a *me* can exist – the real me is not mine but his, and I am the one who does not have a *me*! I am the pretender!' (Morson 2015, 50).

The theme of falseness and pretension is mentioned by Nina's director when he praises the way Lily dances. He says: '[s]he is not faking it', apparently comparing her style with that of Nina. From the very beginning of the movie, Lily seems to be the real Black Swan, with her careless, sensual and free personality. Nina, not having any of these personality traits, does indeed seem to fake them when she tries to transform herself. The passage here, then, is not organic but implies pretence. Soon, Nina's wish to appear as the 'other' rather than 'becoming' one gets out of her control, placing her in a different mental state after a period of transition. Thus, the oscillation ends as she becomes trapped in a single state. At the end of the film, she kills herself by metaphorically killing the White Swan inside her as she fails to maintain two opposite forces in herself. Thus, the dissociation ends with self-annihilation.

Conclusion

Dissociation, as a result of daily stress and social requirements, is quite a natural outcome, both as a passage from one psychological state to another and as a mental transformation. Some models of DID, such as PTM and SCM, as well as the thoughts of Moskowitz (2011a; 2011b) and the theories of Deleuze and Guattari (1983), demonstrate the complexity of this phenomenon. Various terms regarding human psychology are incapable of fully defining their objects, and indicate the impossibility of naming or categorizing certain conditions. As Moskowitz rightly states, the disorders that are considered diseases may not actually be illnesses – at least not in every case (Moskowitz 2011b). What we call a disease may reflect our personal ideology and subjective thoughts about concepts such as reality, normality and so on. After all, there is not, and cannot be, any single objective thought on these abstract terms. Things that are normalized by society (such as abuse and pressure) may not actually be normal, while the reactions to, and consequence of, this stress (such as dissociation) may be totally normal and natural. An ambivalence resides in every human being, and it is normal to have multiple selves, rather than one single centred self, although in some cases (such as Nina's situation), it would be hard to deal with these opposite forces (especially when they are pushed by external factors, rather than experienced naturally). As a result, the subject may prefer to remain singular, even if it means self-destruction. Indeed, Nina's inability to have multiple selves seems to become her tragic flaw, since a true Swan Queen has to become both Odile and Odette instead of choosing one. It is also important to emphasize the importance of the concept of passage, which both defines dissociation and enables us to better understand its complex nature. One can only embrace one's multiple selves by defining dissociation as a passage from one mental state (or role) to another, rather than seeing it as a pathological phenomenon or anomaly. In that sense, the Swan Queen can be seen as a perfect symbol of this ambivalence and reconciliation.

Notes

1. Deleuze and Guattari's approach to schizophrenia is almost metaphorical and emphasizes the mistake of oversimplifying such complex disorders by labelling them. They do not try to blame society, normalize or justify such a condition. As they state: '[w]hen we say that schizophrenia is our characteristic malady, the malady of our era, we do not merely mean to say that modern life drives people mad. It is not a question of a way of life, but a process of production' (Deleuze and Guattari 1983, 34).
2. *Swan Lake* has many different endings (see Performing Arts School of Classical Ballet 2016).
3. 'While the majority of hallucinations reported in primary psychotic disorders are auditory, they may also be visual, olfactory, tactile, or gustatory' (Teeple et. al 2009, 27). Although Moskowitz claims: '… auditory verbal hallucinations or voices (and some passivity phenomena such as thought withdrawal or insertion) should, on the balance of the evidence, be considered dissociative rather than psychotic in nature' (Moskowitz 2011a, n.p.).
4. There are various ideas regarding the behaviour of the director, Thomas, although in this chapter I consider it to be abuse. As Julie Sexeny comments: '[h]e reframes her notion of perfection to include letting go and the value of surprise. But when he suddenly kisses her and she bites him in return, it is unclear what to make of this. Is this an abuse of authority? Is he, like her mother, crossing boundaries in order to control her? Or does he cross a boundary with her precisely in order to test her ability to draw a line between them?' (Sexeny 2015, 53).
5. In various scenes, the audience witnesses the problematic and pathological relationship between Nina and her mother. As Julie Sexeny states: 'Nina's control of her own self – especially her body – is reflected in the control her mother (Barbara Hershey) exerts over her. Even though she is a young adult, her mother wakes her and puts her to bed, feeds and dresses her, cuts her nails and surveys her body for any signs that she has cut or scratched herself' (Sexeny 2015, 53).

Filmography

Black Swan (Darren Aronofsky; US 2010).

References

APA (American Psychiatric Association). 1994. *DSM-IV: Diagnostic and Statistical Manual of Mental Disorders 4th Edition*. Washington, DC: American Psychiatric Press.
APA (American Psychiatric Association). 2013. *DSM-5: Diagnostic and Statistical Manual of Mental Disorders 5th Edition*. Washington, DC: American Psychiatric Publishing.
Arciniegas, David B. 2015. 'Psychosis', *Continuum: Lifelong Learning in Neurology* 21 (3): 715–36.
Brinker-Gabler, Gisela. 2012. *Image in Outline: Reading Lou Andreas-Salomé*. New York: Continuum International.
Deleuze, Gilles and Félix Guattari. 1983. *Anti-Oedipus: Capitalism and schizophrenia*. Minneapolis: University of Minnesota Press.
Donaldson James, Susan. 2010. '"Black Swan": Psychiatrists diagnose ballerina's descent', *ABC News*, 20 December. Accessed 16 February 2022. https://abcnews.go.com/Health/Movies/black-swan-psychiatrists-diagnose-natalie-portmans-portrayal-psychosis/story?id=12436873.
Dostoyevsky, Fyodor. 1972. *Notes from Underground & The Double*. Harmondsworth: Penguin.

Lilienfield, Scott O., Steven Jay Lynn, Irving Kirsch, John F. Chaves, Theodore R. Sarbin, George K. Ganaway and Russell A. Powell. 1999. 'Dissociative identity disorder and the sociocognitive model: Recalling the lessons of the past', *Psychological Bulletin* 125 (5): 507–23.

McAllister, Margaret and Donna Lee Brien. 2015. 'Haunted: Exploring representations of mental health through the lens of the Gothic', *Aeternum: The Journal of Contemporary Gothic Studies* 2 (1): 72–90.

Merriam-Webster Online. 2022. 'Passage'. Accessed 16 February 2022. https://www.merriam-webster.com/dictionary/passage.

Morson, Gary Saul. 2015. 'Me and my double: Selfhood, consciousness, and empathy in *The Double*'. In *Before They Were Titans: Essays on the early works of Dostoevsky and Tolstoy*, edited by Elizabeth Cheresh Allen, 43–60. Brookline, MA: Academic Studies Press.

Moskowitz, Andrew. 2011a. 'On the relation between trauma, dissociation, psychotic symptoms and schizophrenia'. European Society for Trauma & Dissociation, June. Accessed 16 February 2022. http://estd.org/relation-between-trauma-dissociation-psychotic-symptoms-and-schizophrenia.

Moskowitz, Andrew. 2011b. 'Schizophrenia, trauma, dissociation, and scientific revolutions', *Journal of Trauma & Dissociation* 12 (4): 347–57.

Performing Arts School of Classical Ballet. 2016. 'Ballet lessons: What is Swan Lake about?', 21 June. Accessed 16 February 2022. https://pascb.com/ballet-lessons-swan-lake/.

Sexeny, Julie. 2015. 'Identification and mutual recognition in Darren Aronofsky's *Black Swan*'. In *Embodied Encounters: New approaches to psychoanalysis and cinema*, edited by Agnieszka Piotrowska, 51–9. London: Routledge.

Shelley, Mary. 1994. *Frankenstein*. New York: Dover.

Stevenson, Robert Louis. 1991. *The Strange Case of Dr Jekyll and Mr Hyde*. New York: Dover.

Teeple, Ryan C., Jason P. Caplan and Theodore A. Stern. 2009. 'Visual hallucinations: Differential diagnosis and treatment', *Primary Care Companion to The Journal of Clinical Psychiatry* 11 (1): 26–32.

Thompson, Anne. 2010. 'Aronofsky talks the "nightmare" of getting "Black Swan" made', *Indiewire*, 15 September. Accessed 16 February 2022. https://www.indiewire.com/2010/09/aronofsky-talks-the-nightmare-of-getting-black-swan-made-238424/.

Wilde, Oscar. 2005. *The Picture of Dorian Gray*. Clayton, DE: Prestwick House.

11
Passage and flow: oceanic dystopia in the self-conscious Anthropocene

Florian Mussgnug

The water is rising on us. In 2020, the United Nations Intergovernmental Panel on Climate Change (IPCC) estimated that sea levels will rise by approximately half a metre in the twenty-first century if drastic cuts to carbon emission are imposed now. Without such cuts, oceans are likely to rise twice as much by 2100 (IPCC 2019).[1] Large floods are predicted to occur with increasing frequency, especially in tropical regions. Indeed, it is expected that these vulnerable areas – the 'tropic of chaos', in Christian Parenti's words – will be hit simultaneously by multiple connected natural disasters, due to complex weather systems and feedback loops (Parenti 2011). Warmer oceans, for example, not only accelerate the melt of ice sheets in Greenland and Antarctica, but also absorb less heat from the atmosphere, and thereby increase the likelihood of heat waves and droughts. Similarly, sea-level rise and more frequent flooding will inundate farmland, cause crop failure and thus push climate refugees into other regions. Such cascades have a particularly devastating impact on coastal communities, and it has been suggested that rising sea levels may leave hundreds of millions of people without a home by 2050.[2] And this is just the beginning. Science journalist Peter Brannen neatly sums up the long-term consequences of unchecked global warming:

Within a couple of centuries much of Florida will drown. So too will Bangladesh, most of the Nile Delta, and New Orleans. In the centuries beyond, if our experiment with the climate goes unchecked, so too will much of New York City, Boston, Amsterdam, Venice, and countless other temporary shelters of humanity. (Brannen 2017, 260)

How is this troubling prospect considered and communicated in twenty-first century literature? In her recent, important monograph, *Allegories of the Anthropocene* (2019), postcolonial theorist and environmental scholar Elizabeth DeLoughrey has described fluidity, mutability and risk as the emerging hallmarks of a new oceanic imagination, which she contrasts with the predominantly land-based imaginaries of twentieth-century nature writing (DeLoughrey 2019). Sea-level rise is only one of the many existential threats that result from global heating, but it has attracted particular attention in literature and the media, as perhaps the most visible sign of an unfolding planetary catastrophe. Pictures of flooded cities and landmarks are a familiar trope in political campaigns for sustainability and behavioural change.[3] Similarly, rising sea levels and floods have featured in many recent novels, including – since the publication of DeLoughrey's study – John Lanchester's *The Wall* (2019), Kassandra Montag's *After the Flood* (2019), Pitchaya Sudbanthad's *Bangkok Wakes to Rain* (2019), Carys Bray's *When the Lights Go Out* (2020), Richard Flanagan's *The Living Sea of Waking Dreams* (2020), M. John Harrison's *The Sunken Land Begins to Rise Again* (2020), Andrew Hunter Murray's *The Last Day* (2020) and M.R. Carey's *Rampart Trilogy* (2020a; 2020b; 2021), among others. As DeLoughrey points out, the ocean, which makes up seventy per cent of the surface of Earth, has finally entered our stories, through a steady 'increase in books, films and photography representing the ocean (including the poles) as an active agent, as well as an expansion in technologies and sciences dedicated to both studying and mining the minerals of the seabed' (DeLoughrey 2019, 134). The sea is no longer considered external to human societies, but features with growing frequency as humanity's impoverished and perilous future habitat.

Building on DeLoughrey's work, my chapter discusses two recent examples of oceanic climate fiction – Clare Morrall's *When the Floods Came* (2016) and Helen Marshall's *The Migration* (2019) – through the dual conceptual lens of 'passage' and 'flow'. I have chosen these two related concepts because of their specific engagement with spatial and temporal scales, and I will consider them here as literary themes and allegorical forms, adopting the critical method that DeLoughrey, in turn, derives from Walter Benjamin and Gayatri Chakravorty Spivak. Allegory, as DeLoughrey explains, is an adaptive and fluid mode, and therefore especially suited to the experiences of rupture and entanglement that define our post-holocenic cultural present (DeLoughrey 2019, 9). In my discussion, I will employ 'passage' – a term that evokes the imperial cartographies and biopolitical violence of colonialism and slavery – to shed light on contemporary transnational chains of ecological, political and cultural interdependence (see Drabinski 2019). By contrast, 'flow' will serve to explore a latent but growing desire, in twenty-first century literature, for new horizons of posthuman vitality. 'Passage', in other words, marks the political importance of climate fiction as a critique of globalization, whereas 'flow' evokes the ocean as a force that transcends existing human social categories, boundaries and limits, and that can activate new relations with non-human nature. These attitudes will be exemplified, respectively, by the two aforementioned British novels, which similarly feature the sea as a dynamic, intimate and threatening force: not an 'alien ocean', in Stefan Helmreich's words, but an encroaching, uncanny presence that disrupts the flow of everyday life (Helmreich 2009).

Morrall's *When the Floods Came* and Marshall's *The Migration* belong to a highly recognizable popular genre that political scientist Lucy Sargisson has described as climate dystopia. Both novels are set in Britain, in an unspecified, catastrophic near future, and focus on contrasting individual responses to the climate emergency. They raise questions about responsibility and agency in our present, and reflect on contemporary environmental challenges, 'sketching key problems to extremes and placing them in an imaginary future' (Sargisson 2012, 98). For this reason, the two novels may also be described as 'critical dystopias', according to Tom Moylan's influential definition: their vision of the future is strictly focused on the concrete level of lived experience (Moylan 2000). In both texts, environmental catastrophe unfolds in the home, and in surprisingly ordinary settings: a tower block in Birmingham; a family house in suburban Oxford. Rising sea levels and flooded wastelands, for Morrall and Marshall, are not harbingers of a future menace, but part of the quotidian, in a manner that collapses the difference between personal and planetary scale. *The Migration* and *When the Floods Came* imagine strikingly ordinary domestic futures, which hold up a 'shocking mirror' of cognitive estrangement – in Darko Suvin's words – to our present, and thereby seek to invite behavioural change, and to expose the flaws and contradictions of contemporary climate politics (Suvin 1979, 57). The two writers also engage with the particular generic conventions of young adult fiction.[4] In both novels, the conflict between laconic endurance (nostalgia) and radical political and aesthetic reorientation (activism) is played out in strictly generational terms, according to a set of tropes that is also influential in twenty-first century climate protest movements.[5] In Morrall's and Marshall's stories, only the young can truly comprehend the obsolescence of modern civilization and the inadequacy of conventionally tragic responses to global warming – what Timothy Morton has playfully described as the 'default agricultural mode' of climate politics (Morton 2016, 6). Unlike their parents, Marshall's and Morrall's protagonists belong to a generation that was born into the 'weird weirdness' – I quote Morton again – of environmental catastrophe (6).

My reading of the two novels relates 'passage' to *When the Floods Came* and associates 'flow' with *The Migration*. It is not my intention, however, to bestow a unique and specific meaning on the two concepts. Rather, I use both terms, in the words of anthropologist Marilyn Strathern, as poetic and cross-disciplinary *attractors*. What attracts me to 'passage' and 'flow' is their productive ambivalence, as well as their power to engage other terms and concepts, draw in values and disseminate feelings, 'exactly as though everyone knew what was meant' (Strathern 2020, 2). In this respect, 'passage' and 'flow' exemplify the rapidly growing importance of relational thinking in the environmental arts and humanities. They speak to an increasingly common understanding of the human and more-than-human world as a single material and ethical force field: a tangle of relations. Consequently, my interpretation of Morrall's and Marshall's novels highlights how human and non-human ways of being are shaped by the collisions, frictions, confluences and intimacies between species, or, in the words of Stacy Alaimo, by 'the literal contact zone between human corporeality and more-than-human nature' (Alaimo 2010, 2). I also suggest, with Amy J. Elias and Christian Moraru, that 'today's planetary life consists in an incessantly thickening, historically unprecedented web of relations among people, cultures, and locales', and that 'to comprehend the planetary must entail grasping the relationality embedded in it' (Elias and Moraru 2015, xii). This claim is also relevant to the realm of the aesthetic, where art practice has come to be understood as a set of immanent, ever-modulating force-relations that emphasize both relatedness and interruptions in relatedness, across space and time.[6] I echo this fluidity in my use of the disciplinary conventions of literary criticism in this chapter. In a move that explicitly mirrors the shift from *terra* to *oceanus* in twenty-first century oceanic literature, I engage 'passage' and 'flow' as aesthetic openings, to disorient and reorient critical thinking in the environmental humanities, and to challenge established 'territorial' boundaries of disciplinary enquiry. As literary critic Steve Mentz remarks: '[r]ethinking movement as flows and circuits rather than progress or retreat can revivify intellectual communities. Thinking in terms of cyclical flows rather than linear progress makes historical narratives messier, more confusing, and less familiar. These are good things' (Mentz 2020, xvii).

A new cultural dominant

DeLoughrey's analysis of oceanic literature unfolds in the context of a wider political critique of Anthropocene discourse (DeLoughrey 2019). Beyond the specific expertise of earth scientists, the Anthropocene has become a staging ground for debates about environmental justice, race, decoloniality and the crisis of global capitalism. As Jussi Parikka explains, the Anthropocene marks a challenge to the traditional humanities, but it has also served as 'a useful trigger for a variety of approaches that are interested in the nonhuman and post-human' (Parikka 2018, 52). Faced with the gravity of the unfolding planetary environmental crisis, scholars in the arts and humanities have turned their attention to the Anthropocene, both as a temporal and historiographic marker, and as a new periodization of the contemporary.[7] For example, Anthropocene discourse has served as a powerful transdisciplinary vector in comparative literature, cultural studies and the environmental humanities.[8] Earth scientists and biologists have become more attentive to political, economic and cultural structures, in a manner that cuts across established disciplinary boundaries. Similarly, numerous artists have focused on natural processes that are affected by human activities and impinge upon them: extreme weather events, rising sea levels, pollution, mass extinction and so on.[9] As novelist Amitav Ghosh has famously pointed out, 'the climate crisis is also a crisis of culture, and thus of the imagination' (Ghosh 2016, 9). This situation, in which new narratives and controversies are generated out of the limits of earlier debates and disciplinary orientations, can be considered, in Fredric Jameson's terms, as a dialectic moment of passage:

> in which the foregrounding of continuities, the insistent and unwavering focus on the seamless passage from past to present, slowly turns into a consciousness of a radical break; while at the

same time the enforced attention to a break gradually turns the latter into a period in its own right. (Jameson 2002, 24)

Borrowing from North American literary scholar Lynn Keller, I use the term 'self-conscious Anthropocene' to describe this reorientation of scholarly attention and artistic practice since the turn of the century (Keller 2017).[10] Keller's expression serves, in my intention, both as an emergent historiographic label in the arts and humanities, and as the name of a new cultural dominant. I suggest, in fact, that cultural production has been reshaped, over the past two decades, by an increasing awareness of catastrophic environmental degradation, and that new forms, genres and themes have emerged in response to the anthropogenic violation of non-human species and more-than-human habitats. This includes the literary genre of oceanic dystopia, which I examine in this chapter. What attracts me to Keller's terminology, in addition to her specific interest in poetic form, is the fact that the 'self-conscious Anthropocene' displays, but also displaces, anxieties over geological time and stories of origin.[11] Since its inception in 2009, the multidisciplinary Anthropocene Working Group (AWG) has considered three possible beginnings for the Anthropocene: the Columbian exchange, the Industrial Revolution and the so-called 'Great Acceleration' since 1945.[12] From the perspective of literary and cultural studies, these three hypotheses concerning the passage from the Holocene to the 'Age of Man' are perhaps less interesting than the idea of a new Anthropocenic cultural dominant. Where cross-disciplinary discussions about the Anthropocene typically focus on the putative beginning of the new geological era, Keller's terminology, by contrast, focuses critical attention on the period when the Anthropocene comes into view as an influential generative concept: a new cultural dominant. As Keller explains, 'the phrase acknowledges that, whatever the status of the Anthropocene as a geological category …, [the term] signals a powerful cultural phenomenon tied to the reflexive, critical, and often anxious awareness of the scale and severity of human effects on the planet' (Keller 2017, 1–2).

Keller's terminology – and the work of philosopher Donna Haraway (2016) and literary critics Elizabeth DeLoughrey (2019) and Steve Mentz (2019), among others – inform my approach to climate fiction in this chapter. I embrace the sense of extreme urgency that typically characterizes debates about climate change and climate science, but question the teleological structures of thought that have shaped many contemporary accounts of the 'Age of Man'. Instead of focusing, in Mentz's words, on 'the apocalyptic story in which Old Man Anthropos destroys the world', I call attention to the vulnerability and value of human and non-human life on a warming planet, and suggest that the climate emergency needs to be understood as a dynamic opening: an invitation to rethink categories of place and space, not in terms of eschatological closure, but as a state of protracted uncertainty that necessitates and activates new political, artistic and epistemic modes (Mentz 2019, 1).[13] DeLoughrey elaborates on this in *Allegories of the Anthropocene*, where she challenges the universalizing focus on novelty and catastrophic rupture in Anthropocene discourse. For her, this focus threatens to erase plural histories of ecological violence and imperialist exploitation, from transatlantic European colonization to the modern fossil fuel industry. Indigenous and postcolonial perspectives, she argues, hold the power to remind us that the 'catastrophic ruptures to social and ecological systems have already been experienced through the violent processes of empire. In other words, the apocalypse has already happened; it continues because empire is a process' (DeLoughry 2019, 2).

Inundated worlds

How is this tension between traumatic rupture (extreme weather events) and lingering biopolitical violence (colonial mastery) expressed in my examples of twenty-first century oceanic fiction? Clare Morrall's *When the Floods Came* is set in a largely abandoned tower block outside Birmingham, in an area that is frequently flooded and has become inaccessible for months at a time. The protagonist, 22-year-old Roza Polanski, and her family of six lead a seemingly normal life, working online for a Chinese company, feeding on the care packages delivered by North American 'drone drops' and riding their bicycles on empty roads, when water levels are sufficiently low. During flood seasons, the Polanskis play indoor games, watch old films, argue over Roza's wish for a digitally arranged marriage or discuss the sporadic news that reaches them through a heavily censored internet. Rarely, their conversations touch on the pre-apocalyptic past. When Roza's parents, Popi and Moth, reminisce about the world before the floods, and before the pandemic that has decimated the human world population, laconic Roza simply insists that, 'our family has been lucky' (Morrall 2016, 46). And her more reckless sister Delphine proclaims that comparisons with the past are something for old people: '[w]hy can't they just get on with things and forget the world they grew up in? It's never going to come back' (79). Roza and Delphine dream of a different, more adventurous life, but their hopes for freedom come to a bitter end in the second half of the novel. During one of her furtive visits to the abandoned and partly flooded Birmingham Art Gallery, Roza encounters Aashay, a mysterious and handsome young stranger, who introduces her and her siblings to a hidden world of contraband and travelling fairs. Roza is attracted to Aashay, but he finally betrays her trust. Disturbing intimations of child trafficking rumble beneath the surface of Aashay's seemingly welcoming, libertarian community, and in the end the Polanskis have no choice but to seek protection from the remote authoritarian government that has been imposing its care packages and strict surveillance on them since the beginning of the story.

While Clare Morrall sets her novel in a post-apocalyptic future Birmingham, Helen Marshall's *The Migration* imagines a near-future Oxford that slowly but steadily vanishes under the river Cherwell's rising waters. As in *When the Floods Came*, the family at the heart of Marshall's story appears unaware, or stoically indifferent, to the unfolding climate emergency, at least until a mysterious new immune disorder begins to afflict the young. Aunt Irene, a medieval historian, is intrigued by contemporary records of the Black Death, because, she proclaims, 'a disaster that large' would be unimaginable in the twenty-first century: '[t]here wasn't anything in my experience that helped me understand it' (Marshall 2019, 43). The irony, of course, lies in the fact that Irene's Oxford college is literally surrounded by a greater menace – the flood and the pandemic – which remains entirely unaccounted for in this passage, but which subsequently causes the apparent death of two of the main characters. Again, it is the novel's adolescent protagonist, Sophie, who arrives at a radically different understanding of existential risk. In an inundated world, she contends, it is easier to imagine the horrors of the Black Death than to recall the surprising stability and predictability of holocenic ecologies and societies: the world of her parents. 'Don't you feel it?', Sophie asks her friend Bryan, as they both stare at the flooded expanse of Port Meadow, '[t]his ... can't be forever. Maybe the world worked one way for our parents, for their parents – but not for us. It isn't the same' (340). Marshall's darkly imaginative novel develops this intuition through its unexpected, surrealist ending. All hope seems to be gone when Sophie's younger sister Kira succumbs to the pandemic, but ultimately the girls discover that the victims of the new disease – all young people – are not in fact terminally ill, but rather affected by an eerie vitality that is no longer fully human. Their bodies undergo a mysterious metamorphosis, which leaves them transmuted, beyond human recognition, into a new bodily form that appears more suited to survival on an increasingly oceanic planet.

In its final chapters, *The Migration* plays with century-old fantasies of the ocean as a realm of pure nature, a vast blank space outside human control: *aqua nullius*. The sea, according to this cultural tradition, is limitless and unbound. Like Kira's and Sophie's new bodies, the ocean possesses a primordial fertility that lies outside the orbit of history. This is the sensation that Romain Rolland and Sigmund Freud called the *oceanic feeling* (Freud 1962, 11), and which inspired Gaston Bachelard to wax lyrical about the 'substantive nothingness of water' (Bachelard 1983, 6).[14] Helen Marshall pays homage to this tradition when she describes Sophie's final encounter with the sea as a posthuman epiphany of joyful material dissolution: 'I'm pouring out of my body and into the darkness, spread so thin, thin as electrons spinning and spinning, shifting: becoming this: the hidden world, it is me, it is all of us' (Marshall 2019, 377). The ending of *When the Floods Came*, by contrast, appears more pessimistic. Unlike Sophie, Roza remains imprisoned in a claustrophobic, decaying human world that – just like the oceans of our own age – remains entirely regulated by political, economic and military interests. Where Marshall conjures subversive dreams of oceanic freedom, Morrall's watery dystopia examines the noxious legacy of centuries of maritime imperialism and violence. Roza lives in a world of crumbling cities and collapsing ecosystems. Nevertheless, her post-apocalyptic life is firmly shaped by the interdependencies and inequalities of transnational capitalism: she is a recipient of North American humanitarian aid, delivered by military drones, the employee of a Chinese multinational, and, despite her dreams of rebellion, an obedient citizen of the authoritarian and technocratic future Britain, which is governed from Brighton and survives only because of its draconian policies of population control and forced marriage.

The fluidity of the future

Contemporary oceanic fiction offers numerous other, related examples of the tension between darkly romantic fantasies of posthuman transgression ('flow') and the strictures of advanced capitalist globalization ('passage'). Port Meadow and the Thames Valley, for instance, are also flooded in Philip Pullman's *La Belle Sauvage* (2017), where Spenserian fairies coexist with the ruthless enforcement agents of a proto-capitalist theocratic government, the Magisterium. Nathaniel Rich's *Odds Against Tomorrow* (2013) imagines Manhattan under water, seen through the eyes of a risk analyst. *La seconda mezzanotte* (2011), by Italian novelist Antonio Scurati, conjures a mid-century underwater Venice, protected by a large glass cupola for the benefit of wealthy Chinese tourists. Most recently, Ben Smith's skilfully dreary novel *Doggerland* (2019) invites us to imagine life on a vast coastal wind farm, where two Beckettian characters – a boy and an old man – lead a life of monotony and confinement, surrounded by floating debris and a dying ocean. While the silent old man appears to hold some secret knowledge of the environmental catastrophe that hit the mainland, the boy's entire life has been spent offshore, on the bleak archipelago of rusty platforms that functions for both characters as a precarious space of last retreat: a minimal 'aquatopia', in Elizabeth DeLoughrey's words (DeLoughrey 2019, 146). Under the surface, the reader senses a world of collapsing marine ecosystems that is painful to contemplate.[15] At the time of writing, countless species have been overfished to the point of extinction, or have been endangered by the thoughtless destruction of marine habitats. Atomic testing and deep-sea mining have caused irreparable damage. Industrialization and the runoff from sewage and chemical fertilizers have accelerated the spread of anoxic waters, or so-called 'dead zones'. Ocean acidification, deep-sea warming and plastic pollution are destroying complex ecosystems, which have been home to thousands of species. Veteran environmentalist Bill McKibben warns that, by the middle of this century, oceans are likely to contain more plastic than fish, by weight. All the world's coral reefs might be dead by then (McKibben 2019, 46, 50). The future of the sea is bleak, and has perhaps no better symbol than the Great Pacific Garbage Patch, an enormous concentration of floating plastic, which is currently approaching the size of Russia. What will happen to us, asks Mentz, 'when all waters everywhere throb with these same colours, these same plastics, this toxicity?' (Mentz 2019, x).

Oceanic dystopia, in its diverse forms, draws attention to these questions, through its political and ethical critique of advanced globalization and environmental slow violence. Beyond their immediate concern, respectively, with 'passage' and 'flow', all the literary case studies in this chapter share a pressing concern with anthropogenic environmental degradation. It is worth pointing out, moreover, that all the aforementioned novels are set in small and oppressively claustrophobic fictional worlds. In this regard, they develop one of the most characteristic generic conventions of utopian and dystopian writing: spatialization. Ever since Thomas More conceived of his island kingdom, journeys, walls and similar barriers have been a defining feature of utopia.[16] Utopian worlds are usually imagined as physically remote or distant in time, even where their political critique of the contemporary is concrete and specific.[17] As Peter Ruppert remarks, classical utopias are self-contained and static, or at least resistant to uncontrollable and uncontrolled change. In utopian societies, nothing of significance ever happens, or, more precisely, everything significant has *already* taken place (Ruppert 1986, 27). Progress, political experiment and time itself, in any meaningful sense, are banned from 'the good place'. Utopian thinking, for this reason, echoes apocalyptic religion, with its monumental vision of a space beyond history: a Heavenly Jerusalem that functions, as Steven Goldsmith points out, as 'the sublime rupture that occurs when time becomes space, when history meets its final antithesis in both a heavenly city and a book' (Goldsmith 1993, 56).[18] In traditional utopian literature – as in the Church's official interpretation of Revelation – the shift from a temporal to a spatial order functions as a symbol of enduring social power, a source of authority, which lies beyond history, and therefore marks a line beyond which dispute cannot pass.

As this chapter has shown, twenty-first century dystopias, despite their attention to place, break with the tradition of apocalyptic *telos*. Their engagement with fluidity marks the emergence of a new affective register, which runs counter to both religious millenarianism and to the spatializing impulse of twentieth-century utopian and dystopian fiction. Instead of promising catastrophic closure or redemption, oceanic literature urges us to stretch the limits of our imagination towards responsible and responsive local sensitivity: 'situated knowledges', in Donna Haraway's terms (Haraway 1988, 575–99). Its critique of capitalist globalization is always embedded in specific contexts, and foregrounds the importance of the more-than-human world, not as a mere backdrop or context for human stories, but as a co-constitutive presence. In this way, 'passage' and 'flow' enable us to express the fundamental unpredictability of post-holocenic societies and ecologies – and perhaps to regain some of the vital energy that Freud ascribed to oceanic feeling (Freud 1962, 11). Environmental catastrophe, cascading existential risk and planetary entanglement generate a protracted uncertainty, which can find expression in fantasies of rupture or efforts to reorient our political values. Either way, climate fiction illustrates an urgent need for new political and epistemic modes.

Notes

1 For a list of the IPCC's recommendations, see IPCC (2019).
2 A 2018 World Bank study predicts that by 2050, climate change may displace as many as 143 million people from Africa, South Asia and Latin America. See McKibben (2019, 29).

3   Consider, for example, the slogan of the climate justice campaign launched by the United Nations Environment Programme (UNEP) on World Environment Day 2014: 'Raise your voice, not the sea level'.
4   See Hintz and Ostry (2009); Basu et al. (2015).
5   Fridays for Future is a particularly good example. See also Klein (2019, Introduction).
6   See Mussgnug (2018).
7   See Bonneuil and Fressoz (2015); Davies (2016).
8   See DeLoughrey et al. (2015); Heise et al. (2017); Emmett and Nye (2017); Barry and Welstead (2017).
9   See Trexler (2015); Johns-Putra (2019).
10 I explore the significance of Keller's terminology in Mussgnug (2021).
11 Kathryn Yusoff (2018) offers a provocative and illuminating discussion of the erasure of colonial mastery from geological discourse.
12 The Columbian hypothesis was advanced by Simon Lewis and Mark Maslin (2015). See also Thomas et al. (2020); McNeill and Engelke (2016).
13 For further discussion, see Mussgnug (2019).
14 Both texts are quoted in Dening (2004). See also Probyn (2016, Chapter 1).
15 See Alaimo (2016, Chapter 5).
16 See Jameson (1977).
17 See Jameson (2005).
18 See Goldsmith (1993, 56). For a more detailed discussion of utopia and religious apocalypse, see Aichele and Pippin (1998). See also Ferns (1999, 21): 'the fact that time, in any meaningful sense has come to a stop often lends to the traditional utopian narrative a millenarian character'. For my contribution to this debate, see Mussgnug (2013).

References

Aichele, George and Tina Pippin, eds. 1998. *Violence, Utopia and the Kingdom of God: Fantasy and ideology in the Bible*. London: Routledge.
Alaimo, Stacy. 2010. *Bodily Natures: Science, environment, and the material self*. Bloomington: Indiana University Press.
Alaimo, Stacy. 2016. *Exposed: Environmental politics and pleasures in posthuman times*. Minneapolis: University of Minnesota Press.
Bachelard, Gaston. 1983 [1942]. *Water and Dreams*, translated by Edith R. Farrell. Dallas, TX: Pegasus.
Barry, Peter and William Welstead, eds. 2017. *Extending Ecocriticism: Crisis, collaboration and challenges in the environmental humanities*. Oxford: Oxford University Press.
Basu, Balaka, Katherine R. Broad and Carrie Hintz, eds. 2015. *Contemporary Dystopian Fiction for Young Adults: Brave new teenagers*. New York: Routledge.
Bonneuil, Christophe and Jean-Baptiste Fressoz. 2015. *The Shock of the Anthropocene*, translated by David Fernbach. London: Verso.
Brannen, Peter. 2017. *The Ends of the World: Volcanic apocalypses, lethal oceans and our quest to understand Earth's past mass extinctions*. London: Oneworld.
Bray, Carys. 2020. *When the Lights Go Out*. London: Hutchinson.
Carey, M.R. 2020a. *The Book of Koli: The Rampart trilogy book 1*. New York: Orbit.
Carey, M.R. 2020b. *The Trials of Koli: The Rampart trilogy book 2*. New York: Orbit.
Carey, M.R. 2021. *The Fall of Koli: The Rampart trilogy book 3*. New York: Orbit.
Davies, Jeremy. 2016. *The Birth of the Anthropocene*. Oakland: University of California Press.
DeLoughrey, Elizabeth M. 2019. *Allegories of the Anthropocene*. Durham, NC: Duke University Press.
DeLoughrey, Elizabeth, Jill Didur and Anthony Carrigan, eds. 2015. *Global Ecologies and the Environmental Humanities: Postcolonial approaches*. New York: Routledge.
Dening, Greg. 2004. 'Deep times, deep spaces: Civilizing the sea'. In *Sea Changes: Historicizing the ocean*, edited by Bernhard Klein and Gesa Mackenthus, 13–36. New York: Routledge.
Drabinski, John E. 2019. *Glissant and the Middle Passage: Philosophy, beginning, abyss*. Minneapolis: Minnesota University Press.

Elias, Amy J. and Christian Moraru, eds. 2015. *The Planetary Turn: Relationality and geoaesthetics in the twenty-first century*. Evanston, IL: Northwestern University Press.
Emmett, Robert S. and David E. Nye. 2017. *The Environmental Humanities: A critical introduction*. Cambridge, MA: MIT Press.
Ferns, Chris. 1999. *Narrating Utopia: Ideology, gender, form in utopian literature*. Liverpool: Liverpool University Press.
Flanagan, Richard. 2020. *The Living Sea of Waking Dreams*. London: Chatto & Windus.
Freud, Sigmund. 1962 [1930]. *Civilization and Its Discontents*, translated by James Strachey. New York: W.W. Norton.
Ghosh, Amitav. 2016. *The Great Derangement: Climate change and the unthinkable*. Chicago: Chicago University Press.
Goldsmith, Steven. 1993. *Unbuilding Jerusalem: Apocalypse and romantic representation*. Ithaca, NY: Cornell University Press.
Haraway, Donna J. 1988. 'Situated knowledges: The science question in feminism and the privilege of partial perspective', *Feminist Studies* 14 (3): 575–99.
Haraway, Donna J. 2016. *Staying with the Trouble: Making kin in the Chthulucene*. Durham, NC: Duke University Press.
Harrison, M. John. 2020. *The Sunken Land Begins to Rise Again*. London: Gollancz.
Heise, Ursula K., Jon Christensen and Michelle Niemann, eds. 2017. *The Routledge Companion to the Environmental Humanities*. New York: Routledge.
Helmreich, Stefan. 2009. *Alien Ocean: Anthropological voyages in microbial seas*. Berkeley: University of California Press.
Hintz, Carrie and Elaine Ostry, eds. 2009. *Utopian and Dystopian Writing for Children and Young Adults*. New York: Routledge.
IPCC. 2019. 'Summary for policymakers', *IPCC Special Report on the Ocean and Cryosphere in a Changing Climate*, edited by H.-O. Pörtner, D.C. Roberts, V. Masson-Delmotte, P. Zhai, M. Tignor, E. Poloczanska, K. Mintenbeck, A. Alegría, M. Nicolai, A. Okem, J. Petzold, B. Rama and N.M. Weyer. Accessed 29 January 2022. https://www.ipcc.ch/srocc/chapter/summary-for-policymakers/.
Jameson, Fredric. 1977. 'Of islands and trenches: Naturalization and the production of utopian discourse', *Diacritics* 7: 2–21.
Jameson, Fredric. 2002. *A Singular Modernity: Essay on the ontology of the present*. London: Verso.
Jameson, Fredric. 2005. *Archaeologies of the Future: The desire called utopia and other science fictions*. London: Verso.
Johns-Putra, Adeline. 2019. *Climate Change and the Contemporary Novel*. Cambridge: Cambridge University Press.
Keller, Lynn. 2017. *Recomposing Ecopoetics: North American poetry of the self-conscious Anthropocene*. Charlottesville: Virginia University Press.
Klein, Naomi. 2019. *On Fire: The burning case for a Green New Deal*. London: Penguin.
Lanchester, John. 2019. *The Wall*. New York: W.W. Norton & Company.
Lewis, Simon and Mark Maslin. 2015. 'Defining the Anthropocene', *Nature* 519: 171–80.
Marshall, Helen. 2019. *The Migration*. London: Titan Books.
McKibben, Bill. 2019. *Falter: Has the human game begun to play itself out?* London: Wildfire.
McNeill, J.R. and Peter Engelke. 2016. *The Great Acceleration: An environmental history of the Anthropocene since 1945*. Cambridge, MA: Harvard University Press.
Mentz, Steve. 2019. *Break Up the Anthropocene*. Minneapolis: Minnesota University Press.
Mentz, Steve. 2020. *Ocean*. London: Bloomsbury.
Montag, Kassandra. 2019. *After the Flood*. New York: Harper Collins.
Morrall, Clare. 2016. *When the Floods Came*. London: Sceptre.
Morton, Timothy. 2016. *Dark Ecology: For a logic of future coexistence*. New York: Columbia University Press.
Moylan, Tom. 2000. *Scraps of the Untainted Sky: Science fiction, utopia, dystopia*. Boulder, CO: Westview Press.
Murray, Andrew Hunter. 2020. *The Last Day*. London: Hutchinson.
Mussgnug, Florian. 2013. 'No new earth: Apocalyptic rhetoric in Italian nuclear-war literature'. In *Beyond Catholicism: Heresy, mysticism, and apocalypse in Italian culture*, edited by Simon Gilson and Fabrizio De Donno, 195–216. Basingstoke: Palgrave Macmillan.
Mussgnug, Florian. 2018. 'Planetary figurations: Intensive genre in world literature', *Modern Languages Open* 1: 22.

Mussgnug, Florian. 2019. 'Species at war? The animal and the Anthropocene', *Paragraph* 42 (1): 116–30.
Mussgnug, Florian. 2021. 'World literature and the self-conscious Anthropocene', *Literary Research/Récherche Littéraire* 37: 207–14.
Parenti, Christian. 2011. *Tropic of Chaos: Climate change and the new geography of violence*. New York: Nation Books.
Parikka, Jussi. 2018. 'Anthropocene'. In *Posthuman Glossary*, edited by Rosi Braidotti and Maria Hlavajova, 52. London: Bloomsbury.
Probyn, Elspeth. 2016. *Eating the Ocean*. Durham, NC: Duke University Press.
Pullman, Philip. 2017. *La Belle Sauvage*. Oxford: David Fickling Books.
Rich, Nathaniel. 2013. *Odds Against Tomorrow*. New York: Picador.
Ruppert, Peter. 1986. *Reader in a Strange Land: The activity of reading literary utopias*. Athens: University of Georgia Press.
Sargisson, Lucy. 2012. *Fool's Gold? Utopianism in the twenty-first century*. Basingstoke: Palgrave Macmillan.
Scurati, Antonio. 2011. *La seconda mezzanotte*. Milan: Bompiani.
Smith, Ben. 2019. *Doggerland*. London: 4thEstate.
Strathern, Marilyn. 2020. *Relations: An anthropological account*. Durham, NC: Duke University Press.
Sudbanthad, Pitchaya. 2019. *Bangkok Wakes to Rain*. New York: Riverhead Books.
Suvin, Darko. 1979. *Metamorphoses of Science Fiction: On the poetics and history of a literary genre*. New Haven, CT: Yale University Press.
Thomas, Julia Adeney, Mark Williams and Jan Zalasiewicz. 2020. *The Anthropocene: A multidisciplinary approach*. Cambridge: Polity.
Trexler, Adam. 2015. *Anthropocene Fictions: The novel in a time of climate change*. Charlottesville: Virginia University Press.
Yusoff, Kathryn. 2018. *A Billion Black Anthropocenes or None*. Minneapolis: Minnesota University Press.

Part III
Political passages related to identity, othering, supremacy and power

12
The gaze and the city: woman walking down the street

Martina Hrbková

Virginia Woolf and Jean Rhys are authors for whom the city constitutes an essential setting. For Woolf, the dominant city is London; for Rhys, it is Paris. Both of them create female characters whose passage through the space of the city plays an important role in exploring their subjectivity and identity. This chapter considers themes of visibility, self-perception and the internalized patriarchal gaze that these characters experience as they move through the public space of the street and are coded as female bodies. The meaning of passage here is literal in the spatial sense: the passage is the space of the street, as well as the act of passing through it. However, the passage as a section of space and as an act of movement is also charged with relations of power. Through his essayistic work on Charles Baudelaire, as well as his writing compiled in *The Arcades Project*, or *Passagenwerk*, Walter Benjamin (2006, 1999) popularized the figure of the *flâneur* as a topic of interest. The term designates the nineteenth-century male wanderer who leisurely observes the urban scene. The *flâneur* is someone who is keen to find refuge in the crowd. One of his principal characteristics is that he 'makes himself into a registering sensibility' (Gelley 2015, 119) as he walks in the street and looks into the shop windows. For him, the passage is neutral. In contrast, neither the space nor the act is neutral when it comes to the presence and activity of women. Although the narrative styles and moods of Woolf's and Rhys's prose in many ways differ, they are concerned with similar themes, and they both demonstrate how the experience of walking through a city never seems to be casual for women. It is marked by self-consciousness regarding one's physical presence – more specifically, a pervasive and recurrent sense of (self-)surveillance. This is a product of specific power relations, and social and gendered codes. This chapter focuses primarily on the novels *Good Morning, Midnight* and *After Leaving Mr Mackenzie* by Jean Rhys, and *Mrs Dalloway* and *The Years* by Virginia Woolf. However, relevant instances in Woolf's *The Voyage Out*, *Jacob's Room* and *Between the Acts* are also touched upon, as Woolf also alludes to the theme in question within these texts.

Panopticon of patriarchy

In *Ways of Seeing*, John Berger describes the societal dynamic of the gaze within patriarchal society, in which '[m]en look at women. Women watch themselves being looked at' (Berger 2008, 47). It is a scheme in which men are the surveyors and women are not only the surveyed, but they also internalize the feeling of being observed, which makes them automatically monitor themselves. To further illustrate how this dynamic of the power of the gaze works in a more general societal context, and consequently in urban space, it can be related to Foucault's notion of the panopticon, an architectural figure through which he describes the principle of functioning of power in establishing discipline and the control of bodies. The panopticon is a ring-shaped prison with a watchtower in the middle, from which the prisoners in their cells are supervised by a guard who is not visible to them (Foucault 1991, 19). The mechanism creates an opposition between the one who is seen without ever seeing, and the one who sees without ever being seen. The observed individual assumes they are always being observed, which removes the necessity for the observer to be there. The effect is the induction in the prisoner of 'a state of consciousness and permanent visibility that assures the automatic functioning of power' (Foucault 1991, 201). The watched individual thus disciplines themselves. Foucault uses the concept of panopticon to demonstrate how physical institutions such as prisons, schools, the military and hospitals work. However, he adds that the panopticon represents a 'generalizable model of functioning; a way of defining power relations in terms of the everyday life of men' (205), and that panopticism is a 'general principle of a new "political anatomy" whose object and end are not the relations of sovereignty but the relations of discipline' (208).

Therefore, the figure of the panopticon is relevant to understanding how the gaze is used within a patriarchal setting as a tool of discipline with an aim towards the control and restriction of women. It is an aspect of maintaining the status quo of gender relations.

Foucault's description of (self-)discipline relates to Berger's description of the internalizing of the male gaze in women. Berger describes how, '[a] woman must continually watch herself. Whilst she is walking across a room or whilst she is weeping at the death of her father, she can scarcely avoid envisaging herself walking or weeping. From earlier childhood she has been taught and persuaded to survey herself continually' (Berger 2008, 46). In what can be termed the panopticon of patriarchy, the feminine has been subjected to the masculine. As Berger suggests, men's presence has been defined by the power they embody and exercise on others, whereas women are born into a space that is governed by this power (46). This dynamic then extends to the concept of the gaze. Sandra Lee Bartky, in her feminist appropriation of the Foucauldian theory of power entitled 'Foucault, femininity and the modernization of patriarchal power', says that Foucault ignores the 'disciplines that produce a modality of embodiment that is peculiarly feminine' (Bartky 1997, 132). The patriarchal gaze is implicit in the production of such disciplines, which are specific to women.

To better understand the position of a woman as an image to be looked at, as an object of the gaze, it is also useful to look at the history of actual produced images of women. John Berger turns to art history to point out how the notion of a woman as an – often sexualized – object is embedded in Western culture. He points out that the objectification of women in art is especially poignant in paintings of nudes. Berger says that, '[a] naked body has to be seen as an object in order to become a nude' (Berger 2008, 54), suggesting that there is a difference between nakedness and nudity. A nude is an object on display. He also writes:

> In the art-form of the European nude the painters and spectator-owners were usually men and the persons treated as objects, usually women. This unequal relationship is so deeply embedded in our culture that it still structures the consciousness of many women. They do to themselves what men do to them. They survey, like men, their own femininity. (Berger 2008, 63)

In Jean Rhys's novel *After Leaving Mr Mackenzie*, Julia, the main protagonist, looks at a reproduction of a painting of a nude by Modigliani entitled *Reclining Nude* from 1917–18. It depicts a woman reclining on a couch, whom Julia describes as a 'woman with ... a lovely body ... A sort of proud body, like an utterly lovely proud animal. And a face like a mask, a long dark face, and very big eyes' (Rhys 1997, 52). She feels uneasy while looking at the picture, as she thinks about her past and her identity:

> I felt as if the woman in the picture were laughing at me and saying: 'I am more real than you. But at the same time I am you. I'm all that matters to you.' And I felt as if all my life and all myself were floating away from me like smoke and there was nothing to lay hold of – nothing. (Rhys 1997, 53)

The picture instils in her a sense of insecurity and instability as she faces the nude who, with her confident pose, is made to face her male creator – she appears 'to be the result of his being there' (Berger 2008, 54) – as well as other viewers, as if she knows and relishes her purpose being reduced to being gazed at. Julia is both made to and yet cannot identify with the image. She, too, is gazed at daily and made into a visual object up for scrutiny, but her feelings, and those of others regarding her body as an image, are not stable. Her appearance does not remain stable: she experiences good days and bad days, and she ages, which is seen as a negative side effect of the passage of time. Images such as the painting, which depict conventionally attractive youthful bodies, remind women of their own potential to be reduced to an image, and of what they should aspire to.

In *Vision and Difference*, her book on modern art history, Griselda Pollock points out why it has been inconceivable that men's bodies should be a sign of women's sexuality and the territory across which women claim their modernity, as was true for male modernist avant-garde painters, such as Modigliani, with regard to the bodies of women (Pollock 2008, 75). She writes of a 'historical asymmetry – a difference socially, economically, subjectively between being a woman and being a man', which is 'the product of the social structuration of sexual difference and not any imaginary biological distinction' (75). Art, then, provides a helpful historical context for how the concept of a woman as a subject of the gaze is rooted in representations and perceptions of the world.

Watchful city

The theme of a woman being subject to the discipline of the gaze is pertinent to the depiction of women's movement through urban space in Woolf and Rhys. For both writers, the street is an indispensable setting. It is a spatial passage through which one moves, and on to which one projects one's thoughts and impressions. In their narratives, women walk the streets of London and Paris all the time to get around. It is a setting for the exploration of what a character sees or thinks, but the public space of the city street is also where women's sense of the visibility of their bodies is heightened. In her late novel *The Years*, Virginia Woolf alludes to the feeling of being watched and followed as a woman moving through the cityscape. She has her female characters talk about the fear of walking alone at night due to drunken men in the streets. Rose asks her cousins Maggie and Sara, '[d]on't you find it rather unpleasant … coming home late at night sometimes with that public house at the corner?' Maggie replies, 'Drunken men, you mean?' (Woolf 1998, 127). Sara misses this exchange, and enquires what they are talking about:

> 'Another visit to Italy?'
> 'No,' said Maggie. She spoke indistinctly because her mouth was full of pins. 'Drunken men following one.'
> 'Drunken men following one,' said Sara. She sat down and began to put on her shoes. (Woolf 1998, 127)

The phrase 'drunken men' appears three times within the space of a few lines. The whole conversation feels disjointed, its relaying interrupted by descriptions of the women dressing up as they prepare to go outside in the street together. The repeated invocation of men following one in the street is thus interwoven with mundane acts of putting on shoes or clothes, which one performs almost automatically. In a similar manner, being followed, literally or by the male gaze, is presented as part of the ordinary. The repetition of the phrase implies the recurrence of the experience. Regarding Woolf's literary style in her later fiction, Whittier-Ferguson rightly points out that, '[s]carcely a sentence from *The Years* or *Between the Acts*, even if pulled out of context, could be mistaken for something Woolf would have written in the 1920s' (Whittier-Ferguson 2011, 232–3). The political and cultural atmosphere of the late 1930s, and the oncoming war, bring a sense of exhaustion and depletion to Woolf's writing. She moves from writing lyrically about characters' inner lives to the surface level, the ordinary and the mundane. Whittier-Ferguson writes that 'the aesthetic finish of her prose' is 'deliberately marred by repetition, misplaced rhyme, and broken rhythms' (231). Woolf's late style can also be seen as depicting conversation that is faithful to reality, as utterances are often incomplete or interrupted. An interesting aspect of this conversation in *The Years* is its casual and entirely unemotional nature, despite the subject matter. Raising the question of being followed by men in the street is not surprising to any of the women. They all know what the experience entails, either from personal experience or through it being described to them, as is the case for Sara.

Sara recounts meeting a stranger, a woman who conveyed to her the feeling of always being observed within the public space of the city. The woman tells her of eating ice cream under some trees in Regent's Park. Sara recalls what the woman said to her: 'The eyes, she said, came through every leaf like the darts of the sun; and her ice was melted!' (Woolf 1998, 127–8). Sara is told and passes on the story of the indeterminate gaze, the image of the eyes, which, by relation to the story of the drunken men, are tied to the patriarchal gaze. The eyes that rest upon the woman have a fixing and adverse effect. They seem embedded in the material fabric of the city and, as such, their gaze pervades a woman's daily life insidiously. This experience is shared within the collective of the female characters, because it is known by and pertinent to all of them. Its matter-of-fact nature, and the fact that it remains unchallenged, is reflected in the unvexed tone of the passage.

The image of the city as a watchful entity also appears in Jean Rhys's novel *After Leaving Mr Mackenzie*, in which the main female character, 'watched the lights coming out in the Palais de Justice across the river like cold, accusing, jaundiced eyes' (Rhys 1997, 18). In Woolf's and Rhys's novels, such images can be seen as representing the eye of patriarchy. They connote uneasiness and a sense of being observed, which is subtly embedded in the space of the everyday, be it an institution governed by men or something as innocent as trees. As Gillian Rose writes in *Feminism and Geography*, '[t]he everyday is the arena through which patriarchy is (re)created – and contested' (Rose 1993, 24).

The city as having an agency of the gaze illustrates the fact that the power that lends it its effect is not necessarily wielded by individuals – which here would be men looking at women. Rather, it represents the nondescript surveyor within each woman, as described earlier by Berger. It is also what Bartky describes as a 'generalized male witness', who 'comes to structure a woman's consciousness of herself as a bodily being' (Bartky 1997, 145). By endowing the city space with eyes, Woolf and Rhys externalize the internalized gaze. They project it on to the space. The city is shown as watching women as they live and move in it. The gaze itself can be confronted and conveyed as real, because it is rendered palpable as a material element of the city in the form of the trees or the windows of buildings. These kinds of images re-emerge throughout Woolf's and Rhys's novels. With the appearance of a woman on the urban scene, the space of the street is occasionally portrayed as becoming physically oppressive – as if a woman's presence becomes apparent to the city space, which then reacts to it. For example, Rhys describes the sensation of buildings on both sides of a street moving menacingly forward as a character walks past them (Rhys 2016, 23). At times, the passage seems to be suffocating, or even impossible, if one is a woman, while the true cause of such oppressive experience is not palpable, despite its omnipresence.

Between private and public space

This sense of the gaze being embedded in the city space itself recalls the reality of the literal male gaze, which has historically contested women's bodies in such a space, and functioned as an instrument of policing them. The lone female walker has not always been authorized to walk in the streets freely and on her own, and was, instead, confined to private space. Gillian Rose writes that, for White women (the dominant female characters in the novels of Woolf and Rhys are White and middle class), 'one of the most oppressive aspects of everyday space' has been 'the division between public space and private space' (Rose 1993, 24). While Benjamin's *flâneur* could easily traverse the line between the two spheres of the public and the private, women could not. For women, public space has not been historically available as a space for unrestricted movement, let alone leisure. In *The Fall of the Public Man*, Richard Sennett describes how, by the end of the nineteenth century, women were still unable to freely go to cafes or restaurants alone, '[e]ven into the 1880's, a woman alone could not go to a café in Paris or a respectable restaurant in London without arousing some comment, occasionally being rejected at the door' (Sennett 2002, 217). A woman walking alone in the street signified a deviant body, such as that of a prostitute. Such significations are depicted by both Woolf and Rhys in their novels.

Relatedly, Griselda Pollock writes that 'to maintain one's respectability, closely identified with femininity, meant not exposing oneself in public' (Pollock 2008, 97), and, although she writes of the nineteenth century, these prohibitions are shown to reverberate in Woolf's and Rhys's fiction. For the most part, their heroines live in the first half of the twentieth century, and they do walk in the street alone. However, their presence in the street is not devoid of inhibition or contestation. Lisbeth Larsson notes the 'gender hierarchy in terms of walking', which Woolf exposes in her novels: 'In the mapping in her novels, Woolf reveals London's class and gender codes very explicitly. Men and women cannot go where they like, when they like, either historically or at different times of day' (Larsson 2017, 10). The young protagonist in Woolf's debut novel, *The Voyage Out*, is prevented from walking alone in Piccadilly, because the place is associated with prostitution. On the other hand, in *Jacob's Room*, the eponymous hero confidently strolls through Piccadilly between two and three o'clock in the morning: 'The long loop of Piccadilly, diamond-stitched, shows to best advantage when it is empty. A young man has nothing to fear' (Woolf 2008, 153). The free indirect discourse employed here renders its tone and focalization ambiguous. It expresses Jacob's heady and drunken confidence, and his point of view, but it is also an authorial comment on men's privilege of being able to attain this feeling of safety while walking the streets, especially at night. In Rhys's novels, women who walk alone are often apprehended by men, who sometimes mistake them for prostitutes. More gravely, in Woolf's *The Years*, the character Rose is sexually harassed when she goes out to buy a toy as a young girl. At points, both novelists stress that there is no casualness to passing through the street as a woman, and they crucially explore how, as a woman, one comes to be conscious of this reality.

In Woolf's fiction, the best-known city stroller is Clarissa Dalloway, who goes out to 'buy the flowers herself' (Woolf 1992, 1), although by page 25 of the book she is back in her house to prepare for her party. The *flâneur* of *Mrs Dalloway* is really Clarissa's friend Peter Walsh. He is depicted as being able to roam the streets freely without an aim – so much so that he decides to follow a young woman he does not know on what he sees as an innocent adventure. This scenario is reflected in Rhys's work, from the point of view of the women who are often followed by random men. These instances are not portrayed as an adventure, but as a threat to one's bodily autonomy as a woman. To return to *Mrs Dalloway*: in comparison with the *flâneur*, Clarissa's venture in the streets of London is not simply carefree or aimless. In a sense, it is a calculated shopping trip. She goes out to buy her flowers, and then returns. In 'The invisible *flâneuse*', Janet Wolff writes that the characteristics of the modern experience of the fleeting, anonymous encounter and purposeless strolling typical for the *flâneur* do not apply to shopping. Rather, consumerism provided a new arena for the legitimate public appearance of middle-class women in public space (Wolff 1985, 13). In Rhys's novels, female characters often feel self-conscious and uneasy in the city streets, as if they are about to be persecuted. In *Good Morning, Midnight*, the main character, Sasha, narrates going to the Luxembourg Gardens in Paris, where she feels comfortable because an attendant comes up to her and sells her a ticket. In a space defined by such a transaction, she adopts a stable role. She thinks, 'Now everything is legal. If anyone says: '"Qu'est-ce qu'elle fout ici?" I can show the ticket ... I feel safe, clutching it. I can stay here as long as I like ... with nobody to interfere with me' (Rhys 2016, 41). Shopping, window shopping, and casual purchases in general, legitimize women's presence in the public space.

Woolf reflects on this in her essay 'Street haunting: A London adventure', in which the speaker feels she must justify her venture into the streets of London with the purchase of a pencil. Woolf writes:

> So when the desire comes upon us to go street rambling the pencil does for a pretext, and getting up we say: 'Really I must buy a pencil,' as if under cover of this excuse we could indulge safely in the greatest pleasure of town life in winter – rambling the streets of London. (Woolf 2009, 177)

Relatedly, in *Good Morning, Midnight*, Rhys reflects upon the necessity to have a plan and an aim while moving through the city via Sasha's thoughts: '[n]ot too much drinking, avoidance of certain cafés, or certain streets, of certain spots and everything will go off beautifully. The thing is to have a programme, not to leave anything to chance – no gaps. No trailing around aimlessly' (Rhys 2016, 8). The contrast in the styles of the quoted passages is striking. Woolf's essay is light-hearted. Her collective 'we' is not gendered; however, her remark about the compulsion to justify her walk by the purchase of a pencil seems significant. The pleasure derived from walking for its own sake must be concealed by the cover of necessity. This is in line with the history of women having been expected to move through public space with purpose, as loitering or wandering may be seen as morally suspect. The essay's speaker can be linked to Clarissa Dalloway, who, on her way to and from the flower shop, walks along big shopping streets such as Bond Street, and extends her presence in the streets by window-shopping. She seems to belong in this particular city space in part because it is clear she can afford the objects on display.

Rhys's Sasha is more self-conscious than Clarissa, because her self-consciousness stems not only from being a woman-object always observed, but also from her precarious existence and her feeling of being alien as an Englishwoman in Paris. James Williams writes that Rhys's metropolitan novels 'sit in an uneasy relation to the modernist canon of the 1920s and 1930s, engaging in linguistic and other formal experimentation, but doing so with an apparent trepidation which reveals a deep concern for social dynamics and socio-political context' (Williams 2019, 1180). Sasha's stream of consciousness really is a stream of self-consciousness. As she feels like an outsider, her inner monologue does not steer away from her position in her surroundings. As she does not wander freely in the city space, neither does her mind wander spontaneously. Rather, the function of her stream of thoughts is self-soothing and suppressing the doubts that continuously arise within her.

The feeling of it being necessary to have a plan and an aim may make sense in a culture that values productivity, but Woolf and Rhys bring this compulsion up with a degree of anxiety. In different but related ways, they allude to the need for having a purpose in public space as a woman, and for being able to justify one's presence if necessary. The writers depict women's compulsion to mentally map out the city, and the options they have in passing through it, before entering its public space. This compulsion is so internalized that the reasons for it are never reflected upon.

The body as a spectacle

Consumer culture relates to women's bodies in street spaces in more ways than one. When women are observed, they also think of how they are seen, and whether they comply with the current standards of constituting a proper female body. In Rhys's and Woolf's prose, this is often manifested by characters thinking about their clothes or buying new clothes. Clothes affect the way the body is visible. Bartky writes that there are different categories of 'disciplinary practices that produce a recognizably feminine body', and one of them is the display of the body as an 'ornamented surface' (Bartky 1997, 132). In Rhys's *After Leaving Mr Mackenzie*, Julia thinks about buying clothes in moments of discomfort in her journey through the city. If she buys them, her body will look better to the gaze, and she will thus feel more confident and pleasant (Rhys 1997, 19). In 'Feminism, Foucault and the politics of the body', Susan Bordo raises an interesting point about power and pleasure, which in the Foucauldian framework do not cancel each other out. She says that, '[t]he ... experience of feeling powerful, or "in control", far from being a necessarily accurate reflection of one's actual social position, is always suspect as itself the product of power relations whose shape may be very different' (Bordo 1993, 192). Julia buys new clothes to feel powerful. Nevertheless, she ultimately does it in the service of the gaze.

In *Mrs Dalloway*, a character called Miss Kilman walks down the street while feeling her body to be painfully inadequate: '"It is the flesh, it is the flesh," she muttered ... trying to subdue this turbulent and painful feeling as she walked down Victoria Street ... She could not help being ugly; she could not afford to buy pretty clothes' (Woolf 1992, 113). Miss Kilman imagines passers-by despising her for her appearance. The gaze of these passers-by may be real, but it is also half-imagined, as the observed projects her own self-image and her compulsion to self-police on to others. In direct contrast to Miss Kilman, there is Mrs Dalloway's daughter, Elizabeth, who is beautiful, wears very well-cut clothes and is complimented by people in the street. Yet Elizabeth thinks of this as making her life burdensome. Rhys and Woolf portray their characters as being conscious of femininity as relentless spectacle. The societal expectation to perform femininity in accordance with particular norms creates pressure to police the appearance of one's body. No matter the fate of the individual characters, Rhys and Woolf show this to be the experience of every woman walking in the city. The difference between Elizabeth and Miss Kilman is not only that one is more skilled or physically better predisposed to subscribe to standards of attractiveness than the other. It is also that Miss Kilman feels alienated because of her lower class. Class is the reason why she cannot achieve a form of discipline of the body and self-presentation required by the norms for women of her time.

Similarly, in Rhys's *Good Morning, Midnight*, Sasha hears a second-hand account of a mixed-race woman from Martinique, who feels abject when being looked at by other people with scrutiny and contempt in their gazes. Like Sasha, the woman, who also feels uprooted in the world, finds solace in drinking. Upon hearing part of her story, Sasha exclaims, '[e]xactly like me' (Rhys 2016, 77). However, the man telling her the story corrects her:

> 'No, no,' he says. 'Not like you at all ... She said that every time they looked at her she could see how they hated her, and the people in the streets looked at her in the same way ... She told me she hadn't been out, except after dark, for two years.' (Rhys 2016, 77–8)

Like *Mrs Dalloway*, the novel brings awareness to the fact that women's experience is not homogeneous. Furthermore, Rhys shows how the main character becomes aware of this, which is a rare depiction of a White woman attaining a broader awareness of the self in relation to women whose lives are radically different from her own. In her critique of Western-centric feminist attitudes, Gayatri Spivak famously says that, 'I see no way to avoid insisting that there has to be a simultaneous other focus: not merely who am I? but who is the other woman? How am I naming her? How does she name me? Is this part of the problematic I discuss?' (Spivak 1981, 179). Such awareness and seeing another, however, should not only apply to consciously feminist and delineated positions and discussions, but also to encounters within everyday life. Although the focus of the two novelists in question is on White middle-class women, the novels reflect upon how intersections of class, race and gender produce varying experiences, including the experience of passing through urban space. This brief episode in *Good Morning, Midnight* showcases another level of dehumanization of women in public space, in addition to the reality of gender-based objectification. In 'The oppositional gaze', bell hooks discusses how, in visual culture, Black women's bodies have often been represented as being there to serve, and 'to enhance and maintain white womanhood as object of the phallocentric gaze' (hooks 1992, 119). She also reminds her readers of the fact that Black people have been historically punished for the act of looking and, speaking from within the context of the United States, Black men were lynched for merely looking at White women (hooks 1992, 118). No position in relation to power is without context. The negating power of the gaze so far discussed stems from patriarchy, and patriarchy is never unrelated to White supremacy, which forms an equally pervasive socio-economic structure.

Undesirability and invisibility

As has been established, the internalization of the patriarchal gaze translates into a significant sense of visibility and being surveyed, which continuously surfaces in the consciousness of Woolf's and Rhys's female characters. What does it mean, then, that some of the women walking the streets of London or Paris in Woolf and Rhys feel invisible? In Woolf's *The Years*, Sara says that she is unafraid to walk alone through London because she is plain and nobody notices her: 'I can walk over Waterloo Bridge at any hour of the day or night ... and nobody notices' (Woolf 1998, 127). Woolf's Clarissa Dalloway walks through London thinking about the inadequacy of her body, which she translates into invisibility: 'But often now this body she wore ... with all its capacities, seemed nothing – nothing at all. She had the oddest sense of being herself invisible; unseen; unknown' (Woolf 1992, 7). When these characters feel invisible, it is necessary to ask who they are invisible to. This sense of invisibility does not imply transgression of the gaze. The woman must first survey the inadequacy of their existing material bodies to feel invisible. To see oneself as such, one must first engage in the objectification of oneself. Bartky describes the implications of objectification of women:

> To be dealt with in this way is to have one's entire being identified with the body, a thing which in many religious and metaphysical systems, as well as in the popular mind, has been regarded as less intrinsically valuable, indeed, as less inherently human, than the mind or personality. Clearly, sexual objectification is a form of fragmentation and thus an impoverishment of the objectified individual. (Bartky 1997, 35)

To be seen as an object is to be reduced and dehumanized. To feel the demand to participate in this vision is a sign of the panopticon of patriarchy being effective – one arrives at policing and reducing the self in a process that is felt to be quite natural. Invisibility here is not that of Benjamin's *flâneur*, signifying the freedom to roam the city, but rather, it is associated with ugliness, plainness and ageing, which all signify perceived undesirability within the power structures of the patriarchal panopticon. Such invisibility, rather than implying freedom, implies complete erasure of one's being.

Desirability and undesirability are portrayed as significant concerns for Rhys's and Woolf's female characters, and they are often connected to everyday experience in the public space of the city. Interestingly, both Woolf and Rhys portray women who see other women observing themselves, or they have a character imagine how another woman feels about herself. Often, an older woman represents a threatening vision of a younger woman's future. In *Leaving Mr Mackenzie,* Rhys has the main character observe that, '[t]he older women looked drab and hopeless, with timid, hunted expressions. They looked ashamed of themselves, as if they were begging the world in general not to notice that they were women or to hold it against them' (Rhys 1997, 69). Ageing in particular is a pervasive theme for both of the writers discussed. It is connected to the feeling of threat of persecution for not being able to comply with the disciplines of womanhood, and it bears negatively on the psyche. As Susan Bordo says, '[p]revailing forms of selfhood and subjectivity are maintained not through physical restraint and coercion, but through individual self-surveillance and self-correction to norms' (Bordo 1993, 190). Failure to coerce oneself into being a normative feminine body creates anxiety, and one either feels persecuted or like an improper body/

object moving through space. As a consequence of such policing of the female body and failure to discipline it, one's sense of selfhood is threatened. This, in turn, relates to how one perceives space and is able to move through it. In *Space, Time and Perversion*, Elizabeth Grosz draws on Paul Schilder and Roger Caillois's work to explain how body-image plays a role in a subject's capacity to locate themselves in space and to perceive space (Grosz 1995, 87). What happens is not only that a woman's perception of her bodily presence and the self in the public space of the city is affected by the gaze, but also that this bears upon how the city space appears to her – as a space of hostility and instability prior to any experience of confrontation with it. There is, again, a sense of transference of the effect of the gaze on to the city space. A relation between space and the subject is formed by the power of the gaze.

Conclusion

Woolf and Rhys manage to portray in both subtle and explicit ways how the panopticon of the gaze and the discipline of femininity pervade women's everyday passage through cities. It is tempting to look for a transgression of the gaze and its internalization in the novels. Woolf's novels contain more hope than those of Rhys in this regard. Their poetic prose style allows for daring visions. If there is any kind of liberation from the dynamics of power that discipline the female body in the city space, perhaps it is in the passages in which characters are imagined to be absolved of their own bodies and merge with the space of the city itself. In *Mrs Dalloway*, Clarissa imagines herself carrying on a form of existence in the material setting of the city, even after death:

> [s]omehow in the streets of London, on the ebb and flow of things, here, there, she survived, Peter survived, lived in each other, she being part ... of the trees at home ... being laid out like a mist between the people she knew best, who lifted her on their branches as she had seen the trees lift the mist. (Woolf 1992, 6)

Unlike Rhys's anxious characters, Clarissa Dalloway can, in her mind, transport herself elsewhere. As Larsson observes regarding Woolf's employment of stream of consciousness, '[a]s a reader you always feel you are inside someone's thoughts and these thoughts are generally not in the same place as the body that is at the same time bearing them through the streets of London' (Larsson 2017, 116). Significantly, in this passage in *Mrs Dalloway*, Clarissa's thoughts wander into another dimension, but through them she also transposes her body and reimagines her physical existence as more meaningful and freer than that of an ageing mortal and female body.

Both Woolf and Rhys do draw attention to power, which affects women in their passage through the city. Although the scheme of the panopticon seems like a totalizing trap, Foucault says that where there are relations of power, there is space for resistance (Foucault 1988, 12). An important step to resistance is the pointing out of power – the realization of its functioning. When in *In Between the Acts*, Isa senses men observing her, it is unpleasant to her. During one such instance, she thinks, '[s]he felt Dodge's eye upon her as her lips moved. Always some cold eye crawled over the surface like a winter blue-bottle! She flicked him off' (Woolf 1987, 128). The eye here is not merely an image. The unwanted male gaze is embodied in Dodge, and can thus be named and confronted. Isa's conflation of it with a large insect – a fly – as well as her naming her act of confronting it as flicking it off, suggest agency, rather than simply a defensive stance. The unwanted scrutiny is categorically refused as parasitic and unacceptable. Here, Woolf affirms the meaningfulness of the patriarchal gaze being confronted in the arena of the everyday.

In depictions of city strollers within literary tradition, women walkers have been at times reduced to one-dimensional images or tropes without subjectivity. Woolf and Rhys show empathetic portrayals of women watching themselves and being watched as they test their right to the city by walking in it. They portray both enjoyment and displeasure related to passing through the city. To exist within it as a woman is not strictly figured as the experience of the oppressed. Rather, it is shown to be in varying degrees tinged with underlying uneasiness and limitations. Even if the experience of a woman walking down a street is not tainted by negative aspects, such as the material reality of harassment, or worried thoughts and projections, there is an insidious sense of the self versus the body as object, the discipline of self-observation, the policing of one's bodily appearance, as well as of the passage itself, which women confront in their daily movement through city streets. In the context of the city space, the passage as a spatial concept and as an experience proves to be anything but straightforward in terms of human existence and relations within it. The sense of being subject to a gaze is only one aspect of women's experience of navigating and exploring the city. However, it is a sense that women have in common. It is not unfamiliar to any one of them.

References

Bartky, Sandra Lee. 1997. 'Foucault, femininity and the modernization of patriarchal power'. In *Writing on the Body: Female embodiment and feminist theory*, edited by Katie Conboy, Nadia Medina and Sarah Stanbury, 129–54. New York: Columbia University Press.

Benjamin, Walter. 1999. *The Arcades Project*, edited by Rolf Tiedemann, translated by Howard Eiland and Kevin McLaughlin. Cambridge, MA: The Belknap Press of Harvard University Press.

Benjamin, Walter. 2006. *The Writer of Modern Life: Essays on Charles Baudelaire*, edited by Michael W. Jennings. Cambridge, MA: Harvard University Press. Berger, John. 2008. *Ways of Seeing*. London: Penguin.

Berger, John. 2008. *Ways of Seeing*. London: Penguin.

Bordo, Susan. 1993. 'Feminism, Foucault and the politics of the body'. In *Up Against Foucault: Exploration of some tensions between Foucault and feminism*, edited by Caroline Ramazanoglu, 179–202. London: Routledge.

Foucault, Michel. 1988. 'The ethics of care for the self as a practice of freedom: An interview with Michel Foucault on January 20, 1984'. In *The Final Foucault*, edited by James William Bernauer and David M. Rasmussen, 112–31. Boston, MA: MIT Press.

Foucault, Michel. 1991. *Discipline and Punish*. London: Penguin.

Gelley, Alexander. 2015. *Benjamin's Passages: Dreaming, awakening*. New York: Fordham University Press.

Grosz, Elizabeth. 1995. *Space, Time and Perversion: Essays on the politics of bodies*. New York: Routledge.

hooks, bell. 1992. 'The oppositional gaze'. In *Black Looks: Race and representation*, 115–31. Boston, MA: South End Press.

Larsson, Lisbeth. 2017. *Virginia Woolf's London: An investigation in literary biography*. London: Palgrave Macmillan.

Pollock, Griselda. 2008. *Vision and Difference: Feminism, femininity and the histories of art*. New York: Routledge.

Rhys, Jean. 1997. *After Leaving Mr Mackenzie*. New York: W.W. Norton & Company.

Rhys, Jean. 2016. *Good Morning, Midnight*. London: Penguin.

Rose, Gillian. 1993. *Feminism and Geography: The limits of geographical knowledge*. Cambridge: Polity Press.

Sennett, Richard. 2002. *The Fall of the Public Man*. London: Penguin.

Spivak, Gayatri Chakravorty. 1981. 'French feminism in an international frame', *Yale French Studies* 62: 154–84.

Whittier-Ferguson, John. 2011. 'Repetition, remembering, repetition: Virginia Woolf's late fiction and the return of war', *Modern Fiction Studies* 57 (2): 230–53.

Williams, James. 2019. 'Tongue-tied modernism in Jean Rhys's Paris', *Textual Practice* 33 (7): 1179–98.

Wolff, Janet. 1985. 'The invisible flâneuse: Women and the literature of modernity', *Theory, Culture & Society* 2: 37–46.

Woolf, Virginia. 1987. *Between the Acts*. London: Grafton.

Woolf, Virginia. 1992. *Mrs Dalloway*. London: Vintage.

Woolf, Virginia. 1998. *The Years*. London: Penguin.

Woolf, Virginia. 2008. *Jacob's Room*. London: Oxford University Press.

Woolf, Virginia. 2009. 'Street haunting: A London adventure'. In *Selected Essays*, edited by David Bradshaw, 177–87. London: Penguin.

13
Passages: reading before/for responsibility in Elizabeth Bowen's *The Death of the Heart* (1938)

Laura Lainväe

As I read Elizabeth Bowen's *The Death of the Heart* (1938) in 2019, after a recent fire at a French chemical plant in the city of Rouen, the 'oddly transformed air' (Osborn 2006, 187) of the novel aligns with the increasing oddities and worries about the physical air in my lungs, and in the streets. What has happened to the imperceptible air, which I fail to read here and now as I breathe it, I cannot tell. For a plain non-scientific reader, such as I, air seems to signify only when it is odd – when an uncanniness, a sudden strangeness of air, becomes perceptible.

The reading of what escapes our bodily human sensory apparatus is, as Timothy Clark writes, a matter of scale and 'scalar literacy' (Clark 2019, 84). Clark explores the Anthropocene as a kind of passage, an emergent threshold that names a 'border at which what used to be clear human goods begin to flip over into sources of degradation and environmental harm' (46). By viewing the Anthropocene through the concept of *threshold*, which is a passage, Clark shows the potential of this concept to uproot and reconsider the modes of thinking and practices that, although they might once have been adequate, have become destructive.

This reading of *The Death of the Heart* concentrates particularly on the difficulties of reading one of the most complicated phenomena of the

Anthropocene – anthropogenic climate change, through the reading of *air* in its manifold forms. The notion of *passage* (while naming the textual fragments under study), also comes to describe two achievements of the literary writing of a transnational modernist author, Elizabeth Bowen: the deciphering of identity (from Latin *identitas*, *idem* meaning 'same', OED) as a passage, rather than as something immutable; and, through that first deconstruction of the notion of identity, the illumination of other elusive phenomena, such as London's polluted air. The latter phenomenon is directly related to climate change, which, I argue, is less of a change and more of a passage, in the sense that it does not give itself willingly to our human senses, and is thus hard to read. Reading climate change is like reading air.

Bowen was a reader and writer of airs, for, as Walter Sullivan explains, Bowen was 'a novelist of manners' (Sullivan 1976, 144). In *The Death of the Heart*, she combines the reading of social airs, the patterns of social behaviour of the Londoners Thomas and Anna Quayne, and the reading of London's air that, readers will learn, is ill. The reader of air in the novel is a teenage relative of the couple, Portia Quayne, who arrives at their London home after the passing of her parents. Being Thomas's half-sister, but also the result of a love affair that broke up his parents' marriage, Portia's return unearths the painful family history that precedes her.

As Maud Ellmann writes: '*The Death of the Heart* is the story of the Quaynes' ethical awakening: their realization of responsibility to Portia, to the past, and to the dead' (Ellmann 2004, 130). I would only add to this statement that the novel is also concerned with future death. It bears witness to the elusive traces of destructive human activity, for which readers of today must take responsibility. The novel creates a passage, a threshold between now and then, between reality and fiction, in the space of literature, where one is made sensitive to the traces that are otherwise unreadable. It makes visible the traces of what is now called climate change through Portia's diary, which is written from a specifically marginal position, from the sensitive territory between adulthood and childhood, and from the viewpoint of a half-stranger.

I will show how the smog that the character of Portia perceives in London's air is paired with the errors she perceives in Anna's and Thomas's lifestyle and reasoning, egging the readers on towards what Timothy Clark calls 'scalar literacy' (2019, 84), the reading of what does not fully present itself in the present, the reading of *air*.

Air, materialized in stone or wood

Born from a love affair, Portia Quayne first emerges as an embarrassing passage, a story, from the history of the Quayne family, and then as a person only passing through, for her cohabitation with Thomas and his wife Anna in their London home is supposed to be temporary. Having lived in continental Europe with her parents, Portia's Englishness is not rooted in her experience of England or London. In many ways, England is foreign to her, and she does not know all the details of the family's past. The moment the half-foreign Portia crosses the threshold of the Quayne household, evoking a memory of the family history she is part of but not a witness to, her presence in the house becomes a trigger for Anna and Thomas. On the one hand, her presence causes the Quayne family history and patterns of behaviour to resurface. On the other hand, her strangeness also challenges the fixity of their identities, revealing a certain instability at the very core of the notion of identity.

Identity is constructed but, at the same time, it survives those constructions, those fixations (or 'little deaths' as de la Soudière writes), which it cannot sustain, for they become an impasse (de la Soudière 2000, 10), a still life for a life that must go on, evolve. The concept of passage (more so than the notion of change that concentrates on a result), Martin de la Soudière suggests, evokes the idea of renewal, mutation and metamorphosis (9). Such instability characterizes identity also in Bowen's fiction. In her last novel, *Eva Trout*, she asks: 'Anyhow, what a slippery fish is identity; and what *is* it, besides a slippery fish?' (Bowen 2019, 213). In her autobiography, Bowen writes that the main trait of human nature is 'the amorphousness of the drifting and flopping jellyfish in a cloudy tide' (Bowen 1987, 295), which she then compares to our 'obsessive wish to acquire outline, to be unmistakeably demarcated, to *take shape*' (295).

In *The Death of the Heart*, Bowen underlines her characters' attempts at mastery through their denial of identity as a passage. Their efforts to petrify identities into familiar patterns, through the processes of normalization and marginalization, are shown to fail, as identity seems to always already extend itself towards the uninvited, the unforeseeable and the seemingly other. Portia is the strange yet undeniable extension no one saw coming.

Being a member of the extended family, Portia integrates the Quaynes's household as a half-stranger – a half-sister that was accidentally planted within the 'proper' sociocultural network and order of the Quayne family. Her unconventional conception did not follow the traditional concatenation of social rites (engagement, marriage, having children) through which one's social identity is consolidated, yet Portia's identity cannot be reduced to absolute otherness in terms of her nationality, social class or family ties, because she is English and a Quayne. Through her stay (just a passage) in Windsor Terrace, the novel explores and undermines the opposition between two ways of living: the marginalized life that Portia's parents lived roaming continental Europe, which is depicted through flashbacks in Portia's mind, and, thus, in a way, hangs in the air; and the 'proper' English way of life that Anna and Thomas embody, which has been materialized in patterns one is made to follow in Windsor Terrace.[1]

The social constructions within Windsor Terrace are described as 'a perfect web' (Bowen 1998, 103). Containing furniture as well as a housekeeper (Matchett) from Thomas's childhood home, Windsor Terrace refers to a certain materialization and sacralization of manners (airs) of living: to *oikonomia*, or the laws of a house. The novel is packed with images of patterns (puzzles, *moirés*, texts), which recall the haunting sociocultural structure of Windsor Terrace, or what Alfred McDowell calls 'the master-pattern of the world' (1978, 7–8) around Portia.

Through Mr Quayne (Thomas's and Portia's father), Windsor Terrace is portrayed as a 'normal' environment. Mr Quayne felt that Portia 'had grown up exiled not only from her own country but from normal, cheerful family life' (Bowen 1998, 11). Thus, the identity of Windsor Terrace, and the lifestyle it represents, is presented as a norm to which Portia must adapt by erasing her difference. Her failure to make herself disappear, to unwrite the conditions of her birth and its implications, destines her to fail in the integration into a household that does not seek to extend its hospitality to otherness.

This 'normal' environment is an exclusive world of wealthy adults that, instead of offering the 'cheerful family life' that Mr Quayne dreamt of, protects privacy and a sense of superiority over people such as Portia. Portia's strangeness within this sociocultural framework is communicated through various animal comparisons: 'a little crow', 'a kitten that expects to be drowned', 'an excellent lamb', 'a wild creature just old enough to dread humans', 'a bird astray in a room', 'a demented kitten', 'an animal' and 'a little monster' (Bowen 1998, 41, 39, 309, 319, 221, 3, 8). Etymologically, 'Portia' is shadowed by the figure of a pig, from Latin *porcus*, yet she is animalized because she does not respond to the social norms at Windsor Terrace, which reduce her parents' way of life and her origins to piggishness, to a lack of order. According to Anna, Portia, 'the child of an aberration, the child of a panic, the child of an old chap's pitiful sexuality' had been 'conceived among lost hairpins and snapshots of doggies in a Notting Hill Gate flatlet' (274). Anna's mention of Notting Hill Gate, historically a place where a tollgate used to be, locates Portia's conception at a *lieu de passage*, a crossing point or a threshold. The very idea of this flatlet (not even a flat) hovers outside the realm of dignified living, which is rooted in houses such as Windsor Terrace and does not give passage to strangers.

The inhospitality, even hostility, of Windsor Terrace is portrayed by the Quaynes's demand for privacy, the house being 'surrounded by an electric fence – friends who did not first telephone did not come' (Bowen 1998, 92). Unpredictable visitors such as Major Brutt, we are told, 'had been eliminated; they simply did not occur' (92).

The danger of this house becoming something of a *lieu de passage* for visitors, against which various measures have been put in place, veils a more profound worry about the effects of hospitality on one's identity. As Jacques Derrida explains:

> It does not seem to me that I am able to open up or offer hospitality, however generous, even in order to be generous, without reaffirming: this is mine, I am at home, you are welcome in my home, without any implication of 'make yourself at home' but on condition that you observe the rules of hospitality by respecting the being-at-home of my home, the being-itself of what I am. There is almost an axiom of self-limitation or self-contradiction in the law of hospitality. As a reaffirmation of mastery and being oneself in one's own home, from the outset hospitality limits itself at its very beginning, it remains forever on the threshold of itself …, it governs the threshold – and hence it forbids in some way even what it seems to allow to cross the threshold to pass across it. It becomes the threshold. (Derrida 2000, 14)

Derrida makes the link between 'the being-at-home of my home' and 'the being-itself of what I am' (the rules of the house and one's identity) evident through the process of welcoming, which is, at the same time, shown to be the process of the negation of the stranger's identity. Hospitality beyond hospitality (without the self-contradiction Derrida speaks of) would imply coming to terms with the possibility of mutation or metamorphosis that lurks in the notion of passage. As Derek Attridge summarizes it, hospitality towards the other begins with 'a willingness not just to accept the other into one's own domain, but to change that domain, perhaps radically, in order to make the other welcome' (Attridge 2017, 49–50).

Portia's presence in Windsor Terrace itself becomes not only a passage in a spatio-temporal sense (for she is not there to stay); it also evokes the forces of metamorphosis of that passage, and their effect on the world's perception of Anna's and Thomas's identities, as well as her own:

> They had passed on the same stairs, grasped the same door handles, listened to the strokes of the same clocks. Behind the doors at Windsor Terrace, they had heard each other's voices, like the continuous murmur inside the whorls of a shell. She had breathed smoke from their lungs in every room she went into, and seen their names on letters each time she went through the hall. When she went out, she was asked how her brother and sister were. To the outside world, she smelled of Thomas and Anna. (Bowen 1998, 164)

These passages from room to room have tied the characters together through the forced coexistence (Thomas and Anna 'having been by blood obliged to open their door', 164), where continuous intrusions into each other's privacy, touching each other without touching, enmeshing ears, lungs and skin of each body through the same air, have ruined the impermeability of a fixed identity. This coexistence has begun to signify something else; that is, to the outside world, they have become entangled.

The physical site of this contamination of identity – namely, Portia's room – is disturbing to Anna, who has decorated it. Against Anna's best efforts to make it pretty (Bowen 1998, 4), Portia's room has been turned into a sort of animal habitat, which includes arrangements of tiny wooden bears that only Matchett, the housekeeper and archiver of the Quayne family and its furniture, recognizes as something other than a mess. With its tea-sipping little wooden bears, the room takes on a symbolic value, becoming a mockery of Anna's dignified patterns of living (as humans are replaced by bears), as well as an antidote to the order of Windsor Terrace. The command of the normalizing *oikos* is undercut visually by Portia's metaphorical piggishness, her untidiness, which cannot be eradicated from the house.

Through this clashing pattern that materializes Portia's presence and identity in the house, the novel underlines the superimposed norms of Windsor Terrace, materialized in stone and wood, which have the power to control by 'comparison, differentiation, hierarchization, homogenization and exclusion' (Foucault 2004, 185), like the institutions such as prisons and schools described by Foucault. Through 'the master-pattern of the world' (McDowell 1978, 7–8) around Portia at Windsor Terrace, in comparison to which the otherness of Portia's way of life is formed, Bowen shows that a home can also be used as a means of marginalization. However, marginality itself cannot be reduced to vulnerability and passivity.

Secret passages: writing from the margins

The notion of marginality is often used to refer to inferiority and impuissance. 'Marginal' signifies 'subsidiary, on the edge of a society or social unit' (*OED*), 'small and unimportant or insignificant' (*Chambers*). As such, marginality implies the existence of the other, someone who is not on the edge, but who is central and significant. Yet marginality could also be imagined as a border that is a passage between the two, and thus not only what separates and upholds oppositions, but also an in-betweenness from where rigid oppositions and their rule can begin to be questioned. Portia, as the 'port' in her name playfully suggests ('port' from Latin *'portus'*, meaning 'harbour, haven, mouth of a river' or 'recess of the mountains' (*OED*); 'a mountain pass and a gate, a door, basically, therefore, a passage' (Partridge 1991)), finds herself at the margin of two lifestyles (that of her parents, and that of Anna and Thomas), as well as between childhood and adulthood.

In an essay entitled 'On not rising to the occasion' (1956), Bowen writes that 'the child dithers somewhere round the margin', and often must enter a stage with 'a thousand-and-one rules', without clear instructions (Bowen 1987, 67). Portia is shown in a similar situation. She needs to pass, not only from one room to the next, but also in and out of the world of adults:

> Getting up from the stool carefully, Portia returned her cup and plate to the tray. Then, holding herself so erect that she quivered, taking long soft steps on the balls of her feet, and at the same time with an orphaned unostentation, she started making towards the door. She moved crabwise, as though the others were royalty, never quite turning her back on them – and they, waiting for her to be quite gone, watched. She wore a dark wool dress, in Anna's excellent taste, buttoned from throat to hem and belted with heavy leather. (Bowen 1998, 27)

Dressed by Anna, Portia is left to navigate (moving *at a passage*, crabwise, like a text across the page) the complex sociocultural patterns of Windsor Terrace under the piercing gaze of the adults, 'the accustomed actors' (Bowen 1987, 67). The marginal Portia, a half-stranger and a half-child, is burdened by the expectation to respond to adults such as Anna – to behave well, that is, 'never to be conspicuous' (67). Yet her efforts to appear less conspicuous make her appear even more out of place.

Metaphorically, her place as a half-stranger is the very condition of being always already *almost* out of place, for she constitutes the very margin that both ties together and separates her parents' exile and Anna's and Thomas's life in London. A marginal existence, the being inside and outside at once, as Guillaume le Blanc shows, is a life always threatened by social invisibility, voicelessness and the inability to take action in a different manner, that is, without miming the powerful in order to escape the domination (le Blanc 2010, 101–2, 107, 127). Portia's attempt to fit in and fade out of the room, to be a 'good' stranger (that is, the kind of stranger whose otherness is assimilated, nearly erased), is haunted by the contradictory force of her writing, which questions the order she feigns to incorporate through her behaviour.

Portia is shown to walk 'with an orphaned unostentation' (Bowen 1998, 27), which could be read as a deserted lack of pretention, perhaps not quite the renewed pretention yet. That is, her soft steps do not simply dither somewhere around the margin. They are read by Anna and her writer friend, St Quentin, whose perception is charged with the knowledge of her far less humble passages – her diary in which all adults have been observed, archived and judged. Anna, who has secretly read Portia's diary, already suspects that Portia, an 'excellent lamb' (304) walking 'on the balls of her feet' (27), might instead be a wolf in sheep's clothing (in a 'dark wool dress', 27), approaching, à pas de loup, in order to blow Anna's house in.

Portia's dangerousness consists in her audacity to observe and record her observations from her marginal position, thereby transgressing the threshold of a certain humility expected of children: obedience and conformity to the order set by adults. A child, like an animal, is not supposed to talk back. Finding the courage to question the order set by adults is the very rite of passage of teenage years, which Bowen observes in *The Death of the Heart* through Portia, who refuses to be written off as a hidden and shameful passage in her family's history.

Her diary, written for herself, is a form of writing that releases Portia from the obligation to please Anna and other adults, and it allows her to observe without the constraint of having to conform to an already dictated vision. Her secret textual passages are outrageous, because, through the act of writing, she reverses the dialectics of the dominant (the seer) and the dominated (the one being seen), which, as Derrida puts it, has, for a long time, been the relation between humans and animals (Derrida 2002, 382–3), as well as between powerful humans and animalized humans. Suddenly, Portia, the exiled bastard who has been wrapped up in others' stories about her for years, secretly and indirectly returns the gaze. Thereby, she destabilizes those who have reserved for themselves the right to observe and judge others. To make matters worse, she somewhat innocently allows Eddie, her crush, to read her diary passages, thereby opening her secret archives to the public eye. Portia's diary makes the group of powerful Londoners aware of the violence of their gaze, turning them into the objects being seen, analysed and denuded.

Her observations come from the life that has only known dislocation. Up until her arrival in London, Portia's home had been a mosaic of different countries and houses, which puts her on the margin of several territories. This condition is similar to Bowen's own experience as a writer: 'I have thriven, accordingly, on the changes and chances, the dislocations and ... the contrasts which have made up so much of my life. That might be why "my" world (my world as a writer) is something of a mosaic' (Bowen 1987, 283).

Portia's position as a half-outsider and a teenager is not only what causes her marginalization; it also gives her a liminal viewpoint that is fertile soil for reflection. As de la Soudière suggests, we need a place to think alterity, and liminal places – thresholds – encourage such thinking (de la Soudière 2000, 16). While *passage*, from Latin *passus* (meaning 'step'), evokes movement, a threshold names and gives place to that movement, by, in its name, calling for the passage to come: threshold descends from Old English *þerscold*, Old Norse *þreskjoldr*, in which 'thresh-' means 'to tread, trample' (*OED*). The very condition of thinking seems to rely on giving place (your body, or, in the act of writing, the body of a page or a book) to what, in one form or another, started elsewhere (a word learned – always already from others, a passage read and so forth), and is only passing through. This giving place to passages to come is what Derrida evokes in the experience of alterity in thinking. He writes:

> For me, the first way to turn speech over, in a situation that is first of all mine, consists of recognizing by giving passage to a woman's voice or to women's voices that are *already there* in a certain way at the origin of speech or of my speech. (Derrida 1995, 394)

In *The Death of the Heart*, Portia is similarly shown to host what she imagines is her mother's (Irene's) voice or perspective from a threshold of a classroom filled with girls, which enables her to think the difference between the two worlds she has inhabited:

> *Sins* cut boldly up through every class in society, but mere misdemeanours show a certain level in life. So now, not only diligence, or caution, kept the girls' smooth heads bent, and made them not glance again at Irene's child. Irene herself – knowing that nine out of ten things you do direct from the heart are the wrong thing, and that she was not capable of doing anything better – would not have dared to cross the threshold of this room. For a moment, Portia felt herself stand with her mother in the doorway, looking at all this in here with a wild askance shrinking eye. The gilt-scrolled paper, the dome, the bishop's chair, the girls' smooth heads must have been fixed here always, where they safely belonged – while she and Irene, shady, had been skidding about in an out-of-season nowhere of railway stations and rocks, filing off wet third-class decks of lake steamers, choking over the bones of *loups de mer*, giggling into eiderdowns that smelled of the person-before-last. (Bowen 1998, 56–7)

Portia enters a space where one's value is judged by one's air, for 'misdemeanours', we are told, reveal one's place in society. In that classroom, one's air must be meticulously controlled, for this is a world where 'nine out of ten things you do direct from the heart are the wrong thing' (Bowen 1998, 56). While being 'Irene's child' (56), Portia perceives that she herself is not completely like Irene, for she will enter the room Irene would not have dared to enter. Her ability to perceive this room with 'a wild askance shrinking eye' (56) stems from her marginal position, where she can recognize differences by giving passage to a different viewpoint, by feeling 'herself stand with her mother in the doorway' (Bowen 1998, 56–7).

Characters in transit, literally moving or dislocated, are typical in Bowen's work, which the writer herself has commented upon:

> An arrival, even into another room, is an event to be registered in some way. When they extend their environment, strike outward, invade the unknown, travel, what goes on in them is magnified and enhanced: impacts are sharper, there is more objectivity. But then, is this not so with all persons, living or fictional? (Bowen 1987, 286)

Having lived outside the bounds of English life, Portia has the advantage of noticing what others might not perceive. Her liminality gives her the power to decipher and deconstruct the normalized way of life at Windsor Terrace.

Although she was sent to Windsor Terrace because her father believed that ordinary life went on for Thomas and Anna, Portia makes a contrary statement, saying: 'there is no ordinary life' (Bowen 1998, 325). By claiming that there is no ordinary life, no normal way of living, Portia threatens the authority of norms and the power of normalization, for if there is no ordinary life, all life, including that going on in Windsor Terrace, might be extraordinary, that is, not necessarily 'remarkable or excellent', but *extraōrdinārius*, meaning: 'outside (the usual) order' (*OED*). When life is always already out of the ordinary, the very notion of otherness becomes irrelevant, since there is nothing to measure it against. In the absence of ordinary life, Anna and Thomas's life becomes a fiction of normality, a mere desire for the fixity of home and *oikonomia*.

By doubting the norms set by the dominant culture (illustrated by Anna's and Thomas's lifestyle) through Portia's liminal perspective, the novel inspires reflection about the potential larger (national as well as global) implications of the desire for a fixed identity. One of those, I argue, is anthropocentric climate change. It is fuelled both by our discomfort with the idea of change (in the perception of our personal, national and species identity), and by an inability to read climate change from our immediate human perspective. Our immediate perspective relies on an outdated concept of identity as something stable, fixed and linked to our sense of presence (of what is constantly verifiable and recognizable). Identity as such is not useful to our understanding of climate change. However, it can easily be used to discredit it, as James Inhofe (a senator in the United States) infamously demonstrated in 2015, when he brought a snowball to the Senate floor as real-life proof against claims of global warming. Climate change, which is happening on a counter-intuitive scale, cannot be read from a familiar snowball that is here now. Its identity is more complex and elusive – an uncanny passage we cannot read, must read and therefore will have to read without mastery.

In *The Death of the Heart*, complex irregular phenomena in a *habitual* environment are made visible through Portia. From a marginal viewpoint, she perceives the further consequences of the Londoners' lifestyle, namely, the smog. My reading of *The Death of the Heart* shows the correlation between the socio-economic framework of Londoners and air pollution. Bowen's London at the dawn of the climate crisis urges us to imagine and reconsider our impact on the places we inhabit through what Timothy Clark calls 'scalar literacy' (Clark 2019, 84), that is, reading what does not fully present itself in the present.

Traces in the air

The Death of the Heart was published in 1938, just before World War Two broke out and triggered a significant acceleration in the production of energy, crops and meat, which jump-started a rapid increase in CO2 levels in the atmosphere. Bowen could not have predicted the extent of the consequences of the war, but she does already comment on the destructive forces of progress. Pre-war London, where the novel is set, was known for its polluted air; to the twenty-first-century reader, it is readily associated with climate change, which already haunts the air/era of the novel.

In 'A way of life', an essay published in December 1947, and in the light of the post-war economic and fuel crises, Bowen underlines the unsustainability of an outdated model of living. She writes: '[n]o, we did not re-architect our houses while we could, although their coming impossibility foreshadowed itself as early as World War I' (Bowen 2008, 390). She explains:

> It seems symbolic that in our houses, even, we are hampered, and being drained of our needed energies, by an outmoded plan: the average middle and upper-class British home was built for, and remains the expression of, an order, a *material* way of living, now gone for good. Segregation of children; work by servants; importation of ton upon ton of coal. (Bowen 2008, 390)

In *The Death of the Heart*, coal is burnt at full speed. Readers are shown that Windsor Terrace is partially heated by 'the electric fire' (Bowen 1998, 28, 29, 30), Thomas's books are 'electric cleaned' (166) and their privacy is sustained by 'an electric fence' (92) – a telephone. We are told that at Portia's school, 'at the end of the afternoon, in winter, a blue-black glazed blind was run across from a roller to cover the skylight, when the electric lights had been turned on' (53). Portia, who is said to disturb other students by looking at the domed skylight (that 'told the state of the weather, went leaden with fog, crepitated when it was raining, or dropped a great square glare on to the table when the sun shone', 53), is brought down to earth, 'at face-and-table level', by the teacher's sarcastic remark: '[a]re we here to look at the sky?' (53). Thinking is called for, but not about London's air. The coal retrieved from the depths of the earth is in the air, invading lungs and writing stains on windows, yet it is so 'normal' and evasive that only the pen of a half-stranger – Portia's pen – seems to record its oddity.

She writes about it in her journal: '[w]hen I woke my window was like a brown stone, and I could hardly see the rest of the room. The whole house was just like that, it was not like night but like air being ill' (Bowen 1998, 122). Her first sight of smog is met with a sense of danger and childlike curiosity. When Matchett takes her to school through the thick fog, Portia feels that the walk is 'just like an adventure' (122). A day at Miss Paullie's 'felt more like a holiday', with 'lights on all day' (122). The contemporary reader understands all too well the irony of Portia's excitement about this excessive use of electric light, which fuels the poisonous smog outside, which Portia is cautioned not to swallow by speaking (122–3). The element of naivety that accompanies Portia's first experience of this strange phenomenon in hindsight depicts a lack of seriousness towards the matter, resulting in the Great Smog of London in 1952, which killed thousands of people, and many more uncounted non-human animals.

The fog is quickly forgotten by others, and the perception of the fog is facetiously wrapped up in silly mysticism and self-importance by Anna. Portia writes: '[s]he said that whenever there was a fog she always felt it was something that she had done, but she did not seem to mean this seriously' (Bowen 1998, 123). Only Portia seems to pay attention to the traces that this fog has left behind. She writes: '[i]t has left a brown stain' (123). Portia's sensitivity makes her quite a detective. She notices: '[t]he forest is full of blackish air like London, the trees do not look the same in it' (130), while Anna, who sits in the car, reading 'a detective story' (130), is blind to the polluted air in the wood.

The smog that comes and goes seems hardly a menace for Londoners such as Anna and Thomas, for it is, after all, a typical phenomenon in London. One perceives it partially, fleetingly. The same is true for climate change. As Timothy Clark writes:

> We experience phenomena at a (mostly) fairly stable and consistent speed – too slow and our perception would give us an almost static world in which nothing happened – too fast, and everything would blur into indistinctness. We understand distance, height, and breadth in terms of the given dimensionality of our embodied

existence. A particular human scale is inherent to the intelligibility of the Earth around us. (Clark 2015, 29–30)

Climate change does not necessarily come across as a perceptible change, but rather as an *uncanny* passage (which also has become a symbol of climate change, the carbon footprint – a footprint one cannot see with a bare eye). As Freud writes: '[t]he uncanny (*das Unheimliche*, "the unhomely") is in some ways the species of the familiar (*das Heimliche*, "the homely")' (Freud 2003, 134), for it is 'that species of the frightening that goes back to what was once well known and had long been familiar' (124). This lurking, frightening otherness within what is familiar describes the challenges involved in the perception of climate change in our familiar environments. To perceive, as Portia does, that the air is ill, one needs to challenge the human scale, which, I will suggest, could be done through becoming sensitive to a certain *différance* that is in the air. By *différance*, Derrida refers to difference and deferral of the signified: to a certain haunting plurality and even contradiction in a word that fails to present itself in the present, at all times.

To put the fog that Portia perceives into Derrida's terms, the pollution in the fog is an evasive supplementary signified that cannot be observed in the present, for it does not present itself in the present separately from the fog, and it hides itself again, when the fog disappears. However, Portia manages to record the visible trace of pollution in the air before it disappears: 'a brown stain' (Bowen 1998, 123) left behind by the fog. That brown stain is not capable of representing the event that preceded it, the expansive coal burning that goes unwitnessed in its globality. In this sense, the brown stain that is left, but only barely and not for long, recalls Derrida's concept of the cinder, which is what 'remains after a material has burned', but also 'a trope that comes to take the place of everything that disappears without leaving an identifiable trace' (Derrida 1995, 391). As Derrida explains, the body of which the cinder is the trace has totally disappeared; it is non-identifiable to the point that forgetting itself is forgotten, making it 'the trace or step … of what at the same time inscribes the vestige and carries it off' (391). Similarly, of the carbon footprint of Londoners' lives, a stain remains, only for a moment, inscribing the vestige of a much greater trouble.

The greater trouble, climate change, cannot be read in its totality from a mere stain on the window of Bowen's novel. Yet, I believe we can learn a lot about reading climate change from the experience of writing and reading literature such as Bowen's. Literature demands a certain sensitivity towards the *différance* proper to each word in its respective environment (the syntax, plot, context), and commands our imagination to see what is not there. Literature opens us up to the possibility of reading, misreading and rereading the familiar concepts ('passage') and environments (in this case, London) that, by the power of literary writing and reading, can be seen anew. Bowen's *The Death of the Heart* – already alert to strange traces and complex patterns – demands that its readers shift between perspectives, thereby underlining the ambivalence and shortcomings of our knowledge of complex phenomena. The passing smog is part of a larger passage (story) in the narrative of climate change, which is a narrative without an end in sight. Our reading of it is both possible and impossible (if one aims to be an omniscient reader). Reading climate change (like reading smog in the 1930s) demands humility from the reader, who must accept the imperfection of reading a passage that is unfinished, and that gives itself willingly to our human senses.

Bowen also shows that there is something distinctive about the writer's ability to perceive elusive phenomena, but it is not mastery. She writes:

> The childishness is necessary, fundamental – it involves a perpetual, errant state of desire, wonder, and unexpected reflex. The writer, unlike his non-writing adult friend, has no predisposed outlook; he seldom observes deliberately. He sees what he did not intend to see; he remembers what does not seem wholly possible. Inattentive learner in the schoolroom of life, he keeps some faculty free to *veer* and wonder. His is the *roving eye*. (Bowen 1987, 63, my emphasis)

The combination of the kind of sensitivity that keeps some faculty free to veer and wonder, united with childlike intuition and inattentiveness 'in the schoolroom of life' (Bowen 1987, 63), echo in Portia's schoolroom experience, as well as in her 'wild askance shrinking eye' (Bowen 1998, 57). Through this 'perpetual, errant state of desire, wonder, and unexpected reflex' (Bowen 1987, 63), Bowen's novel proposes an alternative gaze at the world of her time that does not give in to the dialectics of the dominant and the dominated.

The roving eye that Bowen evokes possesses certain elements of humility – of not knowing, or being able to plan ahead (control, master). It also suggests a roving 'I'. Bowen's writer is vulnerable in her environment and, through this vulnerability, is open to anything that might make itself known. She writes that 'writers do not find subjects: subjects find them' in a 'state of open susceptibility' (Bowen 1987, 63). This responsiveness to, without mastery of, the unknown, or even the unknowable, is the beginning of thinking.

Derrida explains that, according to the Western philosophical tradition, questioning is 'the essential act of philosophy, of thought, that is to say, the piety of thinking' (Derrida 2000, 12). Yet, he argues:

> But before the question, if one can speak of a before that is neither chronological nor logical, in order for there to be a question there must first of all be an acquiescence, a 'yes'. In order to ask, there must first be a certain 'yes'. This is what Heidegger called *Zusage*, which is more originary than the question. (Derrida 2000, 12)

Bowen's concept of the 'state of open susceptibility' (Bowen 1987, 63) seems to demand the same sort of acquiescence from a writer. The act of writing, as Bowen sees it, is not the matter of approaching a subject from the viewpoint of mastery. The writer is to enter 'a perpetual, errant state of desire, wonder, and unexpected reflex', without a 'predisposed outlook' (63), in order to host the unexpected. The roving eye/I of the writer, open to all sort of veering and wondering, seems to offer a different kind of sensitivity towards one's environment, capable of veering, that is, turning away from a usual direction or pattern (away from the seeming fixity of identities we give to phenomena in order to recognize them, speak of them and conceptualize them).

Nicholas Royle, one of the most influential readers of Bowen's oeuvre, explains that, as the French verb *virer*, meaning 'to turn, to turn around', is deposited at the core of the word 'environment', 'veering' offers a new understanding of the term 'environment' itself (Royle 2012, 2). 'Veer ecology' explores 'how language is changing in response to what has happened and what is happening but also how language can innovate and invent, alter or start differently – to change how people think and feel, and what they do' (Cohen and Duckert 2017, 471). Royle, while holding his page down with a stone from Bowen's Court, her old house that no longer exists, writes:

> Bowen invites us to think about telepathy and literature, telepathy in literature, the telepathy of literature. Novelistic narration is an eerie weave of thought-reading and feeling-sharing, shifting about within and through one body or point of view and another, never at home, never properly 'in place'. (Royle 2012, 126)

The Death of the Heart dislocates its readers, but it also concatenates us to a variety of others who are not quite here, and not quite others. Attridge writes that to read responsibly means 'to trust in the unpredictability of reading, its openness to the future' (Attridge 2017, 180). He evokes a certain readerly hospitality, that is, 'a readiness to have one's purposes reshaped by the work to which one is responding' (113). Like her readers, Bowen's characters cannot escape from the unpredictability of reading. The character of Eddie seems to both recognize and fear the power of art to reshape one's purposes. He does not want to see himself being written about in Portia's diary, and he warns Portia: 'I hate writing; I hate art – there's always *something else* there. I won't have you choosing words about me' (Bowen 1998, 115, my emphasis). Eddie, like Anna and Thomas, is afraid of the *différance* at the core of his identity. He tries to stabilize his identity through his social airs, but he fails, for his identity is always already open to others' perception, and thus lends itself to the haunted experience of reading that threatens to contradict how one wishes to be perceived.

The reading and writing of air/airs, Bowen shows, do not lend themselves willingly to Eddie's desire for fixity. He fails to read the menace of London's air, but also the menace in Portia's air (appearance) of child-like innocence: 'No presence could be less insistent than hers. He [Eddie] treated her like an element (air, for instance) or a condition (darkness): these touch one with their equality and lightness where one could endure no human touch' (Bowen 1998, 211). He only accepts a certain naivety of youth that *he* perceives (without being made 'conscious of the vacuum there must be in his eyes', 211). Thus, he commands: '[y]ou must never show any sign of change' (234), which is an impossible request of a teenager defined by changes. Such narrowness of vision, and the comfort Eddie finds in a reduced system of identification, clash with the elusive presence of fog in the novel. The fog is nothing to Eddie, who is only interested in mastering how he is perceived – his social airs. This very desire for mastery makes him unable to read both Portia and London's air, while Portia's reading of Londoners' airs, as well as London's air, from her liminal viewpoint, manages to reveal strange contaminations in both.

Conclusion

Like Portia, we have inherited the consequences of the mistakes made by previous generations. The destructive traces from the twentieth century, left behind in the biosphere, cannot take responsibility for themselves. It is up to the future of the novel, its readers today, to connect the traces of pollution in London's air to climate change. It is also up to us to underline the traces of destructive ways of living as the cause of climate change, and to alter those patterns.

Bowen could not have known what we know about climate change, but she seems to give her readers a tool for reading this phenomenon – a kind of sensitivity that she calls the 'state of open susceptibility' (Bowen 1987, 63). It is the sort of profound doubt and curiosity that is the antithesis of various efforts to reduce phenomena to what is present and perceptible to the human sensory system. It is the opposite of Inhofe's snowball-vision. Veering with Bowen, as a transformative experience of reading, outwits 'the personal human experience as the basic reality' (Clark 2019, 80–1) considered to be proper to novelistic writing. Reading Bowen's fiction might make one feel and think in an extraordinary manner, that is, not necessarily 'remarkable or excellent', but *extraōrdinārius*, meaning: outside order, outside command. Through what Timothy Clark calls 'scalar literacy' (Clark 2019, 84), addressing what does not fully present itself in the present, *The Death of the Heart* challenges the way one experiences environments. There lies the power of certain literary writings to expand, question and alter our perception of complex phenomena. Through Portia's observations of London's air, the novel seems to sensitize its readers to the subtle forces of an unidentifiable trouble.

Bowen's view on the amorphousness of identity paves the way for thinking about uncanny phenomena that do not respond to our normal categories and range of perception. Climate change is omnipresent, and yet we do not perceive it at all times. Climate change becomes visible as a change only when we are able to look at a broader pattern on a vast timescale. To a regular person, climate change appears less as a change and more as a passage one must read without mastery. It is that passing, returning, strangeness that builds up in the scientific data, but also comes from stories that bring us closer to understanding climate change.

Through the brown stain recorded in Portia's diary, the evasive, hardly perceptible pollution resurfaces and haunts the twenty-first-century reader, who has a different perspective on smog and its irreparable damage. Portia's diary becomes a shaky shared ground, a passage, between other characters and Portia, but also between the novel and its contemporary readers, constituting a gateway between reality and fiction, but also a temporal passage between the twentieth and twenty-first centuries that makes the invisible concatenation of pollution visible.

Note

1   In one passage in particular, Bowen 'dematerializes' Portia while Londoners stay put: '[s]he felt blotted out of the room, as little present in it as these two others truly felt to be' (Bowen 1998, 285). The fleeting images of Portia's journey from continental Europe to London emerge as if out of thin air: 'She saw that tree she saw when the train stopped for no reason; she saw in her nerves, equally near and distant, the wet trees out there in the park. She heard the Seale sea, then the silent distances of the coast' (285). Appearing 'equally near and distant' (285), the depictions of Portia's life with her parents hang in the air. They are memories of a life that is no more, and that was never rooted in a specific place or custom.

References

Attridge, Derek. 2017. *The Singularity of Literature*. London: Routledge.
Bowen, Elizabeth. 1987. *The Mulberry Tree: Writings of Elizabeth Bowen*, edited by Hermione Lee. 1st American edn. San Diego, CA: Harcourt Brace Jovanovich.
Bowen, Elizabeth. 1998. *The Death of the Heart*. London: Vintage.
Bowen, Elizabeth. 2008. *People, Places, Things: Essays*, edited by Allan Hepburn. Edinburgh: Edinburgh University Press.
Bowen, Elizabeth. 2019. *Eva Trout or Changing Scenes*. New York: Anchor Books.
Clark, Timothy. 2015. *Ecocriticism on the Edge: The Anthropocene as a threshold concept*. London: Bloomsbury.
Clark, Timothy. 2019. *The Value of Ecocriticism*. Cambridge: Cambridge University Press.
Cohen, Jeffrey Jerome and Lowell Duckert, eds. 2017. *Veer Ecology: A companion for environmental thinking*. Minneapolis: University of Minnesota Press.
De la Soudière, Martin. 2000. 'Le paradigme du passage', *Communications* 70: 5–31. https://doi.org/10.3406/comm.2000.2060.
Derrida, Jacques. 1995. 'Passages – from traumatism to promise'. In *Points: Interviews, 1974–1994*, edited by Elisabeth Weber, 372–98. Stanford, CA: Stanford University Press.
Derrida, Jacques. 2000. 'Hospitality', *Angelaki* 5 (3): 3–18. https://doi.org/10.1080/09697250020034706.
Derrida, Jacques. 2002. 'The animal that therefore I am (more to follow)', translated by David Wills, *Critical Inquiry* 28 (2): 369–418.
Ellmann, Maud. 2004. *Elizabeth Bowen: The shadow across the page*. Edinburgh: Edinburgh University Press.
Foucault, Michel. 2004. *Surveiller et punir: Naissance de la prison*. Paris: Gallimard.
Freud, Sigmund. 2003. *The Uncanny*, edited by Hugh Haughton, translated by David McLintock. London: Penguin.
Le Blanc, Guillaume. 2010. *Dedans, dehors: La condition d'étranger*. Seuil: La Couleur des idées.
McDowell, Alfred. 1978. '"The Death of the Heart" and the human dilemma', *Modern Language Studies* 8 (2): 5–16.
Osborn, Susan. 2006. 'Reconsidering Elizabeth Bowen', *MFS Modern Fiction Studies* 52 (1): 187–97.
Partridge, Eric. 1991. *Origins: An etymological dictionary of modern English*. 4th edn. London: Routledge.
Royle, Nicholas. 2012. *Veering: A theory of literature*. Edinburgh: Edinburgh University Press.
Sullivan, Walter. 1976. 'A sense of place: Elizabeth Bowen and the landscape of the heart', *The Sewanee Review* 84 (1): 142–9.

14
Thirdspace and hospitality: migratory passage and the labyrinth of national (in)difference in Rachid Boudjedra's *Topographie idéale pour une agression caractérisée* (1975)

Eric Wistrom

The aim of this chapter is twofold. Using Edward Soja's theory of Thirdspace and 'real-and-imaged' places, we will study the representation of blocked passage in Rachid Boudjedra's 1975 novel *Topographie idéale pour une agression caractérisée*. In so doing, a particular emphasis will be placed on the author's characterization of the Parisian Métro as both a metaphor for the physical movement of transnational migration and a metonymic symbol for the French migrant condition. This will lead to an extended discussion of the threshold of tolerance that underlies the novel's conception of postcolonial social interaction, which will draw heavily from Jacques Derrida's Fourth and Fifth Seminars on hospitality, as well as from Émile Benveniste's philological work on the Latin word *hostis* (Benveniste 2016, 61–74; Derrida and Dufourmantelle, 2000). While our discussion will centre on the complicated history of Franco-Algerian migration in the early 1970s – specifically on the *ratonnades* of 1971 and 1973 – the chapter will also invoke broader changes in the French national consciousness over the past half century as they have informed contemporary political rhetoric on immigration and integration.

To that end, it is useful to briefly outline the challenges of framing the French national consciousness in a postmigratory context. In a March 2007 interview with *Le Monde*, historian Pierre Nora stated that Ernest Renan's theory of the nation was dead in contemporary French society (Gherardi 2007). No longer defined by a solidary will to live together as 'constituted by the memory of collective sacrifice' (Smith 2015, 63) and bound by a memorialized cult of ancestors, France's national discourse could no longer be characterized as possessing a continuous sense of filiation between the historical past and the future. Rather, Nora saw it as inhabiting 'a perpetual state of the moment' engendered by a new national trialectic of 'memory, identity, and heritage' (Gherardi 2007, n.p.)[1] – a shift in nationalist cognition, which led to his ultimate conclusion that '[i]t is not France that is eternal, but [rather] Frenchness' (Gherardi 2007, n.p.). Within this framing of national identification, memory serves as a means of reconstituting the past in an emancipatory action that erodes the historical notion of identity and generates a new heterogeneous model that is reliant upon the stratified interaction between national myth and the collective memories of subnational groups. To put this more plainly, national identity has become increasingly decentralized in the postcolonial era, largely as a result of the 'memorial hegemony' (Nora and Chandernagor 2008, 15) of identity politics, whose 'recent naïve tendencies seem ... to prefer in certain ways memory, which is taken to be more authentic, more "true" than history' (Le Goff 1988, 10) itself. Rather than the documentary aspect of historical fact, it is thus the perception and manipulation of historical memory that has become important in today's political landscape. In Nora's words, collective memory has been reduced to 'that which remains of the past in the lived experiences of groups, or that which groups do with the past' (Nora 1978, 378).

While one could certainly argue for an increasingly narrow view of nationalist identity, given the contemporary rise of populist movements across Europe – movements which do, in fact, resemble certain aspects of Benedict Anderson's (2006) discursively created imagined communities – Nora was quick to point out that reactionary movements[2] tending to nationalist regression have been unsuccessful in reinstituting a collective sense of uniform identity that could offer 'a communal bond to each segment of the heterogeneous French population' (Gherardi 2007, n.p.). Rather, such disparate notions of subnational belonging represent the small, the marginal and the decentralized – the interstitial parts of the larger collective.

It is, however, important to note that it is not just the historical framing of national identity that has altered the political landscape as a product of the 'radicalization of memory' (Nora and Chandernagor 2008, 15); so, too, has our perception of culture changed in relation to the phenomenon of transnational movement. In this vein, Edward Said stated that the monolithic image of culture:

> has now shifted from the settled, established, and domesticated dynamics of culture to its unhoused, decentered, and exilic energies, energies whose incarnation today is the migrant, and whose consciousness is that of the intellectual and artist in exile, the political figure between domains, between forms, between homes, and between languages. (Said 1994, 332)

In light of this idea of decentred creative energy, I would like to suggest that there exists a dialectic engagement of both the real and the imagined – of various perceptions and conceptions of the temporal, the spatial and the social – in Nora's determination of identity as a restitutive corollary of memory. As will be developed in this chapter, I hold this association to be indicative of a state of liminality[3] existing at the heart of the postcolonial national ethos. Moreover, this dialectic is central to understanding how the biopolitics of transnational migration have been perceived over the past century, given that the progressive insertion of minority voices into the national dialogue has manifestly changed how the theoretical notion of Frenchness has been conceived in the post-war era. The fluidity at the centre of this shifting national optic poses a fundamental question: have we truly become more inclined to multiculturalism and migratory integration in the face of an increasingly decentralized conception of nationhood? Or, have we been progressively plunged into a state of radical binary – viewing the Other as a threat not only to our cohesive sense of national belonging, but also to our constructed sense of ontological being?

Rachid Boudjedra's 1975 novel *Topographie idéale pour une agression caractérisée* provides a unique perspective on this very question. Having been published roughly 13 years after Algeria gained its independence in 1962, the novel's theme of migration is socially coded in the wake of a complex series of interwoven events: the successive waves of post-World War Two immigration during the period of reconstruction known as the *Trente Glorieuses*, which led to thirty years of unprecedented economic growth of the French economy; the steady rise of unemployment in the late 1960s, which was complicated by the civil unrest of May 1968 and the 1973 oil crisis; and the lasting effects of the Algerian War of Independence on the French national consciousness, which culminated in the *ratonnades*[4] of 1971 and 1973. The novel's publication in 1975 also retrospectively takes into account the tensions surrounding the politics of Franco-Algerian migration in the early 1970s – related both to France's decision to suspend labour migration in 1974 in response to its ongoing economic crisis and changing public attitudes regarding immigration (Laurens 2008, 70), and to Algeria's decision to suspend immigration to France following the rise of racially motivated attacks against Algerians and the nationalist politics of 'Arabization' undertaken by the government of Houari Boumediene (Meynier and Meynier 2011, 224). To understand the complexities inherent in the novel's portrayal of migratory passage, one must recognize the complicated historical context that exists behind the textual narrative that is progressively weaponized by the 'radicalization of memory' (Nora and Chandernagor 2008, 15) as a means of establishing and upholding migratory difference.

As will be shown, the reconstitution of these historical events, heavily inflected by subnational group memory and long-standing racial prejudice inherited from the colonial era, plays an integral role in establishing a differential sense of identity that separates the self from the Other, and engenders a characteristic sense of hostility and aggression within the confines of the Parisian Métro. As stated by Boudjedra in a 1976 interview, the Métro serves as an ideal topography for the development of this idea, given that its subterranean labyrinth amplifies hostility to difference through its closed system, which forces interpersonal contact at the same time as serving as a metonymic symbol for the French migrant condition (Boudjedra 1976). Moreover, its tunnels lead the protagonist along a set of predetermined avenues, which, while giving the protagonist a sense of personal agency, nonetheless lead him towards his eventual death, which is inflicted upon his Orphic exit from the underground at the Porte de Clichy.

In this vein, Boudjedra's conceptualization of passage addresses not only the physical spatiality of transnational movement of an unnamed migrant worker lost in the bowels of the Parisian Métro, but also the ambiguous state of errancy brought about in a third space of sociocultural exchange – a theoretical space which, to borrow from Edward Soja and Homi Bhabha, is 'brought about in the rebalanced trialectics [of being] of spatiality-historicality-sociality' (Soja 1996, 10), so as to challenge the monolithic image of 'the historical identity of culture as a homogenizing, unifying force' (Bhabha 2004, 54). The marriage of these two theorists must at first seem strange; after all, there is a definite need to separate Bhabha's focus on ambivalent areas of discourse in cultural enunciation from Soja's decidedly more spatial focus, which draws heavily on the work of Henri Lefebvre. Whereas Bhabha's theory of Thirdspace is defined discursively as a production of meaning from within two competing frames of cultural or symbolic reference, Soja's Thirdspace is defined by a production of space that is at once 'real-and-imagined'. While Thirdspace indeed holds a discursive element, this discourse is fundamentally spatially mediated, and is thus produced through the interrelation of three 'spaces': that of perceived space (also referred to as spatial practice, or Firstspace), which is composed of empirically measured configurations of physical space; that of conceived space (also known as representations of space, or Secondspace), which is composed of projections into the empirical world from the spatial imaginary; and that of lived space (also known as spaces of representation, or Thirdspace), which is produced through a dialectical engagement of the real and the imagined (Soja 1996, 53–82). More specifically, if perceived space is defined by perspective and epistemology, and is thus largely dependent on the materiality of 'real' spatial forms, conceived space is defined by thought and cognition, and is thus oriented towards mental forms existing in the spatial imaginary. Taken together, Thirdspace can be understood as 'an-Other way of understanding and acting to change the spatiality of human life, a distinct mode of critical spatial awareness that is brought about in the rebalanced trialectics of spatiality-historicality-sociality' (10). Through this trialectic interaction, Thirdspace comes to form a 'real and imagined lifeworld of experience, emotions, events, and political choices … marked out materially and metaphorically in *spatial praxis*, [as] the transformation of (spatial) knowledge into (spatial) action in a field of unevenly developed (spatial) power' (31, emphasis in the original). It is important to specify that Soja's use of the term 'trialectic' should be understood as not only encompassing 'a triple dialectic, but also a [new] mode of dialectical reasoning that is more inherently spatial than the conventional temporally-defined dialectics of Hegel or Marx' (10). This distinction is important, for Soja's more spatially oriented vision of trialectical exchange relying on a dialectic of the perceived and conceived – of the real and imagined – is particularly apt for understanding the intersubjective and intersocietal negotiations that are to be encountered in Boudjedra's novel. Put more plainly, the Métro can be read as both a physical space and a metaphysical space capable of representing the threshold of national indifference and difference before the positional liminality of social interaction.

It is within this conceptual framing – viewing the protagonist's itinerant passage through the labyrinth of the Parisian underground not only as a physical movement, but also as a metaphysical commentary on the state of transnational migration before the dominant discourse of postcolonial nationalism – that I ask the following: how is the Thirdspace of postcolonial migration affected by the politics of national indifference and difference in *Topographie*, and to what extent do postcolonial contact zones encourage a rebalancing of the spatial, historical and social paradigms of cultural exchange?

Blocked passage and the suspension of affiliation

The politics of social interaction of *Topographie* can be envisioned in one of two ways. There is of course the notion of radical binary, wherein the novel's unnamed migrant (referred to here as the protagonist) is seen as a subaltern Other – a manifest negation of everything that comprises the essence of normatively established Frenchness – who is relegated to a position of sociocultural inferiority at the periphery of socio-economic integration. This is perhaps the most explicit form of racially posited intercultural exchange in the novel, and it can be aptly described as the 'us-and-them' mentality. While the notion of what exactly constitutes 'us' remains a dynamic and fluid construct built upon a superimposed network of intersectional identities, the notion of Otherness is often essentialized into a much simpler construct. Given the difficulty in establishing what exactly constitutes 'us' at any specific moment in time, Otherness is often perceived as the existence of fundamental difference – a typed negation of what we conceive of as integral to our own socially derived sense of being. This is not to say that Othering is an inherently simple act. Quite the contrary: the recognition of difference involves a 'play between the metaphoric/narcissistic and metonymic/aggressive moments in colonial discourse', as 'there is always the alienating other (or mirror) which crucially returns its image to the subject; and in that form of substitution and fixation that is fetishism there is always the trace of loss, absence' (Bhabha 2004, 116). Rather than presence – or the unilateral production of positive difference – I would like to suggest that it is in fact the generative notion of absence – the possibility for a reductive negation of the Self – that enables dialectical Othering. Otherwise stated, Othering implies a production of discourse situated between positive – the Other is/has something that I do not – and negative – the Other is lacking something that I am/have – conceptions of referential difference. As explained by Bhabha:

> Stereotyping is not the setting up of a false image which becomes the scapegoat of discriminatory practices. It is a much more ambivalent text of projection and introjection, metaphoric and metonymic strategies, displacement, over-determination, guilt, aggressivity; the masking and splitting of 'official' and phantasmatic knowledges to construct the positionalities and oppositionalities of racist discourse. (Bhabha 2004, 117)

When we speak of Othering, it is necessary to take into account the ambivalent space of enunciation surrounding oppositional aggression. More specifically, stereotyping involves the splicing of real and imagined knowledge into a system of positionalities, and it is through this positional framing within an inscribed system of knowledge that one produces a sense of Foucauldian power. In a similar vein to Said's thesis that the transformation of latent orientalism into manifest orientalism produced a characteristic vision of the Orient that was largely self-referential (Said 1979, 201–25),[5] racist discourse relies on a positional and affective knowledge of the Other that self-referentially buttresses its system of beliefs through heuristics and cognitive bias. As stated by Soja:

> Everything, including spatial knowledge, is condensed in communicable representations and re-presentations of the real world to the point that the representations substitute for the real world itself ... Such subjectivism reduces spatial knowledge to a discourse on discourse that is rich in potential insights but at the same time filled with illusive presumptions that what is imagined/represented defines the reality of social space. (Soja 1996, 63–4)

It is within this context that the novel's title – *An Ideal Topography for a Characterized Aggression* – can be understood: the space of representation is transformed into a site of localized aggression through the interrelationship of spatial practice and the spatial imaginary. In so doing, the Parisian Métro comes to embody a 'real and imagined lifeworld of experiences, emotions, events, and political choices' (Soja 1996, 31) that represents an ideal topography for a characterized aggression on two interrelated fronts: if the Métro's halls metaphorically allow for the concentration of racist ideologists in much the same way that they physically funnel travellers through their subterranean labyrinth, the

Métro's confined pathways also play a generative role in the production of violence through a characteristic form of spatial conditioning that predisposes social actors to conflict and aggression. Once again returning to Boudjedra's qualification of the Métro as a metonymic symbol for the French migrant condition (Boudjedra 1976), we can tie this 'real-and-imaged' spatiality to Arnold van Gennep's (2019) theory of liminality in ritual passage: the migrant becomes an intruder once they enter into the 'real-and-imagined' spatiality of the Métro – having undergone a rite of separation from their place of origin (Algeria), yet not having been incorporated into their place of destination (France) – given that their liminal suspension of affiliation threatens the host community's sense of ontological stability. Otherwise stated, the migrant's participation in a rite of passage questions the basis of incorporated sociality, for in the liminal phase of passage:

> the very moral foundation of sociability can also be broken down, and with devastating consequences. The *communitas* that comes out of liminality may be recognized as a deeply bonded human collectivity; but whether this collectivity engages in loving care toward the other or in violent destruction we really cannot to say [*sic*] in any general way. (Thomassen 2014, 84, emphasis in the original)

Here, liminality does not intrinsically imply marginality, as liminality always implies some sense of transition – as stated by Thomassen, '[i]f it is not about transition, it is not about liminality' (Thomassen 2014, 15). However, in certain cases of blocked passage, liminality can indeed involve experiences of marginality. This is not a productive marginality, like the one praised by Bhabha and Soja. Rather, this is a place of exclusion, violence and subaltern alienation.

This manner of viewing the Other is especially prevalent in the protagonist's death scene, wherein he – having been lost in the underground labyrinth of the Parisian Métro for the entire day, due to his illiteracy – approaches a group of young men to ask for directions, only to be savagely murdered:

> He didn't yet have the time to relieve himself of his excitement, of his jubilation, of that vital impulse that had propelled him beyond the labyrinth in an incredible rush, cut clean by an aggression of which he all too quickly understood the meaning; not needing to hear them repeat that it had been a long time since they had caught

an immigrant so typical, so stereotypical, with his suitcase filled with stinking nonsense, ravenous microbes and subversive booklets threatening the very foundations of their civilization. (Boudjedra 1975, 158)

In this excerpt, the protagonist – largely devoid of characterization – is reduced to an anonymous type upon which the young men's aggression can be concentrated. Yet, despite the detail given to the assault and murder, no real motivation is given as to why the protagonist was targeted. Indeed, it appears that the only justification relies on the fact that he: (1) is 'a typical immigrant'; (2) carries a suitcase; and (3) possesses something that threatens the bedrock nature of French society. This causality is certainly vague and unconvincing. However, if one reads this scene in conjunction with a previous statement on page 78, in which the protagonist's suitcase is described as 'the very expression of his journey', the causality established between the bag – the metaphoric representation of his migration – and the murder would seem to signal that it is in fact the protagonist's foreignness – an innate negation to the men's conception of postcolonial national identity – that provides the only convincing explanation. The unstable binary surrounding Algerian migration to France in the years following the 1962 Évian Accords can be seen to a certain extent as instigating a sense of perpetual liminality that serves a generative role in the production of violence in the novel. While the Algerian government did vigorously defend the right of Algerian citizens to work abroad in France prior to 1973, it also showed itself to be somewhat accommodating of French policies that sought to limit (im)migration from North Africa. Where the French government was concerned, '[t]he fear of "concentrations" gave birth to the concept of a "threshold of tolerance"' (Cohen 2012, 21–2) with respect to Maghrebin populations. In both cases, the blocked possibility of passage – being stunted in a liminal stage of suspended affiliation – tends towards marginalization and exclusionary politics by way of which hospitality comes to be circumscribed by binary views of resolute foreignness. One has the impression that if the protagonist had simply chosen to stay in the relative obscurity of the Parisian underground – out of sight, and out of mind – the young men would have been perfectly content to assault or murder another passing migrant in his place, for there is not anything particular about the protagonist that can explain this outburst of violence. Rather, it can only be seen as the characterized expression of pure hatred for racial and social difference. While taking place 11 years after independence, the situational agency of the young men in Boudjedra's novel echoes the colonial attitudes given in an anecdote by Frantz Fanon, who stated that:

> one of these good French folks declared on a train where I was sitting: 'May the truly French values live on and the race will be safeguarded! At the present time we need a national union. No more internal strife! A united front against the foreigners [and turning to me] whoever they may be.' (Fanon 2008, 101)

The idea of keeping race pure signifies a damning attitude with regard to the Other: in all instances, a binary separation is to be upheld between the postcolonial cult of the nation and the foreign Other.

This interpretation is further supported by Boudjedra's decision to include a list compiled by the Association of Algerians in Europe of 11 deaths that occurred in 1973 following the outbreak of *ratonnades* in Marseille (Boudjedra 1975, 161). The report lacks any human dimension, giving only the name, age, family status, and place and cause of death. In short, the victims are given only categorical descriptions common to many abbreviated news formats, such as *fait divers*: their ages range from 16 to 43 years; their family statuses vary from being single to having six children; and, while seven died in Marseille, the remaining four died throughout France in Perreux, Metz, Maubeuge and Tours. Their causes of death also vary greatly: while five died from gunshot wounds, one died after suffering a traumatic brain injury, one was discovered drowned, three are listed as having died after being physically assaulted with no other explanation given, and one is said to have died of 'natural causes' after being taken into police custody. These categorical descriptions serve an important purpose: apart from the fact that the men were all Algerians (that is, foreigners) and political demonstrators, the men's only unifying characteristic was their link to transnational migration and postcolonial difference.

Now let us return to our protagonist. Note the parallel between these categorical descriptions and the description of our 'typical immigrant' on page 158. Lacking any distinguishing characteristics apart from his suitcase and uneven shoulders, his very essence becomes reduced to that of an itinerant object that threatens the young men's notion of communal identity. Even the limited physical description of the protagonist's shoulders serves to return the reader's attention to the bag that he is carrying – a bag which, we should remember, exists as a metonymic symbol for the protagonist's state of errancy. And here, we can now return to Nora's statement that opened this chapter: the question of memory and identity is highly implicated for the young men, who act exclusively as a function of their own cognitive bias and sense of conceived identity. Living in 'a perpetual state of the moment' (Gherardi 2007, n.p.), the men's sense of identity is largely predicated on the traumatic memory of the Algerian War, and the evolving nature of the French ethos, which saw a progressive insertion of minority voices into the national dialogue through the transition from a politics of assimilation towards a politics of integration – the latter of which was championed in the 1980s as the dominant model of social discourse on immigration (Chemin 2016). Combined with the economic stress of the 1973 oil crisis, the arrival of the migrant Other is thus perceived by the young men as an attack on their constructed sense of social and cultural identity – therein unifying the three constituent parts of Nora's national trialectic of 'memory, identity, and heritage' (Gherardi 2007, n.p.). While the text does not describe the young men individually – instead characterizing them collectively as a 'horde' – one can form an idea of their character through their opposition to the protagonist, in much the same way that Boudjedra indicated in the previously referenced 1976 interview that the protagonist's fictional hometown – le Piton – was to be taken as the metaphoric antithesis to the Parisian Métro: the young men are most probably White, could be characterized as *Français de souche*, and have an established communal identity formed on binary hierarchies of European superiority that were in many ways inherited from the ethnographic tropes and cultural mythologies of the French colonial empire. In this instance, one sees a complete failure in the politics of migration: there is no possibility of cultural exchange to be found in this space of interaction, given that it is immediately superseded by a sense of foundational difference that turns to violence. As such, the concept of liminality here fails to produce a sense of transformative, transcendental agency. Rather, Thirdspace transforms the oppositionality of racial discourse into violent action that is situated in a field of unevenly distributed social power. According to René Girard's theory of foundational violence, 'once the spiralling movement of escalating conflict and violence has started, there is only one possible solution: an innocent must be identified as guilty, excluded and killed, and in this way unanimity can be restored to society' (Thomassen 2014, 103). As in Albert Camus's *L'Étranger*, it is ultimately the unnamed Other who serves this sacrificial role (Camus 1989).

Hospitality and the threshold of tolerance

All this being said, it would be easy to dismiss this view of intercultural interaction as being coded to a specific event or series of events – namely, those of the *ratonnades* of 1973. However, it is important to recognize that Boudjedra broadened the political scope of his novel from that of simple binaries of overt hostility to include subliminal acts of bias carried out in everyday interactions, noting that, while he himself had not lived the same experiences as migrant workers, he had faced similar experiences of racism (Boudjedra 1976). And here we arrive at the second form of social interaction seen in the novel, which is similarly facilitated by the 'real-and-imaged' spatiality of the Parisian Métro: a faculty of characterized hostility that is far more subtle in its manifestation and that does not exclusively rely on the idea of fundamental difference. Rather, it straddles the interpretative edge of social interaction and national indifference, serving as a liminal state between conditional acceptance and hostility. In this case, the illusion of integration is extended only as a transient construct operating out of an immediate necessity for the Other – with the threshold of indifference and difference being quantified by the Other's perceived value to society as defined by their productive utility within the labour market. Given that perceived value is an extrinsic value and can widely fluctuate, even those who would initially be indifferent to our protagonist's existence can ultimately come to exhibit patterns of aggression similar to those that arise from binary relationships from the moment in which the protagonist's perceived value is eclipsed by their arbitrary measure of difference. This idea of marginalism is not the same as the marginality discussed in the previous section. Rather, it centres on Gossen's First Law of diminishing marginal utility – namely, that as one factor of production increases as all others are held constant, the extra output gained by adding a subsequent unit progressively decreases. After a certain level of output has been achieved, the migrant's marginal productive utility passes a 'threshold of tolerance', whereupon the host society's indifference to his presence can turn to a radical sense of positional difference. For a textual example of this phenomenon, let us look to the liminal characterization of the postmigratory state of socio-economic integration:

> It will teach him to want to work hard, to truly merit his salary building houses for others so that they can then rub shoulders with him in the street or in the metro; they won't notice him, they'll look

> down on him, beat him, murder him: in every way he's trapped like a rat and while he can say that he left the labyrinth (having arrived safe and sound) he doesn't know what awaits him ... (Boudjedra 1975, 118)

Note that our protagonist is only treated with relative indifference due to his productive utility – that is to say, his ability to work and produce for his host society – in a movement that progressively reduces his essence to that of a base economic factor of production. Socially coded under the auspices of a new form of colonial exploitation, this evaluative edge of social indifference can quickly change to aggression when the migrant worker is no longer needed as a means to an end. In this instance, it would appear that our protagonist being welcomed into the postcolonial social economy is primarily contingent upon the added economic value that he can bring to the greater social equation, and, from the moment in which the inconveniences of his existence surpass this perceived value, the host society's sense of tolerance and indifference can rapidly devolve into a state of unfettered hostility.

Certainly, all of this could be dismissed as being indicative of the confines of the Parisian Métro, which, given the title of the novel – *An Ideal Topography for a Characterized Aggression* – conveys the idea that space can produce attitudes in a manner not dissimilar from Soja's trialectics of 'real-and-imaged' Thirdspace. However, the final words that 'he doesn't know what awaits him' would seem to nuance this interpretation, instead showing that this threshold of indifference and difference is not specific to any one geographic location – even if space *can* have a generative effect on aggressivity – but is rather indicative of the postcolonial migrant condition as a whole:

> He doesn't know what awaits him because, even though the labyrinth is a test in itself, there's not only that. There are still the construction sites, the blast furnaces, the kilometres of streets to sweep, the tons of snow to clear, the mines and other dark holes that will come to term; all of that, in the optimistic assumption that the police don't bother him, the housing owner doesn't mess with him, the kids don't stick out their tongues at him, the bugs don't eat his skin, the curses don't go to his head, the brave and valiant men don't kill him on the side of a dark road because – he would have by that time learned the language – he has a bad accent ... (Boudjedra 1975, 180)

An exceedingly negative and fatalist conception of postmigratory hospitality for sure, the language in this description is filled with references to aggression and desperation. In many ways, Boudjedra's portrait of the migrant condition exists as an accumulation of traumatic experiences that gradually erode the space between national indifference and difference, ultimately leading to the exhaustion of the migrant's economic utility until the point beyond which he is discarded as a worn mechanism of industry. The progressive approach towards this threshold presents a more treacherous portrait of postcolonial integration than that which was presented in the binary perspective of the previous section. Instead of simply casting the migrant into a perpetual state of abject Otherness, this new model offers the illusion of acceptance founded upon sublimated tendencies of bias that remain ready to surge beyond the threshold of consciousness into overt acts of aggression and hostility. The fictions underlying this myth of integration ultimately show themselves to be an incredibly dangerous prospect: by their inherent refusal to overtly acknowledge the institutionalized forms of their subliminal bias, they encourage a self-perpetuating system of inequality and unstated aggression. The novel's depiction of the protagonist as being nothing more than a simple factor of production that comes to be progressively dispossessed of his humanity – being forced to overcome an accumulation of obstacles to his integration until he is murdered for an arbitrary measure of difference – is painfully indicative of this new model of colonial exploitation: the migrant's very essence becomes reduced to that of his productive output; and, given the continual influx of new capital into the labour market via post-World War Two policies of immigration, his perceived value becomes reduced to that of a disposable factor of production. When his marginal productive value is eclipsed by his existential cost due to the diminishing point of returns, the illusion of tolerance that has been temporarily extended to him is quickly revoked – revealing in its stead a seething undercurrent of hostility that comes raging to the surface.

The dialectical engagement of the potentiality of space as having a generative role in the production of violence with the arbitrarily assigned value of the migrant's marginal utility is inherently problematic insofar as the prospect of hospitality is concerned. In speaking of the characterized hostility of the Métro, one can speak of geographies of proximity – both in the real and the imagined senses of the term – as a causal way of modelling the spatial reality of Soja's Thirdspace, and the positionality to which Bhabha makes reference in his analysis of the production of discriminatory discursive practices. In her response to Jacques Derrida's

Fourth Seminar, and his position that '[a]n act of hospitality can only be poetic', Anne Dufourmantelle stated that:

> Derrida's obsession, in this philosophical narrative woven around that fine theme of hospitality, takes its time in drawing the contours of an impossible, illicit geography of proximity. A proximity that would not be the opposite of an elsewhere come from outside and surrounding it, but 'close to the close,' that unbearable orb of intimacy that melts into hate. If we say that murder and hate designate everything that excludes closeness, it is insofar as they ravage from within an original relationship to alterity. (Derrida and Dufourmantelle 2000, 2, 4)

Note that this idea of an unbearable orb of intimacy that melts into hate to produce violence has certain parallels with the theory of marginal productive value. In a manner similar to the marginalism of the threshold of national indifference and difference, Dufourmantelle's orb of intimacy is gradual and progressive; it erodes the liminal spatiality of migratory transition to the point at which the possibility of passage becomes irremediably blocked and suspended. Unfortunately, one cannot necessarily state at which point this transformation will take place, given that this measure is extrinsic and arbitrarily assigned. However, Dufourmantelle poses an important question that gives us a sense of phenomenological grounding upon which we can continue to build our analysis:

> So what happens when our eyes halt on the words: 'hospitality, proximity, enclave, hate, foreigner…'? Even if for an instant we find some 'elsewhere' in them, they are soon assimilated to a landscape marked by the seal of our *habitus* of thinking and our memory. (Derrida and Dufourmantelle 2000, 28, emphasis in the original)

With her reference to a '*habitus* of thinking and … memory', we have returned to our initial *point de départ*: memory and cognition have come to be intertwined not only with the production of one's innate sense of identity, but also with the way in which one may position oneself in relation to the Other. Given the importance of unconditional hospitality in Derrida's Fourth and Fifth Seminars, to which Dufourmantelle is responding, the important question now becomes how this referential orientation might affect the possibility of unconditional hospitality – per Derrida, a moral imperative that is defined by a radical openness to the

Other, and which, contrary to conditional hospitality, does not place conditions on its acceptance, nor is guided by expectations of reciprocity.

Hospitality and thirding (in)difference

If the novel offers any hope that the modalities of sociocultural exchange could possibly rebalance the spatial, historical and social paradigms of postcolonial contact so as to encourage a more positive model of transcultural interaction founded upon a sense of unconditional hospitality, it would appear to exist in the benevolence of the few select strangers who help the protagonist along his journey. However, even these select instances of humanitarian outreach are shown to have a threshold of tolerance in the novel – with every benevolent character ultimately abandoning the protagonist due to their own hectic schedules and personal preoccupations. The various witnesses who interact with the unnamed migrant show a stunning unawareness of his person when interviewed by the police, apart from base generalities: '[h]e had a suitcase, in rather sorry shape, and he struggled to give me something. I tell you: [he was] very pleasant. But not a word! Was he mute? Oh! I ask that for myself. I remember that. And now he is dead' (Boudejdra 1975, 185). While the migrant is undoubtedly present in this description, his character is deprived of any human element and exists as a foreign, typed and itinerant object. While 'pleasant enough', his inability to speak allows the host to simply tolerate his presence, without truly recognizing the human dimension of his existence, given that their interpersonal communication is superficial and ephemeral. The somewhat reticent statement given by this same witness later in the interview that 'I shouldn't have abandoned him' (186) thus seems to ring somewhat hollow. If it is only after the migrant's murder that one feels any sense of solidarity with his person, one has to ask if this sense of contrition is truly authentic, for this sense of solidarity cannot be associated with the migrant's passage from social liminality to communal integration, but rather only with the abstracted notion that human life is something that should generally be preserved – an abstraction that, in its infinite generality, does not really say much of anything about the host's responsibilities vis-à-vis the foreigner. Note the witness's post hoc solution formulated one sentence later: 'I should have warned him: all these daily murders … I should have told him to go home. He would have been hurt, but at least he'd be alive right now' (186). One has the impression that if the witnesses would again find themselves in the same situation, they would show a similar state of apathy and indifference, for there does not appear to be any tangible effort – or rather, any tangible desire – on their part to rebalance the trialectics of intercultural exchange. On the contrary, the essence of the witness's statement could be paraphrased as saying that the migrant should simply go home. It is therefore interesting to add that Derrida identified 'the problem of hospitality [as] coextensive with the ethical problem. It is always about answering for a dwelling place, for one's identity, one's space, one's limits, for the *ethos* as abode, habitation, house, hearth, family, home' (Derrida and Dufourmantelle 2000, 149, 151, emphasis in the original). Statements such as 'I should have told him to go home' thus serve to circumvent the ethical, for they rely on an internal justification to shirk one's responsibility to behave hospitably.

Such a stance implicitly lays claim to the right to relegate the Other to the peripheries of social consciousness in an action whereby the host – now protected by a 'real-and-imagined' geography of proximity – comes to feel morally justified in their complacency before the trials and tribulations of the foreigner. As demonstrated earlier in this chapter, such a movement effectively blocks passage and engenders a liminal state of suspended affiliation, which can lead to violence. In light of this situational ambiguity, it is perhaps unsurprising that Derrida – in drawing on the philological work of Émile Benveniste on the Latin word *hostis* (literally, stranger/foreigner *or* enemy) – stated that the foreigner may be 'welcomed as guest or as enemy [through] [h]ospitality, hostility, *hostpitality*' (Derrida and Dufourmantelle 2000, 45, emphasis in the original). If we are to answer 'for one's identity, one's space, one's limits, for the *ethos*' (149, emphasis in the original) of hospitality to be found in the margins and interstitial contact zones of postcolonial society, I would like to suggest that this is to be found in this somewhat ambiguous third concept: *hostpitality*. Only by Thirding the construct of (in)difference can one move beyond its implicit schemata of binary positionality in favour of a new dialectical model that tends towards social transformation and mutual understanding. In short, such an action would require a reconceptualization of the liminal stage of migratory passage and postmigratory rite(s) of integration into host societies.

If there would be any attempt to renegotiate the ethical spatiality of this relationship – if one can ever effectively speak of such an abstract notion – it would necessarily rely on the fabrication of a new system of solidary relation that would be more inclusive in its enunciation and distribution of institutional power. Although the fabrication of such a system is not possible in Boudjedra's narrative due to the specificity of its textual matrixes that are coded in the historical events and social reality of its era, the novel nevertheless raises important questions that allow for the discussion of its possibility.

Conclusion

To return one last time to Nora's interview that opened this chapter, the idea that the contemporary notion of Frenchness relies upon the interrelated constructs of memory and identity is at once its most important and its most damning factor. In comparison to Renan's largely voluntary vision of nationhood, in which the importance of wilful forgetting was as important to national integrity as the faculty of remembering, the increasingly prominent role accorded to subnational memory in the determination of national identity has rendered the idea of forgetting largely impossible – a dangerous proposition in our increasingly transnational era, in which individual differences can easily become magnified by political rhetoric to become sources of oppositional identity. If forgetting is no longer an option, the creation of a more productive model of migratory integration will necessitate the active production of a new spatiality of interaction, in which the trialectics of being can be reconfigured to provide new manners of understanding the Self and the Other.

This admittedly does not say much. Indeed, the need for this new mode of understanding would seem to cut to the very core of my analysis, for such a distinction between the Self and the Other would appear to rely on an inherent philosophy of difference that I have up to this point attempted to contest. What I would thus like to advocate is not a rejection of difference, but rather a reframing of the optics of hospitality from a binary and oppositional perspective to a more ambiguous model of transnational movement that liberates and hybridizes the right to interstitial belonging. Such a contrapuntal reading of postcolonial integration has perhaps been best articulated by Edward Said and Paul Virilio: '[p]recision, concreteness, continuity, form – all these have the attributes of a nomadic practice whose power, Virilio says, is not aggressive, but transgressive … From this perspective then all things are indeed counter, original, spare, strange' (Said 1994, 332). To move beyond aggression – to reframe the trialectics of being into a new model of transformed vision and power – a new manner of viewing the spatiality of human life must be formed on the basis of a reframed right/rite of passage in our increasingly cosmopolitan and transnational modalities of social coexistence.

Notes

1. My translation. Unless a translator is explicitly referenced in the bibliographic references, all translations are mine.
2. More specifically, Nora referenced Jean-Marie Le Pen, President of the National Front from 1972 until 2011.
3. By liminal, I am referencing Arnold van Gennep's tripartite structure of ritual passage, which is divided between 'preliminal rites (rites of separation), liminal rites (rites of transition), and postliminal rites (rites of incorporation)' (van Gennep 2019, 11). Liminality will be central to two interrelated ways of conceptualizing passage in this chapter: that of a sociocultural and political liminality that saw an evolution of the French national ethos in the 1970s, whose political discourse on migration gradually shifted from a politics of assimilation to a politics of integration (Chemin 2016); and that of the protagonist's suspension of affiliation during his transnational migration, which is poetically represented by his passage through the subterranean labyrinth of the Parisian Métro.
4. *Ratonnades* – literally, 'rat hunts' – were racially motived attacks carried out against ethnic minorities and other marginalized social groups. In its origins, the term referred exclusively to the physical violence carried out against Maghrebins, with the term *raton* – 'little rat' – having been a pejorative term for North Africans.
5. More specifically, Edward Said outlined two phases of orientalism that defined the European relationship with the Orient: first, that of a latent orientalism that was defined by a rather uniform field of accumulated knowledge, which was itself based on a large corpus of ethnographic work; second, that of a manifest orientalism that was defined by the projection of imperial power and policy, and that was in many ways facilitated by the accumulated knowledge of latent orientalism. Of particular note is the interrelationship between these two systems of knowledge, which produced a characteristic vision of the Orient that was largely self-referential, and that operated within an established critical tradition (Said 1979, 201–25).

References

Anderson, Benedict. 2006 [1983]. *Imagined Communities*. London: Verso.
Benveniste, Émile. 2016. 'Hospitality'. In *Dictionary of Indo-European Concepts and Society*, translated by Elizabeth Palmer, 61–74. Chicago: Hau Books.
Bhabha, Homi. 2004 [1994]. *The Location of Culture*. London: Routledge.
Boudjedra, Rachid. 1975. *Topographie idéale pour une agression caractérisée*. Paris: Éditions Denoël.
Boudjedra, Rachid. 1976. 'Sur "Topographie idéale pour une agression caractérisée"' [Interview]. Accessed 29 January 2022. https://www.sam-network.org/video/sur-topographie-ideale-pour-une-agression-caracterisee.
Camus, Albert. 1989. *The Stranger*, translated by Matthew Ward. New York: Vintage.
Chemin, Anne. 2016. 'Intégration ou assimilation, une histoire de nuances', *Le Monde*, 11 November. Accessed 29 January 2022. https://www.lemonde.fr/idees/article/2016/11/11/integration-ou-assimilation-une-histoire-de-nuances_5029629_3232.html.
Cohen, Muriel. 2012. 'Regroupement familial: L'exception algérienne (1962–1976)', *Plein droit* 95: 19–22. https://doi.org/10.3917/pld.095.0019.
Derrida, Jacques and Anne Dufourmantelle. 2000 [1997]. *Of Hospitality: Anne Dufourmantelle invites Jacques Derrida to respond*, translated by Rachel Bowlby. Stanford, CA: Stanford University Press.
Fanon, Frantz. 2008 [1952]. *Black Skin, White Masks*, translated by Richard Philcox. New York: Grove Press.
Gherardi, Sophie. 2007. 'Pierre Nora: Le nationalisme nous a caché la nation', *Le Monde*, 17 March. Accessed 29 January 2022. https://www.lemonde.fr/societe/article/2007/03/17/pierre-nora-le-nationalisme-nous-a-cache-la-nation_884396_3224.html.

Laurens, Sylvain. 2008. '"1974" et la fermature des frontières: Analyse critique d'une décision érigée en *turning-point*', *Politix* 82: 69–94.
Le Goff, Jacques. 1988. *Histoire et mémoire*. Paris: Éditions Gallimard.
Meynier, Pierrette and Gilbert Meynier. 2011. 'L'immigration algérienne en France: Histoire et actualité', *Confluences Méditerranée* 77: 219–34.
Nora, Pierre. 1978. 'La mémoire collective'. In *La Nouvelle histoire*, edited by Jacques Le Goff and Jacques Revel, 398–401. Paris: Bibliothèque du CEPL.
Nora, Pierre and Françoise Chandernagor. 2008. *Liberté pour l'histoire*. Paris: CNRS Éditions.
Said, Edward. 1979. *Orientalism*. New York: Vintage.
Said, Edward. 1994. *Culture and Imperialism*. New York: Vintage.
Smith, Anthony D. 2015. 'Icons of nationalism'. In *Building the Nation: N.F.S. Grundtvig and Danish national identity*, edited by John A. Hall, Ove Korsgaard and Ove K. Pedersen, 51–78. Montréal: McGill-Queen's University Press.
Soja, Edward. 1996. *Thirdspace: Journeys to Los Angeles and other real-and-imagined places*. Malden: Blackwell.
Thomassen, Bjørn. 2014. *Liminality and the Modern*. London: Routledge.
Van Gennep, Arnold. 2019 [1960]. *The Rites of Passage*, translated by Monika B. Vizedom and Gabrielle L. Caffee. Chicago: University of Chicago Press.

15
Passage into new realities: Albania(ns) at the turn of the nineteenth and twentieth centuries through the eyes of European travel writers

Oriol Guni

The description of the passage of Western European travel writers into Ottoman Albanian-populated territories at the end of the nineteenth century resulted in an abundance of images that have impacted representations of Albanians to this day. Situated in Ottoman Europe, or the Balkans, Albanian-populated areas were of great interest to Western travel writers, mainly due to political and cultural concerns: the Ottoman Empire was going through successive existential crises. The so-called 'sick man of Europe' was disintegrating, as its European areas were increasingly falling under the influence of nationalism and European powers.

The Albanian areas of Ottoman Europe at the end of the nineteenth century represent a liminal space, as all of the Balkans entered a new stage in this period. The first decade of the twentieth century would result in the establishment of new nation states and the complete removal of the Ottoman Empire from European geography. The end of the nineteenth century also represents a liminal phase within Albanian-inhabited areas and culture, as Albanians faced new realities that would effect these political and cultural changes.

The concept of liminality made its appearance in 1909, after Arnold van Gennep published his ground-breaking work *Rites de Passage*, in which he highlighted the pertinence that shifts and adjustments bear for any given culture or society (van Gennep 1960). The concept of liminality has experienced a re-emergence in the last decade to explain various social and cultural changes. According to one recent definition, liminal stages are 'in-between situations and conditions that are characterized by the dislocation of established structures, the reversal of hierarchies, and uncertainty regarding the continuity of tradition and future outcomes' (Horvath et al. 2009, 3). As liminality 'refers to moments or periods of transition during which the normal limits to thought, self-understanding and behaviour are relaxed, opening the way to novelty and imagination, construction and destruction' (Thomassen 2014, 1), it has to be stressed that in the current discussion of travel writing about Albanians at the end of the nineteenth century, the concept of liminality is relevant due to the representations of structural changes that the region underwent in the period under survey, something that also led to the shifting of hetero-images of Albanians. Notwithstanding the recurrence of old images, the travelogues also opened up new possibilities for a novel European imaginary geography through a disruption of the borders of an older Ottoman territory. This chapter investigates whether the images created in this period placed Albanians on a novel imaginative map, or left them in a liminal imaginative geography triggered by the political events of the time.

One of the most persistent problems of travel writers is their ability to masterfully misrepresent what they experience and witness during their travels. Ansgar Nünning has highlighted this most enduring feature of travel writing as 'its pretense that a journey, the places visited, and the experiences had during a journey can be more or less unproblematically represented in a report in linguistic form' (Nünning 2009, 131). Due to the fact that it is impossible to challenge, prove or disprove the claims made by travellers, critical analyses of travelogues have portrayed them as enjoining 'a license to invent what they liked and to impose it on a credulous audience' (Carey 2015, 3–4). Nünning has also made it clear that the reality represented in travelogues 'is neither unmediated nor authentic, but rather the result of a multi-layered transformation process' (Nünning 2009, 145). Describing the experience of travel as a 'process', Nünning emphasizes that 'the events of a journey are turned into a more or less coherent story and narration, which, in turn, is characterized by strategies of perspectivization and rhetorical strategies' (145).

These problems accompanying travel writing have prompted many theoretical responses, ranging from Edward Said's (1978) concept of 'orientalism' and Maria Todorova's (1997) concept of 'balkanism', Mary Louise Pratt's postcolonial critique of colonial-era travel writing, and many other scholarly interventions (Pratt 1992). In the case of travel writing about Albania(ns), the first two approaches are most pertinent. Maria Todorova argues that, in their passage to the Balkans, Western visitors have created a persisting notion through their rhetorical strategies, which Todorova labels balkanism. Todorova states that 'the Balkans have served as a repository of negative characteristics upon which a positive and self-congratulatory image of the "European" and "the West" was built' (Todorova 1997, 188). While differentiating balkanism from Said's orientalism, Todorova stresses that, while the latter is 'discourse about an imputed opposition, balkanism is discourse about an imputed ambiguity' (17), while stressing that 'the Balkans are left in Europe's thrall, anticivilization, alter ego, the dark side within' (188). Todorova also expounds upon the features that Western travel writers have attributed to Balkan peoples, such as 'male', 'primitive', 'crude' and 'dishevelled' (14), enmeshing thus a 'concreteness' (14), 'as opposed to the intangible nature of the Orient' (11). For hundreds of years, Europeans strived to differentiate between members of so-called civilized society, on the one hand, and barbarians, primitives and savages, on the other hand, with the clear intention of labelling themselves civilized nations (Jezernik 2004). According to other scholars, stereotypes about the Balkans resurface whenever outside observers are compelled by the urge of political exigencies to recirculate them (Goldsworthy 2006).

Another key feature of the representations of the Balkans in European literary productions, according to K.E. Fleming, is that the Balkans are represented as a block: 'Balkan countries are more or less interchangeable with and indistinguishable from one another, that there is a readily identifiable typology of politics and history common throughout the Balkans, that there is such a thing as a Balkan ethnic or racial' kind (Fleming 2000, 1218). Fleming adds that 'the Balkans are represented, perceived, and studied' according to a principle that the areas in question 'are both fully known and wholly unknowable' (1219). The Balkans, for some British travel writers of the nineteenth century, represented an exploration of the origins of Europe through recurring ancient Greek images, while for others it was a boundary where the first oriental images began to take shape (Goldsworthy 2006).

Alongside images related to balkanism, orientalist phantasms simultaneously structure many of the representations of Albanians in this period. Said considered orientalism a way of seeing the Other that involves imagining, emphasizing, exaggerating and distorting differences of Oriental peoples and cultures as compared to those of the West, pointing thus to allegory (Said 1978). As Neval Berber has shown in her study of British travel writing in Bosnia-Herzegovina of the later part of the nineteenth century and beginning of the twentieth century, balkanism is not sufficient for outlining a clear picture of the images that Western European travellers constructed in relation to specific Balkan Muslim populations (Berber 2010).

Now we have come to the core of this chapter – namely, the paradox that lies at the heart of travel writing about Albanians at the turn of the twentieth century. The convergence of balkanist and orientalist readings of Albania(ns) illuminates a first paradox: Albania occupies a liminal zone, neither strictly European nor strictly Ottoman. If you depart from Turkey, you are sure that, after visiting Albania, you are going to Europe. If you depart from Europe, you are sure that you will find Turkey in Albania. Actually, there are resonations of such a view of the Balkans in a more general way, such as 'no longer Orientals nor yet Europeans' (Bakić-Hayden 1995, 920).[1] On the same line of argument, Larry Wolff contends that such an ambiguous, liminal positioning was applied to the whole of Eastern Europe, while Western Europe was constructing an image of its own: 'Eastern Europe was located not at the antipode of civilization, not down in the depths of barbarism, but rather on the developmental scale that measured the distance between civilization and barbarism ... Eastern Europe was essentially in between' (Wolff 1994, 13).

When we read about the co-mingling of hybrid identities in the travel narratives of the end of the nineteenth century, the authors in general fail to nuance what they see. This is not unusual, of course – there is a general tendency to interpret phenomena through pre-existing frameworks and, hence, subordinate or conceal disruptive intermingling elements within the contact zone. Nünning has proposed an application of Paul Ricœur's procedural mimesis model to travel writing and, more specifically, to address the question of the existence of a 'gap between the journey and report about it, i.e. between the reality and verbal representation' (Nünning 2009, 131). According to Nünning, 'prefiguration, configuration and refiguration' – which are also the three levels of mimesis and form a 'three-dimensional model' – are crucial to put into coherence what the travellers conceptualize as pre-existing ideas, what they encounter on the ground during their travels, and how, in the end, they reconfigure the reality that they have pre-conceptualized: 'those literary configurations or stagings of travel can affect the reader and thus also have repercussions on the extra-literary reality (refiguration)' (132).

Indeed, reading the narratives of travel writing about Albania(ns) for the ways that the authors negotiate the prefabricated balkanist and orientalist tropes, inscribing them against what they see on the ground, is a very telling example of what Nünning observes about travelogues. As we will see with some of the examples in this chapter, Albania is a site of continuity and disruption, a contact zone of religions and cultures that defies easy categorization – and, certainly, for the travel writers of the time, defies easy interpretation.

Elements of balkanism

Barbarism and savagery

The travelogues of the period painstakingly highlight the barbarism and savagery that the travellers encounter among the natives. Fanny Janet Blunt, in *The Peoples of Turkey*, draws a link between the barbarian nature of Albanians and the wild nature of the land they inhabit. Citing the 'mountainous character of the country, and the turbulent and warlike disposition of its inhabitants', Blunt states that the area is still unexplored and poorly cultivated, and she also sees a pervading neglect of what she considers 'rich and fertile valleys', while also highlighting that 'the streets are narrow and badly paved, and look dismal and deserted. The bazars and shops are inferior to those of most of the towns of Turkey. They contain no variety of objects for use or ornament beyond those absolutely necessary for domestic purposes' (Blunt 1878, 63).

In another telling passage, Blunt describes the houses as 'scanty, poor, and comfortless' (Blunt 1878, 67). Although Blunt describes the Albanians as a warlike nation, she stresses that they are not prone to conscription as regular soldiers:

> But, as a rule; the Albanian objects to ordinary conscription, and avoids it, if possible, by a direct refusal to be enrolled, or else makes his escape. When on the road to the seat of war, a regiment of Albanians is a terrible scourge to the country it passes through; like locusts, they leave nothing but naked stalks and barren ground behind them. (Blunt 1878, 79)

This passage implies that, despite their fighting capabilities, the primitiveness of the Albanians makes it impossible for them to form an army, triggering thus a deeper and wider trope about the population in question, namely, that they are intrinsically unable to create feasible social structures and interiorize or produce any sort of modernization – modernization being, in that era, the differentiating norm between civilized and primitive cultures.

Blunt also creates a binary of savagery and barbarism, on the one hand, and devoted friendliness and respect, on the other: 'if a Gheg has once tasted your bread and salt or owes you a debt of gratitude or is employed in your service, all his terrible qualities vanish and he becomes the most devoted, attached, and faithful of friends and servants' (Blunt 1878, 71). Notwithstanding her admiration for the natural advantages of the area, Blunt claims that these advantages have 'remained stationary', and not understood by what she calls 'the semi-savage population that inhabits it' (64). The neglect of the natural advantages bears the implication that any sort of modernization was impossible for this people. The latter is a recurring theme in travelogues of the era. For example, Henry Fanshawe Tozer, a British traveller and writer, lamenting how a branch of the Drin River detached from its main line, blames this 'injury' on 'the face of country' on the prevailing 'barbarism and neglect' (Tozer 1869, 285). The trope of savage Albanians is adopted by the British travel writer Edward Frederick Knight as well, when he expresses his concern about the insecurity of travelling 'among the savage Arnauts [the Turkish name for Albanians] without knowing ten words of their language – madness' (Knight 1880, 221).

Knight seems to enjoy the singing of an Albanian bard in one of his fragments, saying that '[t]hese Albanian songs are not unpleasing, barbarous as is their music' (Knight 1880, 240). Knight delves into similar romantic connotations when he describes the ferocity coupled with good nature in the person of Nik Leka, an Albanian chieftain: 'a splendid specimen of a barbarian warrior; very handsome, with an expression that curiously combined great good-nature with a certain amount of latent ferocity' (247). The idea of the savage leader presented by Henry Fanshawe Tozer is quite clear: '[h]e is reported to have a good influence in the country, while a more civilized man might very possibly have no influence at all' (Tozer 1869, 303). Notwithstanding the sympathy imputed to the so-called Albanian leader, the theme undergirding all the aforementioned texts is the constant emphasis on the innate inability of the natives to overcome a pervading primitiveness and primitive worldview.

Blood feuds

The balkanism trope also surrounds another recurring motif in the travel writings of the era considered. Blood feuds are linked with the presumed barbaric nature of the natives. Emile Wiet, in one of his insights about Albanians, while combining barbarism, savagery and the inability to comprehend religion, creates the impression that even the customs and characteristics of the natives he observes are forged by the savage practice of blood feuds:

> The character and customs of the inhabitants of the diocese match the barbaric situation in which they live since many centuries. The Vendetta [blood feud], this terrible curse of Albania, is exercised in an inexorable way here. The Mirdites [inhabitants of Mirdita] believe themselves to be fervent Catholics. The villagers make the divine service to consist in elevation and they only use the expression: *I saw mass*, to say that they attended. (Wiet 1866, 275, emphasis in the original)[2]

The combination of these elements has, as its primary effect, the idea that, in Wiet's narrative about Albanians at the end of the nineteenth century, nothing is explained outside the register created by tropes related to primitivism. In general, this is an intertextual tendency that, as we will shortly see, has been adopted by a number of travel writers. It says a lot about the passage of valorizing images from one author to another, and about how the texts of the travellers are shaped by a discourse that is formed as a result of the transfer of representations from one author to another.

Blood feuds, or vendetta, comprise another element that is placed on the map of the images about Albanians, and that apodictically completes the set of representations that make up an inherently primitive society and culture. For example, Fanny Janet Blunt, along the same lines as Wiet, implies that vendetta is so deeply ingrained in the Albanian life that the style of the houses is that of fortresses, although these fortresses, according to her, do not serve as logistics for blood feuds, 'for it is a point of honour with an Albanian never to incur the disgrace of shedding a man's blood in his own house; but the moment he crosses the threshold, he is at the mercy of his foe' (Blunt 1878, 66). While citing the case of an Albanian chieftain being 'in terror of his life', Blunt highlights that the blood feuds have also taken their toll on the primitive hierarchs of the natives (66). Theodor Ippen links the ubiquitous vendetta to an 'innate ferocity': 'Whenever grounds for feuding are lacking', he says, 'the restless spirit of these would-be knights-errant is vented in highway robbery!' (Ippen 1892, 114).

According to the British travel writer Edward Frederick Knight, who travelled to the mountains of today's northern Albania, the population was decimated due to blood feuds. Stressing that for the locals it is a disgrace to die in bed, Knight claims that their wish is to die in this way, in a characteristic love of death with honour. Knight praises the people of several areas for their industrious skills with metals, although this is framed as a product of the industry of blood feuds and war, since the lauded artefacts are mainly 'gold-hilted and jewelled yataghans and pistols' (Knight 1880, 118). This love of death and industrious nature in producing guns and arms is complemented by what another travel writer, the French August Dozon, describes as a love of guns, expressed in the multitude of gunsmith shops: 'one really feels that this is really Albania', he stresses (Dozon 1875, 612). Bérard, while describing what he calls a 'gravestone fair' in the city of Kavaja, paints the most persisting image of the Albanian of the travelogues of this era, that of an Albanian carrying a rifle and walking along with shouts and knife. He proclaims that '[i]n this country of never-ending vendettas', his interlocutor, a certain Osman Aga, 'is most obliged to contemplate a little bit about his future' (Bérard 1893, 44). However, there is a moment of pause in this cycle of deadly blood feuds. Fanny Janet Blunt offers a binary that pushes further the balkanist trope in question: '[t]he social relations of the Albanians', she writes, 'are limited to two ideas, *vendetta* and *bessa* [sic] (peace)' (Blunt 1878, 80, italics in the original). In another elucidating paragraph, she explains that:

> The *bessa* [sic] or truce is the time Albanians allow themselves at intervals to suspend their blood feuds; it is arranged by mutual consent between the contending parties, and is of fixed duration and strictly observed: the bitterest enemies meet and converse in perfect harmony and confidence. (Blunt 1878, 85, italics in the original)

At first glance, the traditional pledge of honour, *besa*, seems to construct a humanized depiction of the Albanians, but the fact that it has been presented only as a social truce from the perpetual bloody business seems to place it under the shadow of, and subservient to the mechanism of, *vendetta*. This fragment shows that even humanizing features are placed into a discourse impregnated with negative valorizations of the Albanian

Other, showing that a distinctive feature of the discourse on Albanians of the period is presented along the lines of balkanist tropes.

Illiteracy and aversion to education

Widespread lack of education, and illiteracy, is another motif that recurs quite frequently in the travel literature of the period, and that is associated indiscriminately with the nation in general, making it an inescapable feature of the culture observed. Falling into the trope of savagery and barbarism, illiteracy is presented in a similar light to vendetta, or blood feuds, at least in terms of permeating all social relations. As opposed to vendetta, which is mentioned directly, aversion to education is implied. While presenting a series of economic opportunities that the abundance of minerals and hot springs offer to Albania, Fanny Janet Blunt links the ignorance of the populace with local native superstitions:

> ... the country people are totally ignorant of their properties, and take the waters indiscriminately for any ailments they may happen to have, and, in obedience to the old superstitious reverence for the spirits of the fountains, even drink from several different sources in the hope of gaining favour with their respective nymphs. (Blunt 1878, 64)

In another revealing observation, Blunt delights in the wild beauty of nature, but links it closely to the neglect of agriculture of the inhabitants, although the author here nuances her observation, and claims that this condition is true for all of the Ottoman Empire. However, claiming that this is especially true for Albania, Blunt represents the culture as the epitome of backwardness in this aspect (Blunt 1878, 63).

To the widespread lack of education, Dozon adds the general aversion to work. As his depiction of the landscape offers a desolate picture, he jumps to the conclusion that the lack of cultivated land is due to the laziness of the people and the contempt for agricultural labour. He also links these two traits to the sad misery that is characteristic of the lower classes (Dozon 1875).

In a passage that implies that Albanians cannot create an infrastructure to educate themselves, Blunt initially singles out the former Pasha of Ioannina, Ali Pasha, for transforming the southern areas and 'found(ing) schools and libraries', but then points out that 'these were partly destroyed by his followers' (Blunt 1878, 68–9), while she does not offer any clue as to who destroyed the other part. Then she moves to the trope of romanticizing Greeks, so beloved by British travellers of the time, and stresses 'the excellent schools and syllogae that have been established and are said to be doing wonders in improving and educating the new generation of Epirus' (69).

Women as 'mules'

As the sensual oriental nuances in relation to women are absent in the travel writings considered, the balkanist trope of woman as inferior and as male is ubiquitous. The French diplomat Emile Wiet, in his considerations of the inferior rank of Albanian women in general, says that an Albanian woman is a mere slave, 'destined to suffer all his whims and to perform the most painful works. She is never called by her name, but by the qualification *mori*' (Wiet 1866, 284). The passage continues by revealing that 'infidelity of the woman is punished by death, and the sentence is executed by the closest of her relatives' (284).

In her observation on why Albanian women are armed, Fanny Janet Blunt depicts them as equal participants in the all-encompassing vortex of blood feuds: 'that they may be able to join in the brawls of their male relatives, and fight by their side' (Blunt 1878, 82–3).

Depicted in the same way as Albanian men in relation to their participation in the social whirlwind of blood feuds, women are also described as serving another role: that of accompanying travellers that wish to pass through the country: '[t]he respect entertained for women accounts for a strange custom prevalent among Albanians … Thus accompanied, the traveller may proceed with safety into the most isolated regions without any chance of harm coming to him' (Blunt 1878, 83). Although Blunt praises the natural beauty of Albanian girls, the author then states that the social status of marriage pushes her to the exact contrary of beauty:

> She then begins to dye her hair, to which nature has often given a golden hue, jet black; she besmears her face with a pernicious white composition, blackens her teeth, and reddens her hands with henna; the general effect of the process is to make her ugly during youth, and absolutely hideous in old age … On my inquiring the reason of this strange custom of some Albanian ladies, they laughed at my disapproval of it, and told me that in their opinion it is only the fangs of dogs that should be white! (Blunt 1878, 83)

The lack of willingness to offer some nuances, characteristic of travel writers in the Balkan territories, as Maria Todorova has highlighted, also permeates the works of some other writers of the period that have been examined in this study. In the travelogues of Henry Fanshawe Tozer, women are presented as being treated in the Ottoman territories in Europe as mules. While expressing his indignation at the sight of women bearing huge boxes and their husbands walking in front them during his travels in Albania, Tozer recalls a story that he says was told to him by a friend, a certain Sir Henry Ward, who experienced a similar situation in Corfu, nowadays Greece:

> As he was riding, one day, into the country, he overtook a man who had laden his wife with a very heavy bundle of faggot-sticks; he remonstrated with him, and said, 'Really, my good man, it is too bad that you should load your wife in that way; what she is carrying is a mule's burden.' 'Yes, your Excellency,' the man replied, 'what you say it quite true, it *is* a mule's burden: but then, you see, Providence has not provided us with mules, and He *has* provided us with women.' (Tozer 1869, 207)

What is problematic in the fragments analysed here is not whether the phenomena that prompted these images existed or not, but that the images are not presented alongside their context, and are inextricably linked to some inner Albanian quality. Moreover, the hetero-images offered by the travel writers are placed in a general discourse that explains everything related to Albanians according to the prevailing tropes of the time.

Religion as 'facade'

The lack of willingness to offer any nuances, characteristic of travel writers in the Balkan territories, as Maria Todorova has highlighted, even permeates the way in which the natives are juxtaposed to religiousness. The celebrated English travel writer and poet, Lady Mary Wortley Montagu, in her letter dated 1 April 1717, narrates that the Albanians seem to have the most particular religion of all she has seen. Elaborating on her encounter with some Albanian soldiers, she claims that the soldiers, while 'utterly unable to judge which religion is best', see fit to follow both Christianity and Islam, 'and go to the mosques on Fridays and the church on Sundays, saying for their excuse, that at the day of judgment they are sure of protection from the true prophet' (Montagu 1861, 290–1).

While falling prey to a fallacy that she herself highlights when speaking about travellers of the time in the Ottoman Empire – namely, the fact that most of the travellers have arrived at generalized views about entire populations while their sole encounters were with lower classes and not the nobility or merchants (Montagu 1861) – Montagu derives her conclusion from some loose accidental conversations with some soldiers, who cannot be said to be representative of an entire nation. The corollary here is clear: Albanians are unable to determine which religion is the true one. Historian Noel Malcolm (2002, 84) has claimed that, in generalizing her view of Albanians, Montagu became the *locus classicus* for Western writers that dealt with the religiousness of Albanians, dismissing entirely the contextual peculiarities that are typical for Albanians, such as religious syncretism and other phenomena.

However, Montagu's image seems to have made its passage to the travel literature of the nineteenth century considered here. While speculating on the religions of Albanians in general, the French diplomat Victor Bérard writes that 'similarly to their mosques, the religion of these Albanians is all a façade' (Bérard 1893, 46). Describing a convent of dervishes, where some rituals are accompanied by bouts of drinking, Bérard ridicules their religiousness, adding that '[t]hey achieve a less religious state of intoxication every day with *raki* and German liquor. They forget none of their ablutions and purifications of [ritual] law; but our canned pork did not inspire any repugnance among them' (46). In the same vein, but this time through a passage linked with the aforementioned love of war, Henry Fanshawe Tozer presents the native's relationship with religion through a handpicked native proverb: '[w]here the sword is, the creed is also' (Tozer 1869, 202). He writes that his native companion claims that Muslims that abstain from drinking are 'unfaithful to their creed' (202). These words, effectuating an en masse excommunication of Albanian Muslims, place Tozer in a position that is more suitable to a scriptural Muslim scholar.

Returning to Bérard: when he encounters a work of religious generosity – a bridge constructed at the expenses of a local legendary figure known as the Bachelor Pilgrim – he does not see it as an expression of nobility. In a very telling formulation that essentializes the Albanians into all the elements of the balkanist discourse, the French traveller writes:

The greatness of his bridge prompted us to dream about the greatness of his crimes ... however, we would have forgiven him all the murders, robberies, violations and *Albanian things* that he had committed, had he completed his artwork with a road, even a cobblestone one. (Bérard 1893, 75, emphasis in the original)

Noel Malcolm, a modern historian, points out that when the religiousness of Albanians, and their purported indifference, is taken into consideration by contemporary writers, it is clear to them that in the case of Albanians, there is a mixing of some different phenomena (Malcolm 2002). According to Malcolm, outside observers tend to see complex social phenomena among Albanians of any era through a simplifying lens that does not account for the realities historically lived by the natives of the different periods:

> ... these include the syncretism of folk religious practices, the tolerance (and doctrinal syncretism) of the Bektashi, the much rarer phenomenon of crypto-Christianity ..., the social system of northern Albania clansmen ..., and the perfectly normal practice of Muslim men taking Christian wives without requiring their conversion to Islam. These are all different factors, too easily blurred into a single syndrome of 'indifference' by casual outside observers. (Malcolm 2002, 84)

Todorova cites a similar instance, that of Alexandre-Maurice, who writes that the peculiar symbiosis between Christianity and Islam, similarly to that which Montagu presents, was better than the religious wars in Hungary and Transylvania. Nevertheless, he states that this tolerance was due not to any innate noble traits of the Albanians' character, but to the 'ignorance and simplicity of a people without education' (Todorova 1997, 77). 'This "blindness" as he defined it was due to the fact that "these unfortunates are so far from civilization, because they possess none of the passions which prejudice renders so common and incurable elsewhere"' (77).

The travelogues analysed here reinforce the old hetero-image of religious indifference/ignorance imputed to Albanians, and even bring it further by coupling it with the trope of barbarism. While ignoring contextual nuances, the travel writers recycle an old image by equipping it with new nuances constructed as a result of new discursive circumstances. The strengthening of the balkanist discourse during the second half of the nineteenth century caused a reshaping in accordance with new narratives of a trope that had originated almost two centuries earlier.

Orientalist elements

Todorova's framework, while very useful, is centred on Christian Balkan people. However, not all categorizations of balkanism apply to Albanians, since the majority of them are Muslims. However, in order to get a clear picture of the representations of Albanians of the time, it is useful to nuance these analytic categories with orientalism to more accurately read these representations. As we have seen in our previous examples in relation to balkanism, there is an absence of sensuality, usually so characteristic of orientalist discourses. However, in the notes of Maximilian, the Emperor of Mexico, we see an identification of an average Albanian city with the 'Orient', despite the lack of sumptuous luxury. While writing about the city of Durrës, Maximilian depicts colourful Turkish figures, huge turbans and long beards, while also sticking to the ubiquitous oriental pipe and coffee; he also cites their Muslim fatalism, as they do not do anything to encourage buyers (Maximilian 1867).

While elaborating about another city, Victor Bérard draws upon an orientalist trope. Describing the city as Muslim, he claims that, since 'orientals' always think of war, the city is built in an area that is more secure than the coast (Bérard 1893). 'Islam flees the sea that is dear to the Giaours [Christians]', he claims, adding that 'along the coast, the water is never good, security is never perfect, they prefer the green lands, the low hills or the flowing springs for ritual ablutions and where large trees offer shade for long siestas and quiet conversations' (44). There is a sharp tension here between, on the one hand, a love for 'long siestas and quiet conversations' in the pastoral landscape of an orientalized Albania and, on the other hand, the trope of the barbaric and warlike.

In the travelogues of Henry Fanshawe Tozer, there is a paradox that goes along the lines of orientalism: that of religious respect for water, while human life is considered very cheap. 'Orientals', he claims:

> are very curious on the subject of the quality of their water; indeed, they are as great connoisseurs of water as any Western epicure can be of wine. Both in Albania and elsewhere I have heard one spring distinguished as *light* (ελαφρόν) and another as *heavy* (βαρύ), where the traveller can distinguish no difference in the taste. No one can doubt, after observing this, that it requires no refinement of

criticism to understand Pindar's meaning when he said, 'Water is the best of things.' (Tozer 1869, 209, italics in the original)

August Dozon adds to this series of images his perception of Muslims in the town of Liaskoviki, modern day Leskovik, as fanatics, and cites their reluctance to allow a church to be built in their city (Dozon 1875).

The orientalist images created by the travel writers of the period in question lack only the tropes of overt sensuality and despotism. However, they retain part of the register of the orientalist discourse, namely, religious fanaticism, idleness and fatalism, creating a binary that constructs a single Albanian Other that is represented by the collapsing of two different, but still similarly alienating, discourses: orientalism and balkanism. In short, the Albanians in this period came to represent another liminality within the greater liminality of the Balkans in general: differently from the other populations of the peninsula, they were not represented through the single lens of balkanism, but through the compounded, although limited, tropes of orientalist provenance.

Negotiating the passage of Albanian territories into a new geography

The travel artefacts of the period that we analyse here were written and published only a few decades before the enthronement of the German Prince Wied as sovereign of Albania in 1914. Vesna Goldsworthy has pointed out that the import of royal European families in the state formation of the newly established Balkan countries 'offered an easily comprehensible set of icons' (Goldsworthy 1998, 43), signalling a drive towards Europeanization. But before this clear move to Europeanization took place, there were several strategies of identification of the territories in question with Europe in travel literature about Albanians. When discussing British travel literature about the Balkans of the nineteenth century, Goldsworthy contends that the entire period has been perceived by outside observers as one during which the Ottoman Empire was detached from and then 'return[ed] to Europe' (Goldsworthy 2006, 32).

One of these strategies is a geographical identification with European geography and detachment from Ottoman scenery. Henry Fanshawe Tozer, for example, draws similarities between the lake of Ochrida and Italian lakes, adding that it is impossible for a traveller to imagine himself in 'the midst of the wild stern regions of European Turkey' (Tozer 1869, 202). In a similar fashion, August Dozon singles out Tirana as geographically comparable with Normandy and Lombardy, stressing that such a landscape is quite rare in Turkey. Then, while visiting another city, he pushes the European identification further, mentioning Venetian historical buildings (Dozon 1875). A similar trajectory seems to have been pursued by Victor Bérard during his travel to the coastal city of Durrës, which he presents as 'a bizarre mixture of Turkish edifices and Italian shops amidst Frankish and Byzantine battlements. It seemed as if the Turks had installed only yesterday in this Venetian city' (Bérard 1893, 6). Although previous scholarship has claimed that when travel writers to the Balkans draw geographic parallels between European and Balkan sceneries, they do so to accentuate irony and, thus, to reinforce balkanist tropes (Hammond, 2004), the texts examined in this study do not always make room for these similarities to be analysed along this line of thought. What needs to be stressed here is that, more than irony, some of the geographical similarities underline, and, moreover, bring to the fore, the insecurities of the travellers in the face of the political liminal phase that the area was experiencing at the time. Such similarities in scenery might also be considered as a way to stress that the area, despite its recent history and its present culture, is still Europe. In some revealing notes of approximation between Albanians and Europeans, August Dozon, while visiting Korça, links its rise to the well-being of Christians. Dozon says that, thanks to contacts with Europeans, the Christians of the area showed two different characteristics that he identifies as European: 'they have brought back a certain inclination for material and intellectual progress which is manifested in the construction of houses according to the European style and in the efforts to proliferate education' (Dozon 1875, 604). Here, Dozon offers a panorama of an abandoned territory and a people left to their own fate. The corollary is clear: the Ottoman government has no right to rule the area, due to its neglect. The fragment implies that this Albanian territory has practically started its passage from an Ottoman imaginary geography to a new one.

After presenting the Ottoman government as caring neither for Muslims nor for Christians, Dozon explains how the locals administer everything on their own, and how educational 'assistance will be given to everyone, without distinctions of religious belief' (Dozon 1875, 604). What is noticeable in the fragment is that Dozon ascribes a common denominator to both Muslims and Christians, namely Albanianness, and these Albanians are not identified with the Ottoman government. Instead of the common Muslim–Christian oppositional binary, which figures quite frequently in writings about the Ottoman Empire of the era, Dozon points to an acceptance by Albanian Muslims of the Europeanization of the culture of the area, and also hints that the oppositional binary does not bear any significance in this case. We are allowed to say without hesitation that this period was a liminal phase in terms of the relation of Albanians with the imaginative European geography that the travellers had in mind. The old structures were relaxed, and thus opened the way for new opportunities to reconstruct the whole definition of the borders of the European map, and to newly situate Albanians in that novel imaginative geography. Whether this attempt has resulted in a novel map of imaginative Europe remains to be investigated in studies focused on travel literature of the beginning of the twentieth century.

Conclusion

Western travel literature about Albanians at the turn of the twentieth century bears a series of images and representations that vary from balkanism to orientalism. The writers seem to have conceptualized the Albanian Other along the lines of barbarism and savagery, illiteracy, lack of desire to be civilized, an innate incapability to internalize religiousness and a dehumanizing approach towards women that reduces them to animals. Although there is a presence of orientalist approaches in the construction of images about Albanians, the tensions between these approaches and those grounded in balkanism are not very clear at first sight.

In portraying hybrid identities in these narratives, the authors generally fail to nuance what they see. Pre-existing frameworks that are used to explain phenomena pose a recurring problem in travel literature and, as such, these frameworks have an impact on how native populations are viewed and represented, and also make impossible any emergence of elements that disturb the main discourses undergirding the narrative about the contact zone. At best, the disruptive elements which have the potential to reconfigure pre-existing frameworks are hidden between the lines and affect the authors' overall narrative only peripherally. Indeed, reading these narratives for the ways in which the authors negotiate prefabricated balkanist and orientalist tropes and inscribe them into what they see on the ground is a fascinating paradox. The narratives reveal both balkanist and orientalist features, on the one hand, and the inclination to situate Albanian territories outside Ottoman geography, on the other hand. While their preconceived strategies tend to be grounded on the civilizing mission of the European man, and the representations constructed are in stark contrast with what European values represent, what they see deep among the natives seems to prompt them to apply a strategy of detaching Albanians from an Ottoman geography, while envisioning their passage into a European periphery. The example from August Dozon shows a clear strategy in which Albanians are very prone to certain values that the travel writers identify as European. Instead of the regular Muslim–Christian oppositional binary, Dozon's observations show that this oppositional binary is not significant in the case of Albanians, since their Albanianness is presented as having greater importance within, and impact upon, their social realities (Dozon 1875). Presenting Albanians as liminal Others at this stage of history, the Western authors of the period were clearly perplexed, at certain points, as to whether to place Albanians into an Oriental imaginative geography or into a European one. While balkanist tropes came to be implemented as a full discourse only after the Balkan Wars (Todorova, 1997), and as the flux of images of the period prior to World War One included a range of oriental images (Neuburger, 2004), we might conclude that the travel writers analysed here were faced with a crucial dilemma: whether to extend the imaginative European geography to include Albanians as an inner Other, or to leave Albanians outside this geography in the form of an 'oriental' Other. This liminal attitude presented by the travel writers of the period created stark tensions through different sorts of hetero-images.

The persistent failure of the Ottoman Empire to offer an accommodating political approach to the natives implies that the area needs a new political configuration. Along with political concerns, the cultural negotiations of the writers create the persistent idea of a space that seems primed to be filled with Eurocentric values. The space is also represented as disposed to import European values, and to be included in a European imaginary geography. All of this not through the intervening 'civilizing mission' of the Western man, as had been the case with travel writers writing about the colonized areas of the world, but through the native's interiorized 'civilizing mission'.

While teasing out these paradoxes and ambivalences, one cannot overlook the fact that all the representations and images about Albania(ns) were written and read during, or only some decades away from, the redefinition and restructuring of the Balkan states along the lines of European nation states that consolidated with the break-up of the nineteenth-century empires.

Notes

1 See Bakić-Hayden (1995, 920). Bakić-Hayden here evolves an argument that has been addressed by Todorova (1997).
2 Translations are mine.

References

Bakić-Hayden, Milica. 1995. 'Nesting orientalisms: The case of former Yugoslavia', *Slavic Review* 54 (4): 917–31.
Bérard, Victor. 1893. *La Turquie et l'hellénisme contemporain*. Paris: Félix Alcan.
Berber, Neval. 2010. *Unveiling Bosnia-Herzegovina in British Travel Literature (1844–1912)*. Pisa: Pisa University Press.
Blunt, Fanny Janet. 1878. *The People of Turkey: Twenty years' residence among Bulgarians, Greeks, Albanians, Turks and Armenians, by a consul's daughter and wife*, edited by Stanley Lane Poole. London: John Murray.
Carey, Daniel. 2015. 'Truth, lies and travel writing'. In *The Routledge Companion to Travel Writing*, edited by Carl Thompson. London: Routledge.
Dozon, Auguste. 1875. 'Excursion en Albanie', *Bulletin de la Société de Géographie*. Paris: Société de Géographie.
Fleming, K.E. 2000. 'Orientalism, the Balkans, and Balkan historiography', *American Historical Review* 105 (4): 1218–33.
Goldsworthy, Vesna. 1998. *Inventing Ruritania: The imperialism of the imagination*. New Haven, CT: Yale University Press.
Goldsworthy, Vesna. 2006. 'The Balkans in nineteenth-century British travel writing'. In *Travel Writing in the Nineteenth Century: Filling the blank spaces*, edited by Tim Youngs. London: Anthem Press.
Hammond, Andrew. 2004, 'The uses of Balkanism: Representation and power in British travel writing, 1850–1914', *Slavonic and East European Review* 82 (3): 601–24.
Horvath, Agnes, Bjørn Thomassen and Harald Wydra. 2009. 'Introduction: Liminality and cultures of change', *International Political Anthropology* 2 (1): 3–5.
Ippen, Theodor. 1892. *Novibazar und Kossovo: Das alte Rascien, eine Studie*. Vienna: Alfred Hölder.
Jezernik, Božidar. 2004. *Wild Europe: The Balkans in the gaze of Western travellers*. London: Saqi Books.
Knight, E.F. 1880. *Albania: A narrative of recent travel*. London: Sampson Low, Marston, Searle & Rivington.
Malcolm, Noel. 2002. 'Myth of Albanian national identity: Some key elements'. In *Albanian Identities: Myth and history*, edited by Stephanie Schwandner-Sievers and Bernd Jürgen Fischer. Bloomington: Indiana University Press.
Maximilian. 1867. 'Ein Stück Albanien'. In *Aus meinem Leben: Reiseskizzen, Aphorismen, Gedichte von Maximilian, Kaiser von Mexiko*. Leipzig: Duncker & Humblot.
Montagu, Mary Wortley. 1861. *The Letters and Works of Lady Mary Wortley Montagu*. London: Henry G. Bohn.
Neuburger, Mary. 2004. *The Orient Within: Muslim minorities and the negotiation of nationhood in modern Bulgaria*. Ithaca, NY: Cornell University Press.
Nünning, Ansgar. 2009. 'On the manifold prefiguration/premeditation of the representation of reality in the travelogue: An outline of a narratological theory, typology and poetics of travel writing', *Comunicação & Cultura* 8: 127–49.
Pratt, Mary Louise. 1992. *Imperial Eyes: Travel writing and transculturation*. London: Routledge.
Said, Edward. 1978. *Orientalism*. New York: Pantheon.
Thomassen, Bjørn. 2014. *Liminality and the Modern: Living through the in-between*. Burlington: Ashgate.
Todorova, Maria. 1997. *Imagining the Balkans*. Oxford: Oxford University Press.

Tozer, Henry Fanshawe. 1869. *Researches in the Highlands of Turkey, Including Visits to Mounts Ida, Athos, Olympus, and Pelion, to the Mirdite Albanians, and Other Remote Tribes*, Volume 1. London: John Murray.

Van Gennep, Arnold. 1960 [1909]. *The Rites of Passage: A classical study of cultural celebrations*. Chicago: Chicago University Press.

Wiet, Emile. 1866. 'Le diocèse d'Alessio et la Mirdite: Extrait d'un mémoire de M. Wiet, consul de France à Scutari', *Bulletin de la Société de Géographie*, 271–88.

Wolff, Larry. 1994. *Inventing Eastern Europe: The map of civilization on the mind of the Enlightenment*. Stanford, CA: Stanford University Press.

16
Unmaking silence and futureS in the midst of 'The passing dreams of choice' (Audre Lorde)

Susan Arndt and Xin Li

FutureS

The British sociologist Barbara Adam carried out extensive research on social narratives about time and the future. Winding up a decade of research, she suggests that the future is performed as fact, fiction, fortune and fate (Adam 2010; Adam and Groves 2007). Indeed, the future is a *fact* inasmuch as it bears notions of being in becoming. After all, it may be a fact that we, even the sun, are all going to die; or maybe not, since the universe will continue to exist four-dimensionally, no matter what. Yet since we neither exactly know nor completely control what will be/come, could the future ever be a fact-fact? The same goes for *fate*. There are certainly things that are beyond control, but fate is about the total absence of agencies and scopes of decision making. Yet is there really something that exists beyond a total lack of decision making? In other words, is there anything that is fate only? Moreover, the future can also be explained and perceived as *fortune* – depending on our degree of happiness. However, fortune is never a mere 'fortune-given' thing, but wo*man-made, determined by very earthly parameters.

Therefore, anything we might consider to be fortune and fate is also very much about power, and the privileges and options thus (not) granted. For instance, being born within the fortress of Schengen-Europe (or not) is less about fortune or fate, than about power constellations that buy or disclose options of living into a self-determined future. Last, the *fictional* aspect of the future holds true inasmuch as it does not exist beyond being imagined. Such fictionalized meaning matters, because it creates social matters in powerful ways. Thus, rather than reading the future as fortune or fate, or fact or fiction, we argue that the future exists within and beyond the imaginary, and we embrace a silence related to not knowing the future (yet).

As such, futureS do not exist in the (simplicity of any) singular, and this is largely for three reasons. First, futureS are causally intersected with both the past and the present. Second, futureS are intersected and moulded by complexities and coexistences of glocal encounters of conflicting, competing and complementary agencies, interests, contingencies, possibilities and options in the un/making and (not) sharing of futureS. Throughout global histories, some futureS have buttressed each other, while some have deflated each other, and others have prevented each other's existence; some have advanced and some have hindered others. There are futureS that neither did nor will ever happen, because one futurE thwarted the other – and in this instance the capital 'E' puts emphasis on this erasure of given pluralities. Consequently, and third, futureS (as moulded by and moulding the category of analysis 'FutureS') are made and shared unevenly by power-coded agencies. As internet visionary William Gibson suggests, '[t]he future is already here, it's just not very evenly distributed' (1999, n.p.). Indeed, every struggle about power, freedom and justice is about futureS, and every struggle about futureS is about gaining access to power, freedom and justice. After all, futureS' polyphony, complexity, reflexivity and relationality are coded by the structures and discourses of power, along the grammar of racialization, gender, sexuality, religion, health, ability, age and nation. Such coded social positions determine, to a high extent, the degree of impact and agency a person or collective may have in shaping (their own and other people's) individual and collective futureS. Ultimately, however, the struggle over futureS is not determined by power constellations alone. Rather, both power and futureS can be negotiated and un/made by agencies. Contextualized by power and powerlessness, privileges and deprivation, ethics and unscrupulousness, responsibility and the lack thereof, agencies desire and fear, fight and sustain, accept and negotiate, experience and forget, as well as build and destroy futureS. In fact, agency is power's most virulent protagonist and antagonist at the same time.

So what do futureS have to do with silence? To the extent that some futures were prevented from happening, they were silenced. This, however, is not a passive clause issue. After all, silencing is done just as much as silence is always inhabited and can be undone from within or beyond. White supremacy has suppressed the becoming of futureS in the colonies, forcing the colonized into a waiting room of history, claiming that the West was always the future of the colonized. Yet this waiting room is a Western narration. It is true that colonization had the power to violate, exploit and suppress colonized societies. And yet they kept on existing. While the West was eager to narrate this space as empty (a mere fiction), these spaces continued to exist in constant negotiation with the silencing of autonomous futures. Here, Silencing becomes a Silence that is a passing – passing in terms of undoing silence and generating dreams that are about alternatives and choices in the midst of narratives that silence.

By looking into Marlene Nourbese Philip's, Samih al-Qasim's and Audre Lorde's engagements with silence and its poetics of passing into futureS, this chapter examines how silenced spaces in the dominant historical narrative harbour a resistance to imposition and a potential for negotiations of futureS. The paradox etched in silence as a potential space of crafting possible futureS culminates in Audre Lorde's notion of passing – where the past entangles with and nurtures alternative futureS in the Sankofa act of remembering.

Silence as a poetics of passing into futureS: Marlene Nourbese Philip and Samih al-Qasim

Silence has temporal dimensions. It is simultaneously an open call for futureS yet to materialize and a beckoning toward unspoken pasts that are beyond retrieval. For Maurice Blanchot, what is silent is that which cannot be contained and will not allow itself to be said. It eludes us, yet drives the demand for more language (thus futureS-making). In his commentary on Bonnefoy, Blanchot articulates the relevance of silence to time and the desire for literary creation and, thus, futureS-writing:

> 'How can I', he asked, 'in my speech, capture this prior presence that I must exclude in order to speak, in order to speak it? The eternal torment of our language ... when its longing turns back toward

what it always misses, through the necessity under which it labors of being the lack of what it would say.' (Blanchot 1993, 36)

For Blanchot, language is an inevitable act of exclusion, a negation of immediacy ('the prior presence that I must exclude to speak'). Paradoxically, language 'labors' under its longing for silence and 'what it always misses', despite the impossibility of that need ever being satiated. What drives one to tell a story, to address the lost knowledges and the unspoken histories, and to narrate futureS into materialization is, according to Blanchot, the desire for a return to the 'prior presence' of silence and immediacy, before the imposition of an exclusive and totalizing order.

Silence is thus both historical and futureS-oriented – it complicates linear perceptions of time, history and narration through the paradox it embodies. Drawing from Blanchot's thoughts on silence, one may argue that it is exactly the silence of the Atlantic, of the 'unspoken, unrealized pasts that haunt the historical present' (Bhabha 2004, 12), which invites and commands the postcolonial desire to give a voice to it, to integrate it into present narratives about the past and into the imagination and materialization of a postcolonial futurity. Silence (such as that of the Middle Passage) thus invites narrations that are always and already an act of futureS-making, of engaging and resisting the current structures of domination.

Karmen MacKendrick, in her reading of Blanchot and silence, highlights the temporal dimension of the latter's theorization of silence, assigning it to temporalities of past, present and future (MacKendrick 2014). In its temporal dimension relating to the past, silence is read (clearly under Blanchotian influence) as 'that which we find ourselves unable to remember or forget – from which we shall see that it has returned, before and after, already' (MacKendrick 2014, 36). In its present aspect, silence is, according to MacKendrick, the element that empties presence; in its future aspect, silence is the call, the waiting (for speaking and writing), and thus an invitation for futureS-making. MacKendrick's elaboration on silence's temporal dimensions mainly focuses on the aporia at the heart of what Blanchot calls 'the disaster' (Blanchot 1986), emphasizing the disruptive function of silence as the presence of absence that simultaneously invites and resists narration and mastery. Thus, the past, present and future become entangled in a fuzzy movement where none can be linearly located. In the Blanchotian framework, that movement is cast in terms of an 'eternal recurrence' (MacKendrick 2014, 19), where the desire for language is perceived to be self-destructive, as it can only result in the eternal return to the aporia. It should be noted that the Blanchotian framework may prove to be inadequate for postcolonial considerations of the process of Otherization, domination and erasure, and the deep entanglement of power with the linear and progressivist perception of time. Power and time – these two aspects work in tandem in a mechanism of self-affirmation. Postcolonial critics have pointed out that the critique of the construction of historical or future-oriented narratives must also be a critical reflection on the construction of time and temporality itself – on the Hegelian progressivist presumptions that allow history to be understood as a linear progress, an ongoing process where humanity evolves from nature to culture, from body to mind, from barbarism to civilization. Such presumptions provide a base for the naturalization and maintenance of racist structures, and other forms of domination and hierarchy.

In a piece of experimental poetry in Marlene Nourbese Philip's formally hybrid novel *Looking for Livingstone: An odyssey of silence* (1991), the poetic voice ponders the relationship between the reductionist nature of language and the making of futureS:

>   the word discovers
>
>   Word
>
>   mirrored
>   in Silence
>   trapped
>   in the beginning was
>
>   not
>
>   word
>   but Silence
>   and a future rampant   with possibility
>
>
>   and Word (Philip 1991, 40)

In the postcolonial effort to articulate and include unspoken and unrealized perspectives in their imagination of futureS, unquestioning use of language only leads to the confirmation of the 'Word', the regime of truth and knowledge. The beginning of the poem presents a metaphor that points to the futility of attempts to imagine futureS within the bounds of the master narrative – for to resist words with counter words without reflecting on their reductionist and essentialist qualities will only lead to the reinforcement thereof. Language is not an unmediated reflection of meaning ('mirrored' is an intertextual reference to the Lacanian notion that the emergence of the subject, or their ascent to the realm of the symbolic, is predicated upon mediation, alienation and separation); it distorts and silences along the power axes of domination. The construction of 'the Word', which symbolizes the single narrative of truth, is built on practices of reduction and exclusion. The silencing of potential and alternative futureS is a necessary condition for its emergence. Musing on the paradox of language and silence, of how history is written through the erasure and silencing of other possible futureS, the poem disrupts linear and progressivist notions of time, as the prospect of futureS 'with rampant possibility' is already arrested at the 'beginning' of the past.

Contesting the construction of silence as an inscription of violence or a symbol of passivity, the poem envisions 'Silence' as a way of passing into futureS without reducing 'rampant possibility'. Adrienne Rich invokes a similar metaphor in her poetry. In her 'Twenty-one love poems IX', Rich relates silence to the symbolism of a pond: '[y]our silence today is a pond where drowned things live' (Rich 1976, ix). The 'drowned things', the excluded and the missing in the historical metanarrative, can only 'live' in the 'pond' of silence, as any articulation would necessarily threaten erasure. Silence thus represents an ethical alternative in the passing to a postcolonial futurity. For both Rich and Philip, silence comprises a possible critical vehicle for passing into futureS in an open, multiple, self-reflexive and non-totalized manner.

Philip's and Rich's vision of silence as a vehicle of passing into futureS is echoed in Palestinian poet Samih al-Qasim's works. Writing about resistance and futureS of Palestine, for example, al-Qasim famously writes in his two-line poem entitled 'Eternity':

> Leaves fall from time to time
> But the trunk of the oak tree
> (Al-Qasim, in Darwish et al. 1984, 78–9)

The oak tree has always been a symbol of strength and resistance in Lebanese and Palestinian contexts. Invoking the symbolisms of the falling leaves and 'the oak tree', the poem reaches for the painful memories of the Israeli occupation while writing into possible futureS of the Palestinian resistance. The reaching-for and writing-into, though, are not invested in the volume of words, but in a profound silence.

In the poem, the indication of pain and struggle is realized through the falling of leaves from the trunk, which provides water, nutrients and the support system for them to live and to be colourful and prosper – an embodied metaphor for the losses and separation suffered by the Palestinian people, who are forcibly relocated from their homeland. A sense of prolonged despair and forlornness is suggested through the construction of an eternally mundane fact of life: leaves fall from the trunk as part of the cycle of life, nothing can be done to change that. Like the falling of the leaves, the displacement of the Palestinian people seems to have been projected as an eternal part of life – nothing can be changed. And yet, as we proceed to the second line of the poem, as the falling leaves hit the ground, they become nutrients for the trunk – after the fall, life begins. Memory of the past nourishes and calls for the emergence of possible futureS (indicated in the line 'but the trunk of the tree'), a passing (emergence) that is conveyed through the silence at the end of the second line, which does not designate a beginning or end. The unspoken past nourishes and calls for futureS in the historical present, where the making of futureS (the act of narration and imagining possible futureS) is always and already taking place.

The passing into futureS of the Palestinian resistance culminates in a profound silence at the end of the second line – a way of writing into futureS that critically engages with the construction of time, history and narration. Khalid A. Sulaiman, in *Palestine and Modern Arab Poetry* (1984), reads silence as a form of indirect approach common to Palestinian resistance poetry. Such a reading would result in a regretful flattening of the aesthetic richness of silence. Instead of laying out a single vision of the future or solution for the Palestinian–Israeli conflict, the poem resorts to silence as an aesthetic form of futureS-making – through a refrainment from, and critical engagement with, the ontologically dualistic construction of Palestine and Israel in the discourse of conflict and confrontation. While addressing the theme of separation and dislocation, the poem envisions futureS of Israeli–Palestinian relations not in terms of dualism and confrontation, but in terms of interdependence and entanglement. The physical and symbolic entanglement of the tree and the leaves, along with the poem's adoption of silence as a passage into open-ended, plural and non-totalizing futureS, form a challenge to the ontological presumptions that underlie the notion of Israeli–Palestinian conflict. Here, through silence, the poem performs a resistance that goes beyond the power-invested logic of Palestinian–Israeli confrontation.

Hope is as vulnerable as it is powerful: Audre Lorde's 'A litany for survival' (1978)

Audre Lorde's poem 'A litany for survival' (1978) addresses the survival of those who were never meant to survive – thus passing from being neglected the right to survive into new futureS. European and American futureS, as we know them today, were built on the erasure of African, Native American and Asian futureS. Early modern Europe, eager to prosper economically, explored and conquered foreign territories. Having arrived in what Europe's colonial rhetoric calls the 'New World', Spain, Portugal and Britain destroyed these rather 'old' worlds' societal and economic structures. They murdered the First Nations of the Americas, declaring their homes as *terra nullius*, waiting to be settled and controlled by *White* Europeans. Driven by White greed for unpaid labour, millions of Africans were enslaved and deported to these new colonies and Europe. Thus, Maafa, the European enslavement of Africans, inaugurated the Industrial Revolution in Europe and North America, while locally grown economic structures in the Americas, Africa and Asia were being destroyed by it. The futureS as paved by the Industrial Revolution thwarted and reoriented collective and individual futureS of people of colour and their societies across the world. White European fictional imaginations and sciences played a role in selling these White atrocities as progress in the name of civilization. People of colour were declared by Europe's racism as lacking humanity, in an endeavour to justify the unjustifiable, that is, treating them in an inhuman way. This narrative comprised the claim that progress and freedom are designed for White Christian men only, turning 'their Europe' into a blueprint of everyone's futurE. Most infamous in this respect are Georg Wilhelm Friedrich Hegel's *Vorlesungen zur Geschichte* (Lectures on the Philosophy of History), held between 1805 and 1831.[1] Hegel suggests that Africa has no history, because it has no social dynamics, movements or developments (Hegel 1833-6, 162-3) and, hence, no (understanding of) 'the future'. Moreover, he claims that Black people do not have any sense of freedom, or of being human (139–40). This is rather irritating, coming from a philosopher of freedom, even more so since he made these claims after the Haitian Revolution (1791–1804). In a questionable attempt to explain away the obvious contradiction, he suggests in a strange dialectic that this revolution is but a proof of the alleged 'disregard for life', and hence the absence of humanity on the part of Black people (159). Ultimately, hardly more is needed to back up the claim that colonial narrations about Africa/ns not being human, not knowing freedom and not desiring 'future' do not do any justice to given societal structures across the African continent and the emerging diasporas elsewhere (Farr 2004, 143–58). The Haitian Revolution is just one outstanding example of anti-Maafa resistance and its strivings for freedom, independence and futureS during the deportation of enslaved Africans and on the plantations in the Americas, and other places where Black people were enslaved. Maafa, and all the White narrations thereof, forced millions of enslaved Africans into death; millions of enslaved humans lost their lives, because they chose the path of resistance. Yet some eventually decided to walk the path of resistance and, even if they were forced into sacrificing their lives for the cause of freedom, they are the ones who built futureS for others, offering survival to millions of enslaved people and their descendants. It is because of centuries of Black resistance, eventually backed up by abolitionism and White agencies, that those 'who were never meant to survive', as Audre Lorde's lyrical I in 'A litany for survival' (1978) puts it, did so against all odds of Maafa. Millions of enslaved Africans survived, precisely because there was resistance that insisted on futureS, which White Maafa supremacy had hoped to erase – to silence.

The chronotopical setting of Lorde's poem might be ambiguous and open, but to (also) read it into Maafa, and the memory and futureS thereof, is very suggestive. Reading the poem with reference to Maafa, the lyrical I bemoans lost memories and forgotten dreams that are able to keep hopes, which in turn generate agencies. This idea is expressed by the conjunction of the terms dream*hopes, triggering a desire for memory as a breeding ground for dream*hopes, speech beyond being silenced, and resistance in the pursuit of Black futureS.

Throughout the poem, the lyrical I inhabits a passage that keeps connecting it with a 'we' and an 'us'. The lyrical I integrates him*herself into the collective, and thus identifies with the 'those of us' that opens the poem and functions as an anaphor that bridges the first and second stanzas, while also having its very own profile. It could be read homographically as 'those of US', turning it into an African American US – a 'we' sharing the experience of Maafa and its legacy in the absence of White solidarity. Yet the 'those of us' is eventually used differently in both stanzas. The 'us' in the 'those of us' in the second stanza is an 'all of us' that indeed refers to *all* Black people (the enslaved and their descendants) 'who were never meant to survive' (II/10), that is, both those who survived the erasing silence and those who did not. The first stanza's 'those of us', however, refers to the enslaved who decided ('crucial and alone', I/3) to perform resistant agencies for survival – either their own or a collective survival (that might not have happened) – by speaking against the silence:

> For those of us who live at the shoreline
> standing upon the constant edges of decision
> crucial and alone
> for those of us who cannot indulge
> the passing dreams of choice
> who love in doorways coming and going
> in the hours between dawns
> looking inward and outward
> at once before and after
> seeking a now that can breed
> futures
> like bread in our children's mouths
> so their dreams will not reflect
> the death of ours:
> For those of us
> who were imprinted with fear
> like a faint line in the center of our foreheads
> learning to be afraid with our mother's milk
> for by this weapon
> this illusion of some safety to be found
> the heavy-footed hoped to silence us
> For all of us
> this instant and this triumph
> We were never meant to survive. (Lorde 1978, 31)

The second stanza uses the 'all of us' in passive sentences, thus featuring 'all of us' as the object without agency that is dominated by the subject (position) in possession of an agency that is all about silencing the sentence's object. Translating this cyclical passage that intersects silence and being silenced into the context of Maafa, the 'heavy-footed' (II/7) would be White supremacy hoping that the weapon (II/5) of dispersing fear (II/2) will keep the 'all of us' (II/8) (as a metaphor for enslaved persons) away from dream*hoping and the agencies thus accessible by employing the weaponry of causing fear via violence. In Maafa's very own oxymoronic rhetoric, fear is spread along with an 'illusion of some safety' (II/6) as a ticket into (allegedly granted) survival. This illusion is the bread that eventually triggers change – and hence the very scape of passing from being silenced to the overcoming thereof.

This illusion was learned by the 'those/all of us' (II/1, 8) 'with our mother's milk' (II/4) that has 'imprinted' the 'us' with 'fear' (II/2), furrowing it 'in the center of our foreheads' (II/3) as a faint worry line. Yet, it was this very illusion that killed safety and survival, as Lorde's lyrical I suggests: just as the past paralyses the Angel of History's wings, giving the past even more power about the now, the White 'weapon' (II/5) of spreading 'fear' (II/2) managed 'to silence us' (II/7) – Black memories, dream*hopes and, therefore, agencies for resistance – and to strengthen White supremacy in the process.

While the second stanza positions the 'us' as the object of a passive clause, the 'those of us' (I/1, 4) in the first stanza is positioned in the active voice, and is hence an actor in terms of building new passages into alternative futureS. This corresponds with the fact that the first stanza's 'those of us' did not buy this 'illusion of some safety' (II/6), but rather insisted on the possibility of dream*hoping, thus securing an 'instant' and 'this triumph' (II/9): the survival of Black dream*hopes and their agencies amid the death of millions of individuals, and their being silenced by fearful violence. In doing so, it is marked as being 'alone' (I/3) – and hence as being much less than the second stanza's 'those of us'. Thus, it might not refer to all African Americans, but above all to 'those of us' who live 'alone' (I/3) on the 'shoreline' (I/1) and on 'constant edges of decision' (I/2), because they 'cannot indulge / the passing dreams of choice' (I/4–5). The shoreline is a scape of passing, and so are the edges of decision. It is in these transcendental spaces of passing that dreams of choice can survive. They pass, yet do not pass away. They pass into a survival that breaks off the silence into a future that can be moulded in an emancipatory way.

Thus, this 'those of us' (I/1, 4) positions this very passing, that is, travelling, via dream*hopes as a 'crucial' (I/4) strategy of choice and agency. This very 'us' is the 'us' that keeps insisting on dreams and agencies thus granted; however peripheral and small, they are a crucial source of agencies that accept the invitation to have 'dreams of *choice*' (I/5) and to make 'decisions' (I/2) – in the face of given limits and dangers, as represented by the 'shorelines' (I/1) and 'edges' (I/2) as horizons of passing. These spatial metaphors of 'shoreline' and 'constant edges' in the middle of the 'doorways coming and going' (I/6) position these crucial dreams, however, as small, fragile and lost. And they are these things, because they fight against being silenced, forgotten and erased.

The second stanza's 'mother's milk' (II/4) that taught fear as a ticket to survival is complemented here with another means of nourishing:

'bread in our children's mouths' (I/12). This bread might dissolve, but not without leaving traces. The melting bread is not about ending only, but also about beginning – since it keeps filling the children's stomachs and souls, not with the fear in their mother's milk, but with the bread's promise of survival, eager to conceal the 'death' of the parent's/ancestor's dreams (I/13–14). It is melting and hence passing, but while vanishing into silence, the dreams energize hopes and respective futureS. Just as much as the Akan Adinkra of Sankofa (Kayper-Mensah 1976, 4) is all about gazing at and addressing the past in order to build the future, Lorde's lyrical I favours a now that can and does dream*hope into 'breed'ing 'futures' (I/10–11) – and Lorde uses 'futures' in the plural here, which is still rarely done today. These 'futures' are, as suggested by the lyrical I, able to start from scratch by not reflecting on 'the death of ours' (I/14), that is, disappointed dream*hopes in the face of violated lives and futureS.

Lorde's lyrical I seeks to replace the silence with dream*hopes for futureS. The old dream*hopes left to loneliness (might) have been killed, but they did nevertheless survive – melting 'like bread in children's mouths' (I/12), and yet nourishing new dream*hopes and their futureS in the process. These dream*hopes pass in Black agencies, empowering them. Therefore, Lorde's idea to *breed* futureS is – somewhat antithetically to the Angel of History's paralysed stagnation that allows the futurE to be the past's fate – intrinsically linked to futureS as being made with affection, and freed from – and yet attached to – the obstacles as represented by the shorelines of loneliness and danger. After all, the repetitive 'those of us' (I/1, 4; II/1) inhabits a cyclical 'always' in which past and future coexist in a scape of passing into each other: '[f]or those of us who live ..., stand ..., love ... in the hours between dawns ... at once before and after' (I/1–9). This simultaneity of before and after integrates the past into futureS and futureS into the past, cyclically and, even more so, causally.

The third stanza is the longest, consisting of 17 lines. It recalls the second stanza's fear, reciting as a leitmotif 'we are afraid' (III/1, 3, 5, 7, 9, 11, 13, 17), whose constant repetition recalls the Angel of History getting stuck in the pains of history and the subsequent now beyond messianic power and agency, however weak:

> And when the sun rises we are afraid
> it might not remain
> when the sun sets we are afraid
> it might not rise in the morning

when our stomachs are full we are afraid
of indigestion
when our stomachs are empty we are afraid
we may never eat again
when we are loved we are afraid
love will vanish
when we are alone we are afraid
love will never return
and when we speak we are afraid
our words will not be heard
nor welcomed
but when we are silent
we are still afraid. (Lorde 1978, 31–2)

This repetition of 'we are (still) afraid' (III/1, 3, 5, 7, 9, 11, 13, 17) marks the importance and centrality of the fears caused by White Maafa violence in a threatening cycle of a past repeating itself from sunrise to sunset, obstructing every access to, and agency (however weak) for, both the now and the morning: 'when the sun rises we are afraid / it might not remain / when the sun sets / we are afraid it might not rise in the morning' (III/1–4). There is also fear that sated stomachs may develop indigestion, or that hungry bellies will remain empty (III/5–8). Love can disappear, never to return again (III/9–12). Although the third stanza hosts only three passive clauses, there is still an absence of agency, which is in line with the fact that the most recurring active clause ('we are afraid') ascribes a predicative 'are afraid' to the subject 'we'. Thus, although being a subject, the 'we' is ultimately 'afraid', and hence nothing but the passive object of the second stanza, that is, the 'those of us / who were imprinted with fear' (II/1–2) by the subject of 'heavy footed' (I/7) White supremacy. Poetologically, the fact that many active and a few passive clauses ultimately both address passivity, that is, the absence of agency, emphasizes the cause of it: intimidation and fear cause paralysis (as was the case with the Angel of History). This line of thought resembles *la tautologie* (tautology), one of Roland Barthes's rhetorical figures of myths in *Mythologies*: '[C]'est comme ça, parce que c'est comme ça' (Barthes 1957, 262). Stuck in this tautology of 'it is like this, because it is like this', with a cyclical absence of causes and agencies, even love cannot be thought of as something that the subject can commit, only as something that happens to the subject to cause pain: 'when we are loved we are afraid / love will vanish' and 'never return' (III/9, 10, 12).

In subversion to this agenda, the four last lines of the third stanza manage to call the vicious cycle by name, which marks the beginning of overcoming it: 'when we speak we are afraid / our words will not be heard / nor welcomed' (III/13–15). However, when one remains silent, as a result, silencing causes a silence that, ultimately, denies itself every dream*hope for safety beyond fear, even an illusory one: 'but when we are silent / we are still afraid' (III/16–17). Ultimately, the first stanza's urgency of speaking up at the shorelines, even if alone (I/3), is evoked as a 'crucial' (I/3) intervention.

The last stanza's 13 words in three lines return to the first stanza's agency with a wording that eventually overwrites the second stanza's pessimistic ending with the fourth stanza's dream*hoping into futureS:

> So it is better to speak
> remembering
> we were never meant to survive. (Lorde 1978, 32)

While 'future' is singled out in the first stanza, line 11, the fourth stanza's middle line gives prominence to only one word as well: 'remembering'. There is an awareness in remembering, at which Lorde is hinting. To remember we were silenced is turned into a source of empowerment, generating the desire to break out, in order to survive for new futureS. So, while the last line suggests 'we were never meant to survive' (IV/3), it is somewhat antithetically turned on its head by making the very last word call out: 'survive' – a 'Yes, we did.' Even though Maafa did not plan survival for Black people, it was fought for by the Sankofa 'us' of the first and fourth stanzas that managed to survive into new futureS, thanks to *remembering* as a mode of passing actively from past to futureS that continuously revive the lost and silenced ones.

The various stanzas in 'Litany for survival' transcend into each other, while celebrating the power of passages. Passages are about agencies that start intervening into social inequalities by mapping dream*hopes and respective paths to alternative futures. Change is not happening, meaning that change does not happen all of a sudden out of the blue. Change is made and paved; and paving it means opening up passages that need to be inhabited and moulded. Then, and only then, can futureS that frame equality be mapped.

Conclusion

We are what we narrate. We will be what we will have narrated. Narration here comprises silence as a rhetorical and ethical strategy that knows about the power of pausing, passing and (re)presenting. Marlene Nourbese Philip, Samih al-Qasim and Audre Lorde poetically speak to the complex and paradoxical dynamic of silence and its potential for (un)making futureS. Thus defined, silence is not about absence, but presence. Silence is not a void, but a scape. Silence is not about surrender, but resistance. It abodes rampant possibilities – silence is both a site where potential futureS are arrested, and a site where alternative futureS take shape – it is both a space of suppression and a productive site of passage where temporalities and agencies entangle in a web of power constellations that harbour the hope of futureS making.

Note

1   He held the lectures in 1805/6 in Jena, 1816/17 and 1817/18 in Heidelberg, and at various places between 1819 and 1831. Based on notes by Hegel and manually written transcripts of the lectures, Karl Ludwig Michelet reconstructed and edited the lectures in the years 1833–6 as *Georg Wilhelm Friedrich Hegel's Werke. Vollständige Ausgabe durch einen Verein von Freunden des verewigten. Vorlesungen über die Geschichte der Philosophie.*

References

Adam, Barbara. 2010. 'Future matters: Challenge for social theory and social inquiry', *Cultura e comunicazione* 1: 47–55.
Adam, Barbara and Chris Groves. 2007. *Future Matters: Action, knowledge, ethics.* Leiden: Brill.
Barthes, Roland. 1957. *Mythologies.* Paris: Edition du Seuil.
Bhabha, Homi K. 2004. *The Location of Culture.* London: Routledge.
Blanchot, Maurice. 1986. *The Writing of the Disaster*, translated by Ann Smock. Lincoln: University of Nebraska Press.
Blanchot, Maurice. 1993. *The Infinite Conversation*, translated by Susan Hanson. Minneapolis: University of Minnesota Press.
Darwish, Mahmud, Samih al-Qasim and Adonis. 1984. *Victims of a Map: A bilingual anthology of Arabic poetry (Adonis, Mahmud Darwish, Samih al-Qasim)*, translated by Abdullah al-Udhari. London: Al Saqi Books.
Farr, Arnold. 2004. 'Whiteness visible: Enlightenment racism and the structure of racialized consciousness'. In *What White Looks Like: African-American philosophers on the whiteness question*, edited by George Yancy, 143–58. New York: Routledge.
Gibson, William. 1999. 'The science in science fiction'. In *Talk of the Nation* [Audio Interview], 30 October. Accessed 14 February 2022. https://www.npr.org/2018/10/22/1067220/the-science-in-science-fiction.
Hegel, Georg Wilhelm Friedrich. 1833–6. *Georg Wilhelm Friedrich Hegel's Werke: Vollständige Ausgabe durch einen Verein von Freunden des verewigten: Vorlesungen über die Geschichte der Philosophie*, edited by Karl Ludwig Michelet. Berlin: Duncker und Humblot.
Kayper-Mensah, Albert W. 1976. *Sankofa: Adinkra poems.* Accra: Ghana Publishing Corporation.

Lorde, Audre. 1978. 'A litany for survival'. In *The Black Unicorn*, 31–3. New York: W.W. Norton.
MacKendrick, Karmen. 2014. *Immemorial Silence*. Albany, NY: SUNY Press.
Philip, Marlene Nourbese. 1991. *Looking for Livingstone: An odyssey of silence*. Toronto: Mercury Press.
Rich, Adrienne Cecile. 1976. *Twenty-One Love Poems*. Emeryville: Effie's Press.
Sulaiman, Khalid A. 1984. *Palestine and Modern Arab Poetry*. London: Zed Books.

Index

arcades, shopping arcades 6, 7, 8, 10, 12, 19–26, 28, 31, 32fn2–3, 93
  Arcades Project (Passagenwerk) 12, 19, 21, 22, 27, 31, 32fn1–2, 40, 52fn4, 202
acoustics 19–20, 22–4, 27, 28, 30, 32fn3–5
  acoustic event 26
  acoustic atmosphere 26
acting 77, 85, 121, 124, 127, 129–30, 241
actor(s) 12, 72–5, 78–86, 91, 100, 119–25, 127–130, 130fn9, 131fn15, 225, 244, 287
agency 82, 100, 136, 188, 207, 216, 240, 245, 247, 278–9, 286–90, 291
air 23, 48, 58, 127–8, 218–23, 227–31, 234–6
Al-Qasim, Samih 14, 279, 282, 291
Albania(ns) 10, 14, 257–74
Alighieri, Dante 159–65, 167–9, 170fn2–3
alterity 226, 251
Anthropocene, anthropogenic 186–7, 190–2, 195, 218–19
anthropology, anthropological, anthropologists 4, 5, 59, 136, 149, 156
Aronofsky, Darren 13, 173–4, 180, 182
art of living 138, 141–3, 151fn13
atmosphere 12, 25–7, 30, 61, 112, 186, 206, 229,
  atmospheric space 26
Austin, John L. 76, 105, 114, 116

Bachmann-Medick, Doris 4, 5, 90–1
Bakhtin, Mikhail 61, 64, 82, 117fn15
Bal, Mieke 3–4, 69fn10, 106, 110–11, 131fn17
Balkan 49–50, 257, 259–60, 267, 270–2, 274
  balkanism 14, 259–61, 263–6, 268–74
Bartky, Sandra Lee 204, 207, 211, 214
Baumbach, Sibylle 4, 6
Benjamin, Walter 2, 7–8, 12, 19–27, 29–32, 32fn1, 32fn4–5, 32fn7–8, 40, 52fn4, 91, 93, 122, 125, 127, 130fn5, 188, 202, 208, 214
Bérard, Victor 264, 266, 268, 270, 272
Berger, John 14, 203–5, 207
Bergson, Henri 156
Berlin School 36
Bhabha, Homi 14, 240–4, 250, 280
Bildungsroman 2
bilingualism 57

Blanchot, Maurice 279–81
Blunt, Fanny Janet 261–6
Böhme, Gernot 12, 26
border regime 49–51
Boujedra, Rachid 14
Bowen, Elizabeth 14, 218–35, 236fn1

care of the self 134–45, 148–9, 150fn6, 150fn8, 150fn10, 151fn16
Casetti, Francesco 36, 38–9
Change 3, 5, 7, 20, 30, 43, 45, 58, 61, 64, 68, 74, 76, 80, 91, 93, 106, 122, 144, 149, 152fn15, 155, 158–60, 167, 169, 180–1, 187–8, 196, 220, 222, 226, 233–5, 241, 283, 286, 290
  climate change 186–7, 191, 219, 228, 230–2, 235, 237, 239, 249
  status change 1–2
city 23–4, 27, 30, 37–8, 41, 44, 47, 52fn4, 52fn6, 53, 66, 93, 96, 99, 141, 143, 146, 179, 187, 196, 202–3, 205–12, 214–15, 216, 218, 264, 270–2
Clark, Timothy 218–19, 229–31, 235
climate 13, 186–93, 196, 229
  climate change 186, 191–2, 196fn2, 197fn3, 219, 228–32
  climate refugees 186
cultural memory 3, 23, 36, 41, 46, 48, 52, 96, 238–40, 247, 251, 254, 283, 285
consumer culture 211
contact zone 14, 74–5, 189, 242, 253, 260–1, 273
cultural grid 90, 93, 95, 98–100
  cultural memory 3, 23, 36, 41, 46, 48, 52, 96, 238–40, 247, 251, 254, 283, 285
  cultural translation 10, 12, 89–91, 93, 97, 100
Cunqueiro, Álvaro 12, 56–68, 69fn22
Cynic philosophy 135–6, 138, 144–9, 151fn18

De la Soudière, Martin 220, 226
death 36, 42, 48, 78, 112, 120, 128, 134, 142, 157–8, 160–1, 163–4, 167–8, 170fn3, 170fn5, 193, 204, 215, 219–20, 240, 244, 246, 264, 266, 285–8
Deleuze, Gilles 150fn1, 177–8, 181, 183, 184fn1

INDEX   293

DeLoughrey, Elizabeth 187–8, 190–2, 195, 197fn8
Derrida, Jacques 14, 41, 46, 76-7, 81, 222, 226, 231, 233, 237, 250–1, 253,
discipline 1, 3–5, 11, 69fn10, 100fn4, 137, 151fn17, 203–5, 212, 214–15
dislocation 66, 226, 258, 283
dissociation 13, 173–83,
Döblin, Alfred 98
Dozon, August 264–5, 271–2, 274
dream*hoping 286–7, 290
Dufourmantelle, Anne 237, 251, 253
dystopia 48, 186, 188–9, 191, 194–6

Eastern Europe 260
Eliade, Mircea 62, 155–6
Enroth, Erik 12, 106–7, 109–14, 116, 116fn1
environment 9, 12–13, 46, 48, 122, 178, 181, 187–91, 195–6, 197fn3, 218, 221, 227–8, 231–3, 235
environmental humanities 190
Ette, Ottmar 90–3, 95, 98–9, 100fn2, 100fn6
exile 20, 25, 37, 65, 146, 165, 221, 225–6, 239

female body 202, 211, 215–16
film 12, 35–52, 53fn11, 73–5, 78–9, 81–2, 85, 86fn7, 87, 173–4, 180–4, 187, 192
flâneur, flânerie 8, 10, 22, 27, 202, 208–9, 214
flight 36–7, 50–2
flood 13, 62, 92, 158, 186–89, 192–4
flow 13, 174, 178, 182, 186–90, 194–6, 215, 270
Fludernik, Monika 105, 110–11, 113, 115, 116fn8, 117fn12–13
Foucault, Michel 14, 39, 85, 134–150, 150fn5–13, 151fn16–18, 181, 203–4, 211, 216, 223
future 14, 48, 51, 74, 85, 92, 147, 169, 187–8, 193–5, 197fn5, 214, 219, 234–5, 238, 258, 264, 277–81, 283–4, 286, 288, 290
futureS 277–88, 290–1
futurity 14, 280, 282

Geertz, Clifford 11
genre 3, 12, 17, 35, 40, 44–5, 59–68, 173, 182, 188, 191
Ginsberg, Elaine K. 9
global warming 4, 186, 189, 228
Gothic fiction 173–4
Guattari, Felix 177–8, 181, 183, 184fn1

Hades 157, 162, 164, 167
Hall, Mirko M. 20
haunting 40–2, 52, 210, 221, 231
Hegel, Georg Wilhelm Friedrich 241, 281, 284, 291fn1
Heimat 37, 43, 52
Hell 13, 155, 157–69, 170fn5
home(less) 10, 14, 37, 43, 58, 65, 78, 95, 98, 110, 168, 188, 195, 206, 215, 219–22, 224, 226, 228–9, 231, 233, 239, 247, 252–3, 283–4
hooks, bell 213
Hoppen, Franziska 5
hospitality 221–2, 234, 237, 245, 248, 250–4
Hutcheon, Linda 38–9, 63–4

identity 3, 7, 9–10, 14, 37, 41, 76–7, 96, 126, 155, 179–80, 200, 202, 205, 219–23, 234–5, 238–40, 245–7, 251, 253–4
imagined communities 14, 238
in-between 120–1, 124, 126–7, 130, 136, 148, 164, 169, 224, 258
initiation 13, 135, 155, 159, 164
interdisciplinarity 2–4, 6–7, 11, 14, 149, 190
intermediality 27, 38
intimacy 251

journey 2, 6, 36–8, 48, 76, 119–20, 135, 142, 148, 156–7, 159–61, 163–70, 170fn2–3, 195, 211, 236fn1, 245, 252, 258, 260
Jung, Carl Gustav 13, 96, 131fn20, 155–69, 170fn1, 170fn5–6

Kafka, Franz 13, 46, 119–30, 130fn1–3, 130fn5, 130fn7, 131fn11–13, 131fn16–31, 132fn34–52
katabasis 157, 166
Keller, Lynn 191, 197fn10
Knight, Edward Frederick 262, 264

liminality 1–2, 4–6, 9, 11, 13–14, 37, 59, 67, 82, 90, 100, 105–6, 114–16, 119–20, 122, 124, 126, 129–30, 130fn4, 131fn31, 134–7, 140, 142–4, 146–50, 151fn18, 155–63, 169, 226, 228, 234, 239, 241, 244–5, 247–8, 251–3, 255fn3, 257–8, 260, 271–4
   liminal critique 134, 136, 144, 148
   liminal passage 155–6, 169–70
   liminal practice 134–5, 140, 142
Lorde, Audre 14, 277, 279, 284–7, 288–91

MacKendrick, Karmen 280
Malcolm, Noel 268–9
Marshall, Helen 13, 187–9, 193–4
mental health 173
metaphor 1–3, 6, 7–9, 11, 15, 20, 25, 40–1, 45, 48, 91, 93, 106, 110 142, 182–3, 184fn1, 223, 225, 237, 241–7, 281–3, 286–7,
Middle Passage 2, 7–10, 280
migration 2, 8, 10, 13–14, 18, 35, 40, 45, 48–52, 53fn13, 77, 89–100, 100fn8, 110, 116, 187–94, 237–254, 255fn3
mobility 76, 92–3, 155–6, 159
Montagu, Mary Wortley 162, 267–9
Morrall, Clare 13, 187–9, 192–4
movement 6–9, 12, 35–8, 48, 50, 53fn12, 56, 73, 78, 89–95, 99–100, 106, 108, 115, 119, 122, 142, 151fn5, 155, 161, 164, 167, 174, 177, 189–90, 202, 205, 208, 216, 226, 237–8, 240, 242, 247, 249, 253–4, 280, 284
   poetics of movement 6, 89–95, 99–100
music, musical space 21–32, 262

Neumann, Birgit 4–6, 76, 106, 116
Nora, Pierre 238–40, 246–7, 254, 255fn2
Nünning, Ansgar 4–6, 76, 106, 116, 258, 260–1

Ottoman Empire 257, 265, 268, 271–2, 274

panopticon 84–5, 203–4, 214–16
parody 12, 58, 60, 63–4, 67–8
   parody as a tool of passage 58
parrhesia 144, 151fn7
passage, linguistic 73
   passages between the self and Other 14
   Passagen 2, 7–8, 21–2
   Passagen-Werk 12, 21–2, 40, 202
   passing into futures 14, 279, 282–3,
   passing of a threshold 1
   passing of racial and gendered identities 2, 7, 10, 202,
   processes of passage 5
   rite of passage 1, 7, 9, 135–6, 161, 225, 244, 254, 258
   site of passage 291
   symbolic passage 12, 17, 73
   social passage 13–14
   temporal passage 73, 235
patriarchy 203–4, 207, 213–14
   patriarchal gaze 202, 204, 207, 213, 216
performativity 3, 76–7
Petzold, Christian 12, 35–8, 40–51
Philip, Marlene Nourbese 14, 194, 279, 281–2, 291
philosophical exercise 134, 139, 150fn6
   philosophy as a practice 134
pilgrimage 25, 168, 268
Plato 134–5, 138–40, 145–6, 148–9
poetry 14, 56, 60, 63–4, 82, 281–3
post-war 105, 106
postcoloniality 252, 280
Pratt, Mary Louise 75, 259
primitivism 263
prison 12, 62, 72–6, 81–6, 87fn11, 134, 194, 203, 223
progress 20, 22–3, 25, 29, 31, 82, 155, 159, 164, 167, 190, 196, 229, 239–40, 247–51, 272, 281–2, 284
psychoanalysis 177–8
   psychological passage 13
psychology 13, 138, 155, 157, 165, 173, 175, 183
psychosis 174, 176–8, 180, 182

racism 4, 248, 284
realism 29–30, 32fn2, 56, 58, 107, 110, 113
refugee 12, 37–8, 41, 45, 48–51, 52fn4, 53fn12, 186
religion 13, 143, 165, 170fn6, 196, 261, 263, 267–8, 271–2, 278
renewal 155, 167–8, 220
resistance 82, 216, 279, 281–7, 291
rhetoric of the verisimilar 105, 107, 110–11, 113–16, 116fn8,
Rhys, Jean 14, 202–16
rhizomatic movement 78
Rich, Adrienne 14, 282
ritual praxis 2
   rite of passage 1, 7, 9, 135–6, 161, 225, 244, 254, 258
Rosa, Hartmut 12, 19–20, 57, 69fn24
Rose, Margaret 63–4, 207
Rose, Gillian 207–8
Rothberg, Michael 96
Royle, Nicholas 233

Said, Edward 11, 14, 239, 243, 254, 255fn5, 259–60
Schechner, Richard 86, 136
schizophrenia 115, 175–80, 184fn1
Seghers, Anna 12, 35–46, 52, 52fn6
self-transformation 13, 155–6, 165–6, 168–9
Shakespeare 12, 69fn22, 72–86, 87fn8
shoreline 286–8, 290
site of passage 291
Skinner, Quentin 105, 108, 114–15, 116fn1, 116fn6
social passage 13–14
social status 143, 156, 266
Soja, Edward 14, 237, 240–4, 249–50
sonic reproduction 21
spatiality 202, 204, 240–1, 244, 248, 251, 253–4
   private space 44, 208
   public space 44, 51, 146, 202, 206–11, 213–15
   spatial turn 92–3
   spatialization 92–3, 195
speech act theory 105, 114
Spivak, Gayatri 188, 212–13
Statovci, Pajtim 10
status change 1, 2
Stoic art of living 138, 142
street 8, 21, 38, 41–2, 47, 51, 99, 114, 145–6, 202, 205–16, 218, 248–9, 261
study of culture 4, 6, 150, 174, 190
subject 2, 8, 20–7, 31–2, 39, 73, 76, 80, 91, 107, 112, 121, 129–30, 134, 137–49, 155, 164, 174, 181–3, 207, 215–16, 232–3, 242, 270, 282, 286–9
subjectivity 20, 134, 137, 140, 142, 146–7, 149, 150fn5, 151fn17, 176, 182, 202, 214, 216
surrealism 29–30, 32fn2, 56
Szakolczai, Arpad 4–5

theatre 121–3, 125, 127–9, 136
theatricality 13, 119–20, 122–5, 129, 130, 130fn4, 131fn15
Thirdspace 237, 241, 247, 249–50
Thomassen, Bjørn 1, 4, 9, 59, 82, 115, 120, 122, 135–6, 244, 247, 258
transformation 10, 13, 21, 59, 76, 81, 135, 140, 142, 150, 150fn10, 155–60, 165–6, 168–170, 174, 180, 183, 241, 243, 251, 253, 258
transgression 12–13, 105, 109, 116fn4, 146, 155, 157, 194, 214–15
transit 39, 52, 120, 227
   Transit 12, 35–55
   transition 1–2, 5, 9, 10, 12–13, 21–22, 26, 28–9, 35–6, 73, 76, 105–6, 121–2, 135, 140, 145, 155, 159, 163, 167–70
translation 10, 12, 21,38, 74–81, 83, 86, 86fn4, 86fn7, 89–94, 97
   translational turn 90, 99
travel 2–4, 6, 10, 13–14, 28–9, 76, 109–10, 116, 126, 136, 155, 157, 159, 163–4, 167
travelogue 14, 258, 261–2, 264, 267, 269–70

travel writers 14, 257–9, 261, 263, 267, 269, 271–2, 274
travelling concept 1, 3–7, 11, 15, 41, 69fn10, 106, 116
Turner, Victor 1, 4, 9, 86, 135–6, 139, 149–50, 151fn18–19, 156

underworld 23–4, 31, 157, 162–3, 166
urban memory 23
    urban space 12, 14, 27, 50, 203, 205, 213

Van Gennep 1, 4, 9, 135–6, 139, 142, 156, 244, 258
Venten, Rudolf 76–7
Veremej, Nellja 12, 89–90, 95–99
visibility/invisibility 14, 202–3, 206, 213–14, 225

Weimar Republic 106–7
white supremacy 14, 213, 279 , 286–7, 289
Woolf, Virginia 14, 202–16
world literature 76, 90–1, 100fn3-4